The Economics of Financial Services in Emerging Markets

Any enquiry into the nature, performance, role, demerits, growth, efficiency or other aspects of financial services such as banking and insurance activities, requires rigorous estimates of their economic output, that is, the economic contributions made by these firms, as well as by the industries as a whole.

Accordingly, this book condenses several theoretical, methodological, empirical and philosophical issues in conceptualizing, measuring and empirically operationalizing the economic output of the banking and insurance industries. The analytical focus is on both Global and Emerging Markets perspectives. The book synthesizes applied and conceptual evidence to locate the chosen theme's analytical patterns, consensus and disagreements. The selected subject matter is studied within the firm-level and aggregate settings, bringing literature of varied scopes together. Contributions from various international academics, practitioners and policymakers further enrich the narrative.

The book concludes with data-driven case studies that analyse the extent to which the critical performance parameters of the banking and insurance industries in the BRIICS economies – including estimation of aggregate industry-level partial factor productivities, total factor productivity, technical efficiency and returns to scale – vary concerning alternate measures of their output. The present work also provides a brief note on the inputs measurement dimension, following which there is a discussion on the limitations, future scope and conclusions.

This work will be valuable for researchers and policymakers undertaking performance analyses related to banking and insurance activities. It shall provide them with the examination of a plethora of analytical options and related issues on the theory and praxis of output measurement, all finely organized into one single volume.

Bhagirath Prakash Baria is Assistant Professor at the Department of Banking and Insurance, Faculty of Commerce, The Maharaja Sayajirao University of Baroda, India. The broad areas of his interest include macroeconomics of banking, agricultural productivity and performance analysis of banking and insurance industries. The author strongly believes in pluralism in both teaching and research. He has a masters' degree in business economics with two Gold Medals, has published in several reputed national and international journals, won a Young Researcher Award, founded a non-profit educational initiative called The Cafe Economics (TCE), and is pursuing a PhD in the area of International Finance.

Banking, Money and International Finance

28. The Digital Disruption of Financial Services
International Perspectives
Edited by Ewa Lechman and Adam Marszk

29. The Economics and Finance of Commodity Price Shocks
Mikidadu Mohammed

30. Artificial Intelligence and Big Data for Financial Risk Management
Intelligent Applications
Edited by Noura Metawa, M. Kabir Hassan and Saad Metawa

31. The Role of Crises in Shaping Financial Systems
From the Global Financial Crisis to COVID-19
Małgorzata Iwanicz-Drozdowska, Elżbieta Malinowska-Misiąg, Piotr Mielus, Paweł Smaga, and Bartosz Witkowski

32. Insurance Market Integration in the European Union
Slawomir Ireneusz Bukowski and Marzanna Barbara Lament

33. The Economics of Financial Services in Emerging Markets
Measuring the Output of the Banking and Insurance Industries
Bhagirath Prakash Baria

34. Innovative Finance for Technological Progress
Roles of Fintech, Financial Instruments, and Institutions
Edited by Farhad Taghizadeh-Hesary, Roohallah Aboojafari and Naoyuki Yoshino

35. Understanding the Polish Capital Market
From Emerging to Developed
Edited by Marek Dietl and Dariusz Zarzecki

For more information about this series, please visit: www.routledge.com/series/BMIF

The Economics of Financial Services in Emerging Markets

Measuring the Output of the Banking and Insurance Industries

Bhagirath Prakash Baria

Routledge
Taylor & Francis Group
LONDON AND NEW YORK

First published 2023
by Routledge
4 Park Square, Milton Park, Abingdon, Oxon OX14 4RN

and by Routledge
605 Third Avenue, New York, NY 10158

Routledge is an imprint of the Taylor & Francis Group, an informa business

British Library Cataloguing-in-Publication Data
A catalogue record for this book is available from the British Library

Library of Congress Cataloging-in-Publication Data
Names: Baria, Bhagirath Prakash, author.
Title: The economics of financial services in emerging markets : measuring the output of the banking and insurance industries / Bhagirath Prakash Baria.
Description: Abingdon, Oxon ; New York, NY : Routledge, 2023. | Series: Banking, money and international finance | Includes bibliographical references and index.
Identifiers: LCCN 2022027726 (print) | LCCN 2022027727 (ebook) | ISBN 9780367712136 (hardback) | ISBN 9780367712143 (paperback) | ISBN 9781003149828 (ebook)
Subjects: LCSH: Financial services industry—Developing countries. | Banks and banking—Developing countries. | Insurance—Developing countries.
Classification: LCC HG195 .B367 2023 (print) | LCC HG195 (ebook) | DDC 332.109172/4—dc23/eng/20220616
LC record available at https://lccn.loc.gov/2022027726
LC ebook record available at https://lccn.loc.gov/2022027727

ISBN: 978-0-367-71213-6 (hbk)
ISBN: 978-0-367-71214-3 (pbk)
ISBN: 978-1-003-14982-8 (ebk)

DOI: 10.4324/9781003149828

Typeset in Bembo
by Apex CoVantage, LLC

To,
Maa Saraswati
Prof. K. Shanmugan
Ela

Contents

Acknowledgements

No research work can be undertaken without direct and indirect contributions from various people. Many people have contributed to the culmination of an idea in this work. Their help and efforts are embodied in the pages that will follow.

I first express my sincere thanks to Dr Hersch Sahay, who allowed me to access various data sources that I otherwise couldn't have. He was kind enough to let me utilize some of his resources for this work. Sincere regards are also due to Dr Meeta Rathod for helping undertake the plagiarism check for the manuscript. My deepest regards are due to the esteemed experts who agreed to contribute their rich insights and opinions to this work. These experts from across different nations have immensely enriched this work. Despite being extremely preoccupied, the experts put their time and effort into creating insights and narratives that will help readers explore the theme through a practitioner's lens. I submit my sincere gratitude to Dr Barendra Kumar Bhoi, Dr Edoardo Pizzoli, Prof. Debashis Acharya, Prof. Frauke Kreuter, Prof. Justin Paul, Prof. N. R. Bhanumurthy, Dr Pronab Sen, Dr R. B. Barman, Prof. Ram Pratap Sinha and Prof. Zhu Haiju. They all lent their years of hard work, experience, and expertise to the pages to follow. It would be a serious error to miss thanking Dr Sofia Devi for helping me connect with Dr Barendra Kumar Bhoi and Prof. Justin Paul. She was kind enough to let me utilize her academic network. Thankfulness is also due to Prof. K. Shanmugan, who lent his time and expertise to comment on several portions of the book, particularly the empirical parts. I want to submit my gratitude to Prof. K. V. Bhanumurthy, who provided rich insights on the problems of adopting aggregated perspective in production analysis. His discussions have helped me recognize several strengths and limitations of the empirical work undertaken in this book. Warm regards are also due to Prof. Madhusudan Raj, who helped in connecting with Prof. Zhu Haiju and who also provided valuable inputs on the subject matter. At this juncture, I must also thank the anonymous referees from Routledge, who provided extremely useful comments on this work in the early stages. The comments were very insightful and were duly incorporated into this work. It must also be humbly put on record that my University Library – Smt. Hansa Mehta Library lent great help in providing access to premium databases through which it was possible to build the database of studies surveyed in this work.

While these wonderful people have shaped various portions of this book, some have played a foundational role throughout the journey. Kristina Abbotts, Senior Editor (Economics, Economics, Finance, Business & Industry), and Christiana Mandizha, Editorial Assistant (Economics), Routledge, are among them. Both of them guided me throughout this journey. They were always available for help, queries and any other issues that an author might typically face. Not only that, but both were extremely tolerant of my continuous queries with long emails and frequent delays. The positive aura that they reflected throughout this journey has played a pivotal role in my journey on this wonderful project. I submit my most sincere thanks to both of them. It will be incorrect to miss thanking my dear wife, Devanshi, for constantly being there every single day and night that I worked on this manuscript. She was always there by my side, ranging from lending help in collecting and organizing the data to preparing infinite rounds of coffee throughout the night. Last but not the least, I convey my earnest gratefulness to the Routledge publishers for providing an invaluable platform for me as an author.

The responsibility for errors, if any, is solely mine.

Bhagirath

Contributors

Barendra Kumar Bhoi Ex-economic policy expert for the Central Bank of Oman; Ex-Principal Adviser at the Reserve Bank of India; Mumbai, India

Debashis Acharya Professor in the School of Economics, University of Hyderabad, Hyderabad, India

Edoardo Pizzoli Statistician at the Italian National Institute of Statistics; Associate Researcher at the University of Luxembourg, Esch-sur-Alzette, Luxembourg

Frauke Kreuter Professor at the Ludwig-Maximilians-University of Munich; Head of the Statistical Methods Group at Institute for Employment Research (IAB); Professor at the University of Maryland, Baltimore, USA

Justin Paul Editor-in-Chief of the International Journal of Consumer Studies; Faculty Member at the University of Puerto Rico, San Juan, USA

N. R. Bhanumurthy Visiting Fellow, Foundation Maison des Sciences de l'Homme, and the McGill University; Vice-Chancellor, Dr B. R. Ambedkar School of Economics University, Bangalore, India

Pronab Sen Former Chief Statistician of India; Programme Director for the International Growth Centre's India Central Programme, New Delhi, India

R. B. Barman Former Executive Director at the Reserve Bank of India; Ex-Vice Chairman of the Irving Fisher Committee on Central Bank Statistics, Bank for International Settlements; Advisor to the National Payments Corporation of India, New Delhi, India

Ram Pratap Sinha Associate Professor at the Government College of Engineering and Leather Technology, Kolkata, India

Zhu Haiju Professor at the Zhejiang Gongshang University, Hangzhou, China

Foreword

Economic production presumes the existence of well-defined inputs and outputs and their technological linkages. These linkages culminate into a production function. Observing the classical assumptions of the firm theory, the study of service as a means of production requires adaptation of the assumptions that regard tangibility. Within the financial services industry, the specification of inputs and measurement of outputs is a demanding task. In particular, banking and insurance firms further complicate this by relying on implicit services; these violate several postulates of a well-behaved production function and raise questions on applying traditional production theory to contemporary practice. Such research has significant implications for both firms and governments.

There has been significant growth in the financial sector among emerging economies, contributing to overall economic growth. The future points to the sector expanding its impact as it rapidly advances financialization and services to consumers in the economy. In literature, the issues, analytical dimensions, and empirical perspectives are spread across voluminous literature that requires proper coherence and structure. Undoubtedly, their assimilation into a single reliable source has definitely been missing in the extant literature. Addressing this gap, the present book synthesizes a large body of theoretical and empirical literature on output measurement in banking and insurance, and the scope is to relay relevant work to this puzzle in a condensed format. The book studies output in the financial sector at both the firm and aggregate levels. The underlying motivation is to summarize the wide differences in the output measurement schools regarding banking and insurance activities. Given the special focus on emerging market economies, the book can be utilized by a large audience in both the developing and advanced nations as a singular reference for studying various aspects of the central theme of this work.

While surveys of literature exclusively focus on reviewing the extant wisdom, this book also moves beyond it by providing fresh perspectives on the subject matter from the viewpoint of carefully selected experts. The contributions by experts on the subject matter enrich the analysis by including debates on the frontier in output measurement of financial services. Finally, the book also provides empirical case studies on the sensitivity of various performance indicators of banking and insurance industries to alternative measures of their output. These case studies focus on the BRIICS countries and the advancement of the financial services sector therein. These empirical case studies, parametrically and non-parametrically, examine the sensitivity of key performance indicators such as partial factor productivities, total factor productivity, technical efficiency, and returns to scale to different output measures. Readers should not build bias from the case studies; rather, they should find new ideas and topics for discussion.

M. Kabir Hassan, PhD
Graduate Coordinator for PhD Program in Financial Economics, professor of Finance, Hibernia Professor of Economics and Finance, Bank One Professor in Business, and Hancock Whitney Chair Professor of Economics, Department of Economics and Finance, University of New Orleans, New Orleans, Louisiana

Preface

Sitting in the corridors of Smt. Hansa Mehta Library, my colleague Dr Sofia Devi and I came up with a question: where do we locate a single systematic source for issues in output measurement for the banking and insurance industries? This concern was raised as we were working on a particular theme where identifying the correct output measures was necessary. After some preliminary survey of the literature, it was clear that this subject was spread across a very voluminous literature. It was unrealistic to locate any single reference work that could summarize it in a compact form. This was when the idea of writing this book emerged, and the pages that follow embody this fundamental concern. After that meeting, Dr Sofia got engaged in her research commitments, and I somehow got fascinated by this issue. It struck me that if the large body of evidence could be systematized into a reference volume, possibly, many analysts would find it useful. It could also serve as an introduction to output measurement issues, which was definitely missing. However, a standard review of the literature was surely not enough. This issue deserved much more than a literature survey due to the sheer diversity of thought. Accordingly, the work on the structure of this book began. After a long series of informal consultations with many people working in this area, I finally realized that a 'mixed method' strategy was necessary to do justice to this topic.

Accordingly, the work on this manuscript began with full vigour. My earlier notes on this matter served as the beginning point for this journey. As work progressed, the manuscript evolved. There was simply too much knowledge to be captured into a single book! Careful assessment of the evidence, sources, empirical data, expert consultations, and intuition helped frame the key premises of this book. The journey of writing this book was a dramatic one with many movie-like ups and downs. However, nature has its own ways of evolving us into the beings we are expected to be. The work kept progressing, albeit at a different pace at different times. And finally, the manuscript emerged out of the long months of hard work. Passion, love and sincerity have been mixed together to present this humble work to you, my dear readers. I hope that this book is able to help you, in some or the other way, in your journey as a researcher and an analyst.

Bhagirath

1 Setting the analytical background

1.1. Background and introduction

The theory of firm attempts to explain the existence of firms from diverse analytical angles such as the sociological, administrative, political, economic, and others. In the present context, the economic theory of the firm and its place in the theory of production are critical. The economic theory of the firm[1] as applied to production theory may be traced to the seminal work of Adam Smith (Curwen, 1976), who made a distinction between the productive and unproductive sectors of the economy. Services were characterised as non-productive sectors, with the underlying notion that they consume the surplus value rather than contribute to it. As the marginal utility theory began replacing the old concepts of economic value, so did the theory of firm begin recognising services as value-creating rather than only value-consuming activities.[2] Despite admitting services as value-adding activities, the discourse on production theory has found it challenging to analyse services with the theoretical finesse that it can achieve in the study of tangible goods.

The fundamental problem in analysing services under the traditional theory of production and firm[3] is that the production process in services does not lend itself easily to quantification. Intangibility is the primary cause of this. The intangible nature of services results in the unobservability of their production processes, and further complications are created by the overlapping and interlocking nature of their production functions.[4] Such complexities in analysing the production function imply difficulties in conceptualising and measuring the output of service industries. Vuorinen (1998) summarises the output measurement problems in service industries as follows. First, quality is inseparable from quantity in services (Adams et al., 2002). Quantitative movements in outputs and inputs embody qualitative movements too. They cannot be separated easily in case of services due to the aforementioned problems. Hence, any measure of output or input in service industries will always contain information on the quality of the same. Increases (decreases) in inputs and output can be purely technical or caused by qualitative improvements (deteriorations). Second, the nature of services does not permit the storability of its output, which causes problems in defining proper economic relations between the inputs and

DOI: 10.4324/9781003149828-1

outputs (Blois, 1985). Third, quality considerations override the quantity of services for consumers and society. Thus the nature of service markets is quite different from the tangible goods markets, where quantity and quality both may be traced to the changes in the physical composition of the goods, which is mainly unobservable in the case of services. Fourth, quality has to be conceptualised in the technical sense and via human and social dimensions. Such an approach naturally complicates the measurement of quality in services and thus further obscures the derivation of the pure quantity measure of output.[5]

Among the more significant service sector, the emergence of intermediation[6] services has raised more challenges for the theory of output in production economics. Whether financial or otherwise, intermediation has been recognised in the economics literature as a source of private and social gains because of its comparative advantages over the direct exchange. Reduction of transaction, search, monitoring, and bargaining costs, along with a better capability to handle problems such as adverse selection, moral hazard and credible commitments in trade contracts (Spulber, 1999), have enabled intermediaries to thrive across the breadth and depth of market economies. Economic theory recognised the nature and importance of intermediaries in a market economy long ago. However, with the structural shift across economies towards a higher share of services in the aggregate output, due recognition was given to the role of intermediation-service providers as not only arbitragers but also creators of diverse values. Consequently, the theory of the firm has also undergone innovations and modifications to account for various kinds of intermediaries necessary for the efficient functioning of any market economy.

Among these intermediaries, banking and insurance firms are the primary focus of this work.[7] Banking firms intermediate via the deposit-credit-asset channel, and insurance firms perform intermediation via the premiums-claims-asset channel, as will be explained in Chapters 3 and 4. The nature of production by banks and insurers is further complicated because they not only intermediate but also transform and sell services at each stage of the intermediation process. Thus, for illustration, banks not only transform deposits into credit and sell loan services to borrowers, but they also sell deposit related services to those who lend their money to banks in the form of deposits. Similarly, insurers not only pool the premiums and transform them into claim payments but also sell the risk coverage service to those who pay premiums to the firm in the first place. These concerns have led to newer debates within the theory of the firm, whereby analysts have tried incorporating the peculiar characteristics of these firms into their traditional analysis. Accounting for risk and uncertainty in production; imperfections in markets (Campbell & Kracaw, 1980); unobservable and indirect services; specialised input requirements at different stages of production (Bylund, 2017); adverse selection and moral hazard problems; interdependent production; implicit pricing; and non-marketable services are some of the fundamental ways in which traditional firm theory has been adjusted to analyse the production behaviour of banks and insurers. The need to recognise these dimensions seems more significant, particularly when performance analysis for these firms is undertaken. Performance analysis consists of diverse issues such as different efficiencies, partial and total factor productivities, financial performance, profitability analysis, competition and market power analysis, and other related matters. There is voluminous literature on the performance analysis of banking and insurance firms. This literature provides rich insights into how banks and insurers perform on different parameters across diverse spaces (cross-sectional units) and times (temporally). A persistent disagreement among the analysts has been to conceptualise, specify, and measure the output of banks and insurers at the firm and industry levels.

While disagreements have also occurred on the specification of inputs and the choice of empirical methods, the literature on banking and insurance performance analysis suggests that the extent of difference of opinion is the largest on the issue of output measurement (Eling & Luhnen, 2010). The sheer variations in the performance estimates obtained by various studies, as analysed later, motivate one to ask to what extent are these differences due to differences in output measurement and to what extent are these due to other considerations? Literature in banking and insurance has shown considerable similarity in the inputs vector required in the performance analysis and indicates a noticeable degree of homogeneity in methodological choices. When inputs specification and empirical methodology are held constant, the differences in performance estimates seem primarily caused by the variations in the output vector used across these studies. While this matter has received attention in the literature, a singular reference that summarises the voluminous literature in this regard is missing. The present work adopts a three-dimensional strategy to study the output measurement issue in banking and insurance performance analysis literature with this motivation. The first strategy is to provide a detailed survey of the output specification and measurement approaches in the literature on banking and insurance. This is undertaken in Part I. The second strategy is to enrich the findings from the literature survey by providing insights and opinions of practitioners in the subject matter, which is provided in Part II. Finally, the debates on output measurement in the literature are examined through the prism of empirical case studies. These case studies offer a fresh perspective on how the aggregate performance parameters of banking and insurance industries vary under alternative output measures, with particular attention to the significant emerging market economies (EMEs). Part III of the present work provides these case studies. When put together, this three-dimensional strategy of analysing the output measurement issue in banking and insurance literature offers a unique perspective beyond a traditional survey of the literature.

1.2. Theory of output measurement: features of an ideal output measure for banking and insurance activities

While the chapters ahead shall explore and examine many aspects of the output measurement debate in the banking and insurance literature on performance analysis, the essence of these debates can be summarised in the features that the literature considers essential for an ideal output measure in the current context. These features have been extracted from the survey of literature presented in Part I. The discussion below informs the crux of the output measurement debates in banking and insurance literature. These characteristics represent the broad expectations from an ideal measure of output in the extant literature on banking and insurance performance analysis. They are not the final word on the matter but an indication of how analysts have theorised the idea of bank and insurance output in the literature. The banking and insurance output measures discussed in Chapters 3 and 4 have been criticised on several postulated features below. The task of the analyst is then to attempt to build an output measure that fulfils as many of these requirements as possible. These ideas are elaborated on later but presented here to provide a preliminary overview of the critical problems in measuring the output of banking and insurance firms and industries.

Product-mix representativeness

The ideal output measure of a banking or insurance firm is expected to fully reflect the changes in the composition of the output, i.e. the product mix. At the firm level, this implies that the emergence of new products (services) or changes in the relative share of each service in the total output must be reflected in the chosen output measure. At the industry (i.e. aggregate) level, intra-industry shifts in the industry's total production should induce subsequent changes in the selected output measure. If the output measure is invariant to such changes, then it may not truly represent the actual production conditions of the firm or industry.

Quality-adjusted measure

The chosen output measure for banking or insurance production should be net of quality effects, i.e. unaffected by the quality changes. As Hughes and Mester (1993, p. 295) state: "ideally, the y (output) vector in the production transformation should be measured as quality-adjusted output". The rationale for this requirement is that the changes in output embody essential information for measuring various performance indicators such as efficiencies, productivities, scale and scope economies, and profitability, among others. These indicators are estimated by utilising the information on output level and its changes. Suppose the chosen output measure embodies the effects of quality changes. In that case, the difference in output will not represent the pure change in production quantity but will be distorted by quality improvements or deterioration. This may lead to over- or underestimation of various performance indicators.

Robustness to regulatory interventions

Ideally, the composition and determination of the chosen measure of banking or insurance output should not be distorted by non-market forces such as regulation. This occurs in cases such as when the so-called 'Averch and Johnson effect' exists, as discussed in further chapters. This requirement is necessary because of the heavy regulation of the banking and insurance industries in most major advanced and emerging economies. Observed output and its movements may be induced by changes in regulations such as monetary policy in the case of banking and solvency and reserve requirements in case of insurance. Such variations in output measure may be independent of the underlying production conditions and thus may distort the inferences on efficiency, productivity and other performance indicators. A classic illustration of this phenomenon is the loan amount, frequently used as an output measure in banking literature. Increases (decreases) in loans disbursed may be due to loosening (tightening) of interest rates by the central bank. However, such changes in output do not necessarily represent any meaningful change in the quantum of production by the banks. Instead, such changes in output occur outside the scope of the production function and thus cannot be meaningfully analysed in performance analysis.

Endogenous to the production function

The technological relationship implied by a production function must hold in both economic and empirical senses for an output measure to play a meaningful role in any performance analysis that directly or indirectly estimates a production function. When an output measure is subjected to frequent and large exogenous shocks, its viability as an element of the production, cost, profit, revenue or other functions is questionable. At times, such exogenous changes in output may be mistaken for technological changes.[8] This implies that the changes in the ideal output measure should represent the underlying market forces of demand and supply rather than exogenous or non-market forces as far as possible. Consider an illustration from the insurance literature. At times, the amount of reserves has been used to measure the insurance firm's output. However, reserves may change even when the numbers of policies and policyholders and even premiums have not changed. This may simply be due to risk aversion behaviour on the part of the insurers in the light of unexpected adverse shocks. The higher the degree of risk aversion of an insurer, the greater such changes may not necessarily reflect actual output movements (Wise, 2018).

Methodological robustness

Performance estimation has generally been undertaken in the banking and insurance literature using the production frontier approach. As discussed later, a host of parametric and non-parametric techniques have been utilised. When different methods within the parametric or non-parametric schools are used, differences in the performance estimates are natural. However, a desirable characteristic of the chosen output measure(s) is that these differences should be as minor as possible or within a tolerable limit. This will ensure that different empirical methods do not change the estimated results by an unacceptable margin if the same output measure is used across all the methodological innovations.

Availability of multiple proxies

The concept of output, its measure and the actual data used to proxy it may have considerable divergences. Empirical exercises are data sensitive, preventing an analyst from perfectly measuring the preferred concept of output. Literature on banking and insurance performance analysis has invariably relied on proxying the theoretical output concepts by rough proxy measures. For illustration, the amount of technical reserves maintained by insurers has been used to represent the risk-bearing services provided by insurance firms to their consumers. While it is the quantum of risk-bearing services in which one may be interested, it must be measured using the available data. Technical reserves have been employed as one such measure.[9] However, the amount of losses paid or claims are also possible candidates and have been used frequently in the literature, as shown in Chapter 4. Thus, multiple proxies can help an analyst choose an output measure that best represents the underlying output concept in a given context. This also implies that the empirical results on various performance indicators should remain broadly consistent irrespective of the proxy variable representing a given output measure.

Maximisation criterion

Production theory demands that output must be subject to conscious (microeconomics) or unconscious (macroeconomics) maximisation. Any measure of production for banks or insurers must be such that the economic agents should strive to maximise it within a rational framework rather than minimise it. This point may seem trivial, but it has critical importance for banking and insurance literature. As shown in Chapters 3 and 4, researchers have used measures such as Non-Performing Loans and the amount of loss paid as output measures for banks and insurers, respectively. These output measures cannot be easily justified because their maximisation does not seem rational economically. Some studies have dodged this problem by theorising such output measures as 'bad output'. Still, a production function that minimises both the inputs and the 'output' cannot yield economically meaningful performance parameters. Gaganis et al. (2013, p. 431) summarise this notion by asserting "that more output should be preferred to less" in any rational production process. Similarly, Brockett et al., 2005 suggest that performance estimates should improve when, *ceteris paribus*, output increases or inputs decrease, or both co-occur.[10]

Based on an output specification approach rather than ad hoc

As elaborated on in Chapter 3, the literature in the current context has treated the problem of output measurement as first a problem of output specification. Well-established specification approaches exist in the literature. They include production, value-added, intermediation, asset, user cost, national income and other approaches. Ideally, the choice of the output variable must emerge from the chosen specification approach rather than being ad hoc. The approaches mentioned earlier are the fundamental theories of banking and insurance production. Hence, choosing output measures that correspond to a specific theory has been deemed a better strategy in the extant wisdom than the ad hoc or the subjective approach. These matters will be discussed in detail later.

Reflect the size of the firm or the industry

At the firm and industry levels, the quantum of output is also utilised to measure how large or small that firm or industry is. There is a strong positive correlation between the size of a firm and its output level. This has been one of the primary motivations for choosing output measures in the extant literature on banking and insurance performance analysis (Wise, 2018). A similar observation applies at the industry level. Literature on the present theme has found it necessary to use such measures of output that can directly signify the economic size of the firm or industry. Economists consider the real value of production in the goods market as the correct representation of the level of activities undertaken by a firm or industry.[11]

High correlation with other possible alternatives

As discussed previously earlier, the same output concept may be captured by different measures in the case of the banking and insurance industries. Empirically, if the alternative proxies are strongly correlated with each other, preferably positively, then the task of choosing an output variable becomes primarily dependent on data availability. The analyst can then select that proxy variable with higher data availability. Both the banking and insurance literature have implied this expectation.[12] For example, in insurance output literature, the risk coverage output can be proxied by the amount of claim or loss or the reserve. In such cases, the *a priori* belief is that the chosen variable strongly correlates with other possible proxy variables. Thus, there is not much information loss in the performance analysis. In practice, such beliefs have been presumed rather than proven empirically. The analyst uses her subjective understanding and prior evidence to make such a leap of faith in choosing the correct output measure for a given output concept.

Existence of an optimal corresponding price index

One of the thorniest issues in output measurement debates on banking and insurance performance analysis has been the deflation of the current price value-measures of outputs. As found in Chapters 3 and 4, no single ideal price index can be used as an optimal deflator specifically for banking and insurance firms or industries. In highly disaggregated studies that focus on branches of an individual firm or a few firms within a particular banking or insurance industry segment, it is possible to use directly observable prices of individual output items. It may also be feasible to construct price measures using observable data. However, the performance analysts have struggled to locate such a price index and have instead employed the aggregate CPI and GDP deflators. Theoretically, these two deflators are far from the reality of price dynamics in the banking and insurance industries. However, the lack of data on a suitable price index has forced such a choice in the literature. An ideal output measure is thus expected to have a corresponding price index which is well-defined and rigorously measured. Hardly any measurement of banking or insurance outputs can qualify this criterion.[13]

Ability to handle the multi-output nature of banking and insurance activities

An ideal output measure is expected to account for the multi-output nature of banks and insurers (Greenbaum, 1967; Clark, 1984). This is especially important at the aggregate levels of analysis, where industry-level output is estimated through aggregation across firm-level outputs. The banking and insurance industry provides many services to its consumers. When a specific kind of service is aggregated across firms, such as aggregating the total deposit amount across all the banks, there still can be considerable heterogeneity in the type of products provided under each of these services. For example, the amount of total deposits will aggregate banks' diverse set of facilities and products to current, savings and term deposit customers. The service vector may be different for each of these customer segments. However, when the total deposit amount is used as an output, the service vectors are collapsed and merged through aggregation procedures. Weighting factors are used to undertake the same. Thus, an ideal output measure should possess such aggregation weights that the full scale of heterogeneity in banking and insurance outputs can be captured while aggregating them into industry-level measures.

Stable and rigid definition

The chosen output measure must exhibit a stable and consistent representation as an output variable. The methodology chosen to specify the output variable must not be subject to temporal or spatial instability. If that is the case, the output measure may switch to an input and vice-versa, which will not allow dynamic or even comparative-static performance analysis. Such a problem may occur, for example, while employing the user cost approach to measure banking or insurance outputs (Berger & Humphrey, 1992).

Fully endogenous to the firm

The preferred output measure should be freely changeable by the banking or insurance firm. This is necessary for performance issues such as technical, cost, profit and other efficiencies, and scale and scope economies. The variations in the ideal output measure should be under complete control of the bank or the insurance firm under consideration. Subsequently, the industry should be capable of freely changing the quantity of output at aggregate levels. Thus, the underlying production function should allow the output measure to be scalable as per the firm's or the industry's choice. When this is not the case, alternative specifications of the production/cost/profit function are required to consider the rigidity of output. Berger and Mester (1997) discuss such issues when estimating the "alternative profit function" that allows output quantity constant while allowing variations in output prices.

Unitary influence factor

Boer (1999) and Inklaar and Wang (2013) elaborate on the influence factor in output measurement for banking and insurance industries. They argue that when a particular measure is employed as an output measure, the assumption is that the underlying service content of the output measure varies proportionally to the quantum of the output measure itself. The relationship between the observed quantitative variations in the chosen output measure and the unobservable changes in the underlying service content is broadly defined as the influence factor by Boer (1999), who suggested that the preferred influence factor should be 1. Hence, a 10 percent increase in the amount of deposits would imply that the quantum of services provided by banks has also increased precisely in proportion. Inklaar and Wang (2013) criticised the value-based measures of bank output on this account. They state that the value-based measure of aggregate banking sector output "assumes that every (real) euro or dollar corresponds to a constant flow of financial intermediation services over time" (p. 96). Similar criticisms have been raised by Wang and Basu (2005).

1.3. Final remarks

With the background laid out and the fundamental ideas briefly elaborated, the following chapters will develop the narrative using the three-dimensional strategy discussed in section 1.1. This monograph has been divided into three parts, and each part focuses on the issue of output measurement in the performance analyses literature for banking and insurance. Part I examines this matter from the angle of a detailed survey of literature where approximately 500 high-quality studies are analysed and compactly summarised separately for the banking (Chapter 3) and insurance (Chapter 4) literature. The methodology for the literature review in this work is explained in Chapter 2. After that, Chapter 5 elaborates on some extended issues about the subject that are not given much space in the core review chapters. Part II then expands the scope of this literature review by incorporating the insights and opinions of selected experts in the form of edited contributions. Chapter 6 explains the methodology adopted for this task. Chapter 7 provides the selected contributions representing experts with diverse policy, academic and professional backgrounds related to output measurement for the banking and insurance industries. Part III then examines the issue of empirical implications when different output measures are used for studying key performance parameters of aggregate industry-level labour and capital productivities, total factor productivity, technical efficiency and returns to scale. Chapter 8 undertakes the exercise for the aggregate banking industry, while Chapter 9 complements the same on the insurance industry. Finally, Part IV examines the inputs measurement issue in the present context (Chapter 10), while Chapter 11 summarises and concludes this study.

Notes

1 In economic terms, a firm may be defined as a nexus of contractual relations among individuals for mutually beneficial economic gains (Jensen & Meckling, 1976).
2 Works by Carl Menger, William Stanly Jevons and Léon Walras laid the foundations of the newer theory of firm in production economics wherein the distinction between the tangible and the intangible sectors could be relaxed. Thereafter, Marshall, Clark, Knight and particularly Cournot helped finalize the profit maximization perspective of firms producing tangibles and intangibles in competitive markets. In the 1930s, however, the earlier works of Pierro Sraffa re-emerged in the efforts of Robinson and Chamberlin, who modified the strict profit maximization conception of firms and allowed for non-competitive tendencies in the behaviour of firms. Somehow, the profit maximization framework under competitive markets has continued its dominance as the major approach in empirical works on firm theory. See Curwen (1976) for an elaborated perspective on these matters.
3 Bylund (2017) suggests that the theory of firm and production are two sides of the same coin itself. However, one may subsume the theory of firm as a special case of the theory of production because production can occur outside the firms also.
4 Overlapping production functions imply that the clean decomposition of the production process into different stages across the value chain is not feasible. The same vector of input-output flow may coincide across different stages in the value chain of service industries. Interlocked production functions imply that in many cases, the individual production functions of various services (products) being produced by a firm are so complexly webbed together that disaggregating the production function for total output across its components may become unrealistic.
5 An illustration with reference to banking services may be provided here. A common practice in the literature on banking performance is to use loan-loss provisions (non-performing assets provisions) as an indicator of loan quality. This is netted out of the gross loans on the books of the bank, and a quality-adjusted output measure is derived. However, this is a crude measure of loan quality and is one-dimensional because it assumes that higher NPA provisions imply lower loan quality. In many cases, the loan quality may not be determined only by the loan-loss provisions; rather the loan losses themselves may be caused by exogenous shocks which are unrelated with loan quality per se. This measure also focuses on outcome rather than output. Banks might be highly diligent in screening and monitoring loans but might face loan losses nonetheless. In this case, the outcome of the screening and monitoring services is negative, though the output might still be positive given that the loan losses recorded could have been higher

if the given level of diligence was not followed. Agu (1988) examines the problems in output measurement in services with special reference to commercial banking firms.

6 The general concept of intermediation is captured by the so-called 'intermediation hypothesis' as examined in Spulber (2009). The author explains that intermediation occurs when consumers do not exchange directly but via firms. Such a viewpoint considers firms as intermediaries by definition. However, intermediation has a more specific conception wherein not all firms are intermediaries. Under this perspective, firms that transform the resources purchased from one set of economic agents and sell these transformed services to another set of economic agents are regarded as intermediaries. Banking and insurance firms qualify for this definition.

7 Banking and insurance firms are inherently different. Despite both of them being intermediaries in the larger financial system, the nature of their production and services are very different. This fact is recognized throughout this work. Thus, both the industries are treated separately as can be ascertained from the index of contents itself.

8 Endogeneity implies that the output variable is determined within the production function and that the variations in output are not explained significantly by any factors other than inputs and residual technology. However, this may not always be the case.

9 The input-output dilemmas in banking and insurance output measurement are elaborated on in Chapters 3 and 4, respectively.

10 This feature is also required by various frontier methods, such as the isotonic assumption in DEA which states that outputs and inputs must possess positive correlation (Nourani et al., 2017).

11 Finance and accounting disciplines generally utilize other measures, such as market capitalization, for example, as a representation of the level of activities and size of a firm/industry. Economists, on the other hand, prefer measures that closely correspond to the real production by the firm or the industry. This is due to the recognition by economists of the fact that financial size and economic size may be different on account of many non-real forces (such as market speculation, boom-and-bust cycles, and other sources of noise in the financial system) that may cause divergence between the economic and financial scales.

12 This is also important because many researchers use a single measure of output in banking and insurance literature rather than a vector. If the chosen variable has a strong positive correlation with the other measures that have not been included, the performance parameters could still be helpful and provide meaningful, practical insights without much of an information loss.

13 Some researchers have stressed the need for output measures that do not contain any price component. Such volume measures of output are generally difficult to locate in the case of many advanced economies, let alone the emerging market economies (EMEs). In reality, the value-based measures dominate the banking and insurance literature and these are mainly composed of price and quantity elements. The removal of the effects of the price component from a composite value measure is the problem of deflation in banking and insurance performance literature.

References

Adams, R. M., Röller, L.-H., & Sickles, R. C. (2002). *Market power in outputs and inputs: An empirical application to banking*. Wissenschaftszentrum Berlin (Discussion Paper FS IV 02–33). https://nbnresolving.org/urn:nbn:de:0168-ssoar-113399

Agu, C. C. (1988). On the performance analysis: The definition and measurement of bank output in Nigeria. *Savings and Development*, *12*(2), 107–126.

Berger, A. N., & Humphrey, D. B. (1992). Measurement and efficiency issues in commercial banking. In *Output measurement in the service sectors* (pp. 245–300). University of Chicago Press. www.nber.org/books/gril92-1

Berger, A. N., & Mester, L. J. (1997). Inside the black box: What explains differences in the efficiencies of financial institutions? *Journal of Banking & Finance, 21*, 895–947.
Blois, K. J. (1985). Productivity and effectiveness in service firms. *Service Industries Journal, 4*(3), 45–60.
Boer, S. D. (1999). *A volume index for the output of the Dutch banking industry based on quantity indicators*. Statistics Netherland (National Accounts Occasional Paper No. NA-094).
Brockett, P. L., Cooper, W. W., & Golden, L. L. (2005). Financial intermediary versus production approach to efficiency of marketing distribution systems and organisational structure of insurance companies. *The Journal of Risk and Insurance, 72*(3), 393–412.
Bylund, P. L. (2017). *The problem of production: A new theory of firm*. Routledge.
Campbell, T. S., & Kracaw, W. A. (1980). Information production, market signalling, and the theory of financial intermediation. *The Journal of Finance, 35*(4).
Clark, J. A. (1984). Estimation of economies of scale in banking using a generalized functional form. *Journal of Money, Credit and Banking, 16*(1), 53–68. https://doi.org/10.2307/1992648
Curwen, P. J. (1976). *The theory of the firm* (Vol. 1). MacMillan. https://doi.org/10.1007/978-1-349-15645-0
Eling, M., & Luhnen, M. (2010). Efficiency in the international insurance industry: A cross-country comparison. *Journal of Banking & Finance, 34*, 1497–1509. https://doi.org/10.1016/j.jbankfin.2009.08.026
Gaganis, C., Hasan, I., & Pasiouras, F. (2013). Efficiency and stock returns: Evidence from the insurance industry. *The Journal of Productivity Analysis, 40*, 429–442. https://doi.org/10.1007/s11123–013–0347-x
Greenbaum, S. I. (1967). Competition and efficiency in the banking system – empirical research and its policy implications. *Journal of Political Economy, 75*(4), 461–479.
Hughes, J. P., & Mester, L. J. (1993). A quality and risk-adjusted cost function for banks: Evidence on the 'too big-to-fail' doctrine. *The Journal of Productivity Analysis, 4*, 293–315.
Inklaar, R., & Wang, J. C. (2013). Real output of bank services: What counts is what banks do, not what they own. *Economica, 80*(317), 96–117. https://doi.org/10.1111/j.1468–0335.2012.00942.x
Jensen, M. C., & Meckling, W. (1976). Theory of the firm: Managerial behavior, agency costs and ownership structure. *Journal of Financial Economics, 3*, 305–360.
Nourani, M., Devadason, E. S., & Chandan, V. (2017). Measuring technical efficiency of insurance companies using dynamic network DEA: An intermediation approach. *Technological and Economic Development of Economy, 24*(5), 1909–1940. https://doi.org/10.3846/20294913.2017.1303649
Spulber, D. F. (1999). *Market microstructure: Intermediaries and the theory of the firm*. Cambridge University Press.
Spulber, D. F. (2009). *The theory of the firm: Microeconomics with endogenous entrepreneurs, firms, markets, and organisations* (1st ed.). Cambridge University Press.
Vuorinen, I., Järvinen, R., & Lehtinen, U. (1998). Content and measurement of productivity in the service sector: A conceptual analysis with an illustrative case from the insurance business. *International Journal of Service Industry Management, 9*(4), 377–396. http://dx.doi.org/10.1108/09564239810228876
Wang, J. C., & Basu, S. (2005). *Risk bearing, implicit financial services, and specialisation in the financial industry*. Federal Reserve Bank of Boston Public Policy (Discussion Paper No. 06–3).
Wise, W. (2018). Life insurance company efficiency: Best method and proxies. *Insurance Markets and Companies, 9*, 6–19. http://dx.doi.org/10.21511/ins.09(1).2018.02

Part I

Survey of evidences

Theoretical and empirical issues

2 Qualitative and quantitative aspects of the survey of literature

2.1. Sample versus population dimensions of literature survey

Theoretically, a literature review can broadly be conducted under the ad hoc and the systematic approaches. Ad hoc methods primarily rely on the subjective understanding of the reviewer regarding the various critical elements of a survey of the literature. These elements include the sources of the studies, choice of databases for performing search queries, keywords to be used, inclusion-exclusion criteria to be employed, and the issues analysed under the review exercise.[1] On the other hand, systematic approaches establish a replicable format for constructing the sample of studies which shall then be subjected to rigorous theoretical and empirical analysis.[2] In both approaches, a sample of studies is used to derive insights into the significant agreements, disagreements, theoretical issues, empirical methodologies, causal connections among variables of interest and other prevalent dimensions in the extant wisdom. However, the reliability of the insights from both these approaches differs considerably due to the role of subjectivity and associated biases that would inevitably be embodied in the nature of the sample that is selected for review. While both the approaches are subject to such problems, the systematic approaches allow the readers to gauge the broad extent of these biases due to their replicability and use of well-defined procedures. In the ad hoc methods, a reader cannot locate the significant sources of biases due to the lack of any structured process in selecting and analysing studies. Thus, systematic approaches are more reliable when the literature survey is the primary focus. In contrast, ad hoc approaches may be used in empirical works that wish only to provide a broad glimpse of major works undertaken earlier. Given the scope and objectives of this work, a broadly systematic approach to the literature survey is adopted herein. Further discussion shall clarify the nature of the review work undertaken in this work.

Irrespective of the approach to literature review adopted, any review work engages in constructing a set of studies that the reviewer believes truly and sufficiently represents the extant wisdom on the topic of interest. Unless an issue is highly specialised,[3] it is challenging to undertake a census of the studies, and thus, the reviewer must inevitably select a sample of studies for assessment. This is particularly important for social sciences and economics, where elimination

DOI: 10.4324/9781003149828-3

by scientific experiments of older models is essentially not permissible.[4] Thus, out of the population of studies on a particular topic, a set of studies is selected using an ad hoc or a systematic procedure. We may term that as the sample of interest. Recognising this population-sample dimension in a review exercise allows one to consciously construct a set of studies that minimises the biases that a high degree of subjectivity can bring into the review.[5] While such biases will not be eliminated, their extent can be kept under tolerable limits, thus allowing the reviewer to summarise the extant wisdom with more excellent reliability. The underlying population of ideas that a reviewer aims to summarise can be better captured by the selected sample if an explicitly defined procedure is followed from the very beginning of the exercise. Moreover, such an approach allows the reviewer and their readers to recognise the limits of the insights drawn from the review work. Despite both the theory and technology for conducting such reviews, minimal studies have followed such an approach to assessing the chosen theme. One of the objectives of the present work is to fulfil this gap.

2.2. Review strategy

The importance of a scientifically undertaken review of literature cannot be overstated. As Gough et al. (2012, p. 3) note, "Reviews can inform us about what is known, how it is known, how this varies across studies, and thus also what is not known from previous research". The extent to which these expectations can be fulfilled depends on how well the review exercise is framed from the very beginning. Thus, this section clarifies the stages through which the sample of studies was constructed.[6]

The entire process of building the sample was divided into the following stages. In stage I, the keywords, databases[7] and inclusion criteria were specified. The primary concern was to collect studies focused on various performance measures of banking and insurance activities. This included studies centred on productivity, efficiency, profitability, competition and related aspects of banking and insurance activities. The first set of studies was collected in stage II, totalling approximately 500 studies for banking and insurance-related issues combined. In stage III, a rolling sample was formed by selecting studies from the reference list of each of these 500 studies. This was done using the pre-defined inclusion criteria. This increased the sample size to approximately 1,000 studies, covering an extensive range of banking and insurance performance analysis issues and output measurement. The sample was cleaned for duplication, repetition, and irrelevance in stage IV. This yielded 872 studies. In stage V, a fixed-weighted quality score was developed by quantifying five main parameters so that the scores ranged between 0 and 100 on an ordinal scale. The parameters included the publisher (weight assigned was 0.3), database where the source was listed (weight given was 0.2), citations for the individual literature as per popular databases (weight assigned was 0.1) and whether the literature focused on issues of interest (weight given was 0.1) and the depth of discussion on the chosen output variables (weight assigned was 0.3).

The 872 studies were reviewed in detail and ranked on these five parameters. The weighted score for each of these studies was estimated. After that, studies were grouped into seven groups based on the score value: very high, high, moderately high, moderate, moderately low, low, and very low.[8] Studies scoring below the moderate group were eliminated from the sample. This yielded approximately 650 studies for banking and insurance issues combined. As the scores also varied within each group, a threshold score of 450 was selected as a cut-off value. All studies below this score from within the moderate group were further eliminated. This yielded 450 studies – 260 on banking performance analysis and 190 on insurance performance analysis. This work has included these studies, though all 872 pieces of evidence were reviewed. This was done due to space restrictions.[9] The 872 studies on various aspects assumed critical for output measurement analysis were examined in detail. The quantitative summary of the finally selected 450 studies is presented in the next section in Tables 2.1 and 2.2. Some of the primary criteria used are reflected therein.

2.3. Quantitative summary of the selected sample of studies

Tables 2.1 and 2.2 summarise the nature of studies that have been selected for analysing banking and insurance output measurement.[10] The range of coverage in terms of sources is visible in the tables. Not only journal articles but also PhD theses and books are covered. However, journal articles dominate the sample. For both the samples, as shown in Tables 2.1 and 2.2, studies that focus on industry-level analysis using firm-level data dominate the sample. This is possibly a reflection of the extensive use of panel data in the literature. Firms as a unit of study also correspond closely to the main empirical methods employed in the literature. Performance analysis is generally applied to data on individual decision-making units, and this is reflected in the analytical approach used in the literature. Efficiencies, productivities and scale economies dominate the sample on banking related studies. Methodologically speaking, traditional data envelopment analysis (DEA), stochastic frontier approach (SFA), ordinary least squares (OLS) method and ratio-based empirical approaches dominate the selected sample, as reflected in Table 2.1. In contrast, analysis of efficiencies and productivity occupies the insurance sample's largest share, as shown in Table 2.2. Regarding empirical methodologies for insurance performance analysis, the distribution of studies in the insurance sample is mainly similar to that of the banking sample. Regarding the geographical distribution, advanced and emerging economies are the main focal points for the selected studies in both the samples, as shown in Tables 2.1 and 2.2. For the banking sample, advanced economies have a sizeably larger share, though coverage of emerging economies is quite broad for both the samples. The geographical spread achieved here is extensive and has not been covered in any literature review in the present context.[11]

Table 2.1 Quantitative summary of the sample studies on banking performance

Dimensions	*Sub-dimension*	*Frequency*
Source	Journal	229 (88%)
	Working Paper	14 (5%)
	Book Chapter	5 (2%)
	Discussion Papers	4 (2%)
	PhD thesis	3 (1%)
	Others (conference papers; edited volume; occasional paper; unpublished)	5 (2%)
Analytical approach	Industry level	16 (6%)
	Industry-level (using firm-level and other unit-level data)	202 (78%)
	International (using country-level aggregate data)	2 (1%)
	International (using firm-level and other unit-level data)	10 (4%)
	Unit level (branch and individual accounts)	3 (1%)
	Sectoral	14 (5%)
	Review of evidence	7 (3%)
	Others (theoretical analysis, mathematical economics, and other approaches)	6 (2%)
Rating based on ranking scale	Very high	89 (34%)
	High	95 (37%)
	Moderately high	60 (23%)
	Moderate	16 (6%)
Decadal distribution	1950–1959	1 (0.4%)
	1960–1960	5 (1.9%)
	1970–1979	14 (5.4%)
	1980–1989	19 (7.3%)
	1990–1999	59 (22.7%)
	2000–2009	79 (30.4%)
	2010–2019	61 (23.5%)
	2020 and later	22 (8.5%)
Issue of analysis	Technical efficiency	60
	Cost efficiency	59
	Economies of scale (including returns to scale)	48
	Total factor productivity	41
	Bank output measurement	23
	Profit efficiency	17
	Economies of scope	13
	Performance analysis	13
	Profitability	13
	Allocative efficiency	11
	Scale efficiency	11
	Partial factor productivity	9
	Others	8
	X-efficiency	6
	Technical change	6
	Pure technical efficiency	5
	Revenue efficiency	5
	FISIM (financial intermediation services indirectly measured)	3
	Market power	3

Dimensions	*Sub-dimension*	*Frequency*
	General efficiency analysis	3
	Cost elasticity	3
	Overall technical efficiency	2
	Competition	2
	Technology gaps ratio	2
	Cost gap ratio	1
	Quality efficiency	1
	Fuzzy efficiency	1
Empirical framework	**Non-parametric**	
	DEA (data envelopment analysis)	
	Traditional DEA	71
	Emerging DEA	11
	DFA (distribution free approach)	8
	TFA (thick frontier approach)	2
	Parametric	
	SFA (stochastic frontier approach)	32
	MLE (maximum likelihood)	
	One-stage MLE	21
	Two-stage MLE	1
	Regression	
	OLS (ordinary least squares)	24
	SUR (seemingly unrelated regression)	22
	Panel regression	13
	Fuzzy regression	1
	COLS (corrected OLS)	1
	GMM (generalised method of moments)	2
	Others	
	Index numbers	
	Traditional	3
	Emerging	3
	Ratios	24
	Others	18
Geographical distribution	Advanced economies	148
	Emerging economies	96
	Developing and non-emerging	6
	Underdeveloped	2
	Transition	5
	Global	10
Stock-flow dimension of the chosen output variables	Only stock	135 (52%)
	Only flow	31 (12%)
	Both	76 (29%)
	Ratio of flow to stock	14 (5%)
	Ratio of stock to stock	2 (1%)
	Others	2 (1%)
Nominal-real dimension of the chosen output variables	Nominal	169
	Real (constant price)	70
	Real (volume)	23

(*Continued*)

Table 2.1 (Continued)

Dimensions	*Sub-dimension*	*Frequency*
Nature of data	Cross sectional	58
	Time series	26
	Panel	
	Unbalanced	18
	Balanced	4
	Unclear	119
	Pooled	15
Temporal dimension of the sample periods (No. of years)	Mean years	10
	Median years	8
	Minimum years	2
	Maximum years	37
Frequency of sample period	Annual	187
	Quarterly	8
	Monthly	2
	Daily	2
Deflators employed for the chosen output variables	Consumer Price Index	25
	Gross Domestic Product deflator	28
	Gross National Product deflator	4
	Wholesale Price Index	4
	Others	4
Output measurement dimensions	Loans	196 (75%)
	Deposits	107 (41%)
	Investments	83 (32%)
	Income measures	71 (28%)
	Non-traditional measure (off-balance-sheet output)	66 (25%)
	Assets	84 (32%)
	Sectoral and national income measures	14 (5%)

Notes: 1. The total number of studies is 450, of which 260 are on banking performance analysis. 2. In some cases, the percentage (%) values shall not be equal to 260 due to multiple counting of a given study in several sub-dimensions and rounding off of percentage values.

Source: Author's survey of the literature.

A contrasting feature between both the samples is that the banking sample has primarily employed the stock measures of banking output while the insurance sample uses flow measures. This is probably a reflection that stock output measures are preferred in banking literature, given the historical development of banking output measures. However, nominal output measures are the most preferred choice in both samples. This again reflects the lack of an optimal price index for banking and insurance services. There also rages a debate on conceptualising the price of banking and insurance outputs and the optimal method to measure the same using micro-level data. This is reflected in the dominance of nominal output variables in the literature. Lastly, as summarised in Table 2.1, the banking sample suggests that loans and deposits are the most frequently employed output measures for banking. At the same time, premiums

Table 2.2 Quantitative summary of sample studies on insurance performance

Dimensions	*Sub-dimension*	*Frequency*
Source	Journal	158 (83%)
	Working paper	7 (4%)
	Book chapter	9 (5%)
	Full book	5 (3%)
	PhD thesis	4 (2%)
	Others (conference papers; monograph; other dissertations; unpublished)	5 (3%)
Scope	Industry level using firm-level data	136 (72%)
	Others	18 (10%)
	Industry-level	8 (4%)
	Sectoral level	8 (4%)
	Industry-level using other units of analysis (policies; intermediaries; groups of firms; geographical areas)	6 (3%)
	Firm-level	6 (3%)
	Review of evidence	4 (2%)
	Sectoral using firm-level data	2 (1%)
Rating	Very high	49 (26%)
	High	45 (24%)
	Moderately high	42 (22%)
	Moderate	52 (28%)
Decadal distribution	Before 1989	4 (2%)
	1990–1999	12 (6%)
	2000–2009	37 (20%)
	2010–2019	125 (67%)
	2020 onwards	9 (5%)
Main issue	Cost efficiency	43
	Technical efficiency	55
	Advertising efficiency	1
	Revenue efficiency	13
	Profit efficiency	6
	Profitability	5
	Economies of scale and scope	8
	Total factor productivity	51
	Partial factor productivity	13
	X-efficiency	1
	Performance analysis	10
	Insurance output measurement	3
	Underwriting cycle	7
	Review of evidence	1
	Allocative efficiency	9
	Others	7
Empirical framework	**Non-parametric**	
	DEA	
	Traditional	86
	Bootstrapped	5
	Dynamic DEA Network	2
	Fuzzy analytic hierarchic process	1
	TFA	1

(*Continued*)

Table 2.2 (Continued)

Dimensions	*Sub-dimension*	*Frequency*
	Parametric	
	SFA	18
	Bayesian SFA	1
	Time series models	4
	OLS	6
	Other regression models	4
	Others	
	Index-based methods (including ratio-based methods)	25
Geographical Distribution	Advanced	91
	Emerging	81
	Developing and non-emerging	6
	Underdeveloped	3
	Gulf Cooperation Council	1
	Islamic	1
	Global	1
	Others	9
Stock-Flow dimension of the output measure	Stock	61
	Flow	153
	Ratio of flow to flow	2
	Ratio of flow to stock	14
	Ratio of stock to stock	6
Nominal-real dimension of output measure	Nominal	85
	Real (constant price)	58
	Real (constant currency)	1
	Real (volume)	9
	Unclear	4
	NA (not applicable)	25
Nature of data	Cross sectional	20
	Time series	15
	Panel	123
	Unbalanced	9
	Balanced	6
	Unclear	108
	Pooled	4
Deflators employed for chosen output variables	Aggregate CPI	51
	GDP deflator	4
	Aggregate WPI	1
	Self-constructed	1
	Output-specific deflators	1
	Unclear	6
Sectoral Focus	Life insurance	102 (54%)
	Nonlife insurance	58 (31%)
	Specific individual industries	18 (10%)
	Property-liability	30 (16%)
	Aggregate	20 (11%)
	Takaful	4
	Financial services sector	2

Dimensions	*Sub-dimension*	*Frequency*
Output variables	Premiums	92 (49%)
	Investments/financial assets	96 (51%)
	Losses	41 (22%)
	Claims	37 (20%)
	Investment income	34 (18%)
	Benefits paid	26 (14%)
	Technical reserves	17 (9%)
	Number of policies sold	7
	Expenses	3
	Sectoral and national income	3
	Amount of time	2
	Number of products	2
	Number of accidents	1
	Number of contracts	1
	Number of claims	1

Notes: 1. The total number of studies is 450, of which 190 are on insurance performance analysis. 2. In some cases, the percentage (%) values shall not be equal to 190 due to multiple counting of a given study in several sub-dimensions and rounding off of percentage values.

Source: Author's survey of the literature.

and investments are the most commonly used output measures for insurance activities. The choice of these variables must largely be seen in terms of data availability. Unsurprisingly, the sectoral and national income measures of banking and insurance outputs are not very popular. This is possibly a reflection of the economic versus national income-based output measurement debates ongoing since the early 1980s (Wolff, 1991).

2.4. Problems in the purposive selection of studies[12]

The ad hoc (or traditional) approaches to literature review are characterised by an unstructured and largely subjective selection of studies. They also generally lack recognition of the sample-versus-population dimension in their survey. This lends the insights derived from such reviews subject to many biases. These biases include, but are not limited to, the researcher bias (Machi & McEvoy, 2022), whereby the reviewer tends to select studies that conform to her subjective ideas and preconceived notions; survivor bias, whereby the reviewer tends to choose studies that have significant citations and thus end up ignoring conflicting views that may not have garnered equal attention; and publication bias (Andrews & Kasy, 2019) whereby statistically significant findings have a higher chance of being included in the sample. Such biases may distort the true underlying consensus and disagreements in the literature. They also make the selected sample unrepresentative of the underlying population of studies that it tries to summarise. While this may not be a problem for empirical researchers aiming to provide a brief commentary on the significant patterns in the literature, it can be a serious limitation for reviews that aim to provide rigorous analysis of the research gaps in the extant wisdom on a topic. Specifically, in banking and insurance output measurement, very few studies exist that undertake a full-scale survey. Furthermore, those existing reviews are largely unclear on their literature selection and sample construction strategies. This makes deriving any kind of generalisation from such reviews very difficult and subject to errors. While it is impossible to eliminate such problems, they can be minimised if the reviewer adopts a structured process and states the same explicitly in clear and straightforward terms.

One must be careful not to equate subjectivity with bias. There are situations when subjective selection of studies can be superior to structured selections. Highly specialised issues are generally well-captured by the expertise of the reviewers in that area. However, the subject matter of this work is a more generalised issue and has been discussed and debated by a large number of researchers from diverse disciplines and ideological schools. Thus, a structured selection of studies with well-defined parameters can help reduce the highlighted biases and possibly allow better generalisations for future research.

2.5. Background on further sections

The following two chapters examine the major output measurement issues in banking and insurance activities. The focus of these chapters is to condense the voluminous literature into broad generalisations that can provide meaningful insights into the consensus and disagreements on this topic. The primary output variables and output specification approaches are analysed. After that, thematic discussions on various issues derived from the survey are discussed.

The idea that a survey of the literature is sufficient in itself is challenged in Part II by incorporating contributions from experts in the areas related to the theme of this work. These experts were carefully selected and interviewed and then were requested to provide their opinions on the central issues in banking and insurance output measurement. The expert contributions serve as first-hand accounts of the beliefs of those involved in critical positions in policy-making and academic research. The experts' profiles are provided in Chapter 7, and the selection and interview strategies are examined in Chapter 6. An analysis of output measurement issues in banking and insurance shall be incomplete without examining how alternative measures change the critical performance parameters. Six major emerging market economies are selected for this purpose: Brazil, Russia, India, Indonesia, China, and South Africa (the so-called BRIICS). Aggregate banking and insurance industries are analysed instead of firms to give a fresh perspective on this issue as the literature has not paid much attention. The same is also motivated by data constraints.[13] After that, Part IV begins by discussing another debated issue in banking and insurance performance literature – namely, the measurement of inputs. The same is discussed in Chapter 10, along with some additional issues. Finally, Chapter 11 concludes the work by recognising the limitations, suggesting the possible directions for future research and deriving tentative conclusions only to be challenged by more able researchers in the coming time.

Notes

1 Given that an increasingly large volume of literature in social sciences is available in digital form, the discussion here assumes that digital literature search is the leading source for selecting studies. In some cases, mainly when the topic is highly specialized, searching in physical databases such as libraries shall be required. The discussion here can broadly be applied in such cases, though considerations of time and costs are not delved deeper here.

2 See Machi and McEvoy (2022) for a compact analysis of the significant elements of a systematic literature review. The authors divide the literature review process into six stages covering various critical aspects of undertaking such an exercise. They stress critiquing the literature to locate research gaps. However, this aspect has not been undertaken in this work. The primary aim of the present work is to summarize and condense the voluminous literature into a single reference. Hence, critiquing it in detail would have expanded the scope beyond the permissible space.

3 This implies that ad hoc approaches shall be more efficient in selecting the set of studies to be analysed because the literature on such specialized topics is expected to be distributed relatively compactly across a limited number of sources. Problems in using such an approach emerge when the subject of interest is more generalized and multidisciplinary.

4 Economic analysis can be approached from two perspectives – the absolutist and the relativist (Blaug, 1990). The absolutist approach considers economic theory from a pure empiricist angle. In this approach, older models are slowly discarded with empirical evidence, and more refined, and scientifically sounder models remain in practice. However, the relativist approach allows for the fact that current empirical proofs may not be sufficient to eliminate one model of economic behaviour in favour of another. Older models may re-emerge later in the same or slightly modified forms to explain new data. The issue of banking and insurance output measurement must be approached from a relativistic angle rather than an absolutist one. Given the lack of universal consensus on even the core set of services provided by banks and insurers, elimination by empiricism is not feasible in this context. Older approaches may very well explain newer data, and current strategies may be unsuitable for explaining present reality.

5 This also allows a reviewer to use quantitative meta-analytic methods, such as meta-regression, to summarize the consensus and disagreement in the literature.

6 The present discussion only highlights this process in brief due to space constraints. The detailed methodology may be obtained from the author upon request.

7 The initial databases included WorldCat, Google Scholar, Scopus, Web of Science and JSTOR. Multiple people and institutions enabled access to these databases and other premium sources, which has been acknowledged in the Acknowledgements section.

8 The rankings are not a final statement of the actual quality of the work. This is a subjective matter. This ranking score method is used only as a tool to classify the more relevant studies from the less relevant ones. Hence, one must interpret these scores and categories in terms of relevance for this study rather than as a measure of their research quality. Some degree of subjectivity is inevitably involved in such a scoring process, but the attempt has been made to reduce this to the best possible extent.

9 The detailed scoring process and scores for all 872 studies and additional notes are happily available from the author on request.

10 The distribution of literature across sources as found here has been corroborated by other studies. Studies of such scope are limited and include the one by Sharma et al. (2013). They, too, find the same journals in their list of top published journals.

11 Review works on banking and output measurement and studies that undertake an empirical sensitivity analysis of performance estimates to alternative output variables are discussed in Chapters 3 and 4.

12 This section has been included based on the valuable suggestions by the anonymous reviewer, for which the author is deeply thankful.

13 The data source called BankFocus (earlier BankScope) of Moody's Analytics has been increasingly used for obtaining firm-level data for banking and insurance industries across the advanced and emerging economies. This data source is constructed from official data and probably other sources. This database has extensive coverage. However, there are concerns about using this database. See Bhattacharya (2003). This was one reason for avoiding the use of this database. Moreover, performance analysis at aggregate levels is largely missing in the literature. Hence, this was another motivation to utilize aggregate industry-level data from official public sources. Future works by the author shall incorporate more disaggregated databases for empirical sensitivity analysis, such as that by BankFocus.

References

Andrews, I., & Kasy, M. (2019). Identification of and correction for publication bias. *American Economic Review, 109*(8), 2766–2794. https://doi.org/10.1257/aer.20180310

Bhattacharya, K. (2003). *How good is the bankscope database? A cross-validation exercise with correction factors for market concentration measures*. BIS (Working Paper No. 133).

Blaug, M. (1990). *Economic theory in retrospect* (4th ed.). Cambridge University Press.

Gough, D., Oliver, S., & Thomas, J. (2012). *An introduction to systematic reviews* (1st ed.). SAGE.

Machi, L. A., & McEvoy, B. T. (2022). *The literature review: Six steps to success*. Corwin, SAGE.

Sharma, D., Sharma, A., & Barua, M. K. (2013). Efficiency and productivity of banking sector: A critical analysis of literature and design of conceptual model. *Qualitative Research in Financial Markets, 5*(2), 195–224. http://dx.doi.org/10.1108/QRFM-10-2011-0025

Wolff, E. N. (1991). Productivity growth, capital intensity, and skill levels, in the U.S. Insurance industry, 1948–86. *The Geneva Papers on Risk and Insurance. Issues and Practice, 16*(59), 173–190. www.jstor.org/stable/41952062

3 Review of evidence on banking output measurement

Global perspective

3.1. Introduction

Concerns with bank output measurement are not new. One can trace the discussions on this matter to as early as the late 1950s. Notable early work on this subject matter can be found in Speagle and Kohn (1958), who summarize the main challenges in constructing an optimal measure of bank output. The factors highlighted by them include the heterogeneity of products, change in the composition of the output mix, product innovations and changes in the quality of the banking services. These concerns remain as profound today as they were decades ago. These concerns emerge due to the multi-product nature of banking firms. More concretely, such concerns are a result of the larger philosophical issues in the measurement of economic phenomenon (Boumans, 2007). The intangibility of production further complicates the matters because cleanly separable production functions cannot be immediately located in the banking value chain. The production process is essentially interlocked, and the underlying production function is itself a product of many interrelated and overlapping production functions spread across different stages in the value chain. Such issues have been well-recognized in the banking literature, which has given rise to alternative approaches to output specification. These approaches are examined in section 3.3. Underlying these specification approaches are different measurements of bank output.[1] Some methods favour volume measures – those that are in quantity terms without any explicit price element. Others profess value measures – those that are in monetary terms with both quantity and price elements. Within both these approaches, different lines of thought have evolved. Such aspects are reviewed and examined in section 3.4. Finally, the most pressing theoretical and empirical issues that have occupied the intense attention of researchers are enlisted and discussed in section 3.5, after which an appendix highlights the evolution of bank output measurement from 1957 to 2022, covering 260 studies.

3.2. Empirical sensitivity of banking performance estimates to alternative outputs

The earliest literature highlighted two significant measures of bank output: balance sheet-based and income account-based (Kalish & Gilbert, 1973;

DOI: 10.4324/9781003149828-4

Agu, 1988).[2] Since then, balance sheet measures have dominated the literature, corroborating the large share of stock measures in the studies sample, as shown in Table 2.1. Despite early warnings against the sole reliance on balance sheet items, their use has continued to be pervasive in banking literature. Speagle and Kohn (1958) provided a way to reconcile this dichotomy of stock-flow measures by suggesting the use of index measures of bank output. While such efforts have been used in literature, their use is sparse at best. Since then, literature on banking performance has employed a rich set of variables that have been justified as the correct measures of the underlying output concept.

While these matters are reviewed in the following sections, one exciting development has been the tests of empirical sensitivity of performance estimates to alternative bank output measures. By the early 1980s, it was explicitly recognized that there could not be a single measure of bank output due to the multi-product nature of banking activities. This led to the need to test the variations in performance estimates brought by alternative output measures employed in the literature. Clark (1984) was one of the earliest attempts in this direction. The author used lending output, lending plus non-lending output and earning assets output to estimate the sensitivity of economies of scale estimates to these alternative output measures. Significant differences in scale economies were found on this account. An early systematic attempt to compare the effects of economic versus national income measures[3] on performance estimates was undertaken by Subramaniam (1985).[4] The author undertook a sensitivity analysis of scale economies in the Australian banking industry using the national income measure, total deposits, total assets (physical plus financial) and total financial assets. In level form, the estimates of scale economies using these alternative measures displayed a strong positive correlation, while in growth rate form, the correlation reduced drastically. Since then, a sizeable set of literature has undertaken such sensitivity analysis. In the 1980s, authors were generally concerned with testing the sensitivity of scale and scope economies using different balance sheet measures. This included notable works by Berger et al. (1987) and Lawrence (1989), while Hunter and Timme (1986) is a noteworthy work with regards to technical efficiency. In the 1990s, the authors' attention was expanded to undertake similar exercises in other advanced economies such as Finland (Kolari & Zardkoohi, 1990) and Norway (Berg et al., 1991). The US continued to garner the most attention in this respect, and notable works were undertaken by Hunter and Timme (1995) and Berger and Humphrey (1997). Berger and Humphrey (1997, p. 198) summarize the crux of the matter when they assert that "inferences regarding efficiency may be importantly affected by how the output is measured, a result usually less dependent upon investigator choice than the availability of data".

The 2000s saw a continuation of this analytical preoccupation. Athanassopoulos and Giokas (2000) undertook empirical sensitivity tests to estimate branch-level intermediation efficiency for alternative volume and value measures of branch output. A notable attempt during this period was made by Tortosa-Ausina (2002), who examined the sensitivity of non-parametric cost efficiency estimates under the intermediation and value-added approaches.[5] The author studied the distribution of the cost efficiency estimates under different output specifications and found that the mean and variability of the efficiency distributions differ substantially across alternative output specifications. In terms of emerging economies, works by Kumbhakar and Sarkar (2003) and Sathye (2003) undertake a sensitivity check for productivity and efficiency estimates respectively of Indian commercial banks. An essential feature of the former study is that it used the number of branches as an output variable and traditional stock variables. However, the latter study used flow output variables regarding interest and non-interest incomes and net loans (gross loans net of non-performing assets). Kumbhakar and Sarkar found significant differences in the estimates of total factor productivity (TFP) for public and private sector banks when branches were included as output variables. Sathye (2003) moves beyond output sensitivity and studies the differences in technical efficiency estimates under alternative inputs-output combinations. Among the two models that they utilize, which are defined under the intermediation approach, the efficiency of the public sector is lower than that of foreign banks in one case and vice-versa in another. A similar attempt was made by Hughes et al. (2000) for scale economies of US commercial banks, which focused on the issue of empirically testing the input or output status of deposits. They assert that the choice of deposits as an input or an output "is a technological question that can be answered by testing whether the data are consistent with the different technological roles of outputs and inputs" (p. 6). Their study concludes that deposits must be treated as an input. However, this finding is tentative and subject to change when studying other periods or countries. Some studies also analysed the differences in technical efficiency estimates using one flow and one stock output variable. De (2004) was undertaken in this spirit. The author undertook sensitivity tests for technical efficiency estimates using the Cobb-Douglas stochastic frontier approach (SFA) with two output measures – viz. gross income (flow) and amount of loans and investments (stock).

The phase of the 2010s saw an improved focus on output sensitivity analysis and the implications of using alternative parametric and non-parametric methods in the production analysis of banks. Lozano-Vivas and Pasiouras (2010) examined the effect of including non-traditional output measures (off-balance-sheet and non-interest income) on cost and profit efficiencies. They found that cost efficiency results improved sizably on having non-traditional outputs, but profit efficiency results showed only a marginal improvement. Similar efforts were undertaken by Feng and Serletis (2010), who checked for the robustness of their efficiency and TFP estimates for US banks by additionally including non-traditional output in their output vector. Both the studies found improvements in their performance estimates, including the off-balance-sheet output. Guarda et al. (2013) brought a fresh perspective on this matter. They used a directional distance function to specify inputs and outputs empirically and then examined the sensitivity of estimated distance function parameters to alternative specifications of the selected output variables. While these studies generally used output variables from both asset and liability sides, Oluitan (2014) analysed the empirical sensitivity of cost efficiency scores to three different asset side variables: the amount of loan, amount of investment, and other earning assets non-interest income. Their findings broadly resonated with the conclusions of past studies. Most of these studies combined loans and investments.

However, Mamonov and Vernikov (2017) checked for the sensitivity of cost efficiency estimates by adding securities investments as a separate output in their trans-log cost function. They, too, found that estimates are quite sensitive to changes in the output vector. Some countries focused on non-advanced economies. This included Thilakaweera (2016), who examined the various economic efficiencies and the Malmquist TFP of Sri Lankan commercial banks under the DEA approach. The stock-flow dimension of output measures was explicitly analysed by adopting both the intermediation approach (stock) and the operating profit approach (Flow). The efficiency and productivity estimates sensitivity to these two output specification approaches are then analysed. Sizeable and statistically significant differences in efficiency and productivity estimates were found between both approaches. Finally, Anwar (2019) examined the sensitivity of parametrically estimated cost efficiency under SFA to alternative asset side outputs in three models. The author found that the cost efficiency estimates were the highest when the standard output specification was used – namely total loans, investments and non-interest incomes compared to more disaggregated measures of loans, investments and non-interest incomes.

In recent times, Boda and Piklová (2021) compared the technical efficiency scores for nine input-output specifications of the intermediation approach, nine specifications of the production-like approaches and three network-integrated specifications of the modelled production function. They found that "intermediation input-output specifications tend to produce higher efficiency scores than production-like specifications" (p. 1551). One can thus conclude that the empirical sensitivity of performance estimates to different outputs in banking has been an area of debate for a long time. This has remained unsettled, though some consensus has begun emerging. These matters will be discussed later, but it is interesting to note that very few studies have undertaken this exercise using alternative outputs and alterative empirical methods. This gap is serious because output sensitivity is expected to change under different empirical methods. This research gap is broadly addressed in Part III of this work.

3.3. Approaches to output specification in the banking literature

This section elaborates on the different lines of thought that have developed on the specification of the "correct" output measure in banking literature. At the outset, one must accept that output specification is contextual and driven by different considerations. Primary among them are the researcher's beliefs concerning the main functions of banks and the availability of data. While the latter is outside of the control of an analyst, the former has induced a large amount of debate and disagreements on how to represent banking output correctly. Different lines of thought have different views. It is not plausible to collapse the differences in beliefs into water-tight compartments of thoughts. However, literature has found it necessary to classify authors' beliefs on output measurement issues into different groups. Each has a specific procedure to ascertain which variables shall be used as output and the rationale. While many researchers elaborated on the theoretical basis underlying these approaches, there have been ad hoc choices on this account too. In several cases, researchers simply adopted a particular output specification approach without really delving into the rationale for their choice. Complete justification is not always provided, and general beliefs are utilised to define the outputs.[6]

The schools of thought on output specification in banking literature have evolved and changed with time and experience. The banking industry has undergone a vast evolution in its services, institutions that provide those services, and policies that govern them. Consequently, different approaches have emerged in the literature. Early traces of this account can be found in Gorman (1969), who delineated two frameworks for output specification in banking: liquidity and transaction approach. The former "measures real output as a weighted average of deflated dollars of demand and term deposits" (Geehan & Allen, 1978, p. 670). The annual average rate earned on bank assets minus the average annual interest incurred on deposits is used as the weighting factor. Alternatively, "the transactions approach measures output as a weighted average of the deflated dollar volume of transactions for the two types of deposits, the weights being base-year interest forgone on deposits of each type" (Geehan & Allen, 1978, p. 671). The value-volume dichotomy is embedded among these two approaches. In a broader sense, the stock-flow debate in bank output measurement seems to have flown from the debates of the 1970s on liquidity versus transaction approaches. After that, another novel[7] classification of output specification approach emerged in Clark (1984), who suggests the following approaches: un-weighted stock outputs, "technically independent production functions" (p. 54) and "weighted index of bank output using information from the income statement as well as the balance sheet" (p. 54). The author suggested these approaches to tackle the issue of non-homogeneous bank production functions. Recognition of value measures, i.e., price and quantity components, increased with time in the literature. Despite the academic strengths of the volume measures, i.e. those having only a quantity component, value measures of output began garnering popularity. Consequently, the specification approaches that recommended their use became more frequent in empirical applications. The 1980s concluded with the suggestion of using both the physical (volume) and value measures together in an indexed measure of bank output. Todhanakasem et al. (1986) suggested two major approaches in this context – physical measures-based production functions or production functions employing multiple output measures via indexing.

During the 1990s, one of the most influential works was undertaken by Berger and Humphrey (1992). They classified output specification approaches into the asset, user cost, and value-added approaches. Coupled with the production and intermediation approaches already in use, these five approaches laid the foundations for all future empirical works on banking performance analysis. In the same spirit, Grigorian and Manole (2002) examined the major approaches as suggested in Berger and Humphrey (1992). Several works emerged during the 1990s and 2000s using these approaches in defining output vectors in bank production analysis. However, the gap between these theoretical economic approaches and the national income accounts remained wide. Hence, in the 2010s, Daisuke et al. (2011a, 2011b) contextualized the economic approaches regarding the national income approach, culminating in the FISIM method of the System of National Accounts (SNA) 2008. Another strongly emerging trend during the 2010s was the shift from single-stage to a multi-stage theorization of the banking and insurance production process. While many works may be quoted on this account, Kouki et al. (2014) provided a fresh perspective by undertaking vertically integrated modelling of the production process in financial services firms such as banks and insurers.[8] The broad consensus in literature post-2020 may be summarised by Shah et al. (2022, p. 8), who assert that "Production approaches are more applicable for branch-level data, while intermediation approaches are for bank-level data". These approaches are summarised in Figure 3.1.

As highlighted in Figure 3.1, specification approaches to bank output can be classified into volume, value, hybrid and national income approaches. The so-called production approach dominates the volume specification, while intermediation (including the asset approach) and value-added approaches dominate the value specifications. The combinations of these approaches yield the hybrid approaches, as explained in the figure. Finally, the national income approach is used for sectoral and aggregate analyses.

Production approach

Underlying any output specification is a specific kind of input-output relationship. The inputs and outputs must be defined consistent with the chosen specification approach. In the production approach, the inputs are labour, capital, and, increasingly also, equity capital. However, labour and capital are the most frequently used inputs. Both deposits and loans are specified as outputs in either volume or value forms.[9] Generally, volume measures of bank output are preferred under this approach. However, the literature has been flexible in specifying the output vector under the production function. Value measures have been used frequently. Both flow and stock measures have been employed, though the early literature stressed that the production approach should employ flow measures of volume output (Colwell & Davis, 1992).

The essential idea in this approach is to theorise banks as typical production units that use standard inputs (labour and capital) to produce traditional outputs (deposits and loans). The current consensus suggests that the production approach is the best choice for branch-level analysis. Intermediation, its

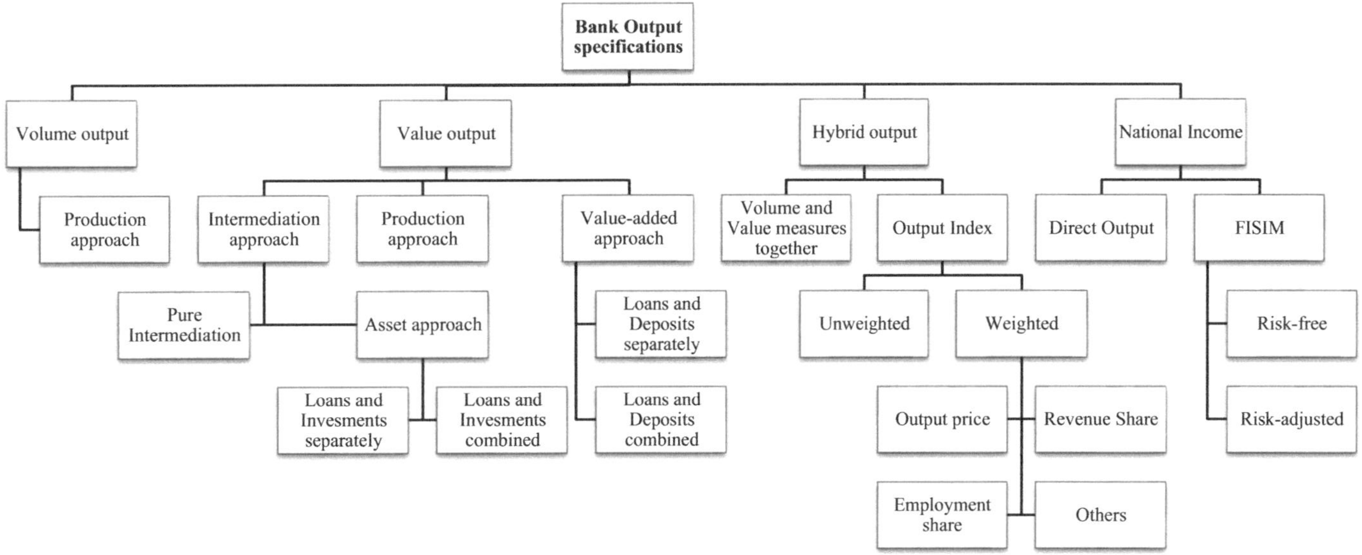

Figure 3.1 Major approaches to banking output specification in the extant literature

Source: Author's analysis based on the survey of the literature.

primary counterpart, is hardly a process under the control of retail branches. The production approach specifies the most basic form of the bank production function, which the literature has modified in different directions to yield alternative approaches. A major criticism of this approach is the utter ignorance of the intermediation function that banks use "the mismatch between lending and borrowing to generate . . . profit" (Daisuke et al., 2011b, p. 7). Because deposits are treated only as output, the liability-asset transformation undertaken by banks is wholly ignored. Essentially, the production approach disregards the interest costs paid on deposits (Shah et al., 2022). This approach is also very much at odds with the core idea of banking, which implies transforming public money into loanable funds. Despite its limitations, this approach provides computational advantages as it can be easily incorporated into a single-stage production function. Its data requirements are also not very strict.[10] This approach has also been utilised as the first stage in a multi-stage production function wherein deposits are produced initially using labour and capital. Subsequently, loans and investments are produced using deposits and other inputs. However, one aspect that seems to be missing in the literature is recognising the production approach as a valuable tool for sectoral levels of analysis. Banks need to be seen as service providers to depositors and borrowers at sectoral levels. The production approach allows the use of deposits and loans both as outputs. Other approaches tend to underplay the deposit services as output and probably overemphasize them as inputs.

In conclusion, the popularity of this approach can be ascribed to lenient data requirements and possibly also to the increasing share of off-balance-sheet output (generally defined as non-interest incomes of banks) in the revenue portfolios of banks. Non-interest incomes include fees, commissions earned, and other such directly charged services of banks. Suppose their share indeed is increasing. In that case, banks could be theorised as production units that process the basic inputs of branches, labour, and equity capital into directly charged services without much theoretical loss.[11]

Intermediation approach

In general, conceptualizing banks as intermediaries accounts for most of the services rendered by banks.[12] It also implies that banks function as transformers of funds rather than simply suppliers of goods, as Hancock (1985) suggested. Under this approach, "banks intermediate deposited and purchased funds into loans and other assets" Berger et al. (1987, p. 508). The purest form of this approach treats deposits strictly as inputs. No, *a priori* empirical test is conducted to decide whether to treat deposits as input or output. "Whenever deposits appear on the input side, commercial banks are viewed as intermediation links between surplus-fund units (depositors) and deficit-fund units (debtors)" (Boda & Piklová, 2021, p. 1553). Hence, this framework sees banks as transformers of deposits (liabilities) into loans and advances (assets). The underlying belief in this approach is that banks possess a competitive advantage in minimizing delegation and monitoring costs compared to other lending models.[13] Thus, their primary source of revenue is assumed to be intermediation services, and this aspect must thus be reflected in the hypothesized production function. This approach implies that banking institutions are primarily engaged in transforming liabilities into assets at the macroeconomic level. Their crucial role in the economy is to allocate scarce loanable funds efficiently.

At least four problems emerge in using the pure form of intermediation approach.[14] First, the services rendered by banks to depositors are ignored in the output vector. Banks provide various fee-based and non-fee based services to the depositors. The quantum of these services is generally assumed to be positively correlated with the deposit amount. Thus, treating deposits as an input contradicts this observation. Moreover, the treatment of deposits as inputs is all the more troublesome, given that "a very substantial and growing portion of the industry's total revenue is received in the form of fee income" (Radecki, 1999, p. 53). Second, at the macroeconomic level,[15] to whom should the intermediation services be ascribed? If depositors are the choice here, then the very idea of intermediation loses context. Deposits being treated as inputs, depositors gain the benefits of the intermediation services, which seems theoretically invalid. If borrowers are assigned the total value of intermediation output, then one ignores the services supplied by banks to the depositors. As discussed later on, these concerns are also at the heart of the national income approach to bank output measurement. The allocation problem for financial intermediation services indirectly measured (FISIM) output directly results from these concerns.

Three, the intermediation process is inherently a two-stage process (Fukuyama et al., 2020). In the first stage, variable and fixed inputs are used to produce deposits, while in the second stage, the deposits are used to produce loans and investments. However, most selected literature studies have theorised intermediation as a single-stage process. This is one matter that has motivated the emergence of newer models such as network DEA (e.g. Yu et al., 2019), dynamic DEA (e.g. Zha et al., 2016), stochastic DEA, two-stage DEA (e.g. Khan et al., 2018) and simultaneous non-linear parametric models (e.g. Kumbhakar & Sarkar, 2003). Fourth and last is the role of monetary policy in the intermediation production function. Banks' transformation of deposits and other funds into assets is conditional on the monetary policy rates in an economy. These rates can induce exogenous shifts in the production function without changing the underlying performance parameters such as efficiency, productivity, etc. Hartwick (1996) provides an overview of this aspect. Studies using the intermediation approach have not accounted for this dimension. Further discussion on this aspect is provided later in this chapter. However, an attempt was made by Triplett and Bosworth (2004a, 2004b) to incorporate monetary reserves in the measurement of bank output. Other than this study, the author could not locate any high-quality work.

Finally, incorporating risk into the intermediation process has been challenged. "Typically in the literature, the cost and profit functions or frontiers are measured without considering the bank's capital structure or bank's choice of risk" (Hughes & Mester, 2008, p. 9). A notable review on this issue was made in this direction by Kenjegalieva et al. (2009), who proposed a risk-adjusted intermediation approach-based output specification. The study highlighted three competitive advantages of banks in terms of managing risks: assessment (information advantages), diversification (pooling of deposits) and risk-taking (deposits as a check on bank's speculative investments). Accordingly, they stressed incorporating three vital explanatory variables: technology, property rights and organizational form. The previous discussion clarifies that a strict specification of production function under the pure form of intermediation approach will cause many theoretical and empirical problems. Researchers have resolved this issue by evolving further extensions of the intermediation approach. The asset approach is one of them and is explored now.

Asset approach

The limitations of the pure intermediation approach have motivated output analysts to incorporate more dimensions of the asset-side of a bank's balance sheet into the output vector. The so-called asset approach is the result of these analytical innovations. The primary difference between the pure intermediation and the asset approach is captured by Leong et al. (2003, p. 198), who state that, "In essence, this stream of thought is a variant of the intermediation approach, but instead defines outputs as the stock of loan and investment assets". Inclusion of investments, specifically financial investments, improves the coverage of the output vector under the intermediation approach and permits the recognition of the shareholders as major consumers of the bank's intermediation process. Along with depositors and borrowers, an additional consumer of the intermediation services is introduced by the asset approach – viz., the shareholders. Banks are not only transformers of deposit funds into loanable funds. They also undertake wealth generation and maximization for their shareholders. This fact is recognized under the banking literature's asset approach to output specification. By including investments as an output in the production function, banks are viewed as transformers of liabilities into loans and liabilities into investments. Two measures of bank output are used under this approach: 1. amount of loans; 2. amount of investments. These two variables are either used separately or combined in the literature. Table 2.1 shows the frequency of use of these variables in the sample studies. Deposits, however, continue to be treated as inputs and the usual problems of the intermediation approach continue to plague this approach. Another improvement in this approach is that non-deposit funds (generally termed as other purchased funds in literature) are recognised as inputs and traditional deposit funds. While the pure intermediation approach considers only deposits as the source of loanable funds, the asset approach can also be extended to include non-deposit sources of funds. In practical terms, this framework generally provides a better fit for productivity and efficiency estimations using bank-level data.

Value-added approach

Concerns with intermediation and production approach gave rise to a new line of thought on bank output measurement, which introduced a data-driven approach to output-input specification of a given variable in the bank's production function. The production approach was improved upon, and instead of ad hoc criteria in choosing the outputs, an empirical approach was suggested by Berger and Humphrey (1992, p. 247), who assert that the value-added approach considers "outputs as those activities that have substantial value-added (i.e., large expenditures on labour and physical capital)". Compared to the intermediation approach, the value-added approach "considers all liability and asset categories to have some output characteristics rather than distinguishing inputs from outputs in a mutually exclusive way" (Berger & Humphrey, 1992, p. 250). Output characteristics are established by operating cost allocations for each liability- and asset-side component. Benston et al. (1982, p. 440) state, "Output should be measured in terms of what banks do that cause operating expenses to be incurred". Hence, if an activity is causing the bank to incur operating costs, it may be termed an output irrespective of whether it is a liability or an asset.[16] This approach is essentially a reframing of the production approach but with the additional restriction of operating cost allocations to each liability and asset item. The value-added approach has been modified to incorporate more aspects of the output vector in banking. Literature has also used value-added specifications, including interest costs or price of deposits, as inputs while considering the deposit amount as an output. This modified value-added approach has perplexed many analysts who criticize the inclusion of deposits on both sides of the production function. Despite some of its limitations, this approach has been the most favoured within the literature. However, very few studies undertake any empirical assessment of the operating costs function to locate those items that should be considered outputs and those that should be defined as inputs. The value-added approach has primarily been ad hoc in the literature. Researchers claim that the selected items (from both the deposits and asset sides) have positive operating cost shares and thus must be considered as outputs. However, hardly any of the reviewed studies empirically justified such an assertion. Concurrent with this approach, another data-driven approach has been frequently used in literature to specify bank outputs, namely the user cost approach, as discussed in the next section.

User cost approach

The emergence of the idea of user cost can be traced back to the works of Donovan (1977) and Barnett (1978), who attempted to construct index measures for the aggregate stock of money supply. The foundation of this approach is well-captured by Hartwick (1996, p. 5), who states that "This approach derives from the practice in the theory of general equilibrium where inputs have negative prices and outputs have positive prices". It is thus clear that the user cost approach utilizes the net contribution of an activity to the total revenue of a banking firm to determine whether it is an input or an output.[17] Positive user cost would imply that the activity is output, while a negative sign would imply that the activity is an input (Hancock, 1985). This approach requires data on net revenue for each banking firm and its disaggregation across various banking services. Individual income and balance sheet items can be specified as input or output in the production analysis. Furthermore, even if such data are available, one needs to estimate the opportunity costs,[18] which will require implicit or shadow pricing methods. The data requirements are strict in this approach, and barring a few advanced economies, such data are generally difficult to obtain, particularly in emerging economies.

Two problems have frequently been discussed in the literature under this approach. First is the instability of the user cost sign (Banker et al., 2010). Second is the problem of accounting for implicit earnings (Berger & Humphrey, 1992). Regarding the first problem, it should be noted that the user cost sign is an empirical issue. It can differ depending on the country, banks, regions, and other aspects. Both temporal and spatial variations in the user cost sign are possible. This makes the output specification using this approach somewhat tentative and unstable. In this case, the output measure may well switch over to input and vice-versa with variations in time and space. The temporal and spatial stability of output measures is difficult to establish in this case. Regarding the second problem, the user cost approach can examine only the observed and direct revenue. This is because the data for such explicit revenues are readily available in banks' income statements. However, there are implicit revenues too that banks earn on intermediation, risk management, wealth maximization and other services. The user cost approach will ignore these services unless the total revenue is modified to include these implicitly priced services too. This is a data-intensive job and will generally be challenging in emerging economies with weak data infrastructure.[19] A criticism often directed at the user cost approach is the lack of explicit specification of the services provided by financial services firms. The user cost sign from the underlying revenue function is used to specify the output. However, there is no guarantee that a particular asset or liability item will always be an input or an output. As mentioned earlier, the user-cost sign is subject to temporal and spatial variations. This makes the input-output specification using user cost of approach ad hoc and possibly even biased.[20] This approach estimates FISIM output under the SNA framework, but its application at the bank and branch levels is complicated. Few studies which have used this approach have not undertaken any empirical estimation of the user-cost sign of the chosen output variables. Instead, they use extant literature and their beliefs in specifying outputs under the user-cost approach.

Index numbers approach

The index numbers approach is a novel and less frequently used method for specifying bank output in the literature. The multi-product nature of banking firms, which was stressed as early as 1959 by Speagle and Kohn, has motivated researchers to use an index of outputs rather than to use single or multiple outputs separately. Noteworthy works using this approach to bank output specification include Benston et al. (1982), Brand and Duke (1982), Clark (1984), Kim (1985), Colwell and Davis (1992), Athanasoglou et al. (2009), and Royster (2012).[21] All these studies undertake weighted indexing. The choice of weights differs from study to study. The popularly used weighting factors[22] in the literature include unit costs, unit prices, gross yields (in the case of assets measures of output), revenue shares, and labour requirements per unit of output. The basic idea behind this approach is that a single output or even multiple outputs separately do not capture the output vector correctly. The multiple outputs should be combined using theoretically consistent index numbers.[23] The choice of outputs can be undertaken using any previously stated approaches. However, the chosen output variables should be combined into an index. Two popular output index numbers in the literature are the Divisia index and the Tornquist index. These indexes are generally considered to be possessing important statistical properties such as being superlative. This allows theoretically consistent aggregation across the chosen outputs. The application of this approach has been limited in the literature, though.

3.4. Output measurement in the banking literature

This section elaborates on and reviews the major output measures used in the literature. Each output measure is presented in a flow diagram that captures the significant mechanics behind its construction and the essential issues highlighted.[24]

Loan outputs

The critical dimensions of the output measures based on loans and advances in banking performance literature are captured in Figures 3.1, 3.2, and 3.3. The figures are prepared in a self-explanatory manner. The fundamental categories of loan-based outputs are classified into three types: 1. stock-based measures, 2. flow-based measures, and 3. other loan-based measures, which is a reflection of how the literature has approached this output measure. Given the distribution of sample studies, as shown in Table 2.1, the stock-based measures, in general, have dominated the banking literature. Generally, the loan amount, either gross of NPAs or net of NPAs, has been employed as a bank output measure. This amount is derived from the balance sheet and is a year-end figure.

The amount of loan and number of loan accounts are the most frequently used measures of bank output in terms of loans-based measures. With regards to the amount of loan, which is by far the most frequently used measure, it has been used in five different ways, namely, as an aggregated measure (weighted or un-weighted), disaggregated measure, in combination with non-loan outputs, in terms of adjustments for interbank loans or as a "bad" output (in the

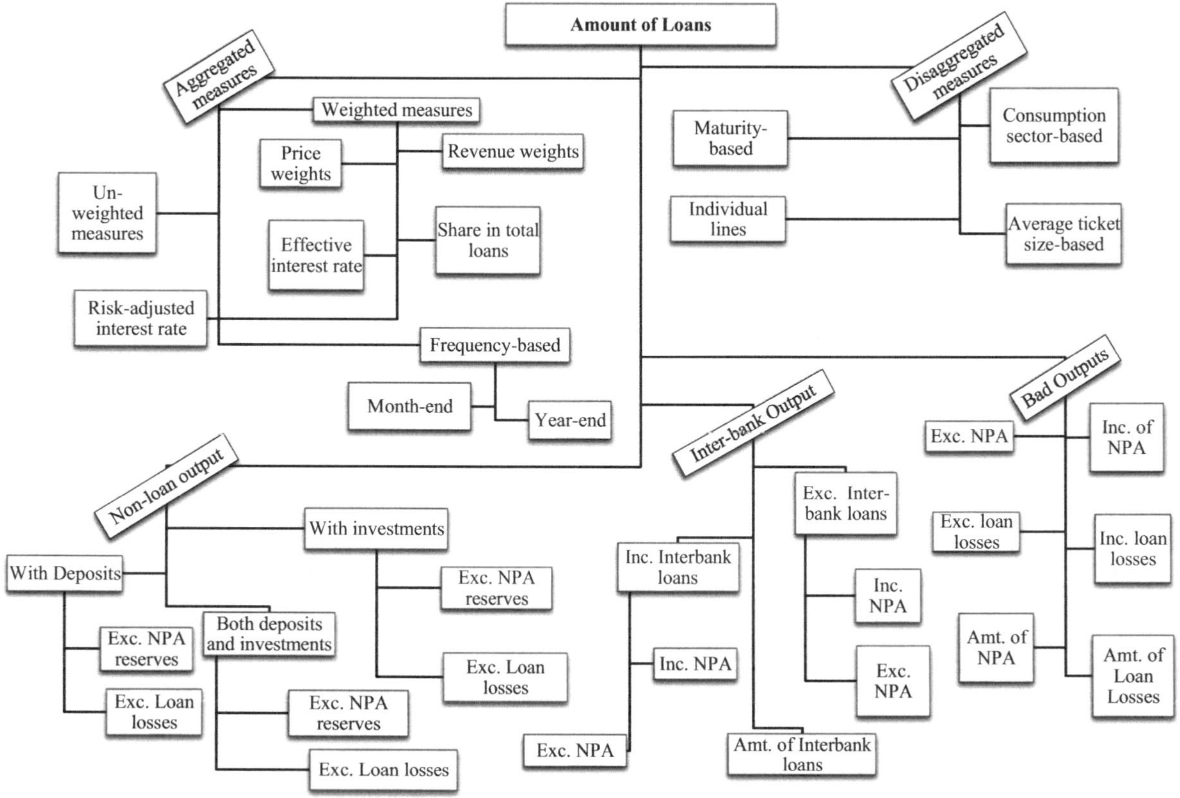

Figure 3.2 Stock measures of loan output in banking literature

Note: "Inc." implies inclusive of, "Exc." implies exclusive of, and "Amt." implies amount.

Source: Author's analysis based on the survey of the literature.

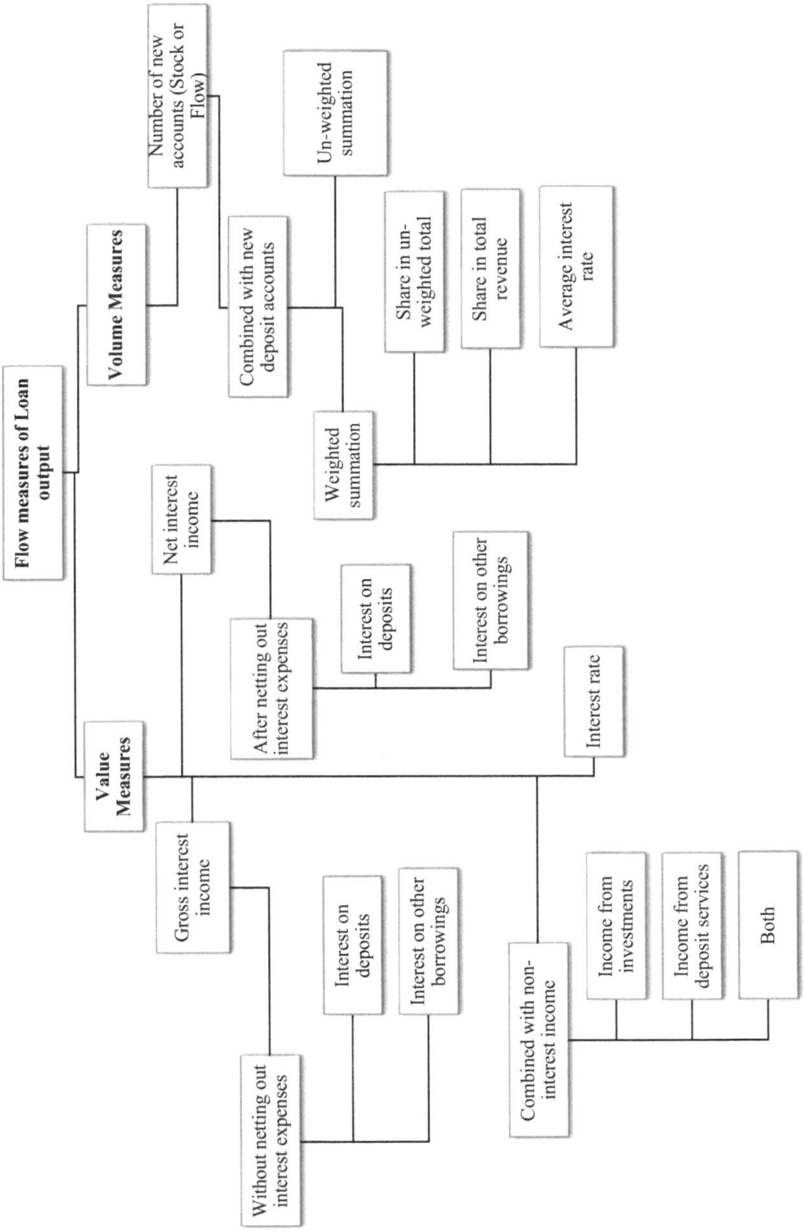

Figure 3.3 Flow measures of loan output in banking literature

Source: Author's analysis based on the survey of the literature.

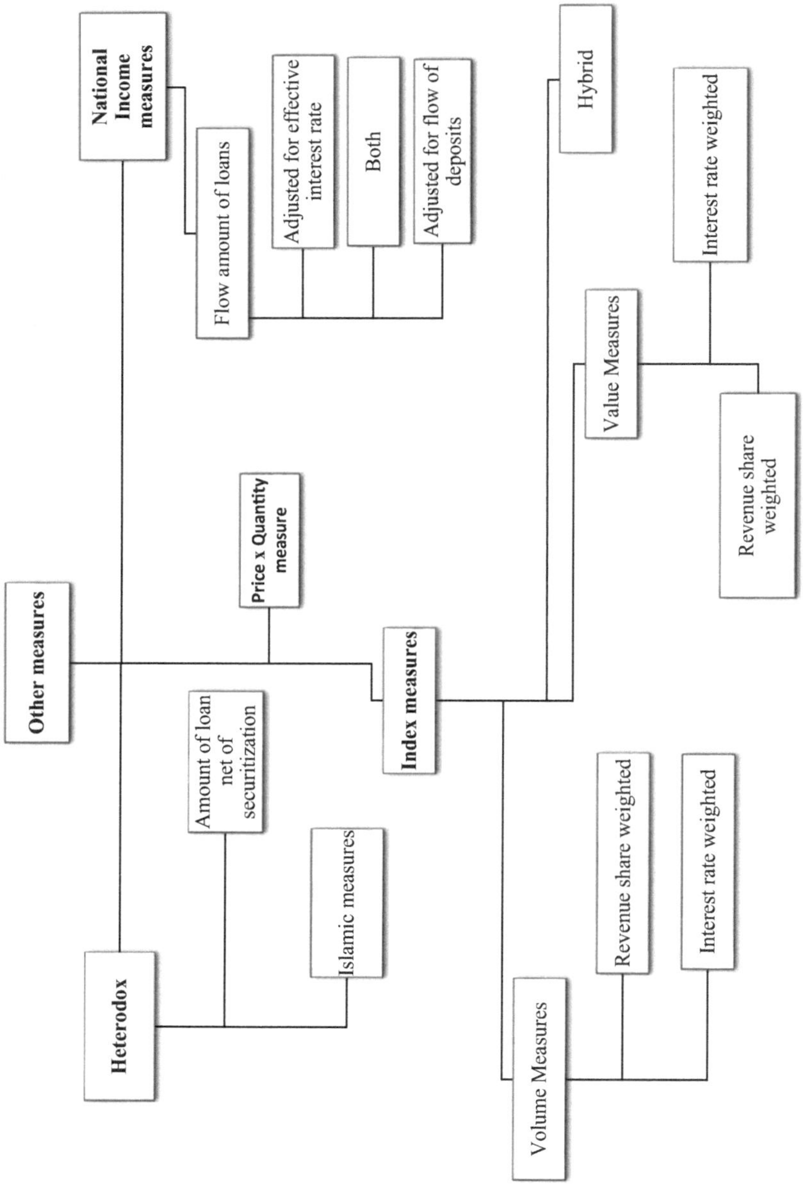

Figure 3.4 Other measures of loan output in banking literature

Source: Author's analysis based on the survey of the literature.

form of NPAs). As examined in the previous section, these approaches to loan output measurement have been used under almost every specification framework. Aggregate measures are at the level of the entire banking industry or the banking firm. Weighted aggregates, in this case, have generally been built using price (interest-rate) weights, revenue-share weights, effective (market interest rate net of reference rate) interest rate weights, share in un-weighted total loans, and risk-adjusted interest rate (where risk is by an interest rate or return on assets or equity).[25] These measures are aggregate in the sense that they represent the sum of all loans with different maturities (short-term and long-term), different lines (real estate, personal, etc.), different ticket sizes (retail and corporate) and diverse consumers (firms, individuals, governments, etc.). Literature has also disaggregated the aggregate amount of loans across these categories and used them separately. This can be examined by looking at the appendix to this chapter. Another frequently used approach is to combine loan output with non-loan outputs. The combination of loans with investments is the most frequently used measure. The aggregation of loans and investments has generally been un-weighted in the literature, i.e. a simple sum of both the components is undertaken to estimate the total bank output.

Further adjustments are made, as shown in Figure 3.2. Adjusting for NPAs has been a serious concern for researchers. When this is done, one has to deal with how to treat the NPAs, i.e. whether to remove them from total loans or treat them separately as "bad" output (subject to minimization rather than maximization).[26] Literature has primarily used the gross loan amount (i.e. including NPAs). It seems to be that incurring losses is a service that banks render to generate good loans (Hartwick, 1996). Another approach has been to combine loans and deposits[27] together.[28] This is a frequently used output measure under the value-added method for output specification, though even the national income approach[29] employs this measure. There has been a lot of debate on whether loans and deposits should be combined. The consensus seems to favour using them separately rather than combining them.[30] Lastly, some novel issues in loan output measurement are treating interbank loans and NPAs as "bad" output in the production function. Studies dealing with the former aspect can be found in Mertens and Urga (2001), Isik and Hassan (2002), Pasiouras et al. (2009), Olson and Zoubi (2011), Kouki et al. (2014), Mamonov and Vernikov (2017), Khan et al. (2020), and Bansal et al. (2022). For the latter issue, some recent illustrations include Fukuyama et al. (2020), and Zaman et al. (2022), among others.

Deposit outputs

Deposits represent the most crucial source of loanable funds for the banking system. Increasingly, however, non-deposit funds such as equity have been gaining increasing attention. Figures 3.5, 3.6, and 3.7 present a systematic representation of the ways in which this output variable has been conceptualized and empirically operationalized in the literature.

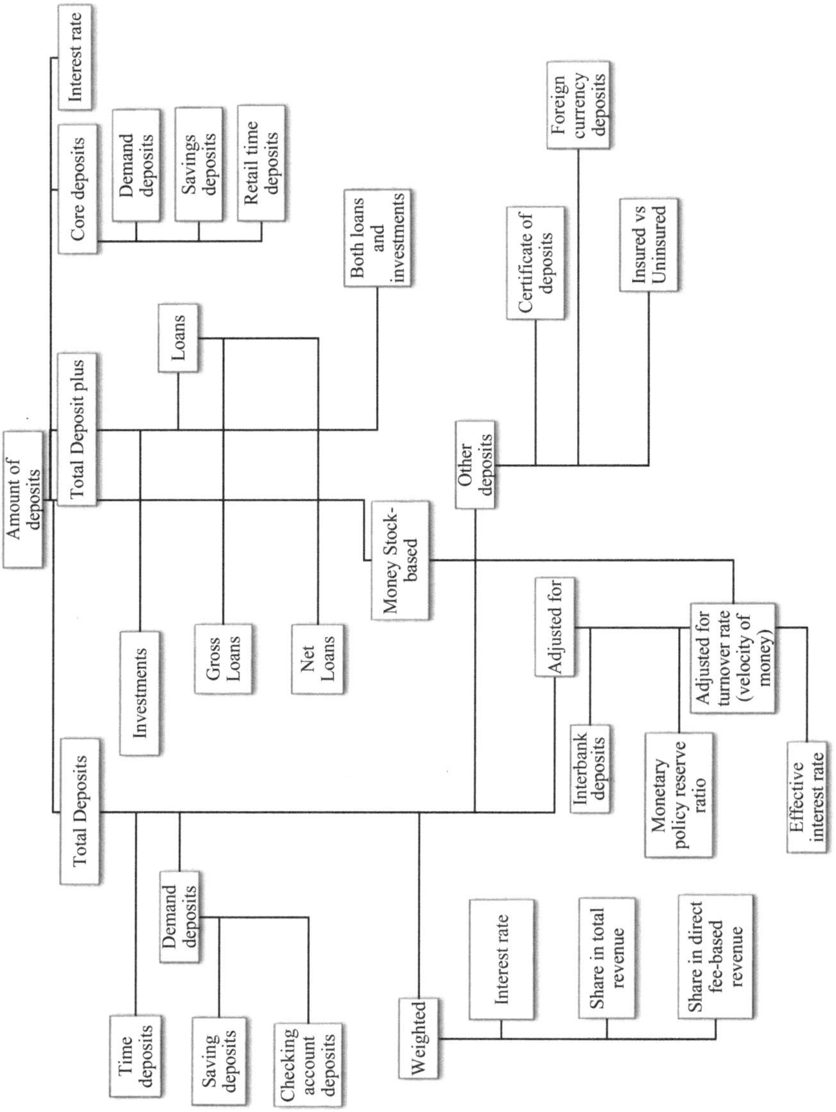

Figure 3.5 Amount of deposits as bank output in the literature

Source: Author's analysis based on the survey of the literature.

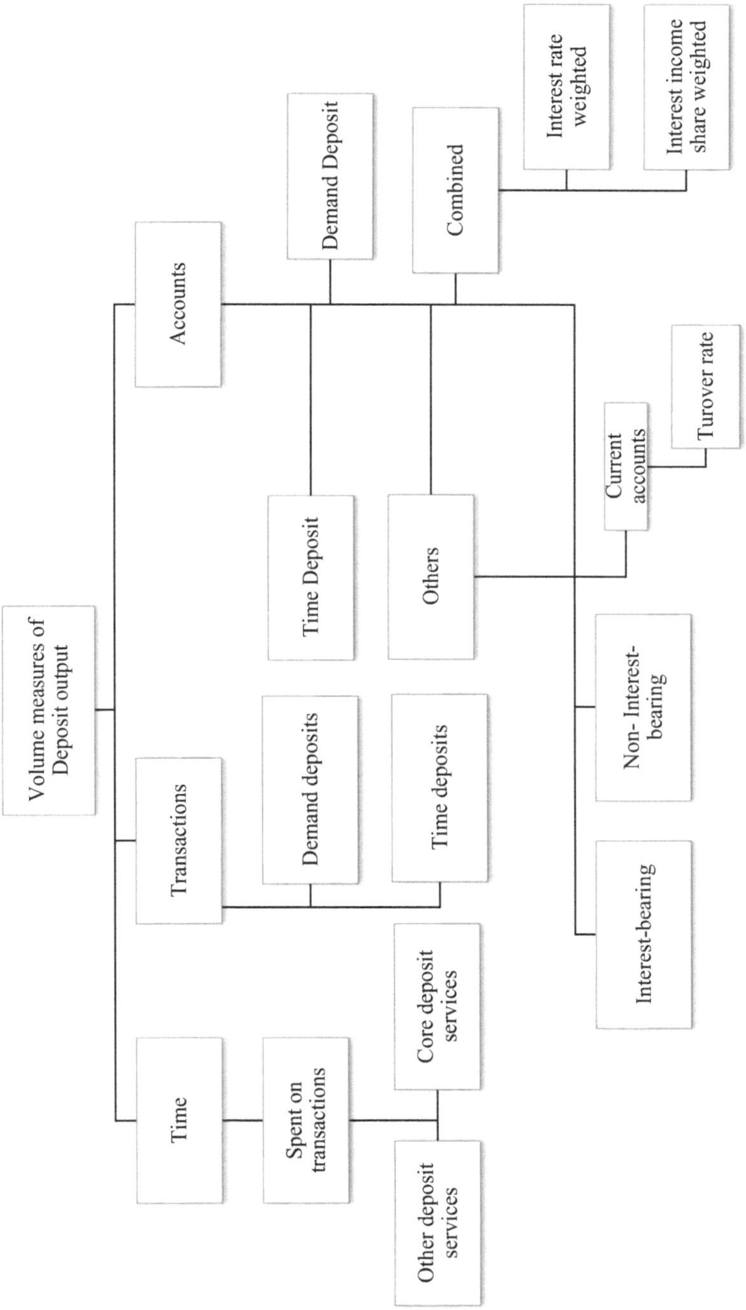

Figure 3.6 Volume measures of deposits as bank output in literature

Source: Author's analysis based on the survey of the literature.

Generally, the sum of demand and time deposits has been used to measure bank output in the literature. However, the use of demand and time deposits separately is also possible, given that the deposit structure may be an essential concern in modelling the production process of banks. When used together, demand and time deposits are aggregated using interest rate, share in total revenue, or direct fee-based revenue as the weighting factor. Banks' deposit services can be associated with two components: those related to maintaining the amount of deposit with the bank and those enabling the amount of customers' transactions through and with the bank (Gorman, 1969). The value of the deposits generally captures these services in the studies on bank performance. In the early studies, analysts have also used other measures of deposits, such as certificates of deposits (Mullineaux, 1978; Todhanakasem et al., 1986; Lawrence, 1989; Noulas et al., 1990; Elyasiani & Mehdian, 1992; Sharpe, 1997; Muldur & Sassenou, 1993; Resti, 1997), and foreign currency deposits (Kim, 1986; Kim & Weiss, 1989; Jagtiani & Khanthavit, 1996). Another novel but recently popular deposit type being included in the output vector of banks is insured deposits (Ohlson et al., 2021). Researchers have used the deposit amount individually, separately with other non-deposit measures or in combination. Loans and investments have been used as non-deposit outputs in the output vector, and the amount of deposit and these three output measures are either combined or used separately. When used together, they have generally been used in an un-weighted form. The value-added approach to output specification generally recommends this kind of output measure. Even the production approach has utilised this kind of bank output measure in the literature.

Finally, the most crucial debate in using deposits in the bank's production function is the so-called input-output dilemma (Agu, 1988). Figure 3.7 examines the significant dimensions of the input-output dilemma in the banking literature. The main issue of contention is whether to treat the amount of deposit as an input,[31] quasi-fixed input[32] or an output.[33] The production approach recommends treating deposits as output, while the intermediation approach stresses its role as an input. The value-added approach recommends appropriately using it on both sides (e.g. interest costs as input and amount of deposits as output). Analysts have also combined them with loans to measure bank output under the value-added approach. User-cost[34] and operating cost approaches recommend that empirical tests be performed to decide whether the amount of deposits is an input or an output in a given context. These two approaches are data-driven and reject any *a priori* conception of deposits being input or output.[35] Finally, in the national income approach, while estimating FISIM, deposits are treated as an output but in terms of the flow of deposit services rather than its stock.[36]

In two-stage models under the intermediation approach, deposits are generally treated as intermediate output and input in the entire production process. In other words, there is no single ideal prescription on how to resolve this dilemma. An alternative input-output dilemma in the literature is whether to treat the number of branches as an input (such as in Adams et al., 2002; Sinha & Chatterjee, 2008;

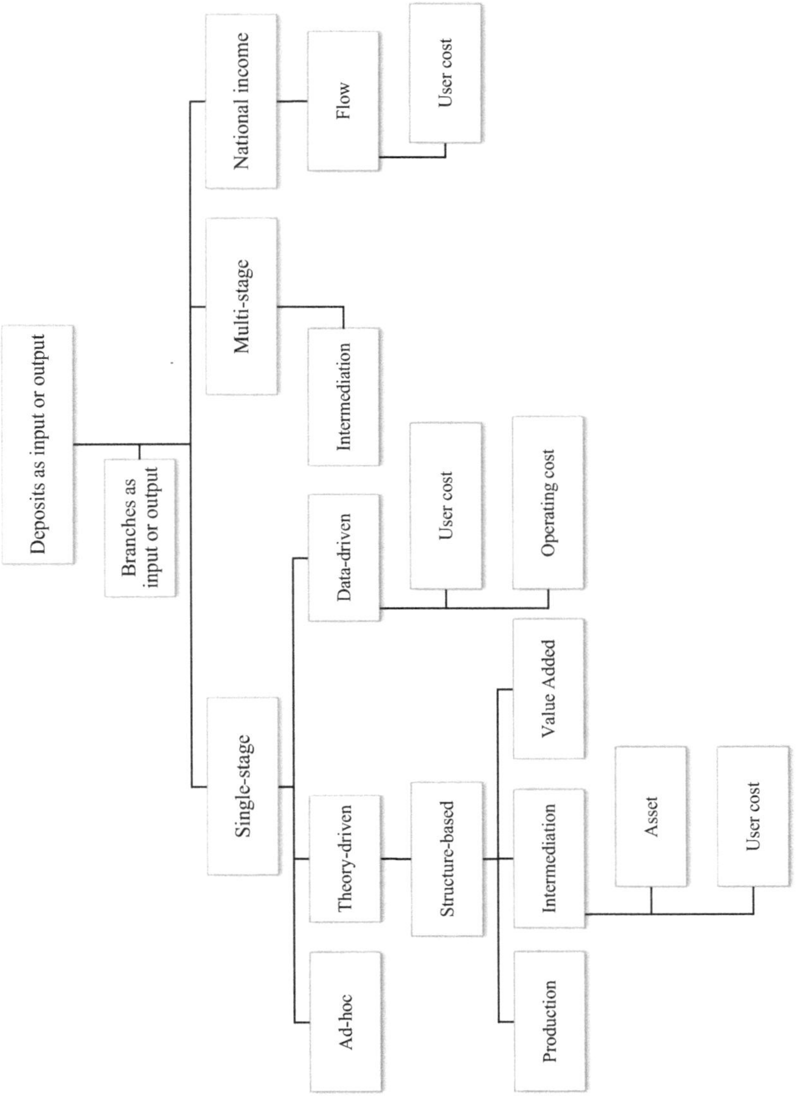

Figure 3.7 Approaches generally employed in literature to resolve the input-output dilemma

Source: Author's analysis based on the survey of literature

Chen et al., 2018, among others) or as an output (such as in Focarelli & Panetta, 2003; Kumbhakar & Sarkar, 2003; Humphrey, 2009, among some others). This dilemma also stands unresolved. Lastly, as shown in Figure 3.6, the literature has also utilized the volume measures[37] of deposit output. Three measures are employed in this context. First is the amount of time spent on handling deposit services. Second is the number of deposit transactions (disaggregated to individual deposit services). Third and last is the number of deposit accounts (combined or disaggregated into demand and time deposit accounts).

Asset output

Amount of loans (as discussed earlier), amount of investments and amount of other assets are the critical asset measures of bank output employed in the literature. Figure 3.8 shows the key permutations and combinations made in defining the asset output of banks in the literature. Assets are those items in the bank balance sheet that create the possibility of future earnings for the banks. Returns may be generated on these items, and thus they are classified as assets. While the amount of loan is the most common asset measure, additional asset items are included and combined with loans to measure the asset output of banks. The amount of bank total assets has generally been defined in the literature as the sum of loans, financial investments, physical assets and other assets (such as loans to the financial sector, unused assets, non-earning assets and interbank assets). The so-called asset approach to output specification, as discussed in section 3.3, recommends using the amount of total assets as the correct measure of bank output. Naturally, deposits are not given a space in the output vector under this framework. However, studies under the value-added approach have used deposits alongside the amount of total assets as bank outputs. More supplementary discussion on this output measure can be obtained from the author upon request.

Investment output

The amount of investments is another frequently employed measure. Figure 3.9 exemplifies the critical aspects of this measure in the literature. Investments in this context are financial investments, i.e. investments made by banks in financial instruments and securities. The amount of investment is used either individually or in combination with loans in the literature. Individually, it is either used as a total consisting of various individual investment items or in disaggregated terms. Literature has adopted different categorizations of investments. They are enlisted in Figure 3.9. The debate seems to hover around the inclusion of risky versus debt investments. How risky investments are included in the investment output impacts the amount of volatility introduced into the output vector. Generally, literature has undertaken un-weighted aggregation of risky and debt investments. Another investment output measure used is the value of liquid assets, i.e. investments with a high degree of liquidity. Some of the notable recent literature using this measure includes Berger and Bouwman

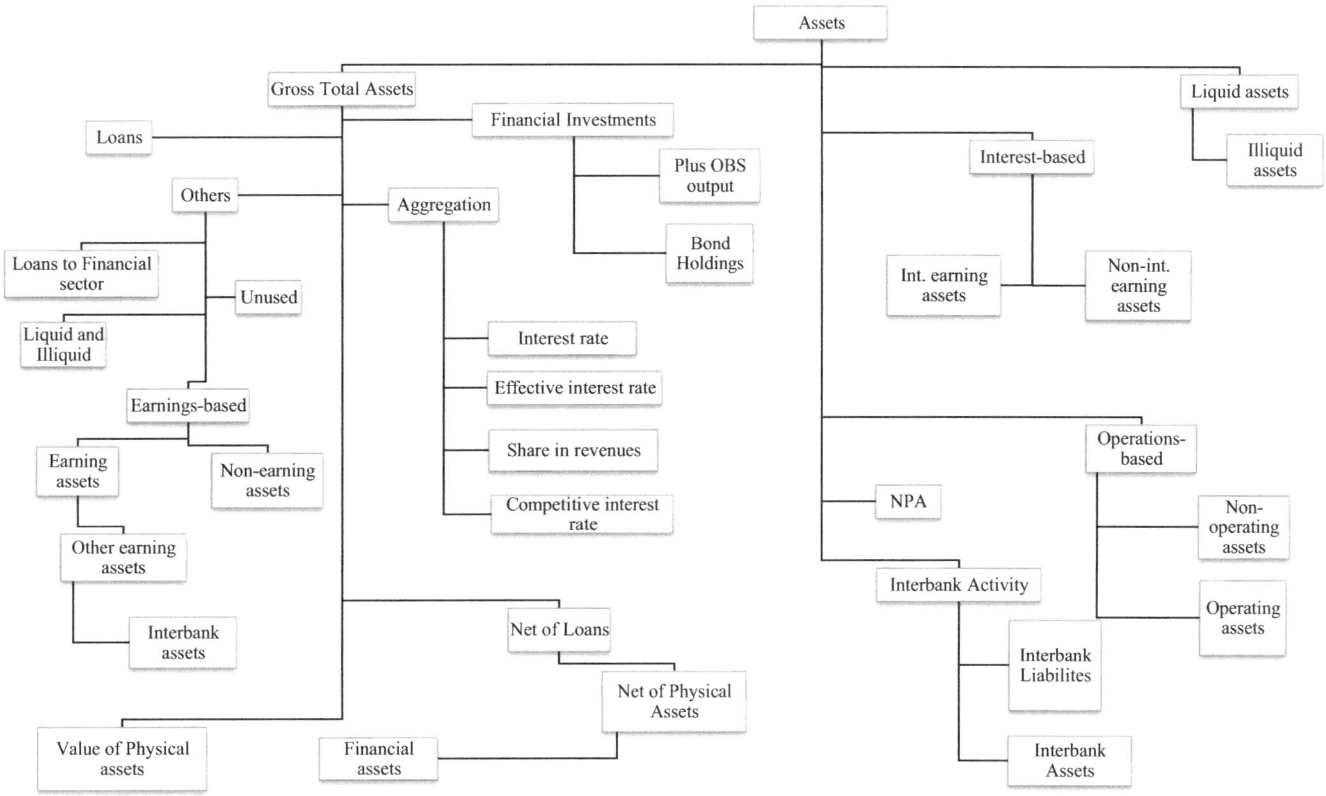

Figure 3.8 Asset measures of bank output in the literature

Source: Author's analysis based on the survey of the literature.

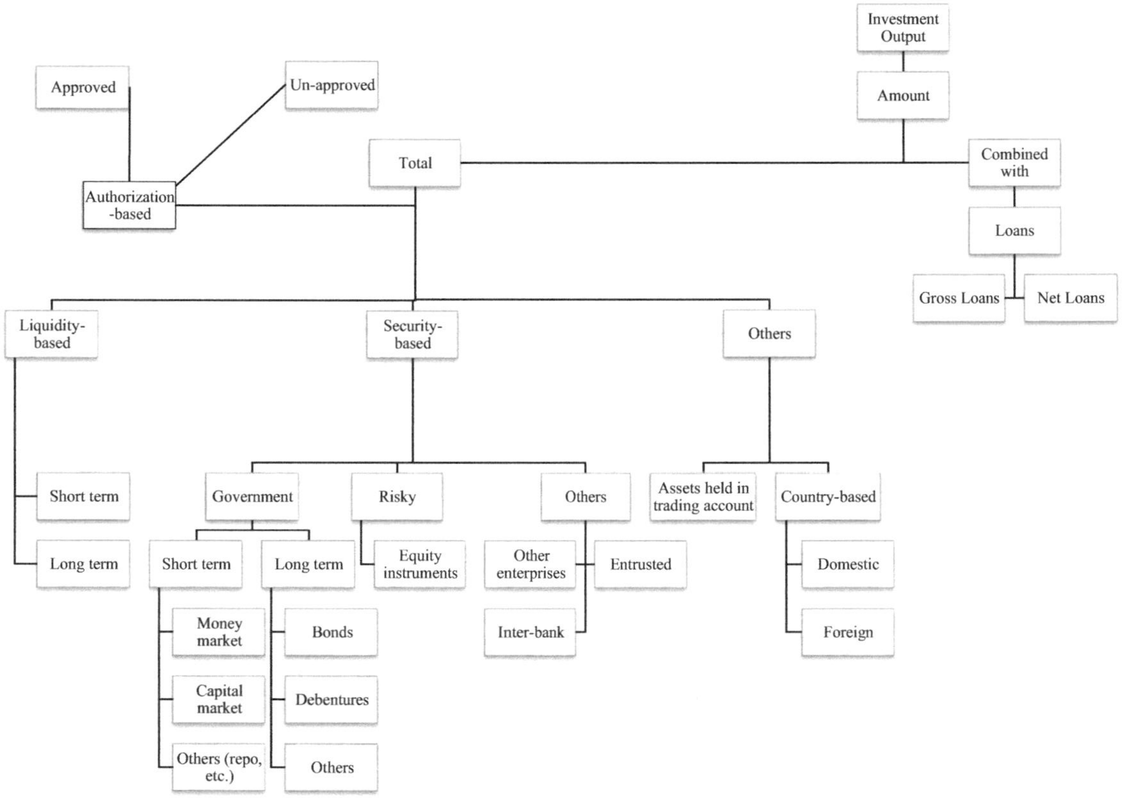

Figure 3.9 Investment outputs used in banking literature

Source: Author's analysis based on the survey of the literature.

(2007), Shih et al. (2007), Banerjee (2012), Davies and Tracey (2014), and Santosa (2022). However, its use can be found in literature from 2000 onwards, as shown in the appendix to this chapter.

Income and off-balance-sheet output

As discussed earlier, a production function requires flow outputs rather than stock measures. However, literature on bank output measurement has found it inevitable to use stock variables. Yet, flow measures of output have evolved in the literature. An early systematic attempt was the SNA (1953) which introduced the FISIM method to estimate the banking sector's output per national income account. At the microeconomic level, some researchers have also attempted to estimate flow measures of deposits and loans. Other than these flow measures, income measures of output have been employed that account for the explicit direct fee commissions charged by banks from depositors, borrowers and other customers. Figure 3.10 explains the effective approaches in this context.

The basic idea behind this approach is to capture the non-traditional services and consequent revenues generated by banks. As per the intermediation approach to output specification, the traditional function of banks is to transform deposits into assets. The interest income captures this and implies that banks generate implicit revenues, which are accounted for through indirect estimation methods such as the FISIM. However, as noted in the literature and will also explained by expert contributions[38] in Chapter 7, the contribution of fee-based output is increasing in the bank's total revenues, and this is being driven by income-based off-balance-sheet items such as fees, commissions, brokerage charges, and other such incomes of banks which are directly recorded in the income statement. One can find the use of this output measure as early as Mullineaux (1978). As shown in the appendix to this chapter, several studies have used this measure. An advantage of this measure is that it is a flow measurement and thus closely corresponds to the demands of the neoclassical production theory. They are termed 'non-traditional' because these services diverge from the traditional notion that the primary function of banks is to transform deposits into assets. The income measure includes both interest and non-interest incomes. In contrast, the off-balance-sheet or the non-traditional measure only includes the non-interest incomes as per the extant literature. At times, non-interest income is adjusted for service charges on deposits and net gains (profit or loss) on speculative investments to yield net non-interest income (such as in Rogers, 1998). Such a measure has been scarcely used in the literature.

Other income measures include the amount of profit (recent examples include Khan et al., 2018; Le & Ngo, 2020; Owusu & Alhassan, 2021; Bansal et al., 2022, among others) and amount of loan adjusted for unearned income (for example, Hughes et al., 2000). Using the off-balance-sheet measures of bank output implies recognising significant structural changes ongoing in the business model of modern banks. This measure is also quite suitable for output

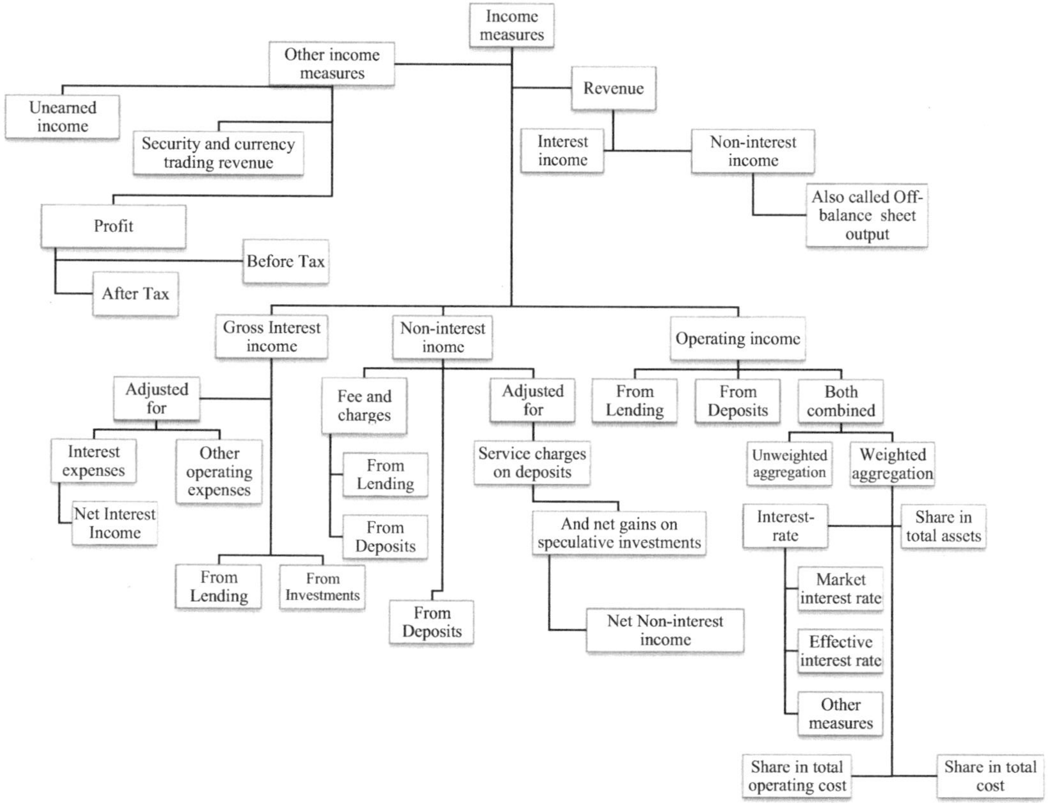

Figure 3.10 Income and off-balance-sheet bank output in the literature

Source: Author's analysis based on the survey of the literature.

analysis of the non-banking financial sector as non-interest income occupies a larger portion of their total revenue.

FISIM output[39]

The essence of the national income approach to bank output measurement is the FISIM approach.[40] This measure tries to capture the output of banks that is implicit[41] in their intermediation activities rather than directly measurable from their income statements or balance sheets. This measure of banking output can be used mainly at the sectoral level and does not directly lend itself to branch-level, firm-level, and intra-industry-level analyses. The main reason for this limitation is that disaggregated measures of this output are not available. However, for macroeconomic analysis of the banking industry, this output measure is quite helpful and provides a reliable summary of the value-added by banks. The primary debate underlying this approach is the choice of the reference rate,[42] also known as the Barnett benchmark rate and the Hancock opportunity cost rate of money (Fixler & Zieschang, 1999). The fundamental debates on the choice of reference rate are summarised in Figure 3.11.

Analysts have used the concept of reference rate to estimate both the FISIM output[43] and disaggregated flow measures of output. In the latter case,[44] the deposit and loan amounts are adjusted for the effective interest rate (market interest rate minus the reference rate). The flow of deposit and loan services is estimated. They are then combined to measure the total FISIM output. FISIM captures the implicit portion of banking output in the national income accounts. While its measurement and accounting procedures have a consensus in the SNA framework, the allocation of the net interest margin (interest received on loans minus interest paid on deposits) to various "business (intermediate consumers) versus households, government, and the rest of the world

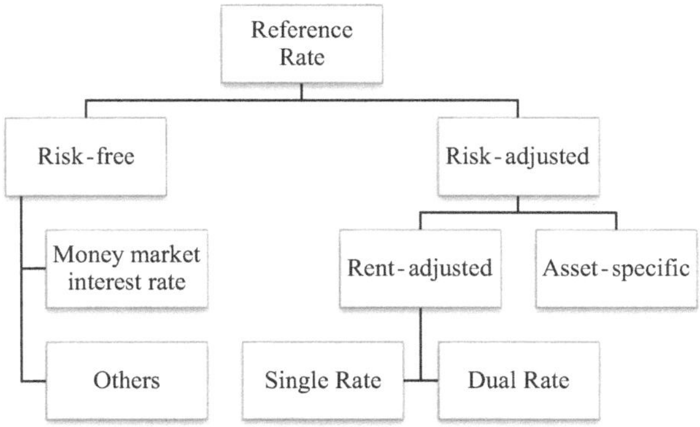

Figure 3.11 Debates on the references rate under the FISIM approach

Source: Author's analysis based on the survey of the literature.

(final consumers)" (Fixler & Zieschang, 1999, p. 547)[45] is still unsettled. An issue that has received considerable attention within the reference rate debates is risk treatment. Traditional SNA-based FISIM estimation relies on a risk-free or minimum risk-based reference rate.[46]

However, several authors have disagreed with this notion and have attempted to incorporate 'risk-incorporated' reference rates into the FISIM framework. Their fundamental argument is that ignoring risk overestimates the FISIM output due to choosing a risk-free (or minimum risk) reference rate such as the treasury bill rate. They also assert that the measurement of opportunity cost with a risk-less reference rate does not capture the actual behavioural dynamics at play. It implicitly assumes risk-aversion on the depositors and borrowers, which may not be applied universally. However, the SNA (1993) defends its use in a risk-free form by stating that "the reference rate to be used represents the pure cost of borrowing funds – that is, a rate from which the risk premium has been eliminated to the greatest extent possible and which does not include any intermediation services". The SNA (2008) goes further and states that "the reference rate should contain no service element and reflect the risk and maturity structure of deposits and loans". Thus, the essential features of a reference rate as per the SNA approach are 1. the underlying asset whose interest rate is used as a reference rate must be risk-free; 2. the underlying asset should not provide any financial intermediation services. One peculiar aspect of the SNA approach to reference rate is that it uses a single aggregate rate for deposits and loans.[47] This has been criticized in the literature, as a single rate will inevitably fail to capture the interest rate structure on deposits and loans.

Furthermore, a single reference rate treats depositors and borrowers as agents with similar risk perceptions, which is not true theoretically or empirically. The very use of a concept like a reference rate has been criticized in literature by arguing that the quantity of financial services and the financial instruments in the market are not necessarily related to each other. The primary assertion has been "that the implicit price of financial services bears no definitive relationship with any reference rate" (Wang & Basu, 2005, p. 1). They also argue that "not all of a bank's net interest income is compensation for its implicit services" (p. 5). The FISIM method is a valuable tool for obtaining a macroeconomic accounting-based nominal measure of banking output but lacks reliable foundations for deriving real banking output (Wang & Basu, 2005).

National income accounts and banking output

Other than FISIM, national income accounts are utilised to estimate a macroeconomic measure of banking output. The same has been presented in Figures 3.12 and 3.13. The primary debate in this regard is whether to use gross output or value-added measures. The main difference between both of them is that of intermediate consumption. Generally, the literature has favoured using the value-added approach for sectoral-level analysis in banking. The broad consensus on this choice seems to be that estimating intermediate consumption for the banking industry is complicated. The gross-output measure is generally available for the financial services industry rather than the banking industry.[48]

Lastly, a major challenge in using sectoral measures of banking output has been the matter of deflation of the nominal output. The main methods used in the literature to deflate nominal banking sector output are highlighted in Figure 3.12.

3.5. Thematic issues in banking output measurement

Given the literature survey undertaken in the above sections, several thematic issues can be extracted, and the same is present in very brief terms below. The readers can access detailed notes on this in the online resources.

Deflation of banking output

Nominal output has been frequently used in banking literature, as explained in Table 2.1. However, many researchers have employed real measures of bank output also. The real measures include volume output measures and constant-price output measures. The volume measures are in pure quantity terms, as discussed earlier. The main problem is converting the nominal (current-price) output to constant-price output. There is no consensus on the ideal deflator for bank output to date. One is presented with a menu of analytical choices, and given the context and purpose, the most feasible deflator is chosen. A reflection of the significant deflators in banking literature has been provided in Figure 3.12. Deflation removes the effects of inflation from the first difference form of a nominal output variable. This means that when the growth of constant-price output is measured, it should represent purely the quantity movements rather than quantity and price movements, as is the case with the growth rate of nominal output. Inflation embodies itself in banking activities under different dynamics not correctly captured by aggregate price indexes such as the Consumer Price Index (CPI), Wholesale Price Index (WPI), GDP deflator and GNP deflator. The frequent use of these indexes reflects the fact that optimal industry-specific deflator for banking services does not yet exist. As discussed by Prof. R. B. Barman in Chapter 7 and Barman and Samanta (2007), many efforts have been undertaken by official agencies in the EU and US to build such a price index. However, there is still no optimal deflator, which is the case with emerging economies. The literature has primarily used CPI and WPI for deflation of nominal bank output at the firm and intra-industry-level and has preferred GDP deflator at the sectoral level of analysis.

Different prices can measure the constant-price value of banking output and the aggregation functions of disaggregate banking outputs: 1. the user-cost price is frequently estimated within the SNA framework (Fixler & Zieschang, 1999); 2. CPI and WPI as crude proxies for banking output price; 3. observed market interest rates (this approach treats observed interest rates as prices of the concerned output measure; deposit interest rate poses a problem here. One can

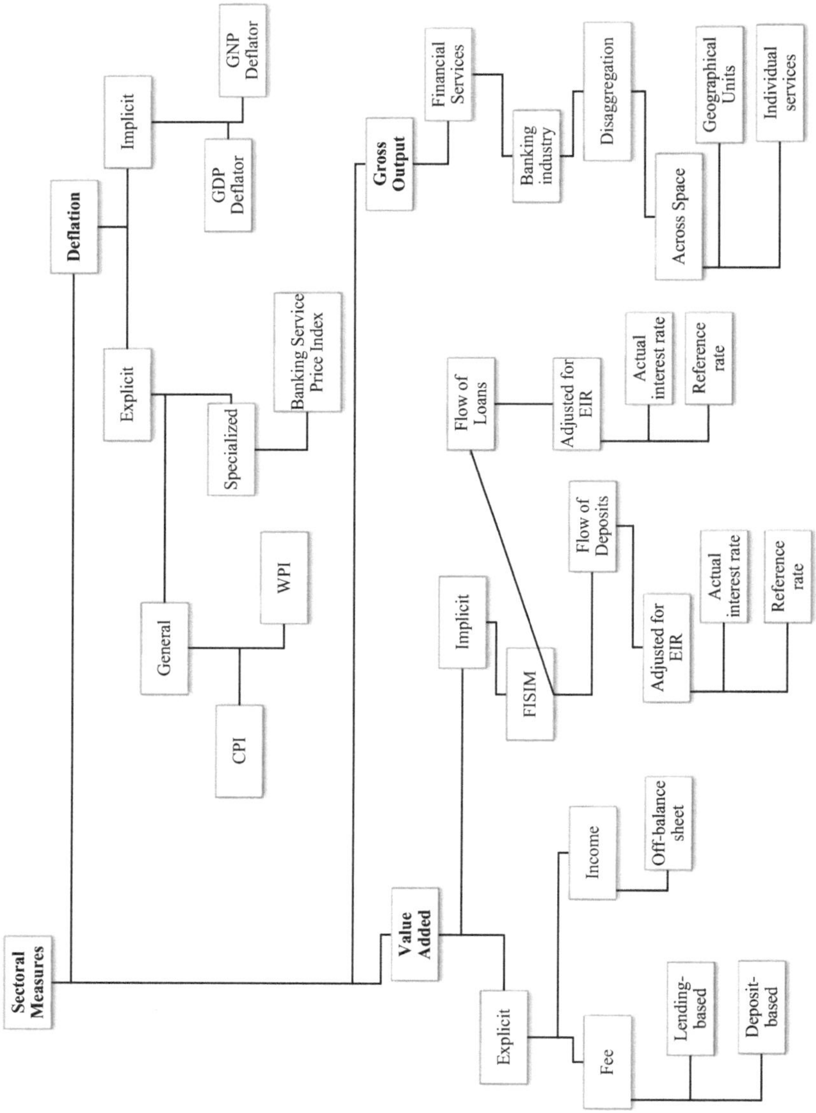

Figure 3.12 National income measures of macro-level banking output

Note: EIR is Effective Interest Rate.

Source: Author's analysis based on the survey of the evidence.

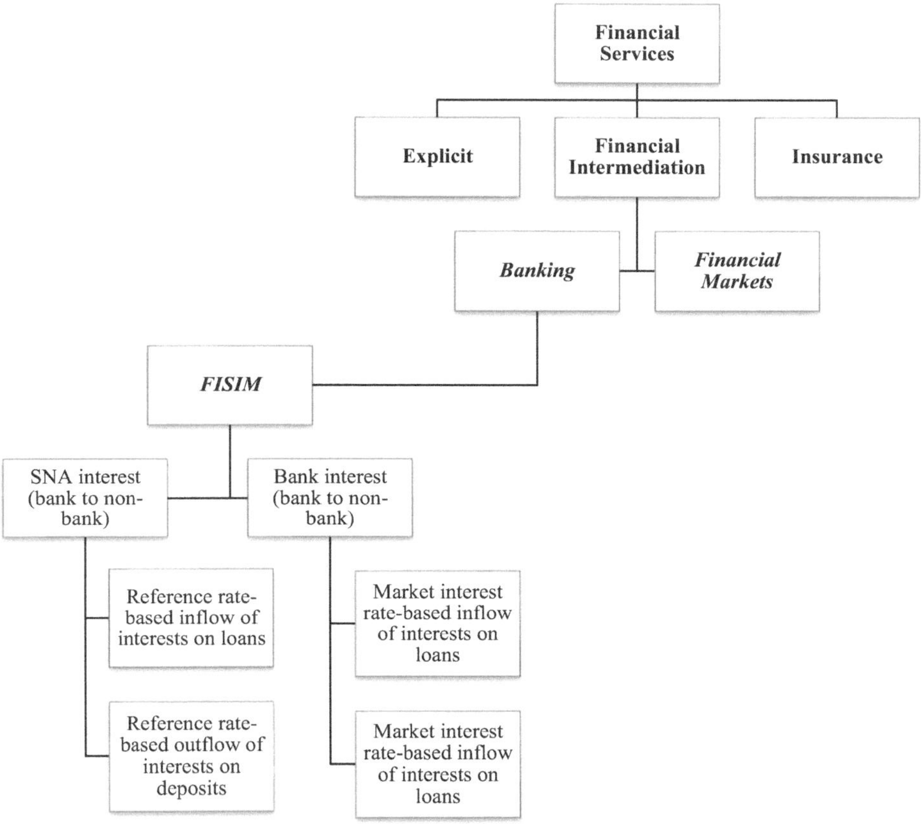

Figure 3.13 Conceptualizing banking output in the SNA framework

Source: Author's analysis based on the SNA 2008 manual.

use the difference between the opportunity cost of holding deposits and the deposit interest rate as a proxy here); 4. operating cost plus margin-based price measures can be used as are traditionally used in manufacturing industry output measurement. The literature has primarily relied on established price indexes such as the aggregate CPI and aggregate GDP deflator. Another thorny issue is the single versus double deflation method.[49] The double deflation method uses two different price indices for output and input deflation, while the single deflation method uses the same price index. Theoretically, double deflation is a superior method as it accounts for more extensive information on the price dynamics in banking – at the side of outputs and inputs. Double deflation deflates outputs and inputs separately; "deflated value-added results from deflated production value minus deflated intermediate consumption of goods and services" (Boer, 1999, p. 5). In other words, inputs and outputs are deflated differently and separately. However, data constraints are more pressing in this method as one requires reliable disaggregated measures of input costs and market prices.[50] Literature has generally used the single deflation approach.[51]

Stock versus flow dimensions in output measurement

Production theory requires the use of flow measures of output. This is irrespective of whether the output is for tangible or intangible goods. In banking literature, stock measures have been dominant. Their use is relatively lesser in the case of insurance firms where flow output data are available and economically meaningful. The use of stock measures implies that the entire amounts of loans and deposits active in a given year are the bank's output and not only the new loans and deposits added during the year. Clark (1984, p. 54) asserted that "a stock concept is appropriate because the relevant stock can only be maintained by the continuous production of intermediation services". However, there are many warnings against using stock measures. Literature has stressed that using stock measures may cause specification errors in the modelled production function (Subramaniam, 1985; Kim & Weiss, 1989). They stress the need for flow measures rather than stock measures, whereas literature has broadly used stock measures found by the survey undertaken in the present work. Hartwick (1996) provides a way out of this by proposing a method to convert stock amounts of deposits and loans into flow measures through adjustment by respective interest rates. This approach is quite similar to what is done under the FISIM method. Another solution is to use both stock and flow variables together in a production function for banks (Resti, 1997). However, this approach does not resolve the matter but finds a middle way. The use of stock variables to measure the output of banks assumes fixed proportionality between the underlying flow of services and each unit of the stock variable, or whatBoer (1999) calls the 'influence factor'. This, too, is a severe criticism levied against this practice. Data constraints continue to maintain the popularity of stock measures of output.

Issues in economic aggregation

Other than the studies that focus on the most disaggregated units of analysis, such as a single banking firm or an individual branch, most analysts have had to face the problem of aggregation. Aggregation is undertaken across space and time (such as converting higher frequency data into annual data) in the literature on banking. Space may be branches, banks, regions, products, etc. The essence of this problem is captured in Benston et al. (1982, p. 440), who state that "the literature on aggregation theory and index numbers concludes that the appropriate way to aggregate quantities of bank output is to (a) estimate the parameters of a 'flexible' aggregator function which captures the substitution and complementarity relationships between all deposit and loan categories or, equivalently, (b) use a statistical index number formula which approximates the results that would have been obtained from a flexible aggregator function". Thus, underlying the issue of aggregation of outputs in banking is the choice of the optimal aggregation function. Generally, linear aggregation functions have been employed in the literature with different weights. The aggregation has been used in banking output literature for two essential purposes: first is to estimate the total output as a composite of heterogeneous sub-components and second for building an index of outputs. Combining outputs of different kinds into an aggregate measure of bank output requires fulfilling various necessary and sufficient conditions, as elaborated in Kim (1986). Very few studies undertake aggregation of banking services within a rigorously defined aggregation procedure while fulfilling the conditions as explained in Kim (1986) or Fisher (1922). The most fundamental condition for meaningful aggregation of bank outputs is separability. It "implies that the marginal rate of transformation between any two elements of the aggregate must be independent of the levels of the variables outside the aggregate" (Kim, 1986, p. 184). Achieving such independence for measures of aggregate output in banking is very difficult given the high degree of interdependencies of banking activities with exogenous non-output factors and the high correlation of bank outputs with general macroeconomic variables. Another major challenge is the problem of aggregation bias, which has a long history in macroeconomics literature. Crudely speaking, aggregation bias occurs when micro-level data patterns are distorted and not represented consistently in the macro aggregate constructed from them. In other words, incorrect specification of variables and the functional relationship between inputs and outputs due to incorrect or theoretically inconsistent aggregation functions can roughly be called aggregation bias. This problem violates the condition of consistent aggregation (Kim, 1986), resulting in a biased measure of aggregate output, which will be incapable of genuinely resenting the level and variations of the underlying individual output measures. As many studies in the literature have used individual bank-level data for analysis, this might not have been a major concern therein. However, this issue deserves sizeable attention for sectoral and aggregate studies. The national income measures of output undertake aggregation while dealing with these problems. Butter (2007) summarises the main procedures used under the SNA.

Some econometric dimensions in the literature

Performance analysis of banks has been undertaken using a diverse set of empirical methods, data types and underlying issues, as examined in Table 2.1. Estimation of the production or cost function has been the most frequently undertaken exercise in the banking literature. Depending on the type of data, researchers have faced econometric challenges. The use of panel and cross-sectional data has been widespread in the literature. For cross-sectional data, dealing with heteroskedasticity has been a concern. Studies have generally adopted two approaches to this problem: the first has been to normalize all the inputs and outputs (all the variables in the cost, revenue, profit or production function) by total assets (e.g. Vennet, 2002, among others), and second has been to use weighted least squares method wherein weights are specified as the total asset variable (e.g. Bos & Kolari, 2005). Another approach has been to use heteroskedasticity-adjusted standard errors in the OLS estimation. For panel data, the main problem has been the lack of balanced panels. This is managed by researchers using appropriate panel econometric models. Generally, production and cost functions have been estimated using panel OLS for panel data.

Researchers have often had to use unbalanced panels due to data constraints. Some studies have used industry-level aggregate data. Using aggregate data, industry-level studies estimate the average production functions rather than firm-specific ones. Generally, these studies employ an OLS or a modified version. But "proximity to an OLS production function does not necessarily mean productivity is maximized" (Colwell & Davis, 1992, p. 119). Yet, researchers have had to accept this constraint due to data limitations and the use of single-stage production functions. For studies using time series data, the usual issues of non-stationarity, unit root and other related matters have been faced by researchers. Given many innovations in time-series econometrics and computation technology, handling econometric challenges for time-series data has not been a major problem for the literature.

Several researchers have used large sample sizes. Given the large volume of data, cleaning the same has been necessary. This is particularly important because outliers can bias the performance estimates. Weill (2004) recommended a novel approach, which used the turkey-box plot method to clean their data before empirically estimating the cost function. Lastly, simultaneity bias has been a problem recognized by many analysts in the banking output literature. Inputs and outputs may be determined simultaneously, and hence their separation in the production or cost function might be incorrect. In this case, literature has recognized at least six approaches: use of trans-log or the more flexible Fourier production and cost functions, use of innovative methods such as the doubly indirect inference method of Kouki et al. (2014) or Fuzzy methods or the indirect inference method of Gourieroux et al. (1993), redefining the variables in the function in different terms (such as in ratio form rather than level form), adopting a multi-stage estimation procedure rather than single-stage estimation procedure (Kouki et al., 2014), avoiding the OLS method which is unsuitable when face with this issue and finally using panel data instead of time-series data.

Monetary policy and the banking production function

Banks are constrained in their intermediation process by monetary policy interventions. Thus, under the intermediation framework, a production function that links the inputs and outputs without accounting for monetary policy might result in biased estimates of performance parameters such as efficiency, productivity, and others. Across the nations, Central Banks are actively engaged in banking sector management, which can induce exogenous changes in the production function of the banks that might be mistaken for productivity and efficiency changes rather than a result of monetary policy shocks. Many analysts state that reserve requirements can shift the production function exogenously, thereby producing residual productivity changes that result from monetary policy shock rather than any genuine advance in technology or efficiency (Greenbaum, 1967). Hence the inclusion of monetary policy as a controlling factor in the production process of the banking sector seems inevitable. Researchers have asserted that efficiency, productivity and profitability changes in the commercial banking sector are mainly explained by monetary policy (Jacob, 1964). Lastly, a very remotely highlighted issue in the literature is the impact of the self-interest maximizing behaviour of regulators on the banking output. Boot and Thakor (1993) analyse the theoretical implications for bank output measurement of such economic behaviour on the part of the banking regulators.

Other issues

The first issue here is true versus observed interest rates in banking literature. Interest rates are used as the price of banking output and hence employed as weights in aggregation functions for building measures of total output. The true measure of interest rate should be free of imperfections in the banking market, particularly should not be affected by monetary policy interventions. Such an interest rate will reflect the actual market price of banking output. However, it is not observable in the real world, and hence one has to depend on observed interest rates, which are strongly affected by non-market forces (Schweitzer, 1972). Market imperfections generally mar observed rates, and one must accept the same as given. These imperfections are not solely due to monetary policy interventions. "Even if there is no central bank regulation on the deposit or lending rates of banks . . . , these rates fail to be market-clearing, owing to various kinds of imperfection in the credit market" (Das & Maiti, 1998, p. 3084). The second issue is the rise of the NBFC sector as a substitute for commercial banking lending.

NBFC segment is increasingly competing with the banking industry as far as the loan segment is concerned and the time deposits are concerned. Ignoring their activities while measuring the performance of the banking segment may not be correct and might distort the results. Similarly, the output of the banking industry might be better measured if the effects of the output of the NBFC industry are taken into account. Limited progress has been made in this regard. Lastly, the banking industry's treatment of payments service output has received some attention in the literature, and some analysts have recommended treating it as a separate output in itself. However, its measurement is challenging and has more extensive data requirements. In this regard, two studies worth noting are Radecki (1999) and Athanasoglou et al. (2009). Readers can refer to these works for more analysis on how to measure the payments service output of commercial banks. Finally, a somewhat lesser debated issue has been the measurement of central bank output and its inclusion in the traditional banking output measures. Bhuyan (2016) summarizes the debate quite well in the context of emerging economies. Accounting for central bank output into the estimates of aggregate output of commercial banks introduces aggregation problems, particularly in determining the optimal weights for aggregation. More fundamentally, both institutions produce very different utilities for the economy and individual agents. Hence, literature has generally treated central bank output measurement as a separate issue in itself rather than subsuming it into the ambit of traditional banking output measurement. Thus, this aspect has not been delved into in detail in this work.

This concludes the survey of literature on bank output measurement. The following section provides an appendix on the evolution of bank output measurement from 1957 to 2022.

Appendix

Evolution of banking output measurement in the extant wisdom from 1950 to 2022

No.	*Citation*	*Issue*	*Output Specification*	*F or S*	*N or R*	*Approach*
1	Farrell (1957)	TE	Value Measure	F	NOM	NA
2	Speagle and Kohn (1958)	LP	Amount of Deposits; Number of cheques handled; Number of debit transactions; Amount of loans and investments; Number of deposit accounts	F, S	R (CP); R (VL)	PRA
3	Benston (1965)	CE	Average number of month-ending deposit; Average number of month-ending loans accounts	S	R (VL)	PRA
4	Greenbaum (1967)	CE	Total earning assets (loans plus investments); current operating earnings; Lending output was defined as the gross yield-weighted sum of the diverse earning assets in each bank's portfolio;	F; S	R (VL), R (CP)	PRA
5	Gorman (1969)	BO; LP	Real Gross Domestic Product (GDP) of Commercial Banking industry	F	R (CP)	PRA
6	Powers (1969)	CE	Sum of amount of lending, non-lending and interest-differential weighted time deposits; For majority firms: Correct measure of Quantity of output = Value of output divided by price; For banking services: Not necessarily so because physical measures will give biased picture as the interest rates (price) component is an inherent part of the banking output; Lending (loans) and non-lending (deposits) outputs need to be estimated using both the price (interest rate) and volume	S	NOM	PRA
7	Khusro et al. (1971)	OE	Amount of Deposits	S	NOM	Reverse INA
8	Benston (1972)	EOS	Highlights following output variables from literature: demand deposits, time deposits, real estate loans, instalment loans, business loans and securities, number of deposit and loans accounts; gross operating income; total deposits; total assets; number of deposit and loan accounts	F; S	NOM	PRA; INA

(Continued)

(*Continued*)

No.	Citation	Issue	Output Specification	F or S	N or R	Approach
9	Murphy (1972)	CE	number of: demand deposit accounts, time deposit accounts, instalment loans, business loans, real estate loans, safe deposits (banking activity); average size of these accounts (within each activity)	S	R (VL)	PRA
10	Schweitzer (1972)	EOS	Financial Assets (investments in equity, government securities, interbank instruments, money market instruments)	S	NOM	INA
11	Coyne (1973)	PRF	Demand deposits; Time deposits; Total Capital accounts	S	NOM	PRA
12	Kalish and Gilbert (1973)	OE	Loans plus investments of banks; revenue of banks adjusted for their market power	F; S	NOM	INA
13	Swamy (1973)	EOS	Total deposits	S	NOM	PRA
14	Singh (1974)	PRF	Balance Sheet total; Deposits and Borrowings combined; Loans and Investments combined	S	NOM	PRA
15	Longbrake and Haslem (1975)	CE	Amount of total deposits	S	NOM	PRA
16	Sato (1976)	ROM	NOM Value added = Value of gross output – Cost of materials or intermediate inputs; Real Value added = NOM Value Added deflated by a Price Index where the choice of price index is the most serious challenge; Single deflation versus Double deflation issues arise; Highlights the properties required in the ideal deflator of value added; Suggests that R value added is an intermediate output and not a final output; Favours Divisia price index for deflation rather than Laspeyer's price index	NA	NA	NIA
17	Sealey (1977)	CE	Amount of Loans; Amount of Securities (investments); Amount of Excess Reserves	S	NOM	INA
18	Geehan and Allen (1978)	ROM	Index of the volume (quantity-based) of 74 non-loan activities (deposit-side); Index of the amount of five major types of loans	F; S	R (VL), R (CP)	PRA
19	Mullineaux (1978)	PRF	Real Estate Loans, Consumer Instalment Loans, Commercial & Agricultural Loans, Safe-Deposit Rental Fees	S	NOM	INA
20	Ojo (1979)	PA	Performance indicators used: Amount of Deposits; Amount of Loans and Advances; Total Earnings; Net Profit Before Tax; Net Profit After Tax	F; S	NOM	PRA

21	Benston et al. (1982)	EOS	Divisia index: 1. of average number of deposit and loan accounts, 2. of average account size for deposits and loans; numbers of deposit and loan accounts; amount of deposits and loans	S	NOM	PRA
22	Brand and Duke (1982)	LP	Output Index = Number of demand deposit transactions; number of transactions on stock exchanges (which imply increased usage of banking services for payments and settlement); amount of time deposits; amount of savings deposits; number of long-term loan contracts; consumer credit operations; real estate loans; trust department services;	F; S	NOM	PRA
23	Angadi and Devaraj (1983)	LP	Total working funds (credits and deposits)	F; S	NOM	PRA
24	Gilbert (1983)	EOS	Amount of demand deposits	S	NOM	PRA
25	Verghese (1983)	PRF	Gross Profit; Net Profit; Operating Margin; Gross Yield; Average Earnings on earnings assets; Average cost of funds; Average excess CRR, SLR; Opportunity cost of CRR, SLR; Cost of Funds	S; Ratio of F to S	NOM	NA
26	Clark (1984)	EOS	Lending output: gross yield-weighted sum of earning assets; Lending plus Non-lending output: lending output + the difference between the bank's total operating income and its operating income from lending; Earning assets output: un-weighted sum of the amounts of bank's earning assets	S	NOM	INA
27	Kim (1985)	EOS	Divisia aggregate of total Bank Output as done in Benston et al. (1982)	S	NOM	PRA
28	Nelson (1985)	EOS	Amount of total deposits produced by each branch	S	NOM	INA
29	Hunter and Timme (1986)	TC; EOS	Main output variable: Sum of all loans, total investment securities, and total deposits less reserves for losses on loans and securities; Alternative measures for sensitivity analysis: (1) total loans, (2) total net loans and deposits, and (3) total loans and securities less reserves for losses.	S	NOM	PRA
30	Kilbride et al. (1986)	EOS	Same as in Clark (1984)	S	NOM	INA
31	Kim (1986)	OA	Output is specified in terms of demand deposits, foreign currency deposit securities, and loans, all of which are calculated as yearly average of monthly balances in inflation deflated terms (by applying the CPI); Deposit related variables are estimated in terms of the "moneyness" concept and thus is defined as the product of money stock [stock variable] and the turnover rate [flow variable])	S; S*F	R (CP)	PRA
32	Owualah (1986)	EOS	Amount of total assets	S	NOM	INA

(*Continued*)

(*Continued*)

No.	*Citation*	*Issue*	*Output Specification*	*F or S*	*N or R*	*Approach*
33	Todhanakasem et al. (1986)	EOS	Rate of interest on total loans	S (PR)	NOM	INA
34	Berger et al. (1987)	EOS	Production approach: number of following accounts: 1) demand deposits, 2) time and savings deposits, 3) Real estate loans, 4) commercial loans, 5) instalment loans; Intermediation approach: Intermediation approach: amount intermediated (meaning unclear; probably implies the amount of assets)	S	R (VL); NOM	PRA; INA
35	Humphrey (1987)	EOS	Amount of total assets	S	NOM	INA
36	Agu (1988)	BO	Amount of Deposits; Amount of earning assets; Number of cheques processed; Amount of cheques processed	F; S	NOM; R (CP); R (VL)	PRA
37	Evanoff et al. (1989)	EOS	Amount of Total Assets; Total Loans; Total Loans and Deposits combined; Total Loans, Deposits and Investment Securities	S	NOM	PRA
38	Kim and Weiss (1989)	TFP	Output is specified in terms of demand deposits, foreign currency deposit, securities and loans, all of which are calculated as yearly average of monthly balances in inflation deflated terms (by applying the CPI); Deposit related variables are estimated in terms of the "moneyness" concept and thus is defined as the product of money stock [stock variable] and the turnover rate [flow variable])	S; S*F	R (CP)	PRA
39	Lawrence (1989)	EOS; EOSCO	Amount of Deposits (includes demand deposits and time deposits, including certificates of deposit, $100,000 and over); Amount of loans (includes real estate loans made and serviced, commercial, consumer, construction, agricultural and other loans); Amount of investments (includes short-term money market instruments and long-term securities held)	S	NOM	PRA; INA
40	Elyasiani and Mehdian (1990)	TE; TC	Loans: (1) real estate loans, (2) commercial and industrial loans, and (3) other loans; Investments: includes all the securities other than those held in the bank's trading accounts	S	NOM	INA
41	Aly et al. (1990)	TE; SE; AE	Amount of: real estate loans; commercial and industrial loans; consumer loans; all other loans; demand deposits	S	NOM	INA

42	Kolari and Zardkoohi (1990)	EOS; EOSCO	Amount of advances outstanding (credit outstanding); Amount of bills outstanding (written orders requiring the bank to extend a specified amount of credit to the borrower)	S	NOM	INA
43	Noulas et al. (1990)	RTS	Loans to individuals for household, family, and other personal expenses; loans secured by real estate; commercial and industrial loans; federal funds sold, securities, total investment securities and assets held in trading accounts	S	NOM	INA
44	Oral and Yolalan (1990)	TE; PRF	Service efficiency outputs: amount of time spent on general service transactions (accounting, control, information, transfers, payments); amount of time spent on credit transactions (contracts, guarantees, credit and risk related procedures); amount of time spent on deposit transactions (commercial accounts, saving accounts); amount of time spent on foreign exchange transactions; Profitability outputs: interests earned on loans; non-interest income	F; S	R (VL); NOM	PRA (Efficiency); INA (Profitability)
45	Berg et al. (1991)	TE	Amount of: demand deposit services; time deposit services; short-term loan services; long-term loan services; other services (brokerage services, property management and the provision of safe deposit boxes)	S	NOM	PRA
46	Goldberg et al. (1991)	EOS; EOSCO	Revenue from brokerage operations (commissions, margin interest and fees from mutual funds sales); revenue from underwriting and capital positioning operations (underwriting fees and gains on trading and investments for firms own accounts); revenue from account supervision (account management fees, research services, mergers and acquisitions and other revenue)	F	NOM	PRA
47	Gropper (1991)	EOS	Amount of: investments; total loans; trust accounts	S	NOM	INA
48	Hunter and Timme (1991)	TCH; RSE; TSB	Amount of loans (Real estate, agricultural, commercial and industrial, personal, credit card and other loan); Amount of deposits (demand deposits, interest-bearing checking accounts, savings accounts and small-time deposits)	S	R (CP)	INA
49	Kolari and Zardkoohi (1991)	EOS; EOSCO	Model 1: Loans [Real estate; Instalment; Commercial and others]; Model 2: Deposits [Demand; Time]; Model 3: Loans and Deposits together	S	NOM	PRA

(*Continued*)

(*Continued*)

No.	*Citation*	*Issue*	*Output Specification*	*F or S*	*N or R*	*Approach*
50	Tachibanaki et al. (1991)	EOS; EOSCO	Output 1: Amount of lending adjusted for interest differential between interest charged and interest paid (interest charged is measured by the interest received through lending and interest paid is measured by the interest paid divided by the total debt minus some receivables, and amount of lending is measured by the amount of total lending; Output 2: Expected profit adjusted for output 1, total cost, discount rate assumed by shareholders, share value of the bank and rate of interest on deposits	S	NOM	PRA (though claimed to be INA by the authors)
51	Berg et al. (1992)	MTFP	Amount of loans: short-term; long-term loans; Amount of deposits: produced (non-bank) deposits [i.e. excludes interbank deposits]	S	R (CP)	PRA
52	Berger and Humphrey (1992)	CE	Amount of – demand deposits; time and savings deposits; Real estate loans; commercial and industrial loans; instalment loans	S	R (CP)	VAA
53	Colwell and Davis (1992)	BO; PFP; TFP	Value Measures (Amount of loans, deposits, investments); Volume Measures (Number of deposit and loan accounts); Index based measures using appropriate weights for aggregating various heterogeneous outputs	F; S	R	PRA; INA; NIA
54	Elyasiani and Mehdian (1992)	OE; AE; OTE; PTE; SE	Amount of: Commercial and industrial loans; real estate loans; other loans; investment securities	S	NOM	INA
55	Hughes and Mester (1993)	EOS; EOSCO	Amount of loans: Commercial real estate loans; commercial loans (C&I loans and loans for securities); consumer loans; other loans; securities, assets in trading accounts, fed funds sold, and total investment securities	S	NOM	INA
56	Mester (1992)	CE	Amount of different information produced by banks (proxied by amount of loans)	S	NOM	INA
57	Dietsch (1993)	EOS; EOSCO	Total Deposits; Total of loans to firms and households; Long-term securities (assets); Interbank market activity (interbank liabilities net of interbank assets)	S	NOM	INA

58	Muldur and Sassenou (1993)	EOS; EOSCO	Cobb-Douglas case: Amount of total assets (Commercial banks); Number of accounts (Savings institutions); Trans-log case: Amount of commercial loans, interbank loans, securities transactions (Commercial Banks); Amount of customer deposits, commercial loans, securities and cash management transactions (Savings institutions)	S	NOM	INA
59	Shaffer (1993)	CE; CMP	Amount of assets (loans, investments, etc.)	S	R (CP)	INA
60	Subrahmanyam (1994)	BO	Amount of deposits; Amount of loans	S	NA	PRA
61	Clark and Speaker (1994)	EOS; EOSCO	Transactions deposits; Purchased Funds; Time Deposits; Investments; Real estate and mortgage loans; Instalment loans; Credit card loans; Commercial and other loans	S	NOM	PRA
62	Keshari and Paul (1994)	TE	Amount of total deposits + Amount of total advances	S	NOM	PRA
63	Sherwood (1994)	BO	Services produce changes and thus the unit of output may be intangible; Highlights the following major difficulties: (1) enumerating the elements of a complex bundle of services, (2) choosing among alternative representations of an industry's output, (3) accounting for the consumer's role in the generation of a service output, and (4) specifying clearly whether what is being worked with is a value-added model or a gross output model; Suggests that service prices are included implicitly in many cases and thus decomposing the observed prices into explicit and implicit components is important; Consumer involvement is inevitable in production (quantum of services versus quantum of outcomes); Highlights the problems in measuring service output when product and process innovations occur	NA	NA	NA
64	Evanoff and Israilevich (1995)	CE	Amount of total loans and securities	S	NOM	PRA

(Continued)

(*Continued*)

No.	Citation	Issue	Output Specification	F or S	N or R	Approach
65	Hunter and Timme (1995)	CE	(1) wholesale loans (average money balance of all commercial and industrial and security loans); (2) consumer loans (average money balance of credit cards and other personal loans, excluding loans secured by residential real estate); (3) Real estate and other loans (average money balance of all loans secured by real estate, agricultural, and other loans not included in other variables); (4) other BO; (5) average money balance of transaction deposit accounts; (6) average money balance of retail non-transaction accounts less than $100,000	S	NOM	VAA
66	Wheelock and Wilson (1995)	TE	Amount of total earning assets (sum of amount of total loans and bond holdings); Amount of demand deposits	S	NOM	INA
67	Zaim (1995)	TE; AE	Total balance of demand deposits; Total balance of time deposits; Total balance of short-term loans; Total balance of long-term loans	S	NOM	INA
68	Batra (1996)	PRF	Gross rates on: loans and advances; investment in govt. and other approved securities; investment in other securities; bills purchased and discounted	F (PR)	NOM	INA
69	Clark (1996)	CE; SE	Commercial and industrial loans (commercial loans, direct leasing, foreign loans, and loans to financial institutions); consumer and real estate loans; total securities (investment securities and trading account securities); core deposits (demand deposits, savings deposits and retail time deposits)	S	NOM	VAA; INA
70	Hartwick (1996)	BO	Net interest income (Interest income from loans and investments combined and net of interest expenses) adjusted for – 1. Service charges, 2. Loan losses (as input ex-ante, and net out of output ex-post), 3. Capital losses (when accounting for equity)	F	R (CP)	INA
71	Humphrey and Pulley (1997)	PRF	Amount of core deposits (demand deposits plus savings and small denomination time deposit); Amount of loans (the sum of the R values of real estate, commercial and industrial, and instalment, including credit card, loans)	S	R (CP)	INA
72	Jagtiani and Khanthavit (1996)	TCH; RSE; EPSE; EPSA	Amount of: deposits; loans and investments; OBS products (OBS guarantees, interest rate and foreign currency swaps, options, and futures and forward contracts)	S	R (CP)	INA

73	Kaushik and Lopez (1996)	PRF	Annual growth rate in Assets – Total and individual items in balance sheet such as interest earning assets, loans and non-interest earning assets; Annual growth rate in Liabilities – Total, Foreign, Domestic (Demand, Other Checkable, Savings), Subordinated notes, Equity capital, Loss provisions	S	NOM	NA
74	Sharpe (1997)	BOP	Amount outstanding in: six-month certificate of deposits; money-market deposit accounts	F	NOM	PRA
75	Berger and DeYoung (1997)	CE	Commercial loans; consumer loans; real estate loans; transactions deposits (transactions deposits include demand deposits, NOW accounts, automatic transfer service accounts, and telephone and pre-authorized transfer accounts); fee-based income (fee-based income equals gross non-interest income less both service charges on deposit accounts and gains/losses from securities and foreign exchange trading)	F; S	NOM	PRA
76	Berger and Humphrey (1997)	EFFS	Production approach (recommended for branch-level data): Number of deposit accounts, loan accounts or deposit transactions, loan transactions, produced in a given year (flow concept); Intermediation approach (recommended for institutions-level data): Flow amount of deposits, loans combined in a given year (flow concept); However, data constraints force the use of stock variables instead of flow variables; Highlights the asset, user cost, and value-added methods of specifying output and notes the debate on treatment of deposits as an input or an output.	F (Ideal); S	NOM	PRA; INA
77	Berger and Mester (1997)	CE; PE	Amount of: consumer loans (instalment and credit card and related plans); business loans (all other loan); securities (gross total assets less loans and physical capital, so that all financial assets are considered to be outputs)	S	R (CP)	INA
78	Bhattacharyya et al. (1997)	TE	Amount of advances (loans); Amount of deposits; Amount of investments	S	NOM	INA
79	Chaffai (1997)	ISTE	Amount of total loans	S	NOM	INA
80	Das and Maiti (1998)	PA	Change (First difference) in the amount of credit flowing from the organised market, particularly from the commercial banks; Change in the amount of deposits with organized commercial banks	F	NOM	PRA

(*Continued*)

(*Continued*)

No.	*Citation*	*Issue*	*Output Specification*	*F or S*	*N or R*	*Approach*
81	Mester (1997)	CE	Amount of: Real estate loans; Commercial loans (commercial and industrial loans, lease financing receivables, agricultural loans, loans to depository institutions, acceptances of other banks, loans to foreign governments, obligations of states and political subdivisions, and other loans); loans to individuals	S	NOM	INA
82	Resti (1997)	CE	Amount of loans: all forms of loans to customers except non-performing loans; Amount of deposits: checking accounts, savings accounts, certificates of deposit with retail customers (excluding interbank CDs); Non-interest income: Net fee-based income, net revenues from security and currency trading	F; S	R (CP)	PRA
83	Anthanassopoulos (1998)	ME; CE	Market efficiency: Liability sales; Loans & mortgages; Insurances & securities; Cost Efficiency: Number of transactions; Liability sales; Loans and Mortgages; Insurance and securities; Number of cards	F; S	R (VL); NOM	PRA
84	Ayadi et al. (1998)	TE	Amount of: total loans; interest income; non-interest income	S; F	NOM	INA
85	Berger and Hannan (1998)	CE	Amount of: Demand deposits; time and savings deposits; Real estate loans; commercial loans; instalment loans	S	NOM	PRA
86	DeYoung and Hasan (1998)	PE	Amount of: total loans; transactions deposits; fee-based financial services (fee-based financial services equals non-interest income less service charges on deposit accounts)	F; S	NOM	INA
87	Durkin and Elliehausen (1998)	EOS; CEL	Number of loans outstanding (that is, serviced)	S	R (VL)	PRA
88	Freixas (1998)	EFFS	Payment volume; Payment value; Net payments system is defined as interbank payments system with net clearing of funds on daily basis; Gross payments system is the settlement of claims by banks through intense use of liquidity; Suggest that net payments system generates a larger risk; Net system saves liquidity (central bank money available with the banks), while Gross system reduces the risk of contagion by one-to-one settlement but intensely uses liquidity	F	NA	NA

89	Grifell-Tatjé et al. (1998)	MTFP	Amount of: loan accounts; savings accounts; checking accounts	S	R (Constant)	VAA
90	Hughes and Mester (1998)	CEL	Real estate loans; business loans (i.e., commercial and industrial loans, lease financing receivables, and agricultural loans); loans to individuals; other loans; amount of earning assets (securities, assets in trading accounts, fed funds sold and securities purchased under agreements to resell, and total investment securities); amount of off-balance-sheet output [credit-risk equivalent amount of off-balance-sheet items (e.g., commitments, letters of credit, derivatives, etc.)]	S	NOM	INA
91	Rogers (1998)	CE; RE; PE	Amount of: demand deposits; time and savings deposits; Real estate loans; other loans; Net non-interest income	F; S	NOM	INA
92	Boer (1999)	FISIM	Mortgages; Consumer credit; Credits granted to enterprises; New credit granted to private enterprises; Total savings account business; Deposit business; Money transfer services (excluding commercial money transfers)	F	R (VL); R (CP)	PRA
93	Camanho and Dyson (1999)	TE; PTE; SE	Number of general service transactions performed by branch staff; Number of transactions in external ATMs; Number of all types of accounts at the branch; Value of savings; Value of loans	F; S	R (VL); NOM	PRA
94	Fixler and Zieschang (1999)	MTFP	Asset side: Cash and Balances Due from Depository Institutions; Amount of Loans; Amount of Securities; Amount of Federal Funds Sold and Securities Purchased; Liability side: Amount of Deposits; federal funds purchased and securities sold	F	NOM	PRA
95	Radecki (1999)	BO	Amount of non-interest revenue (it contains the fee-based income from payments services)	F	NOM	PRA
96	Srivastava (1999)	EOS; CEL	Amount of total deposits; amount of the sum of total advances and total investments	S	NOM	VAA
97	Thanassoulis (1999)	TE; TFP	Finnish bank: Number of transactions processed by human tellers; Number of cash withdrawals; Number of loans processed; Number of transactions effected at automatic teller machines; British bank: Number of mortgage applications; Number of insurance policies sold; Number of new savings accounts; Number of transactions	F	R (VL)	PRA
98	Wheelock and Wilson (1999)	TE; MTFP	Real estate loans; commercial and industrial loans; consumer loans; all other loans; total demand deposits	S	R (CP)	INA

(Continued)

(Continued)

No.	*Citation*	*Issue*	*Output Specification*	*F or S*	*N or R*	*Approach*
99	Altunbas et al. (2000)	TE; SE; XE	Amount of total loans; Amount of total securities; Amount of off-balance-sheet output	S	R (CP)	INA
100	Athanassopoulos and Giokas (2000)	PEF; INE; XEF	Production Efficiency: Number of deposit and transfer transactions; Number of credit transactions; Foreign-receipt transactions; Intermediation Efficiency: savings deposits; current deposits; demand deposits; time deposits; total loans; and non-interest income;	F	R (VL)	PRA
101	Hughes et al. (2000)	EOS	Amount of: liquid assets; short-term securities; long-term securities; loans and leases net of unearned income; other assets	S	NOM	INA
102	Tokle and Tokle (2000)	CMP	Amount of total deposits	S	NOM	PRA
103	Alam (2001)	MTFP	Amount of: Securities; Real estate loans; commercial and industrial loans; instalment loans	S	NOM	INA
104	Altunbaş et al. (2001)	CE; EOS	Amount of: total aggregate loans (all types of loans); total aggregate securities (short-term investment, equity and other investments and public sector securities)	S	R (CP)	INA
105	Karim (2001)	CE	Amount of: commercial and industrial loans; other loans; time deposits; demand deposits; securities and investments	S	NOM	INA
106	Mertens and Urga (2001)	CE; PE; EOS; EOSCO	Amount of: Interbank loans; Consumer loans; Other investments (including government and risky securities, and investment in other enterprises)	S	NOM	INA
107	Okuda and Saito (2001)	EOS	Amount of: interest income (from loans, securities and deposits); Fee-based income (sum of commissions and fees)	F	NOM	INA
108	Adams et al. (2002)	MPR	Amount of: commercial and industrial loans; instalment loans; real estate loans	S	R (CP)	INA
109	Chaudhuri (2002)	PRF	Yield from: loans and advances; Investments	Ratio of F to S	NOM	INA
110	Clark and Siems (2002)	CE; PE; XE	Amount of total credit equivalent amount of OBS transactions (constructed following the guidelines set out by the Basel Committee); aggregate measure of asset equivalence that utilizes the rate of return balance-sheet assets to capitalize the non-interest income from OBS activities; non-interest income; commercial loans, direct leasing, foreign loans, and loans to financial institutions; consumer and Real estate loans; other on-balance-sheet assets (defined as Total Assets minus commercial loans minus consumer and real estate loans)	S	NOM	INA

111	Das (2002)	MTFP	Amount of: Bank credit; total investments	S	R (CP)	INA
112	Devaney and Weber (2002)	PE	Amount of: Real estate loans; four types of commercial and industrial loans (larger than $1million, between $250,000 and $1 million, between $100,000 and $250,000, $100,000 or less); personal loans; securities (investments); transaction account deposits	S	NOM	UCA
113	Grigorian and Manole (2002)	TE	Set 1: revenues (Revenues are defined as the sum of interest and non-interest income), net loans (Net loans are defined as loans net of loan loss provisions), liquid assets (Liquid assets include cash, balances with monetary authorities, and holdings of treasury bills); Set 2: deposits, net loans, liquid assets	S	NOM	VAA
114	Isik and Hassan (2002)	CE; APE	Short-term loans (with less than one year of maturity); long-term loans (loans with more than a year maturity); Risk-adjusted off-balance-sheet items (guarantees and warranties, letters of guarantee, bank acceptance, letters of credit, guaranteed pre-financing, endorsements and other commitments, foreign exchange and interest rate derivatives as well as other off-balance-sheet activities); Other earning assets (loans to special sectors, interbank funds sold, and investment securities which includes treasury bills, government bonds and other securities)	F; S	NOM (Converted to US dollars)	INA
115	Kumbhakar et al. (2002)	LP	Amount of: loans to the public; guarantees; deposits	S	R (CP)	PRA
116	Lozano-Vivas et al. (2002)	TE; CE	Amount of: Loans; Deposits; Other Earning assets	S	NOM	PRA
117	Mohan (2002)	PA	Interest spread; Amount of net profit	F	NOM	NA
118	Tortosa-Ausina (2002)	CE; BO	Intermediation: Amount of – loans (all forms of loans to all categories of customers); Other earning assets (securities and loans to financial institutions); Value-added: Amount of – loans (all forms of loans to all categories of customers); Other earning assets (securities and loans to financial institutions); Deposits (savings, time and transactions)	S	R (CP)	INA; VAA
119	Vennet (2002)	CE; PE	Intermediation approach – Amount of: total loans, total securities (investments); Value added – total interest income, total non-interest revenues	F; S	Converted to ECU	INA; VAA
120	Bhattacharya (2003)	Bank Scope	Statistical distribution of: the log of total assets; market shares; Finds selectivity bias	NA	NA	NA

(*Continued*)

(Continued)

No.	*Citation*	*Issue*	*Output Specification*	*F or S*	*N or R*	*Approach*
121	Fixler et al. (2003)	BO	Total Imputed Output = [Implicit output (Amount of loans*effective interest charged + Amount of Deposits*effective interest paid, effective being net of reference rate) + User cost of own funds (Reference rate*Net Assets, where net assets = total assets – total liabilities)]; User cost of own funds compensates the banks for using equity capital or any other form of self-acquired financial capital	F	NOM	VAA
122	Focarelli and Panetta (2003)	M&A	Size is measured by the amount of total assets; Service quality measures: number of branches per 100,000 inhabitants, average number of employees per branch in each local market, size of the bank	S	NOM; R (VL)	INA
123	Kumbhakar and Sarkar (2003)	CE; TFP	Amount of: fixed deposits; savings deposits; current deposits; investments; loans and advances; Branch output – Number of rural, urban and semi-urban, and metropolitan branches	S	R (CP); R (VL)	VAA
124	Leong et al. (2003)	TE	Amount of: Loans, Interest income, Other income, Risk-weighted financial assets (investments plus OBS output with items weighted as per Basel convention with weights being 0, 10, 20, 50 and 100% percent for five categories of assets)	S	NOM	INA
125	Mohan (2003)	PA	Stock market returns of the banks	Ratio of F to S	NOM	NA
126	Mukherjee et al. (2003)	QE; PE; OE	Quality efficiency: Service quality output variable (constructed using Likert scale responses of 185 customers of nationalized banks tangibility, responsiveness, reliability, assurance and empathy); Profit and overall efficiency: Amount of: deposits (demand, savings and term deposits); advance (bills purchased, cash credit, overdraft, loans); non-interest income (comprising commission, exchange, brokerage, profit from investments, assets deployed and exchange transactions)	F; S	NOM; Subjective Ranking	PRA
127	Rushdi and Tennant (2003)	PRF; LP	Amount of: interest income from bank loans, fee and other income; total R assets	F; S (Assets)	NOM	VAA
128	Sathye (2003)	TE	Model 1 – Amount of: net interest income, non-interest income; Model 2 – Amount of: net loans, non-interest income	F	NOM	INA; VAA

129	Agu (2004)	PA	Amount of deposits; Amount of loans; Operating asset ratio; Operating income ratio	S; Ratio of F to S	NOM	PRA
130	Bossone and Lee (2004)	EOS	Sum of amount of total loans and other earning assets (the average amount at the end of each year)	S	R (CP)	INA
131	Casu et al. (2004)	MTFP	Amount of: total loans; other earning assets; off-balance-sheet activities at NOM value	S; F	NOM	INA
132	Cuesta and Zofío (2005)	TE	Loans (to non-bank sector); Investments (Bonds, cash and other assets); Off-balance-sheet output (non-interest income)	S; F	R (CP)	INA
133	De (2004)	TE	Gross income (equivalent to interest and discount earned plus commission, exchange and brokerage plus other receipts); Amount of total earning assets (total loans and investments at the end of the year)	F; S	R (CP)	INA
134	Fixler (2004)	BO	Deposit-side services; Borrowing-side services; Implicit + Explicit outputs should be included	F	NA	VAA
135	Girardone et al. (2004)	EOS; XE	Amount of: total loans; securities (investments)	S	R (CP)	INA
136	Maghyereh (2004)	PE	Amount of: earning assets (loans and liquid assets & investments); Off-balance-sheet business; other services	S; F	R (CP)	INA
137	Mohan and Ray (2004)	RE	Amount of: loans; investments; other incomes	S	R (CP)	INA
138	Triplett and Bosworth (2004a)	BO; IO	Banking: Gross Output of non-depository financial institutions, Value Added; Insurance: Premiums minus Claims, Risk-adjusted premiums	F	NOM	PRA
139	Triplett and Bosworth (2004b)	BO; FISIM	Criticize the one-stage production functions for ignoring the financial constraints; Inclusion of reserves in the production function is desirable; Incorporate implicit services to depositors in the overall output measure	F	NA	INA
140	Weill (2004)	TE	Amount of: loans; investments	S	NOM	INA
141	Bos and Kolari (2005)	XE; EOS; EOSCO	Amount of loans (aggregate of commercial and industrial, real estate, consumer, agriculture, and other outstanding credit); Amount of investments (securities, equity investments, and all other investments reported on the balance sheet); Off-balance-sheet output (Off-balance-sheet activities are credit items and other guarantees, loan commitments, derivative securities, and other loan and securities exposures not reflected on the balance sheet)	S; F	R (CP)	INA

(Continued)

(Continued)

No.	*Citation*	*Issue*	*Output Specification*	*F or S*	*N or R*	*Approach*
142	Camanho and Dyson (2005)	CE	Production approach: Total value of deposits; Total value of loans; Total value of off-balance-sheet business; Number of general service transactions; Value-Added approach: Total value of deposits; Total value of loans; Total value of off-balance-sheet business.	S; F0	NOM; R (VL)	PRA; VAA
143	Das et al. (2005)	TE; CE; RE; PE	Amount of: investments, performing loan assets, other non-interest fee-based incomes	S; F	NOM	INA
144	Sensarma (2005)	CE	Amount of: fixed deposits; saving deposits; current deposits; loans; investments; and Number of branches	S	R (CP); R (VL)	PRA
145	Tirtiroğlu et al. (2005)	TFP	Sum of amount of real deposits and loan balances	S	R (CP)	VAA
146	Wang and Basu (2005)	FISIM	Stress on the need to incorporate certain minimum levels of risk into the measure of reference rate rather than searching for a pure risk-free reference rate; Reject the practice of using a single reference rate in NIPA and recommend using multiple reference rates to reflect the true nature of FISIM output better; Recommend use of separate reference rates for deposit side and loans side FISIM components	NA	NA	NA
147	Beccalli et al. (2006)	TE	Amount of: loans; earning assets	S	NOM	INA
148	Dick (2006)	PA	Performance indicators used: Loan interest rate; Deposit interest rate; Service fees; Spread; Operating costs; Credit risk; Profit margin	F	NOM	NA
149	Havrylchyk (2006)	CE; AE; TE; PTE; SE	Amount of: Loans; Treasury bonds; Off-balance items	S	NOM	INA
150	Howcroft and Ataullah (2006)	MTFP	Loan-based model: Amount of – loans, investments; Income-based model: Amount of – interest income, non-interest income	S; F	R (CP)	INA
151	Kirkwood and Nahm (2005)	CE	Technical Efficiency: Amount of – Interest-bearing assets, Non-interest income; Profit Efficiency: Profit before tax and abnormal items	S; F	R (CP)	INA
152	Lyroudi and Angelidis (2006)	MTFP	Amount of: total deposits; total customer loans; investments (equity + government securities held by banks)	S	NOM	VAA

153	Nakane et al. (2006)	MPR	Amount of: time deposits; demand and savings deposits; loans	S	NOM	PRA
154	Reddy (2006)	MTFP; TE; SE	Amount: liquid assets; total advances; total deposits; total income (interest plus non-interest income)	S; F	NOM	VAA
155	Tadesse (2005)	EOS; TC	Sum of amounts of Personal loans + industrial loans + investments in cash dues securities	S	NOM	INA
156	Allen and Liu (2007)	CE; EOS	Consumer loans (amount of personal loans for non-business purposes); Non-mortgage loans (amount of secured call and other loans to investment loans dealers and brokers + loans to regulated financial institutions + loans to domestic and foreign governments + lease receivables + reverse repurchase agreements + loans to individuals and others for business purposes); Mortgage loans (amount of residential and non-residential mortgage loans); Investments (amount of other financial assets on a bank's balance sheet); OBS output (non-traditional Asset-equivalent measure of non-interest income-generating activities)	S	R (CP)	INA
157	Ariff and Can (2008)	CE; PE	Amount of: Loans (net loans and interbank lending); Investments (short, long-term and entrusted investments)	S	R (CP)	INA
158	Asaftei and Kumbhakar (2008)	CE	Amount of: current loans; portfolio investment; fee and commission income; and number of branches	S; F	R (CP); R (VL)	INA
159	Berger and Bouwman (2007)	BO	Four measures of liquidity created by banks: cat fat, mat fat, cat nonfat, mat nonfat	S	NOM	PRA; VAA
160	Casolaro and Gobbi (2007)	TFP	Output 1: Composite of three services – i. turnover of current accounts as a proxy for payment services, ii. total amount of deposited securities as a proxy for both safekeeping and asset management, iii. loan guarantees as a proxy for off-balance intermediation activity, Weighting factor for Output 1 is shares in total fees and commission income as weights; Output 2 – outstanding amounts of short-term loans, medium-term loans, long-term loans, deposits	S	R (CP); R (VL)	VAA
161	Chen et al. (2007)	CE; PE	Number of investor accounts	S	R (VL)	PRA

(Continued)

(Continued)

No.	*Citation*	*Issue*	*Output Specification*	*F or S*	*N or R*	*Approach*
162	Dick (2007)	PA; MPR	Major explanatory variables: Amount of deposits; Amount of assets; Real estate loans; Commercial and industrial loans; Loans to individuals; Leases; Non-interest income; Demand deposits; Time deposits; Rate of individual loans; Service charges on deposits	S; F	NOM	PRA
163	Ray (2007)	SZE	Amount of: total credit (net of non-performing loans); Investments; Other income	S	NOM	INA
164	Shih et al. (2007)	PA	Four core measures of bank performance: overall performance, liquidity management, credit risk management, and capital profitability [Core capital ratio; Capital risk ratio; Asset profitability; Doubtful loan ratio; Short-term liquid asset-liability ratio; Risk-adjusted capital adequacy ratio; Ratio of short to long-term debt; Lost loan ratio; Overdue loan ratio; Capital profitability]	Ratio of F to S	NOM	NA
165	Harimaya (2008)	EOS; EOSCO	Amount of: loans and bills discounted; investment securities and trading account securities; total liabilities in trust accounts	S	R (CP)	INA
166	Pelosi (2008)	MTFP	Models for cost minimization function for Banks: Amount of – core deposit (transaction and savings deposits); loans and securities (investments); Model for deposit-taking institutions: Amount of – loans, non-interest income	S; F (non-interest income)	R (CP)	INA
167	Rezvanian et al. (2008)	OE; AE; OTE; PTE; SE; MTFP	Amount of: Loans and Advances; securities (investments); other earning assets	S	NOM	INA
168	Sinha and Chatterjee (2008)	MTFP	Amount of deposits + loans and advances	S	R (CP)	PRA; VAA
169	Sufian (2008)	TE; AE; OE	Amount of: Total Loans; Investment and dealing securities	S	NOM	INA

170	Athanasoglou et al. (2009)	PFP; TFP	Total Output Index (Tornquist): 1. Financial intermediation output – Sum of the amount of loans and deposits adjusted for their effective interest rate (net of reference rate); 2. Payments services output: (a) direct fees for payment services provided and (b) free payment services provided through demand deposits, both weighted through opportunity cost of deposits; Alternative variables used here were number of transactions on a series of payments, including payments through ATMs, credit and debit cards, credit transfers, direct debits and cheques; 3. Other incomes (non-interest income – from fees and securities); All three components are weighted by the percentage share of each component in the value of total BO	S; F	R (CP); R (VL)	PRA
171	Humphrey (2009)	EOS	Point of sale transactions (card and check); bill payments (electronic and paper giro); ATM; Size-standardized branch office networks	S; F	R (CP) but PPP in current price	PRA
172	Illueca et al. (2009)	MTFP	Amount of: Loans (to firms and households); Other loans (Cash and balances with the Bank of Spain, interbank loans); Fixed-income securities (Fixed-income securities, public debt); Other securities (Shares and other equities such as quoted shares, unquoted shares, other equity, mutual funds shares); Non-traditional output (non-interest income)	S; F	NOM	INA
173	Kao and Liu (2009)	TE	Amount of: demand deposits; short-term loans; long-term loans	S	NOM	INA
174	Kenjegalieva et al. (2009)	PA	For incorporating risk in production behaviour: Amount of profit, Return on equity	F; Ratio of F to S	NOM	INA
175	Koutsomanoli-Filippaki and Mamatzakis (2009)	CE; PE	Amount of: loans (net of provisions); other earning assets (government securities, bonds, equity investments, CDs, T-bills, etc.)	S	NOM	INA
176	Pasiouras et al. (2009)	CE; PE	Amount of: Loans; other earning assets; total deposits (customer and interbank)	S	R (CP)	VAA

(*Continued*)

(Continued)

No.	*Citation*	*Issue*	*Output Specification*	*F or S*	*N or R*	*Approach*
177	Seelanatha and Wickremasinghe (2009)	PA	Amount of: Loans; Deposits; Investments	S; Ratio of S to S	NOM	NA
178	Altman et al. (2010)	PA	Amount of loans; Returns on loans	S; Ratio of S to S	NOM	NA
179	Banker et al. (2010)	TE	Amount of: interest revenue; other operating revenue	F	R (CP)	INA
180	Chronopoulos et al. (2010), in Fiordelisi et al. (2010)	TE	Amount of: total customer loans; other earning assets; non-interest income	S; F	NOM	INA
181	Dong (2010)	CE	Amount of: total loans; Other earning assets (investments, interbank assets); Non-interest income	S; F	R (CP)	INA
182	Feng and Serletis (2010)	TE; EC; EOS; TFP	Amount of: securities (all non-loan financial assets, i.e., all financial and physical assets minus the sum of consumer loans, non-consumer loans, and equity); consumer loans; non-consumer loans (industrial, commercial, and real estate loans)	S	R (CP)	INA
183	Hsiao et al. (2010)	OE	Amount of: interest revenue (interest on loans, income from government bonds and corporate bonds); non-interest revenue (services charges on loans and transactions, income from renting and fiduciary activities, commissions, and other operating income); total loans (short-term and medium-term loans)	S	NOM	INA
184	Lozano-Vivas and Pasiouras (2010)	CE	Amount of: loans, other earnings assets, off-balance-sheet (OBS) items, non-interest income	S; F	R (CP)	INA
185	Margono et al. (2010)	CE; EOS; TFP	Amount of: total aggregate loans; total aggregate securities	S	NOM	INA
186	Murillo-Melchor et al. (2010)	MTFP	Amount of: customer loans (all forms of loans performed by banks); deposits (excluding interbank deposits); Securities and equity investments; other earning assets; non-interest income	S; F	NOM	INA; VAA

187	Ray and Das (2010)	CE; PE	Investments (in approved and non-approved securities); Earning advances (NPA adjusted bank credit); Other income (Fee income emanated from the commission, exchange, brokerage, etc.)	S	NOM	INA
188	Weyman-Jones et al. (2010), in Fiordelisi et al. (2010)	BO	Kenjegalieva et al. (2009)	F; Ratio of F to S	NOM	INA
189	Andries (2011)	MTFP	Amount of: total loans; total investments; Other income (non-interest income)	S; F	NOM	INA
190	Curi et al. (2013)	TE	Amount of: interbank loans; customer loans; securities; Off-balance-sheet output (non-interest income)	S; F	R (CP)	INA
191	Daisuke et al. (2011a)	PFP	Output 1: Gross Output = Interest Receipt – Interest Payment; Output 2: B/S Adjusted Output = [Interest Receipt – Interest Payment] × (Loan Outstanding/Deposit Outstanding); Output 3: B/S Adjusted Output – expected average loan losses for next three years	F	NOM	INA
192	Hon et al. (2011)	TE; MTFP	Amount of Loans and Advances combined	S	NOM	INA
193	Huang et al. (2011)	TE; AE	Amount of: total loans; investments; non-interest income	S; F	R (CP)	INA
194	Rajan et al. (2011)	TE; TFP	Amount of: total loans; investments	S	R (CP)	INA
195	Banerjee (2012)	REV	Popularly used: Amount of: deposits; loans; Other earning assets; Less frequently used: net loans; liquid assets	S; F	NOM	PRA; INA
196	Diewert et al. (2011)	BO	Measures of output in terms of services rendered by banks to: 1. Household sector, 2. Banking sector, 3. Non-financial sector and 4. Owner-occupied housing sector	F	NOM	NA
197	Royster (2012)	BO	Tornquist Index of output: Revenue-share weighted index of loan quantity index and deposit quantity index	S	NOM; R (VL)	INA
198	Boucinha et al. (2012)	EOS; CE; CFP	Amount of: total loans (adjusted for securitization); other earning assets	S	NOM	INA
199	Guarda et al. (2013)	BO	Amount of: loans; investments	S	R (CP)	INA
200	Huang and Fu (2013)	CE; CGR; MFCE	Amount of: total loans; total investments	S	R (CP)	INA

(*Continued*)

(Continued)

No.	*Citation*	*Issue*	*Output Specification*	*F or S*	*N or R*	*Approach*
201	Inklaar and Wang (2012)	BO	Count-based (US) versus Balance-based (EU); Quality-adjusted Counts-based output; Reject stock measures in favour of flow measures	F	NA	INA
202	Lee and Kim (2013)	MTFP	Amount of: interest income; fee income	F	NOM	INA
203	Lee et al. (2013)	CE; EOS; EOSCO	Amount of: total loans; investment; non-interest income	S; F	R (CP)	INA
204	Sharma et al. (2013)	REV	Key findings: 1. Intermediation approach is the most popular approach (56 out of 106 used it in their survey); 2. Production approach was the second-highest used (21 out of 106); 3. Stock measures of output dominated the literature reviewed by them; 4. DEA is the most popular methodological choice (66 out of 106 studies)	NA	NA	NA
205	Westhuizen (2013)	MTFP	Amount of: loans and investments; deposits	S	R (CP)	PRA
206	Davies and Tracey (2014)	EOS	Amount of: Liquid assets (cash and equivalents); Total investments (includes securities, trading asset securities, and mortgage-backed securities); Net loans (includes loans given to banks and customers, financial leases, and total portfolio loans, and deducts allowance for loan losses and other adjustments); Other non-loan assets (Total other assets); Off-balance-sheet output (Non-interest income – service activities charge of deposits)	S; F	NOM	INA
207	Kouki et al. (2014)	EOS	Amount of: total loans (except the interbanks loans); Total securities; Total amount of interbank loans	S	NOM	INA
208	Oluitan (2014)	CE	Amount of: Loans; Other earning assets; Non-interest income	S	NOM	INA
209	Tan and Floros (2014)	PRF	Profitability indicator: ROA (ratio of net income to total assets); ROE (ratio of net income to equity)	Ratio of F to S	NOM	NA
210	Tzeremes (2015)	TE	Amount of: Loans; Other earning assets	S	R (CP)	INA
211	Allen et al. (2015)	BO	Key lending variable (dependent variable): R growth in total loans	Ratio of F to S	R (CP)	INA

212	Beccalli et al. (2015)	EOS	Amount of: Loans (Total amount of loans granted by banks, as expressed in the balance sheet); Securities (Total amount of securities, as expressed in the balance sheet); Off-balance-sheet items (comprising managed securitized assets reported off-balance-sheet, other off-balance-sheet exposure to securitization, guarantees, acceptance and documentary credits, committed credit lines, other contingent liabilities, as expressed in the balance sheet, the exact definition used pre-and post-IFRS adoption)	S; F	R (CP)	INA
213	Grover and Arora (2015)	TE	Net-interest margin (i.e., spread); other income; bancassurance income (income earned from -selling insurance policies as a corporate agent)	F	R (CP)	PRA
214	Huang et al. (2015)	MTFP	Amount of: total loans; investments	S	NOM	INA
215	Mamatzakis et al. (2015)	TE; AE	Amount of: Loans; Other earning assets (government securities, bonds, equity investments, CDs, T-bills, etc.)	S	NOM	INA
216	Mamonov and Vernikov (2017)	CE	Amount of loans to households and nonfinancial firms; Amount of retail and corporate deposits (excluding government and interbank accounts); Amount of non-interest income (fee and commission income)	S; F	NOM	PRA
217	Mosko and Bozdo (2016)	CE	Amount of: total loans; other earning assets	S	NOM	INA
218	Phan et al. (2016)	XE	Amount of Loans	S	NOM	INA
219	Salim et al. (2017)	TE	Desirable outputs: Amount of loans, Amount of earning assets; Undesirable outputs: non-performing assets	S	NOM	INA
220	Thilakaweera (2016)	TE; MTFP	Intermediation approach: Amount of loans and advances, Amount of investments; Operating profit approach: Amount of interest income, Amount of non-interest income	S; F	R (CP)	INA; OPA
221	Zha et al. (2016)	TE; CE	Desirable outputs: amount of – interest income, non-interest income; Undesirable output – non-performing loans	F	NOM	INA
222	Abdul-Majid et al. (2017)	CE; TGR	Conventional banks – Amount of loans, other earning assets; Islamic banks: Amount of financing, other earning assets	S	NOM	INA
223	Badunenko and Kumbhakar (2017)	CE; TC	Amount of: interest-bearing assets; other earning assets (investments and securities); fee-based income	S; F	R (CP)	INA

(Continued)

(Continued)

No.	*Citation*	*Issue*	*Output Specification*	*F or S*	*N or R*	*Approach*
224	Batir et al. (2017)	TE; AE; CE	Total loans (Sum of long-term and short-term loans); Off-balance-sheet items (Sum of guarantees, commitments and financial derivative instruments)	S; F	NOM	INA
225	Chen et al. (2018)	TE	Amount of: Total Assets; Fixed Assets; Gross Loans; Total Securities; Total Customer Deposits; Pre-tax Profit; Net Interest Income; Non-Interest Operating Income	S; F	NOM	PRA
226	Feng et al. (2017)	TE; RTS; TFP	Amount of: Consumer loans; Securities (non-loan financial assets, i.e., all financial assets minus the [sum of all loans, securities, and equity]); non-consumer loans (industrial, commercial, and real estate loans); off-balance-sheet items	S; F	R (CP)	INA
227	Wanke et al. (2018)	TE; FZE	Ratios of equity to: assets, net loans, short-term funding, liabilities; ratio of cost to income; ratio net loans to total assets; net interest margin; return on average assets; return on average equity; recurring earning power; interbank ratio; loans; total earning assets; total assets; deposits and short-term funding; other incomes (non-interest bearing); net interest revenue; other operating income; profit before tax; net income	Ratio of F to S	NOM	PRA
228	Babu and Kumar (2018)	TE	Amount of operating profit	F	NOM	PRA
229	Khan et al. (2018)	TE	Total Loans (all the net loans and advances to the customers – net of provision for non-performing loans); Interest/Profit (net interest income for conventional banks and profit/markup for Islamic banks); Investments (investments in government bonds, debentures, treasury securities, and shares of other entities; Other Incomes (non-markup or non-interest income)	S; F	NOM	INA
230	Robin et al. (2018)	PA	Performance indicators: Net Interest Margin (Ratio of net interest income to total assets); ROA (Ratio of net income to total assets); ROE (Ratio of net income to total equities); Yield (Yield on earning assets)	Ratio of F to S	R (CP)	INA
231	Wu et al. (2018)	PE	Amount of: Bad loans (undesirable output); Total loans (desirable output)	S	NOM	PRA
232	Anwar (2019)	CE	Model 1: Total finance, Securities and investment, Other income; Model 2: small business finance, Other finance, Securities and investment, Other income; Model 3: Other finance, Securities and investment, Other income	S; F	NOM	INA

233	Glass and Kenjegalieva (2019)	TFP	Amount of: loans; securities; net interest income	S; F	R (CP)	INA
234	Dincer et al. (2019)	SE	Return on Equity (Net Profit (Losses)/Total Shareholders' Equity); (Return on Assets (Net Profit or Losses/Total Assets); Asset Quality (Total Loans and Receivables/Total Assets); Income Structure – 1 (Interest Income/Total Assets); Income Structure – 2 (Non-Interest Income (Net)/Total Assets)	Ratio of F to S	NOM	INA
235	Nartey et al. (2019)	MTFP	Amount of: loans and advances (total loans and advances offered to customers); other earning assets (securities investments)	S	NOM	INA
236	Otero et al. (2020)	CE	Amount of: Loans; Off-balance-sheet activities	S; F	NOM	INA
237	Yu et al. (2019)	TE	Stage I: Amount of Deposits; Stage II: Loans, Investments, Non-interest income, Undesired output (NPAs)	S; F	NOM	PRA; INA
238	Al-Khasawneh et al. (2020)	CE; SE; PTE; AE; MTFP	Amount of – net loans (net of NPAs); other earning assets (loans to special sectors and interbank loans); investment securities (treasuries and other securities)	S	NOM	INA
239	Colesnic et al. (2020)	TE	Amount of: Earning assets; Net Loans; Impaired loans	S	NOM	INA
240	Fukuyama et al. (2020)	TE; CE	Good outputs – Amount of trading securities, Amount of net loans (net of NPAs); 'bad' output – Amount of non-performing loans ('bad' output)	S	NOM	INA
241	Huang et al. (2020)	LMS	Amount of total assets	S	R (CP)	NA
242	Khan et al. (2020)	EFFS	Amount of – Total loans (both short-term and long-term loans); Other earning assets (loans to special sectors – directed and specialized loans, interbank funds sold, and investment securities – treasury and other securities); Off-balance-sheet items (Guarantees and warranties – letters of guarantee, bank acceptance, letters of credit, guaranteed pre-financing, endorsements and others, commitments, foreign exchange and interest rate transactions, as well as other off-balance-sheet activities)	S; F	NOM	INA

(Continued)

(Continued)

No.	*Citation*	*Issue*	*Output Specification*	*F or S*	*N or R*	*Approach*
243	Mansour and Moussawi (2020)	TE; AE; CE; MTFP	Amount of: total customer deposits; impaired loans	S	NOM	PRA
244	Phan et al. (2020)	PA	Performance indicators: Net Interest Margin (Ratio of net interest income to total assets); ROA (Ratio of net income to total assets); ROE (Ratio of net income to total equities); Yield (Yield on earning assets)	Ratio of F to S	NOM	INA
245	Boda and Piklová (2021)	Output	Major output variables across specifications: interest income, other earning assets, total other operating expense, non-interest expense, total loans, total deposits	S; F	R (CP)	PRA; INA
246	Chen et al. (2022)	TFP	Amount of: investments (equity, securities, other financial assets); total loans	S	NOM	INA
247	Darb and Mohammed (2021)	MTFP	Amount of: Murabaha loan, investment loan, Al-Hassan loan and Al-Musharaka loan	S	NOM	INA
248	Le and Ngo (2020)	PRF	Profitability measures: Net Interest Margin; ROA; ROE; Implicitly includes interests earned on loans plus service charges and fee from depositors)	F; Ratio of F to S	NOM	INA; PRA
249	Ohlson et al. (2021)	MDS	Amount of: insured deposits; uninsured deposits	S	R (CP)	PRA
250	Olson and Zoubi (2011)	CE; PE	Amount of: net loans (net of NPA provisions); securities and other earning assets	S	NOM	INA
251	Owusu and Alhassan (2021)	PRF	Profitability measures: Net Income (net operating income plus securities gains or losses and extraordinary credits or charges less income taxes); Net Interest Income (the difference between interest income and interest expense); Implicitly includes interests earned on loans plus service charges and fee from depositors	F	NOM	INA; PRA
252	Shair et al. (2021)	TE; MTFP	Amount of: loans; interest income	S; F	NOM	INA
253	Syed (2021)	NPAs	Amount of net income; amount of assets; ROA	S; F; Ratio of F to S	NOM	INA
254	Aksoy et al. (2022)	TE	Amount of: Interest income (from credits, banks and securities); Non-interest income (Fees and service charges)	F	NOM	INA; PRA

255	Bansal et al. (2022)	TFP	Stage 1: Amount of deposits; Stage 2: Unused assets of the previous period (total assets minus the sum of required reserves, fixed capital, loans, and securities investments), net profits; Stage 3: Net-interest income, Non-interest income	S; F	R (CP)	PRA; INA
256	Milenković et al. (2022)	TE	Amount of: loans; investments	Ss	NOM	INA
257	Sang (2022)	TE	Amount of: total loans; interest income; non-interest income (including net income from services, net income from trading activities of securities trading, investment and net income from other activities)	S; F	NOM	INA
258	Santosa (2022)	TE	Amount of: total loans; liquid assets	S	NOM	INA
259	Zaman et al. (2022)	MTFP	Amount of: performing loans (gross loans – NPAs); Investments (government and other approved securities both in India and abroad by the banks); Fee-based income (income from exchange transactions, commission, securities, and underwriting)	S; F	R (CP)	INA
260	Shah et al. (2022)	TE; TGR	Amount of: net interest income; non-interest income	F	NOM	INA

Notes: 1. LP – Labour Productivity, BO – Bank Output, OA – Output Aggregation, PRF – Profitability, TC – Technical Change, TE – Technical Efficiency, PE – Productive Efficiency, Production Efficiency, CE – Cost Efficiency, AE – Allocative Efficiency, PTC – Pure Technical Change, EOS – Economies of Scale, EOSCO – Economies of Scope, TCH – Technological Change, RSE – Ray Scale Economies, TSB – Technological Scale Bias, OE – Overall Efficiency, OTE – Overall technical Efficiency, PTE – Pure Technical Efficiency, SE – Scale Efficiency, CMP – Competition, EPSE – Expansion Path Scale Economies, EPSA – Expansion Path Subadditivity, BOP – Bank Output Pricing, EFFS – Efficiencies, ISTE – Input-specific Technical Efficiency, ME – Market Efficiency, CEL – Cost Elasticity, XEF – X-Efficiency, PEF – Production Efficiency, INE – Intermediation Efficiency, MPR – Market Power, PE – Profit Efficiency, APE – Alternate Profit Efficiency, M&A – Mergers and Acquisitions, QE – Quality Efficiency, IO – Insurance Output, SZE – Size Efficiency, PA – Performance Analysis, REV – Review of Evidences, CFP – Cost Function Parameters, CGR – Cost Gap Ratio, MFCE – Metafrontier CE, TGR – Technology Gap Ratio, FZE – Fuzzy Efficiency, LMS – Loan Market Switching, TFP – Total Factor Productivity or Malmquist TFP or Luenberger TFP or Malmquist-Luenberger TFP, MDS – Market Discipline, PRA – Production Approach, INA – Intermediation Approach, VAA – Value Added Approach, NIA – National Income Approach, UCA – User Cost Approach, OPA – Operating Profit Approach, F – Flow variables, S – Stock variables, N – NOM, R – R, R (CP) – R (Constant Price), R (VL) – R (Volume), S (PR) – S (Price), F (PR) – Flow (Price); 2. A further detailed review sheet with more analytical dimensions on each of the studies above and on a larger sample of studies can be availed from the author on request.

Source: Survey of evidence by the author.

Notes

1 Once the appropriate approach to output specification is determined, as discussed in section 3.3, the issue becomes a measurement problem. The analyst must choose the best possible proxy for the underlying output concept as prescribed by the chosen specification approach. This seems to be how literature has conceptualised the bank output measurement problem.
2 Agu (1988) reviews the significant output measures used under the balance sheet versus income statements approaches in the literature on bank performance spanning from the 1950s to the late 1970s.
3 Bankers, economists and national income accountants tend to view the banking activities from different angles. See Stauffer (2004) for an overview of these perspectives.
4 The University of Adelaide, Australia, made this study available and was kind enough to send the soft copy of this work on request. Also, see Tripplet and Bosworth (2004a, 2004b), for more details on this issue.
5 The author studied the distribution of the cost efficiency estimates using the Kernel density method. The author suggested this non-parametric distribution to avoid introducing subjectivity by having to choose a specific functional form, as is the case with parametric distributions. The author asserts that "the need to know the functional form makes the parametric approach barely useful as a descriptive tool" (p. 206).
6 The approaches discussed here define not only the output but inputs as well. Hence, these approaches can be better referred to as production function specification approaches in banking rather than output specification approaches. However, as discussed in Chapter 10, there is a reasonable consensus on the significant inputs employed in a banking production function. Hence, the major differences among these approaches result from incongruence in output specification. That is the approach followed in this work.
7 Another novel approach on this account was the one Leland and Pyle (1977) suggested, which approached bank output measurement under a risk-based approach. They incorporated dimensions such as risk management, adverse selection and information asymmetry into their measurement of banking output. After the Great Recession, this approach gained increased attention, particularly in advanced economies. Another notable study in more recent times on broadly similar lines is Saeed et al. (2020).
8 The discussion here is brief due to space constraints. More works on the approaches highlighted here can be located in the appendix to this chapter and the additional material provided in the online resources.
9 Several approaches use these same variables but are different from the production approach. The basic idea is that both the inputs and outputs should be consistent with what a particular approach suggests. Different approaches may use the same output vector. These dimensions will emerge clearly in further discussion.
10 This statement is true to the extent that value measures are used in the production approach. Data availability on volume measures is challenging in both advanced and emerging economies.
11 This statement can be confirmed only under the assumption that the intermediation component of total bank output is falling or lower than the direct component. However, for aggregate sectoral analysis, if one wishes to focus on the performance of the banking sector in terms of its direct output, the production approach can serve as a helpful tool. In Chapter 8, section 8.3, sectoral analysis of returns to scale for the banking and insurance industries of the BRIICS countries is performed wherein both the production and intermediation approaches are employed. The returns to scale coefficient does not diverge much under both approaches.
12 The fundamental essence of the intermediation approach in the banking and insurance literature is that these intermediaries have a comparative advantage in minimization of the transaction, search and monitoring costs relative to non-banking and non-insurance firms. However, with the increasing digitalization of both these industries, transactions and search costs may be brought down considerably in the coming years. Does that

mean that their intermediation function will become redundant? See Scholtens and Wensveen (2003) for a possible answer to this concern.

13 Diamond (1984) warned at a very early stage that the emergence of non-banking financial companies (NBFC) and the increasing problem of NPAs indicate the falling competitive advantages banks enjoy in resolving the issues of monitoring costs and information asymmetries. This warning still holds, and the implications are examined in section 3.5.

14 See Radecki (1999) for a criticism of the pure intermediation approach.

15 For a compact introduction to intermediation theory, see Inklaar and Wang (2011, 2012). Interestingly, the authors suggest that the flow of funds between depositors and borrowers via the banks should not be considered a measure of output under this approach. Broadly, similar line of analysis is adopted by Colangelo and Inklaar (2010).

16 This also implies that the operating cost shares can be used to aggregate various outputs into a single aggregate/composite index.

17 A compact introduction to user costs concerning banking can be found in Hancock (1985).

18 This is required because net contribution can be estimated only after adjusting for all economic costs, including accounting and opportunity costs.

19 Such an exercise is undertaken across many advanced and emerging economies in the form of FISIM estimation under the SNA framework. However, FISIM estimates are estimated and available at the sectoral level – bank-level and branch-level information.

20 See Wang and Basu (2005) for more details on this dimension. They also provide a way out of this limitation of the user-cost approach. Their work is vital because the imputation of the implicit output of the commercial banking sector in the SNA is based mainly on the user cost framework.

21 Further details on these studies can be found in the appendix to this chapter and the extended review sheet, which may be requested from the author directly.

22 Weights are essential elements of an index number. In his works, Fisher established that rather than the averaging procedure, the choice of weights and other considerations are more serious challenges in the construction of index numbers. While reviewing the classic work of Fisher, namely 'the making of index numbers', Synder (1923, p. 421) comments that "the choice of weights, of material, of the accuracy of the data, of the number of quotations, is of far greater importance, and it is these and not the method of averaging which makes practically all the remarkable differences".

23 This can be undertaken using the so-called acid tests laid down by Fisher (1922).

24 Further detailed notes on each of these output measures for both the banking and insurance activities may be supplied in the online resources or may be availed from the author upon request. Due to space constraints, only the most essential aspects have been presented here.

25 At this juncture, readers might be interested in knowing the specific studies that employ the measures highlighted here. A thematic bibliography and a list of studies for the various output measures discussed throughout this work can be obtained from the author upon request. This was inevitable due to space restrictions. The readers may kindly forgive the author for this presentation arrangement.

26 See Boda and Piklová (2021) for a brief note on this matter. Also see Setiwan et al. (2017).

27 A common criticism against using this approach to output measurement has been the so-called divisibility constraint. "Deposits are typically divisible, liquid and riskless, whilst loans are indivisible, illiquid and risky" (Dong, 2010, p. 131). Thus, combining them can distort the true underlying output, and further allocation of the output to consumption sectors, different lines of business, etc., may not be feasible.

28 Needless to say that this measure of output is inconsistent with the pure intermediation and asset approach to output specification.

29 See Hartwick (1996) for an elaboration on this aspect.

30 This implies that deposits and loans are treated as homogenous services, which is theoretically incorrect. If they are to be weighted, the correct aggregation function must be

defined, and valid weighting factors must be ascertained. This is a debate that has not been settled till date. The broad consensus is to treat them separately as far as possible.

31 Sealey and Lindley (1977) proposed this issue for the first time for a rigorous analysis of deposits as inputs. Similarly, Humphrey and Pulley (1997) defend using deposits as inputs. However, Tripplet and Bosworth (2004b) outrightly reject the notion of deposits being an input.

32 For treatment of deposits as quasi-fixed inputs, please see Flannery (1982). "A quasi-fixed factor of production is one whose cost to the firm in any production period is partly fixed (sunk) and partly variable" (Flannery, 1982, p. 530). The author rejects the notion that deposits are variable inputs and contends that they must be included as quasi-fixed inputs to capture the true production process of banks better. This conception is also based on the premise that demand contraction or external shocks do not allow the banks to freely change the amount of deposit received, especially if the negative demand or external shock is temporary. Banks can't freely change the deposit amount as per extant economic conditions, which requires their treatment as a quasi-fixed input rather than variable input.

33 Deposits are treated as output due to various reasons. One of them is that the explicit revenues on deposits are small, and thus there must be implicit earnings for banks which require deposits to be treated as output (Berger & Humphrey, 1992). Hughes and Mester (1993) have proposed a basic test to decide whether deposits are input or output in a given context. They estimate a variable cost function with deposits as an explanatory variable. If the estimated sign is positive, then deposits are output or else they may be treated as an input.

34 "In the user cost framework the sign of the user cost provides the answer: a negative sign indicates an output status and a positive sign indicates input status" (Fixler & Zieschang, 1999, p. 548). They conclude that as per the evidence, deposits must be treated as output.

35 "It is a technological question that can be answered by testing whether the data are consistent with the different technological roles of outputs and inputs" (Hughes et al., 2000, p. 6).

36 The stock amount of deposits is adjusted for the effective interest rate for inclusion in the FISIM.

37 More details on this matter can be found in the online resources or can be obtained from the author on request. Also see Rakshit and Bardhan (2022) for some dimensions on this aspect.

38 See the contribution by Prof. Barendra Bhoi in Chapter 7.

39 Detailed Notes on the estimation procedures of FISIM output and other supplementary notes are provided in the online resources. Only the most pressing issues in the literature are elaborated on in this section.

40 See Akritidis (2017) and Triplett and Bosworth (2004a, 2004b) for the history and evolution of the FISIM framework in the national income accounting.

41 Several authors have criticized this implicit approach to measuring the implicit output. Instead, they focus on directly estimating the real flow of services. See Wang and Basu (2005) for an illustration of such an approach.

42 For an overview of alternative approaches to estimating the reference rate, see Davtyan (2018).

43 In the most fundamental terms, the equation for estimating FISIM output is $(R_L - R_R)Y_L + (R_R - R_D)Y_D$, where R_L is the chosen rate of interest on loans, R_D is the chosen rate of interest on deposits, Y_L is the amount of loan, Y_D is the amount of deposit and R_R is the chosen reference rate.

44 See Daisuke et al. (2011a, 2011b), who construct a risk-adjusted measure of FISIM output for individual banks and examine FISIM output productivity using data on 368 to 1251 bank-firm groups of Japan across 1976–2005.

45 The authors provide an extensive discussion on the various aspects of bank output regarding the requirements and principles of the national income accounts, particularly the SNA, 1993 manual released shortly before their study.

46 The reference rate was initially conceptualised as the minimum rate of return that accounts for a given risk exposure on an asset, but the SNA adopted a risk-free interpretation (Fixler et al., 2003).

47 Disaggregated reference rates can be used to represent the benchmark rate for each bank with each FISIM-consuming sector (e.g. reference rate between banks and the household sector, banks and manufacturing business, banks and agriculture businesses, banks and services, banks and other banks, banks and Government, etc.). Such efforts are possible only for advanced economies. EMEs are still a long way from undertaking such exercises. For a brief overview on this problem in the context of emerging economies, see Das and Jangili (2017).

48 An emerging database on sectoral and industry-level output measures is the KLEMS project. However, it has not been developed enough to be used on a larger scale. The author could not find any high-quality study on the present theme that employed the KLEMS estimates of value-added and gross output. Moreover, the KLEMS database provides estimates only for the financial services sector and not for the banking industry.

49 For a detailed discussion on double deflation methodology, especially concerning national income accounts, see Vanoli (2005).

50 While this may be possible for labour variables, the controversy on the correct price of capital input makes such an exercise subject to many disagreements. Regulatory data on banking statistics in the emerging economies generally do not get deeper into capital input pricing. Moreover, the pricing of capital input has been a complicated matter and has been raged by many debates. The so-called "fundamental problem of accounting" (Diewert, 2001, p. 3) persists. The analyst has to estimate the same using disparate data sources, which again can be a possible source of measurement error.

51 A unique approach for single deflation of banking inputs and outputs has been suggested by Diewert et al. (2012). The price index of non-monetary assets is proposed as deflators for the liability components in the banking sector's balance sheet constructed by the authors. Even earlier attempts on broadly similar lines may be found in Diewert et al. (2004, 2009).

References

Abdul-Majid, M., Falahaty, M., & Jusoh, M. (2017). Performance of Islamic and conventional banks: A meta-frontier approach. *Research in International Business and Finance, 42*, 1327–1335. https://doi.org/10.1016/j.ribaf.2017.07.069

Adams, R. M., Röller, L.-H., & Sickles, R. C. (2002). *Market power in outputs and inputs: An empirical application to banking*. Social Science Research Network (SSRN Scholarly Paper No. 355100). https://doi.org/10.2139/ssrn.355100

Agu, C. C. (1988). On the performance analysis: The definition and measurement of bank output in Nigeria. *Savings and Development, 12*(2), 107–126.

Agu, C. C. (2004). Efficiency of commercial banking in the Gambia. *African Review of Money Finance and Banking*, 31–50.

Akritidis, L. (2017). *Financial intermediation services indirectly measured (FISIM) in the U.K. Revisited*. Office for National Statistics. www.ons.gov.uk/economy/grossdomesticproduct gdp/articles/financialintermediationservicesindirectlymeasuredfisimintheukrevisited/2017-04-24

Aksoy, E. E. A., Dirik, C., & Göker, İ. E. K. (2022). Opening the black-box of bank efficiency in Turkey with two-stage data envelopment analysis: A study on capital adequacy ratio. *Ege Academic Review, 22*(1), 75–91. https://doi.org/10.21121/eab.1064816

Alam, I. M. S. (2001). A nonparametric approach for assessing productivity dynamics of large U.S. Banks. *Journal of Money, Credit and Banking, 33*(1), 121–139. https://doi.org/10.2307/2673875

Al-Khasawneh, J. A., Essaddam, N., & Hussain, T. (2020). Total productivity and cost efficiency dynamics of U.S. Merging banks: A non-parametric bootstrapped analysis of the fifth merger wave. *The Quarterly Review of Economics and Finance*, *78*, 199–211. https://doi.org/10.1016/j.qref.2020.02.002

Allen, F., Jackowicz, K., Kowalewski, O., & Kozłowski, Ł. (2015). Bank lending, crises, and changing ownership structure in central and Eastern European countries. *Journal of Corporate Finance*. https://doi.org/10.1016/j.jcorpfin.2015.05.001

Allen, J., & Liu, Y. (2007). Efficiency and economies of scale of large Canadian banks. *The Canadian Journal of Economics*, *40*(1), 225–244.

Altman, E. I., Gande, A., & Saunders, A. (2010). Bank debt versus bond debt: Evidence from secondary market prices. *Journal of Money, Credit and Banking*, *42*(4), 755–767.

Altunbaş, Y., Gardener, E. P. M., Molyneux, P., & Moore, B. (2001). Efficiency in European banking. *European Economic Review*, *45*(10), 1931–1955. https://doi.org/10.1016/S0014-2921(00)00091-X

Altunbas, Y., Liu, M.-H., Molyneux, P., & Seth, R. (2000). Efficiency and risk in Japanese banking. *Journal of Banking & Finance*, *24*(10), 1605–1628.

Aly, H. Y., Grabowski, R., Pasurka, C., & Rangan, N. (1990). Technical, scale, and allocative efficiencies in U.S. Banking: An empirical investigation. *The Review of Economics and Statistics*, *72*(2), 211–218. https://doi.org/10.2307/2109710

Andries, A. M. (2011). The determinants of bank efficiency and productivity growth in the central and Eastern European banking systems. *Eastern European Economics*, *49*(6), 38–59.

Angadi, V. B., & Devaraj, V. J. (1983). Productivity and profitability of banks in India. *Economic and Political Weekly*, *18*(48), M160–M170.

Anthanassopoulos, A. D. (1998). Nonparametric frontier models for assessing the market and cost efficiency of large-scale bank branch networks. *Journal of Money, Credit and Banking*, *30*(2), 172–192. https://doi.org/10.2307/2601208

Anwar, M. (2019). Cost efficiency performance of Indonesian banks over the recovery period: A stochastic frontier analysis. *The Social Science Journal*, *56*(3), 377–389. https://doi.org/10.1016/j.soscij.2018.08.002

Ariff, M., & Can, L. (2008). Cost and profit efficiency of Chinese banks: A non-parametric analysis. *China Economic Review*, *19*, 260–273. https://doi.org/10.1016/j.chieco.2007.04.001

Asaftei, G., & Kumbhakar, S. C. (2008). Regulation and efficiency in transition: The case of Romanian banks. *Journal of Regulatory Economics*, *33*(3), 253–282. https://doi.org/10.1007/s11149-007-9041-0

Athanasoglou, P. P., Georgiou, E. A., & Staikouras, C. C. (2009). Assessing output and productivity growth in the banking industry. *The Quarterly Review of Economics and Finance*, *49*(4), 1317–1340. https://doi.org/10.1016/j.qref.2009.08.003

Athanassopoulos, A. D., & Giokas, D. (2000). The use of data envelopment analysis in banking institutions: Evidence from the commercial bank of Greece. *Interfaces*, *30*(2), 81–95.

Ayadi, O. F., Adebayo, A. O., & Omolehinwa, E. (1998). Bank performance measurement in a developing economy: An application of data envelopment analysis. *Managerial Finance*, *24*(7), 5–16. https://doi.org/10.1108/03074359810765589

Babu, M. R., & Kumar, A. M. (2018). Evaluating the nationalization & privatization effect: A case of Indian banking industry. *Banks and Bank Systems*, *13*(1), 11–21. https://doi.org/10.21511/bbs.13(1).2018.02

Badunenko, O., & Kumbhakar, S. C. (2017). Economies of scale, technical change and persistent and time-varying cost efficiency in Indian banking: Do ownership, regulation and heterogeneity matter? *European Journal of Operational Research*, *260*(2), 789–803. https://doi.org/10.1016/j.ejor.2017.01.025

Banerjee, B. (2012). Banking sector efficiency in new E.U. Member states: A survey of cross-country evidence. *Eastern European Economics*, *50*(6), 81–115.

Banker, R. D., Chang, H., & Lee, S.-Y. (2010). Differential impact of Korean banking system reforms on bank productivity. *Journal of Banking & Finance*, *34*(7), 1450–1460. https://doi.org/10.1016/j.jbankfin.2010.02.023

Bansal, P., Kumar, S., Mehra, A., & Gulati, R. (2022). Developing two dynamic Malmquist-Luenberger productivity indices: An illustrated application for assessing productivity performance of Indian banks. *Omega*, *107*, 102538. https://doi.org/10.1016/j.omega.2021.102538

Barman, R. B., & Samanta, G. P. (2007). Measuring banking intermediation services: Issues and challenges for India. *Economic and Political Weekly*, *42*(37), 3754–3763.

Barnett, W. A. (1978). The user cost of money. *Economics Letters*, *1*(2), 145–149. https://doi.org/10.1016/0165-1765(78)90051-4

Batir, T. E., Volkman, D. A., & Gungor, B. (2017). Determinants of bank efficiency in Turkey: Participation banks versus conventional banks. *Borsa Istanbul Review*, *17*(2), 86–96. https://doi.org/10.1016/j.bir.2017.02.003

Batra, A. (1996). Bank profitability with a hybrid profit function – the Indian case. *Indian Economic Review*, *31*(2), 223–234.

Beccalli, E., Anolli, M., & Borello, G. (2015). Are European banks too big? Evidence on economies of scale. *Journal of Banking & Finance*, *58*, 232–246. https://doi.org/10.1016/j.jbankfin.2015.04.014

Beccalli, E., Casu, B., & Girardone, C. (2006). Efficiency and stock performance in European banking. *Journal of Business Finance & Accounting*, *33*(1–2), 245–262. https://doi.org/10.1111/j.1468-5957.2006.01362.x

Benston, G. J. (1965). Branch banking and economies of scale. *The Journal of Finance*, *20*(2), 312–331. https://doi.org/10.2307/2977238

Benston, G. J. (1972). Economies of scale of financial institutions. *Journal of Money, Credit and Banking*, *4*(2), 312–341. https://doi.org/10.2307/1991041

Benston, G. J., Hanweck, G. A., & Humphrey, D. B. (1982). Scale economies in banking: A restructuring and reassessment. *Journal of Money, Credit and Banking*, *14*(4), 435–456. https://doi.org/10.2307/1991654

Berg, S. A., Førsund, F. R., & Jansen, E. S. (1991). Technical efficiency of Norwegian banks: The non-parametric approach to efficiency measurement. *Journal of Productivity Analysis*, *2*(2), 127–142.

Berg, S. A., Førsund, F. R., & Jansen, E. S. (1992). Malmquist indices of productivity growth during the deregulation of Norwegian banking, 1980–89. *The Scandinavian Journal of Economics*, *94*, S211–S228. https://doi.org/10.2307/3440261

Berger, A. N., & Bouwman, C. H. S. (2007). *Bank liquidity creation*. Federal Deposit Insurance Corporation, U.S. (Conference Paper).

Berger, A. N., & DeYoung, R. (1997). Problem loans and cost efficiency in commercial banks – sciencedirect. *Journal of Banking & Finance*, *21*(6), 849–870.

Berger, A. N., & Hannan, T. H. (1998). The efficiency cost of market power in the banking industry: A test of the 'quiet life' and related hypotheses. *The Review of Economics and Statistics*, *80*(3), 454–465.

Berger, A. N., Hanweck, G. A., & Humphrey, D. B. (1987). Competitive viability in banking: Scale, scope, and product mix economies. *Journal of Monetary Economics*, *20*, 501–520.

Berger, A. N., & Humphrey, D. B. (1992). Measurement and efficiency issues in commercial banking. In *Output Measurement in the Service Sectors* (pp. 245–300). University of Chicago Press. www.nber.org/books-and-chapters/output-measurement-service-sectors/measurement-and-efficiency-issues-commercial-banking

Berger, A. N., & Humphrey, D. B. (1997). Efficiency of financial institutions: International survey and directions for future research. *European Journal of Operational Research*, *98*(2), 175–212.

Berger, A. N., & Mester, L. J. (1997). Inside the black box: What explains differences in the efficiencies of financial institutions? *Journal of Banking & Finance*, *21*(7), 895–947. https://doi.org/10.1016/S0378-4266(97)00010-1

Bhattacharya, K. (2003). *How good is the bankscope database? A cross-validation exercise with correction factors for market concentration measures*. Bank for International Settlements (Working Paper No. 133). https://doi.org/10.2139/ssrn.901147

Bhattacharyya, A., Lovell, C., & Sahay, P. (1997). The impact of liberalization on the productive efficiency of Indian commercial banks. *European Journal of Operational Research*, *98*(2), 332–345.

Bhuyan, P. (2016). *Measurement of central bank output – methodological issues for India*. Reserve Bank of India (Working Paper No. 06/2016).

Boda, M., & Piklová, Z. (2021). Impact of an input-output specification on efficiency scores in data envelopment analysis: A banking case study. *RAIRO – Operations Research*, *55*, S1551–S1583. https://doi.org/10.1051/ro/2020040

Boer, S. D. (1999). *A volume index for the output of the Dutch banking industry based on quantity indicators*. Statistics Netherland.

Boot, A. W. A., & Thakor, A. V. (1993). Self-interested bank regulation. *The American Economic Review*, *83*(2), 206–212.

Bos, J. W. B., & Kolari, J. W. (2005). Large bank efficiency in Europe and the United States: Are there economic motivations for geographic expansion in financial services? *The Journal of Business*, *78*(4), 1555–1592. https://doi.org/10.1086/430869

Bossone, B., & Lee, J.-K. (2004). In finance, size matters: The 'systemic scale economies' hypothesis. *IMF Staff Papers*, *51*(1), 19–46.

Boucinha, M., Ribeiro, N., & Weyman-Jones, T. (2012). An assessment of Portuguese banks' efficiency and productivity towards Euro area participation. *Journal of Productivity Analysis*, *39*(2), 177–190. https://doi.org/10.1007/s11123-012-0310-2

Boumans, M. (2007). *Measurement in economics: A handbook*. Emerald Group Publishing Limited.

Brand, H., & Duke, J. (1982). Productivity in commercial banking: Computers spur the advance. *Monthly Labor Review*, *105*(12), 19–27.

Butter, F. A. G. den. (2007). National accounts and indicators, Chapter 8. In M. Boumans (Ed.), *Measurement in economics: A handbook*. Elsevier.

Camanho, A. S., & Dyson, R. G. (1999). Efficiency, size, benchmarks and targets for bank branches: An application of data envelopment analysis. *Journal of the Operational Research Society*, *50*, 903–915. https://doi.org/10.1057/palgrave.jors.2600792

Camanho, A. S., & Dyson, R. G. (2005). Cost efficiency, production and value-added models in the analysis of bank branch performance. *The Journal of the Operational Research Society*, *56*(5), 483–494.

Casolaro, L., & Gobbi, G. (2007). information technology and productivity changes in the banking industry. *Economic Notes*, *36*(1), 43–76.

Casu, B., Girardone, C., & Molyneux, P. (2004). Productivity change in European banking: A comparison of parametric and non-parametric approaches. *Journal of Banking & Finance*, *28*(10), 2521–2540. https://doi.org/10.1016/j.jbankfin.2003.10.014

Chaffai, M. E. (1997). Estimating input-specific technical inefficiency: The case of the Tunisian banking industry. *European Journal of Operational Research*, *98*(2), 314–331. https://doi.org/10.1016/S0377-2217(96)00350-5

Chaudhuri, S. (2002). Some issues of growth and profitability in Indian public sector banks. *Economic and Political Weekly, 37*(22), 2155–2162.

Chen, G., Kim, K. A., Nofsinger, J. R., & Rui, O. M. (2007). Trading performance, disposition effect, overconfidence, representativeness bias, and experience of emerging market investors. *Journal of Behavioral Decision Making, 20*(4), 425–451. https://doi.org/10.1002/bdm.561

Chen, X., Zhang, X., Wang, Y., & Jia, H. (2022). The risk-adjusted profit productivity change in Chinese banks: A comparative analysis of the different type banks. *Managerial and Decision Economics, 43*(2), 523–532. https://doi.org/10.1002/mde.3399

Chen, Z., Matousek, R., & Wanke, P. (2018). Chinese bank efficiency during the global financial crisis: A combined approach using satisficing DEA and support vector machines. *The North American Journal of Economics and Finance, 43*, 71–86. https://doi.org/10.1016/j.najef.2017.10.003

Chronopoulos, D., Girardone, C., & Nankervis, J. (2010). Post-merger bank efficiency and stock market reaction: The case of the U.S. versus Europe. In *New issues in financial institutions management* (pp. 122–135). Palgrave Macmillan. https://doi.org/10.1057/9780230299153_8

Clark, J. A. (1984). Estimation of economies of scale in banking using a generalized functional form. *Journal of Money, Credit and Banking, 16*(1), 53–68. https://doi.org/10.2307/1992648

Clark, J. A. (1996). Economic cost, scale efficiency, and competitive viability in banking. *Journal of Money, Credit and Banking, 28*(3), 342–364. https://doi.org/10.2307/2077979

Clark, J. A., & Siems, T. F. (2002). X-efficiency in banking: Looking beyond the balance sheet. *Journal of Money, Credit and Banking, 34*(4), 987–1013.

Clark, J. A., & Speaker, P. J. (1994). Economies of scale and scope in banking: Evidence from a generalized Translog cost function. *Quarterly Journal of Business and Economics, 33*(2), 3–25.

Colangelo, A., & Inklaar, R. (2010). Banking sector output measurement in the Euro area: A modified approach. *SSRN Electronic Journal*, 1–51. https://doi.org/10.2139/ssrn.1610200

Colesnic, O., Kounetas, K., & Michael, P. (2020). Estimating risk efficiency in middle east banks before and after the crisis: A metafrontier framework. *Global Finance Journal, 46*, 100484. https://doi.org/10.1016/j.gfj.2019.100484

Colwell, R. J., & Davis, E. P. (1992). Output and productivity in banking. *The Scandinavian Journal of Economics, 94*, S111–S129. https://doi.org/10.2307/3440252

Coyne, T. J. (1973). Commercial bank profitability by function. *Financial Management, 2*(1), 64. https://doi.org/10.2307/3665102

Cuesta, R. A., & Zofío, J. L. (2005). Hyperbolic efficiency and parametric distance functions: With application to Spanish savings banks. *Journal of Productivity Analysis, 24*(1), 31–48.

Curi, C., Guarda, P., Lozano-Vivas, A., & Zelenyuk, V. (2013). Is foreign-bank efficiency in financial centers driven by home-country characteristics? *Journal of Productivity Analysis, 40*, 367–385. https://doi.org/10.2139/ssrn.1833327

Daisuke, M., Tomohiko, I., & Keishi, S. (2011a). *Bank efficiency and client firms' productivity*. Economic and Social Research Institute (Discussion Paper No. 273).

Daisuke, M., Tomohiko, I., & Shoji, K. (2011b). *Productivity of banks and its impact on the capital investments of client firms*. RIETI (Discussion Paper Series 11-E-016).

Darb, J. A.-K., & Mohammed, A. A. (2021). Measuring and analyzing the productivity of Islamic banks in Iraq according to the Malmquist productivity index. *Review of International Geographic Education, 11*(7), 1646–1658.

Das, A. (2002). Risk and productivity change of public sector banks. *Economic and Political Weekly*, *37*(5), 437–440 + 443–445 + 447–448.

Das, A., & Jangili, R. (2017). Financial intermediation services indirectly measured (FISIM): The role of reference rate. *Statistical Journal of the IAOS*, *33*, 515–524. https://doi.org/10.3233/SJI-160280

Das, A., Nag, A., & Ray, S. (2005). Liberalisation, ownership and efficiency in Indian banking: A nonparametric analysis. *Economic and Political Weekly*, *40*, 1190–1197. https://doi.org/10.2307/4416367

Das, P. K., & Maiti, P. (1998). Bank credit, output and bank deposits in West Bengal and selected states. *Economic and Political Weekly*, *33*(47/48), 3081–3088.

Davies, R., & Tracey, B. (2014). Too big to be efficient? The impact of implicit subsidies on estimates of scale economies for banks. *Journal of Money, Credit and Banking*, *46*(1), 219–253.

Davtyan, A. (2018). *Estimation of financial intermediation services indirectly measured in Armenia's external accounts*. Irving Fisher Committee – Central Bank of Armenia Workshop on 'External Sector Statistics'.

De, P. K. (2004). Technical efficiency, ownership, and reforms: An econometric study of Indian banking industry. *Indian Economic Review*, *39*(1), 261–294.

Devaney, M., & Weber, W. (2002). Small-business lending and profit efficiency in commercial banking. *Journal of Financial Services Research*, *22*(3), 225–246. https://doi.org/10.1023/A:1019733226515

DeYoung, R., & Hasan, I. (1998). The performance of de novo commercial banks: A profit efficiency approach. *Journal of Banking & Finance*, *22*(5), 565–587. https://doi.org/10.1016/S0378-4266(98)00025-9

Diamond, D. W. (1984). Financial intermediation and delegated monitoring. *The Review of Economic Studies*, *51*(3), 393–414. https://doi.org/10.2307/2297430

Dick, A. A. (2006). Nationwide branching and its impact on market structure, quality, and bank performance. *The Journal of Business*, *79*(2), 567–592. https://doi.org/10.1086/499131

Dick, A. A. (2007). Market size, service quality, and competition in banking. *Journal of Money, Credit and Banking*, *39*(1), 49–81.

Dietsch, M. (1993). Economies of scale and scope in French commercial banking industry. *Journal of Productivity Analysis*, *4*(1/2), 35–50.

Diewert, E., Fixler, D., & Zieschang, K. (2011). *The measurement of banking services in the system of national accounts*. Vancouver School of Economics (Working Paper No. 2011–23).

Diewert, E., Fixler, D., & Zieschang, K. (2012). Problems with the measurement of banking services in a national accounting framework. In *Discussion Papers* (No. 2012-25; Discussion Papers). School of Economics, The University of New South Wales. https://ideas.repec.org/p/swe/wpaper/2012-25.html

Diewert, W. E. (2001). *Measuring the price and quantity as capital services under alternative assumptions*. Department of Economics, The University of British Columbia (Working Paper No. 01–24).

Diewert, W. E., Greenlees, J. S., & Hulten, C. R. (2004). *Incorporating financial services in a consumer price index*. NBER Conference on Price Index Concepts and Measurement, Vancouver, Canada. https://doi.org/10.7208/chicago/9780226148571.001.0001

Diewert, W. E., Greenlees, J. S., & Hulten, C. R. (2009). *Price index concepts and measurement*. University of Chicago Press. www.nber.org/books-and-chapters/price-index-concepts-and-measurement

Dincer, H., Hacioglu, U., Tatoglu, E., & Delen, D. (2019). Developing a hybrid analytics approach to measure the efficiency of deposit banks. *Journal of Business Research*, *104*, 131–145. https://doi.org/10.1016/j.jbusres.2019.06.035

Dong, Y. (2010). *Cost efficiency in the Chinese banking sector: A comparison of parametric and non-parametric methodologies* [Ph.D. Thesis]. Loughborough University. https://repository.lboro.ac.uk/articles/thesis/Cost_efficiency_in_the_Chinese_banking_sector_a_comparison_of_parametric_and_non-parametric_methodologies/9496763/1

Donovan, D. J. (1977). *Consumption, leisure, and the demand for money and money substitutes* [Ph.D. Thesis]. University of British Columbia, Department of Economics.

Durkin, T. A., & Elliehausen, G. E. (1998). The cost structure of the consumer finance industry. *Journal of Financial Services Research, 13*(1), 71–86. https://doi.org/10.1023/A:1007906527814

Elyasiani, E., & Mehdian, S. M. (1992). Productive efficiency performance of minority and nonminority-owned banks: A nonparametric approach. *Journal of Banking & Finance, 16*(5), 933–948. https://doi.org/10.1016/0378-4266(92)90033-V

Elyasiani, E., & Mehdian, S. M. (1990). A nonparametric approach to measurement of efficiency and technological change: The case of large U.S. Commercial banks. *Journal of Financial Services Research, 4*, 157–168.

Evanoff, D. D., & Israilevich, P. R. (1995). Scale elasticity versus scale efficiency in banking. *Southern Economic Journal, 61*(4), 1036–1046. https://doi.org/10.2307/1060739

Evanoff, D. D., Israilevich, P. R., & Merris, R. C. (1989). *Technical change, regulation, and economies of scale for large commercial banks: An application of a modified version of Shephard's Lemma*. Federal Reserve Bank of Chicago (Working Paper No. 89–11). https://ideas.repec.org/p/fip/fedhfi/89-11.html

Farrell, M. J. (1957). The measurement of productive efficiency. *Journal of the Royal Statistical Society, 120*(3), 253–290. https://doi.org/10.2307/2343100

Feng, G., Peng, B., & Zhang, X. (2017). Productivity and efficiency at bank holding companies in the U.S.: A time-varying heterogeneity approach. *Journal of Productivity Analysis, 48*(2), 179–192.

Feng, G., & Serletis, A. (2010). Efficiency, technical change, and returns to scale in large U.S. Banks: Panel data evidence from an output distance function satisfying theoretical regularity. *Journal of Banking & Finance, 34*(1), 127–138. https://doi.org/10.1016/j.jbankfin.2009.07.009

Fiordelisi, F., Molyneux, P., & Previati, D. (2010). *New issues in financial institutions management* (1st ed.). Palgrave Macmillan. https://link.springer.com/book/10.1057/9780230299153

Fisher, I. (1922). *The making of index numbers*. Houghton Mifflin Company.

Fixler, D. (2004). *Incorporating financial services in a consumer price index*. Bureau of Economic Analysis (Working Paper).

Fixler, D., Reinsdorf, M., & Smith, G. (2003). *Measuring the services of commercial banks in the NIPAs changes in concepts and methods*. OECD (OECD National Accounts Experts Meeting STD/NAES(2003)20).

Fixler, D., & Zieschang, K. (1999). The productivity of the banking sector: Integrating financial and production approaches to measuring financial service output. *Canadian Journal of Economics, 32*(2), 547–569.

Flannery, M. J. (1982). Retail bank deposits as quasi-fixed factors of production. *The American Economic Review, 72*(3), 527–536.

Focarelli, D., & Panetta, F. (2003). Are mergers beneficial to consumers? Evidence from the market for bank deposits. *American Economic Review, 93*(4), 1152–1172. https://doi.org/10.1257/000282803769206241

Freixas, X., & Parigi, B. (1998). Contagion and efficiency in gross and net interbank payment systems. *Journal of Financial Intermediation, 7*, 3–31.

Fukuyama, H., Matousek, R., & Tzeremes, N. G. (2020). A Nerlovian cost inefficiency two-stage DEA model for modeling banks' production process: Evidence from the Turkish banking system. *Omega, 95*, 102198. https://doi.org/10.1016/j.omega.2020.102198
Geehan, R., & Allen, L. (1978). Measuring the real output and productivity of savings and credit institutions. *The Canadian Journal of Economics/Revue Canadienne d'Economique, 11*(4), 669–679. https://doi.org/10.2307/134372
Gilbert, R. A. (1983). Economies of scale in correspondent banking: Note. *Journal of Money, Credit and Banking, 15*(4), 483–488. https://doi.org/10.2307/1992163
Girardone, C., Molyneux, P., & Gardener, E. P. M. (2004). Analysing the determinants of bank efficiency: The case of Italian banks. *Applied Economics, 36*(3), 215–227. https://doi.org/10.1080/0003684042000175334
Glass, A. J., & Kenjegalieva, K. (2019). A spatial productivity index in the presence of efficiency spillovers: Evidence for U.S. Banks, 1992–2015. *European Journal of Operational Research, 273*(3), 1165–1179. https://doi.org/10.1016/j.ejor.2018.09.011
Goldberg, L. G., Hanweck, G. A., Keenan, M., & Young, A. (1991). Economies of scale and scope in the securities industry. *Journal of Banking & Finance, 15*(1), 91–107.
Gorman, J. A. (1969). Alternative measures of the real output and productivity of commercial banks. In *Production and productivity in the service industries* (pp. 155–199). NBER. www.nber.org/books-and-chapters/production-and-productivity-service-industries/alternative-measures-real-output-and-productivity-commercial-banks
Gourieroux, C., Monfort, A., & Renault, E. (1993). Indirect inference. *Journal of Applied Econometrics, 8*, S85–S118.
Greenbaum, S. I. (1967). Competition and efficiency in the banking system – empirical research and its policy implications. *Journal of Political Economy, 75*(4), 461–479.
Grifell-Tatjé, E., Lovell, C. A. K., & Pastor, J. T. (1998). A quasi-Malmquist productivity index. *Journal of Productivity Analysis, 10*(1), 7–20.
Grigorian, D. A., & Manole, V. (2002). *Determinants of commercial bank performance in transition: An application of data envelopment analysis*. International Monetary Fund (Working Paper No. W.P./02/146). www.imf.org/en/Publications/WP/Issues/2016/12/30/Determinants-of-Commercial-Bank-Performance-in-Transition-An-Application-of-Data-Envelopment-15965
Gropper, D. M. (1991). An empirical investigation of changes in scale economies for the commercial banking firm, 1979–1986. *Journal of Money, Credit and Banking, 23*(4), 718–727. https://doi.org/10.2307/1992706
Grover, N., & Arora, N. (2015). Revisiting the technical efficiency gains of Indian commercial banks from bancassurance. *Review of Finance and Banking*, 7(1), 19–29.
Guarda, P., Rouabah, A., & Vardanyan, M. (2013). Identifying bank outputs and inputs with a directional technology distance function. *Journal of Productivity Analysis, 40*(2), 185–195.
Hancock, D. (1985). The financial firm: Production with monetary and nonmonetary goods. *Journal of Political Economy, 93*(5), 859–880.
Harimaya, K. (2008). Impact of nontraditional activities on scale and scope economies: A case study of Japanese regional banks. *Japan and the World Economy, 20*(2), 175–193. https://doi.org/10.1016/j.japwor.2006.11.003
Hartwick, J. M. (1996). *The financial capital constraint and the valuation of commercial banking activity*. Queen's University – Department of Economics (Working Paper No. 942). https://ideas.repec.org/p/ags/queddp/273374.html
Havrylchyk, O. (2006). Efficiency of the Polish banking industry: Foreign versus domestic banks. *Journal of Banking & Finance, 30*(7), 1975–1996. https://doi.org/10.2139/ssrn.499922

Hon, L. Y., Tuck, C. E., & Yu, K. L. (2011). Efficiency in the Malaysian banking industry. *ASEAN Economic Bulletin*, *28*(1), 16–44.
Howcroft, B., & Ataullah, A. (2006). Total factor productivity change: An examination of the commercial banking industry in India and Pakistan. *The Service Industries Journal*, *26*(2), 189–202. https://doi.org/10.1080/02642060500369305
Hsiao, H.-C., Chang, H., Cianci, A. M., & Huang, L.-H. (2010). First financial restructuring and operating efficiency: Evidence from Taiwanese commercial banks. *Journal of Banking and Finance*, 7(34), 1461–1471. https://doi.org/10.1016/j.jbankfin.2010.01.013
Huang, J., Matthews, K., & Zhou, P. (2020). What causes Chinese listed firms to switch bank loan provider? Evidence from a survival analysis. *Emerging Markets Review*, *43*, 100678. https://doi.org/10.1016/j.ememar.2020.100678
Huang, M.-Y., & Fu, T.-T. (2013). An examination of the cost efficiency of banks in Taiwan and china using the metafrontier cost function. *Journal of Productivity Analysis*, *40*(3), 387–406.
Huang, M.-Y., Juo, J.-C., & Fu, T. (2015). Metafrontier cost Malmquist productivity index: An application to Taiwanese and Chinese Commercial banks. *Journal of Productivity Analysis*, *44*(3), 321–335.
Huang, T.-H., Shen, C.-H., Chen, K.-C., & Tseng, S.-J. (2011). Measuring technical and allocative efficiencies for banks in the transition countries using the fourier flexible cost function. *Journal of Productivity Analysis*, *35*(2), 143–157.
Hughes, J. P., & Mester, L. J. (1993). A quality and risk-adjusted cost function for banks: Evidence on the 'too-big-to-fail' doctrine. *Journal of Productivity Analysis*, *4*(3), 293–315.
Hughes, J. P., & Mester, L. J. (1998). Bank capitalization and cost: Evidence of scale economies in risk management and signaling. *The Review of Economics and Statistics*, *80*(2), 314–325.
Hughes, J. P., & Mester, L. J. (2008). Efficiency in banking: Theory, practice, and evidence. Draft Manuscript prepared for the Oxford Handbook of Banking.
Hughes, J. P., Mester, L. J., & Moon, C.-G. (2000). *Are scale economies in banking elusive or illusive? Evidence obtained by incorporating capital structure and risk-taking into models of bank production*. Federal Reserve Bank of Philadelphia (Working Paper No. 00–4). https://ideas.repec.org/p/fip/fedpwp/00-4.html
Humphrey, D. B. (1987). Cost dispersion and the measurement of economies in banking. *FRB Richmond Economic Review*, *73*(3), 24–38.
Humphrey, D. B. (2009). *Payment scale economies, competition, and pricing*. European Central Banking (Working Paper No. 1136). https://doi.org/10.2139/ssrn.1522022
Humphrey, D. B., & Pulley, L. B. (1997). Banks' responses to deregulation: Profits, technology, and efficiency. *Journal of Money, Credit and Banking*, *29*(1), 73–93. https://doi.org/10.2307/2953687
Hunter, W. C., & Timme, S. G. (1986). Technical change, organizational form, and the structure of bank production. *Journal of Money, Credit and Banking*, *18*(2), 152–166. https://doi.org/10.2307/1992199
Hunter, W. C., & Timme, S. G. (1991). Technological change in large U.S. Commercial banks. *The Journal of Business*, *64*(3), 339–362.
Hunter, W. C., & Timme, S. G. (1995). Core Deposits and Physical Capital: A Reexamination of Bank Scale Economies and Efficiency with Quasi-Fixed Inputs. *Journal of Money, Credit and Banking*, *27*(1), 165–185. https://doi.org/10.2307/2077857
Illueca, M., Pastor, J. M., & Tortosa-Ausina, E. (2009). The effects of geographic expansion on the productivity of Spanish savings banks. *Journal of Productivity Analysis*, *32*(2), 119–143.

Inklaar, R., & Wang, J. C. (2011). *Real output of bank services: What counts is what banks do, not what they own*. Federal Reserve Bank of Boston (Working Paper No. 11–1).

Inklaar, R., & Wang, J. C. (2012). Measuring real bank output: Considerations and comparisons. *Monthly Labor Review*, 18–27.

Isik, I., & Hassan, M. K. (2002). Technical, scale and allocative efficiencies of Turkish banking industry. *Journal of Banking & Finance, 26*(4), 719–766. https://doi.org/10.1016/S0378-4266(01)00167-4

Jacobs, D. (1964). The impact of examination practices upon commercial bank lending policies. In *Committee on banking and currency*. US Government Printing Office.

Jagtiani, J., & Khanthavit, A. (1996). Scale and scope economies at large banks: Including off-balance sheet products and regulatory effects (1984–1991). *Journal of Banking & Finance, 20*(7), 1271–1287.

Kalish, L., & Gilbert, R. A. (1973). An analysis of efficiency of scale and organizational form in commercial banking. *The Journal of Industrial Economics, 21*(3), 293–307. https://doi.org/10.2307/2098151

Kao, C., & Liu, S.-T. (2009). Stochastic data envelopment analysis in measuring the efficiency of Taiwan commercial banks. *European Journal of Operational Research, 196*(1), 312–322. https://doi.org/10.1016/j.ejor.2008.02.023

Karim, M. Z. A. (2001). Comparative bank efficiency across select ASEAN countries. *ASEAN Economic Bulletin, 18*(3), 289–304.

Kaushik, S. K., & Lopez, R. H. (1996). Profitability of credit unions, commercial banks and savings banks: A comparative analysis. *The American Economist, 40*(1), 66–78.

Kenjegalieva, K., Ravishjankar, G., Shen, Z., & Weyman-Jones, T. (2009). Modelling risk in efficiency and productivity analysis of banking systems. *Undefined*, 1–36. www.semanticscholar.org/paper/Modelling-risk-in-efficiency-and-productivity-of-Kenjegalieva-Ravishjankar/075104d8e6f89e2133afda7c243b32fed8ccd6e8

Keshari, P. K., & Paul, M. T. (1994). Relative efficiency of foreign and domestic banks. *Economic and Political Weekly, 29*(9), M31–M36.

Khan, A., Hassan, M. K., Maroney, N., Boujlil, R., & Ozkan, B. (2020). Efficiency, diversification, and performance of U.S. Banks. *International Review of Economics & Finance, 67*, 101–117. https://doi.org/10.1016/j.iref.2019.12.010

Khan, I. U., Ali, S., & Khan, H. N. (2018). Market concentration, risk-taking, and efficiency of commercial banks in Pakistan: An application of the two-stage double bootstrap DEA. *Business & Economic Review, 10*(2), 65–96. https://doi.org/10.22547/BER/10.2.4

Khusro, A. M., Raghavan, S. N., Ram, K., & Siddharthan, N. S. (1971). Banking efficiency and banking growth. *Economic and Political Weekly, 6*(23), 1150–1152.

Kilbride, B. J., McDonald, B., & Miller, R. E. (1986). A reexamination of economies of scale in banking using a generalized functional form: Note. *Journal of Money, Credit and Banking, 18*(4), 519–526. https://doi.org/10.2307/1992471

Kim, M. (1985). Scale economies in banking: A methodological note. *Journal of Money, Credit and Banking, 17*(1), 96–102. https://doi.org/10.2307/1992509

Kim, M. (1986). Banking technology and the existence of a consistent output aggregate. *Journal of Monetary Economics, 18*(2), 181–195.

Kim, M., & Weiss, J. (1989). Total factor productivity growth in banking: The Israeli banking sector 1979–1982. *Journal of Productivity Analysis, 1*(2), 139–153.

Kirkwood, J., & Nahm, D. (2005). *Australian banking efficiency and its relation to stock returns*. Macquarie University, Department of Economics (Research Papers No. 0508). https://ideas.repec.org/p/mac/wpaper/0508.html

Kolari, J., & Zardkoohi, A. (1990). Economies of scale and scope in thrift institutions: The case of finnish cooperative and savings banks. *The Scandinavian Journal of Economics*, *92*(3), 437–451. https://doi.org/10.2307/3440010

Kolari, J., & Zardkoohi, A. (1991). Further evidence on economies of scale and scope in commercial banking. *Quarterly Journal of Business and Economics*, *30*(4), 82–107.

Kouki, M., Park, S. S., & Renault, E. (2014). Estimating scale economies in financial intermediation: A doubly indirect inference. *Journal of Productivity Analysis*, *41*(3), 351–365.

Koutsomanoli-Filippaki, A., & Mamatzakis, E. (2009). Performance and Merton-type default risk of listed banks in the E.U.: A panel VAR approach. *Journal of Banking and Finance*, *11*(33), 2050–2061. https://doi.org/10.1016/j.jbankfin.2009.05.009

Kumbhakar, S. C., Heshmati, A., & Hjalmarsson, L. (2002). How fast do banks adjust? A dynamic model of labor-use with an application to Swedish banks. *Journal of Productivity Analysis*, *18*(1), 79–102.

Kumbhakar, S. C., & Sarkar, S. (2003). Deregulation, ownership, and productivity growth in the banking industry: Evidence from India. *Journal of Money, Credit and Banking*, *35*(3), 403–424.

Lawrence, C. (1989). Banking costs, generalized functional forms, and estimation of economies of scale and scope. *Journal of Money, Credit and Banking*, *21*(3), 368–379. https://doi.org/10.2307/1992419

Le, T. D. Q., & Ngo, T. (2020). The determinants of bank profitability: A cross-country analysis. *Central Bank Review*, *20*(2), 65–73. https://doi.org/10.1016/j.cbrev.2020.04.001

Lee, J. Y., & Kim, D. (2013). Bank performance and its determinants in Korea. *Japan and the World Economy*, *27*, 83–94. https://doi.org/10.1016/j.japwor.2013.05.001

Lee, T.-H., Liang, L.-W., & Huang, B.-Y. (2013). Do mergers improve the efficiency of banks in Taiwan? Evidence from stochastic frontier approach. *The Journal of Developing Areas*, *47*(1), 395–416.

Leland, H. E., & Pyle, D. H. (1977). Informational asymmetries, financial structure, and financial intermediation. *The Journal of Finance*, *32*(2), 371–387. https://doi.org/10.2307/2326770

Leong, W. H., Dollery, B., & Coelli, T. (2003). Measuring the technical efficiency of banks in Singapore for the period 1993–99: An application and extension of the Bauer et al. (1997) technique. *ASEAN Economic Bulletin*, *20*(3), 195–210.

Longbrake, W. A., & Haslem, J. A. (1975). Productive efficiency in commercial banking: The effects of size and legal form of organization on the cost of producing demand deposit services. *Journal of Money, Credit and Banking*, 7(3), 317. https://doi.org/10.2307/1991625

Lozano-Vivas, A., & Pasiouras, F. (2010). The impact of non-traditional activities on the estimation of bank efficiency: International evidence. *Journal of Banking & Finance*, *34*(7), 1436–1449. https://doi.org/10.1016/j.jbankfin.2010.01.006

Lozano-Vivas, A., Pastor, J. T., & Pastor, J. M. (2002). An efficiency comparison of european banking systems operating under different environmental conditions. *Journal of Productivity Analysis*, *18*(1), 59–77.

Lyroudi, K., & Angelidis, D. (2006). Measuring banking productivity of the most recent European union member countries: A non-parametric approach. *Journal of Economics and Business*, *IX*(1), 37–57.

Maghyereh, A. (2004). The effect of financial liberalization on the efficiency of financial institutions: The case of Jordanian commercial banks. *Savings and Development*, *28*(3), 235–270.

Mamatzakis, E., Tsionas, M. G., Kumbhakar, S. C., & Koutsomanoli-Filippaki, A. (2015). Does labour regulation affect technical and allocative efficiency? Evidence from the banking industry. *Journal of Banking & Finance*, *61*, S84–S98. https://doi.org/10.1016/j.jbankfin.2015.06.012

Mamonov, M., & Vernikov, A. (2017). Bank ownership and cost efficiency: New empirical evidence from Russia. *Economic Systems*, *41*(2), 305–319. https://doi.org/10.1016/j.ecosys.2016.08.001

Mansour, R., & Moussawi, C. E. (2020). Efficiency, technical progress and productivity of Arab banks: A non-parametric approach. *The Quarterly Review of Economics and Finance*, *75*, 191–208. https://doi.org/10.1016/j.qref.2019.02.002

Margono, H., Sharma, S. C., & Melvin, P. D. (2010). Cost efficiency, economies of scale, technological progress and productivity in Indonesian banks. *Journal of Asian Economics*, *21*(1), 53–65. https://doi.org/10.1016/j.asieco.2009.06.001

Mertens, A., & Urga, G. (2001). Efficiency, scale and scope economies in the Ukrainian banking sector in 1998. *Emerging Markets Review*, *2*(3), 292–308.

Mester, L. J. (1992). Traditional and nontraditional banking: An information-theoretic approach. *Journal of Banking & Finance*, *16*(3), 545–566. https://doi.org/10.1016/0378-4266(92)90044-Z

Mester, L. J. (1997). Measuring efficiency at U.S. Banks: Accounting for heterogeneity is important. *European Journal of Operational Research*, *98*(2), 230–242.

Milenković, N., Radovanov, B., Kalaš, B., & Horvat, A. M. (2022). External two stage DEA analysis of bank efficiency in West Balkan countries. *Sustainability*, *14*(2), 978. https://doi.org/10.3390/su14020978

Mohan, T. T. R. (2002). Deregulation and performance of public sector banks. *Economic and Political Weekly*, *37*(5), 393–397.

Mohan, T. T. R. (2003). Long-run performance of public and private sector bank stocks. *Economic and Political Weekly*, *38*(8), 785–788.

Mohan, T. T. R., & Ray, S. C. (2004). Comparing performance of public and private sector banks: A revenue maximisation efficiency approach. *Economic and Political Weekly*, *39*(12), 1271–1276.

Mosko, A., & Bozdo, A. (2016). Modeling the relationship between bank efficiency, capital and risk in Albanian banking system. *Procedia Economics and Finance*, 319–327.

Mukherjee, A., Nath, P., & Pal, M. (2003). Resource, service quality and performance triad: A framework for measuring efficiency of banking services. *The Journal of the Operational Research Society*, *54*(7), 723–735.

Muldur, U., & Sassenou, M. (1993). Economies of scale and scope in French banking and savings institutions. *Journal of Productivity Analysis*, *4*(1/2), 51–72.

Mullineaux, D. J. (1978). Economies of scale and organizational efficiency in banking: A profit-function approach. *The Journal of Finance*, *33*(1), 259–280. https://doi.org/10.2307/2326364

Murillo-Melchor, C., Pastor, J., & Tortosa-Ausina, E. (2010). A bootstrap approach to analyse productivity growth in European banking. *The Journal of the Operational Research Society*, *61*(12), 1729–1745.

Murphy, N. B. (1972). A reestimation of the Benston-bell-murphy cost functions for a larger sample with greater size and geographic dispersion. *The Journal of Financial and Quantitative Analysis*, 7(5), 2097–2105. https://doi.org/10.2307/2329957

Nakane, M. I., Alencar, L. S., & Kanczuk, F. (2006). *Demand for bank services and market power in Brazilian banking*. Central Bank of Brazil (Working Paper No. 107). https://ideas.repec.org/p/bcb/wpaper/107.html

Nartey, S. B., Osei, K. A., & Sarpong-Kumankoma, E. (2019). Bank productivity in Africa. *International Journal of Productivity and Performance Management*, *69*(9), 1973–1997. https://doi.org/10.1108/IJPPM-09-2018-0328

Nelson, R. W. (1985). Branching, scale economies, and banking costs. *Journal of Banking & Finance, 9*(2), 177–191.

Noulas, A. G., Ray, S. C., & Miller, S. M. (1990). Returns to scale and input substitution for large U. S. Banks. *Journal of Money, Credit and Banking, 22*(1), 94–108. https://doi.org/10.2307/1992130

Ohlson, M. P., Lima, G. A. S. F. de, & Takeda, T. (2021). *Deposit insurance and brokerage firms: Impacts on the market discipline of the Brazilian banking industry*. Central Bank of Brazil (Working Paper No. 542).

Ojo, A. T. (1979). Economies of scale in banking: The Nigerian case. *Savings and Development, 3*(4), 277–295.

Okuda, H., & Saito, J. (2001). The production technology of philippine domestic banks in the pre-Asian crisis period: Estimation of cost function in the 1990–96 period. *Hitotsubashi Journal of Economics, 42*(2), 81–101.

Olson, D., & Zoubi, T. A. (2011). Efficiency and bank profitability in MENA countries. *Emerging Markets Review, 12*(2), 94–110. https://doi.org/10.1016/j.ememar.2011.02.003

Oluitan, R. (2014). Bank efficiency in Africa. *The Journal of Developing Areas, 48*(2), 205–221.

Oral, M., & Yolalan, R. (1990). An empirical study on measuring operating efficiency and profitability of bank branches. *European Journal of Operational Research, 46*(3), 282–294. https://doi.org/10.1016/0377-2217(90)90002-S

Otero, L., Razia, A., Cunill, O. M., & Mulet-Forteza, C. (2020). What determines efficiency in MENA banks? *Journal of Business Research, 112*, 331–341. https://doi.org/10.1016/j.jbusres.2019.11.002

Owualah, S. I. (1986). Scale economies and efficiency of bank operations: Further evidence from Nigeria. *Savings and Development, 10*(4), 419–431.

Owusu, F. B., & Alhassan, A. L. (2021). Asset-liability management and bank profitability: Statistical cost accounting analysis from an emerging market. *International Journal of Finance & Economics, 26*(1), 1488–1502. https://doi.org/10.1002/ijfe.1860

Pasiouras, F., Tanna, S., & Zopounidis, C. (2009). The impact of banking regulations on banks' cost and profit efficiency: Cross-country evidence. *International Review of Financial Analysis, 18*(5), 294–302. https://doi.org/10.1016/j.irfa.2009.07.003

Pelosi, T. (2008). *Risk, efficiency and industry dynamics in the Australian banking sector*[Thesis]. UNSW. https://doi.org/10.26190/unsworks/17934

Phan, D. H. B., Narayan, P. K., Rahman, R. E., & Hutabarat, A. R. (2020). Do financial technology firms influence bank performance? *Pacific-Basin Finance Journal, 62*, 101210. https://doi.org/10.1016/j.pacfin.2019.101210

Phan, H. T. M., Daly, K., & Akhter, S. (2016). Bank efficiency in emerging Asian countries. *Research in International Business and Finance, 38*, 517–530. https://doi.org/10.1016/j.ribaf.2016.07.012

Powers, J. A. (1969). Branch versus unit banking: Bank output and cost economies. *Southern Economic Journal, 36*(2), 153–164. https://doi.org/10.2307/1056432

Radecki, L. J. (1999). *Banks' payments-driven revenues, staff reports 62*. Federal Reserve Bank of New York.

Rajan, S. S., Reddy, K. L. N., & Pandit, V. N. (2011). *Efficiency and productivity growth in indian banking*. Centre for Development Studies (Working Paper No. 199).

Rakshit, B., & Bardhan, S. (2022). Does bank efficiency enhance bank performance? Empirical evidence from Indian banking. *Buletin Ekonomi Moneter Dan Perbankan, 25*, 103–124. https://doi.org/10.21098/bemp.v25i0.1844

Ray, S. C. (2007). Are some Indian banks too large? An examination of size efficiency in Indian banking. *Journal of Productivity Analysis, 27*(1), 41–56.

Ray, S. C., & Das, A. (2010). Distribution of cost and profit efficiency: Evidence from Indian banking. *European Journal of Operational Research, 201*(1), 297–307. https://doi.org/10.1016/j.ejor.2009.02.030

Reddy, A. A. (2006). Productivity growth of regional rural banks. *Economic and Political Weekly, 41*, 1079–1086. https://doi.org/10.2139/ssrn.1537538

Resti, A. (1997). Evaluating the cost-efficiency of the Italian banking system: What can be learned from the joint application of parametric and non-parametric techniques. *Journal of Banking & Finance, 21*(2), 221–250.

Rezvanian, R., Rao, N., & Mehdian, S. M. (2008). Efficiency change, technological progress and productivity growth of private, public and foreign banks in India: Evidence from the post-liberalization era. *Applied Financial Economics, 18*(9), 701–713. https://doi.org/10.1080/09603100701222317

Robin, I., Salim, R., & Bloch, H. (2018). Financial performance of commercial banks in the post-reform era: Further evidence from Bangladesh. *Economic Analysis and Policy, 58*, 43–54. https://doi.org/10.1016/j.eap.2018.01.001

Rogers, K. E. (1998). Nontraditional activities and the efficiency of U.S. Commercial banks. *Journal of Banking & Finance, 22*(4), 467–482.

Royster, S. E. (2012). Improved measures of commercial banking output and productivity. *Monthly Labor Review*, 3–17.

Rushdi, M., & Tennant, J. (2003). Profitability of Australian banks: 1985–2001. *Agenda: A Journal of Policy Analysis and Reform, 10*(3), 229–243.

Saeed, M., Izzeldin, M., Hassan, K., & Pappas, V. (2020). The inter-temporal relationship between risk, capital and efficiency: The case of Islamic and conventional banks. *Pacific-Basin Finance Journal, 62*. https://doi.org/10.1016/j.pacfin.2020.101328

Salim, R., Arjomandi, A., & Dakpo, K. H. (2017). Banks' efficiency and credit risk analysis using by-production approach: The case of Iranian banks. *Applied Economics, 49*(30), 2974–2988. https://doi.org/10.1080/00036846.2016.1251567

Sang, N. M. (2022). Impact of the COVID-19 Pandemic on bank efficiency in Vietnam. *Banks and Bank Systems, 17*(1), 13–23. https://doi.org/10.21511/bbs.17(1).2022.02

Santosa, B. (2022). *Indonesian banking efficiency in the post-Asian monetary crisis*. Proceedings of the First Lekantara Annual Conference on Public Administration, Literature, Social Sciences, Humanities, and Education (LePALISSHE 2021). https://eudl.eu/doi/10.4108/eai.3-8-2021.2315127

Sathye, M. (2003). Efficiency of banks in a developing economy: The case of India. *European Journal of Operational Research, 148*(3), 662–671. https://doi.org/10.1016/S0377-2217(02)00471-X

Sato, K. (1976). The meaning and measurement of the real value added index. *The Review of Economics and Statistics, 58*(4), 434. https://doi.org/10.2307/1935875

Scholtens, B., & Wensveen, D. van. (2003). The theory of financial intermediation: An essay on what it does (not) explain. In *SUERF studies*. SUERF – The European Money and Finance Forum. https://ideas.repec.org/b/erf/erfstu/23.html

Schweitzer, S. A. (1972). Economies of scale and holding company affiliation in banking. *Southern Economic Journal, 39*(2), 258–266. https://doi.org/10.2307/1056596

Sealey, C. W. (1977). A further reconsideration of optimal reserve management at commercial banks. *Southern Economic Journal, 44*(1), 117. https://doi.org/10.2307/1057305

Sealey, C. W., & Lindley, J. T. (1977). Inputs, outputs, and a theory of production and cost at depository financial institutions. *The Journal of Finance, 32*(4), 1251–1266. https://doi.org/10.2307/2326527

Seelanatha, L., & Wickremasinghe, G. (2009). Financial reforms in Sri Lanka and their influence on the banking industry. *Bank and Bank Systems, 4*(4), 23–35.

Sensarma, R. (2005). Cost and profit efficiency of Indian banks during 1986–2003: A stochastic frontier analysis. *Economic and Political Weekly, 40*(12), 1198–1209.

Setiwan, C., Hassan, T., Hassan, M. K., & Mohamed, S. (2017). Non-performing loans and bank efficiency of conventional and Islamic banks in the organization of Islamic cooperation (OIC) countries. *Journal of Islamic Economics, Banking and Finance, 13*(4). https://doi.org/10.12816/0051000

Shaffer, S. (1993). A test of competition in Canadian banking. *Journal of Money, Credit and Banking, 25*(1), 49–61. https://doi.org/10.2307/2077819

Shah, W. U. H., Hao, G., Zhu, N., Yasmeen, R., Padda, I. U. H., & Kamal, M. A. (2022). A cross-country efficiency and productivity evaluation of commercial banks in South Asia: A meta-frontier and Malmquist productivity index approach. *PLoS One, 17*(4), 1–17. https://doi.org/10.1371/journal.pone.0265349

Shair, F., Shaorong, S., Kamran, H. W., Hussain, M. S., Nawaz, M. A., & Nguyen, V. C. (2021). Assessing the efficiency and total factor productivity growth of the banking industry: Do environmental concerns matters? *Environmental Science and Pollution Research, 28*(16), 20822–20838. https://doi.org/10.1007/s11356-020-11938-y

Sharma, D., Sharma, A. K., & Barua, M. K. (2013). Efficiency and productivity of banking sector: A critical analysis of literature and design of conceptual model. *Qualitative Research in Financial Markets, 5*(2), 195–224. https://doi.org/10.1108/QRFM-10-2011-0025

Sharpe, S. A. (1997). The effect of consumer switching costs on prices: A theory and its application to the bank deposit market. *Review of Industrial Organization, 12*(1), 79–94.

Sherwood, M. K. (1994). Difficulties in the measurement of service outputs. *Monthly Labor Review, 117*(3), 11–19.

Shih, V., Zhang, Q., & Liu, M. (2007). Comparing the performance of Chinese banks: A principal component approach. *China Economic Review, 18*(1), 15–34. https://doi.org/10.1016/j.chieco.2006.11.001

Singh, S. P. (1974). Profitability of nationalised banks. *Economic and Political Review, 9*(35), M67+M69–M72.

Sinha, R. P., & Chatterjee, B. (2008). Fund-based activity of Indian commercial banks: A Malmquist approach. *Indian Economic Review, 43*(1), 83–102.

SNA. (1953). System of national accounts. *United Nations Statistics Division.*

SNA. (1993). System of national accounts. *United Nations Statistics Division.*

SNA. (2008). System of national accounts. *United Nations Statistics Division.* https://unstats.un.org/unsd/nationalaccount/docs/sna2008.pdf

Speagle, R. E., & Kohn, E. (1958). Employment and output in banking, 1919–1955. *The Review of Economics and Statistics, 40*(1), 22–35. https://doi.org/10.2307/1926477

Srivastava, P. (1999). *Size, efficiency and financial reforms in Indian banking.* Indian Council for Research on International Economic Relations (Working Paper No. 49).

Stauffer, P. (2004). *A tale of two worlds: How bankers and national accountants view banking.* International Association for Research in Income and Wealth.

Subrahmanyam, G. (1994). Measurement of output, scale economies and productivity in banks: A methodological note. *Indian Economic Review, 29*(2), 223–227.

Subramaniam, I. (1985). *A study of the measurement of bank output*[Bachelor Degree Dissertation]. The University of Adelaide.

Sufian, F. (2008). Risks and efficiency in Malaysian banking. *Savings and Development, 32*(1), 7–29.

Swamy, D. S. (1973). Economies of scale in banking: A critique. *Economic and Political Weekly, 8*(8), M13+M15–M16.

Syed, A. (2021). Assessing the impact of banking efficiency, operations, and regulation on banking performance: Fresh insight using dynamic correlated framework on the data set of Russia and Ukraine. *Journal of Eastern European and Central Asian Research (JEECAR), 8*(1), 89–99. https://doi.org/10.15549/jeecar.v8i1.514

Synder, C. (1923). Fisher's 'the making of index numbers'. *The American Economic Review, 13*(3), 416–421.

Tachibanaki, T., Mitsui, K., & Kitagawa, H. (1991). Economies of scope and shareholding of banks in Japan. *Journal of the Japanese and International Economies, 5*(3), 261–281.

Tadesse, S. (2005). Consolidation, scale economies and technological change in Japanese banking. *Journal of International Financial Markets, Institutions & Money, 16*, 425–445. https://doi.org/10.2139/ssrn.681534

Tan, Y., & Floros, C. (2014). Risk, profitability, and competition: Evidence from the Chinese banking industry. *The Journal of Developing Areas, 48*(3), 303–319.

Thanassoulis, E. (1999). Data envelopment analysis and its use in banking. *Interfaces, 29*(3), 1–13.

Thilakaweera, B. (2016). *Efficiency and productivity in Sri Lanka's banking sector: Evidence from the post-conflict era* [Ph.D. Thesis]. University of Wollongong. https://ro.uow.edu.au/theses/4938

Tirtiroğlu, D., Daniels, K. N., & Tirtiroğlu, E. (2005). Deregulation, intensity of competition, industry evolution, and the productivity growth of U.S. Commercial banks. *Journal of Money, Credit and Banking, 37*(2), 339–360.

Todhanakasem, W., Lynge, M. J., Primeaux, W. J., & Newbold, P. (1986). Economies of scale and organization efficiency in banking. *Managerial and Decision Economics*, 7(4), 255–261.

Tokle, R. J., & Tokle, J. G. (2000). The influence of credit union and savings and loan competition on bank deposit rates in Idaho and Montana. *Review of Industrial Organization, 17*(4), 427–439.

Tortosa-Ausina, E. (2002). Bank cost efficiency and output specification. *Journal of Productivity Analysis, 18*(3), 199–222.

Triplett, J. E., & Bosworth, B. P. (2004a). Measuring banking and finance: Conceptual issues. In *Productivity in the U.S. Services sector: New sources of economic growth* (pp. 177–210). Brookings Institution Press. www.jstor.org/stable/10.7864/j.ctt12879w8.13

Triplett, J. E., & Bosworth, B. P. (2004b). *Productivity in the US services sector: New sources of economic growth*. Bibliovault OAI Repository, The University of Chicago Press.

Tzeremes, N. G. (2015). Efficiency dynamics in Indian banking: A conditional directional distance approach. *European Journal of Operational Research, 240*(3), 807–818. https://doi.org/10.1016/j.ejor.2014.07.029

Vanoli, A. (2005). *A history of national accounting*. IOS Press.

Vennet, R. V. (2002). Cost and profit efficiency of financial conglomerates and universal banks in Europe. *Journal of Money, Credit and Banking, 34*(1), 254–282.

Verghese, S. K. (1983). Profits and profitability of Indian commercial banks in seventies. *Economic and Political Weekly, 18*(48), M145–M157.

Wang, J. C., & Basu, S. (2005). *Risk bearing, implicit financial services, and specialization in the financial industry*. Social Science Research Network (SSRN Scholarly Paper No. 917427). https://doi.org/10.2139/ssrn.917427

Wanke, P., Azad, A. K., & Emrouznejad, A. (2018). Efficiency in BRICS banking under data vagueness: A two-stage fuzzy approach. *Global Finance Journal, 35*, 58–71. https://doi.org/10.1016/j.gfj.2017.05.001

Weill, L. (2004). Measuring cost efficiency in European banking: A comparison of frontier techniques. *Journal of Productivity Analysis, 21*(2), 133–152.

Westhuizen, G. (2013). Bank productivity and sources of efficiency change: A case of the four largest banks in South Africa. *International Business & Economics Research Journal, 12*(2), 127. https://doi.org/10.19030/iber.v12i2.7625

Weyman-Jones, T., Boucinha, M., Kenjegalieva, K., Ravishankar, G., Ribeiro, N., & Shen, Z. (2010). Incorporating risk in the efficiency and productivity analysis of banking systems. In *New issues in financial institutions management* (pp. 91–105). Palgrave Macmillan. https://ideas.repec.org/h/pal/pmschp/978-0-230-29915-3_6.html

Wheelock, D. C., & Wilson, P. W. (1995). Explaining bank failures: Deposit insurance, regulation, and efficiency. *The Review of Economics and Statistics*, 77(4), 689–700. https://doi.org/10.2307/2109816

Wheelock, D. C., & Wilson, P. W. (1999). Technical progress, inefficiency, and productivity change in U.S. Banking, 1984–1993. *Journal of Money, Credit and Banking*, *31*(2), 212–234. https://doi.org/10.2307/2601230

Wu, M., Li, C., Fan, J., Wang, X., & Wu, Z. (2018). Assessing the global productive efficiency of Chinese banks using the cross-efficiency interval and VIKOR. *Emerging Markets Review*, *34*, 77–86. https://doi.org/10.1016/j.ememar.2017.10.005

Yu, M.-M., Lin, C.-I., Chen, K.-C., & Chen, L.-H. (2019). Measuring Taiwanese bank performance: A two-system dynamic network data envelopment analysis approach. *Omega*. https://doi.org/10.1016/j.omega.2019.102145

Zaim, O. (1995). The effect of financial liberalization on the efficiency of Turkish commercial banks. *Applied Financial Economics*, *5*(4), 257–264. https://doi.org/10.1080/758536876

Zaman, M. S., Valiyattoor, V., & Bhandari, A. K. (2022). *Dynamics of total factor productivity growth: An empirical analysis of Indian commercial banks*. Social Science Research Network (SSRN Scholarly Paper No. 4040619). https://doi.org/10.2139/ssrn.4040619

Zha, Y., Liang, N., Wu, M., & Bian, Y. (2016). Efficiency evaluation of banks in China: A dynamic two-stage slacks-based measure approach. *Omega*, *60*, 60–72. https://doi.org/10.1016/j.omega.2014.12.008

4 Review of evidence on insurance output measurement

Global perspective

4.1. Introduction

Similar to Chapter 3, this chapter surveys and reviews the literature on insurance output measurement by focusing on the selected studies on insurance performance analysis. Insurance is primarily a tool for protection against fortuitous risks whose outcomes are dichotomous with either a non-profit-no-loss outcome or a loss after an event. Thus, in crude terms, "the purpose of insurance is to protect risk-averse individuals from suffering the full consequences of those actions on the part of nature which affect them unfavourably" (Spence & Zeckhauser, 1971, p. 380). Analysis of various performance parameters of insurance firms and industry, such as their efficiencies, productivities, financial performance, profitability and others, has a long history. A crucial analytical ingredient in the evolution of thought on insurance performance measurement has been the insurance output measurement.[1] There is a wide variety of thought and approaches on this matter.[2] The same are presented in the pages to follow.

4.2. Empirical sensitivity of insurance performance estimates to alternative outputs

Unlike the literature on banking, studies on insurance performance analysis have not delved deeper into the sensitivity of performance estimates to alternative output measures. Even though a few studies were found to have analysed this dimension, it is scarce compared to its banking counterpart, as examined in section 3.2. While the insurance literature has used multiple outputs in their analysis, examination of the sensitivity of those estimates to different output measures does not seem to have been a major concern. This is surprising given that the debates on output measurement are intense in insurance and banking performance analysis. Two works could be found in the literature that assessed this dimension. The first is the work of Leverty and Grace (2010), who examined the empirical sensitivity of properly-liability insures' efficiency estimates to alternative output measures using DEA and range adjusted measure (EAM) of efficiency. They specified outputs in terms of the value-added approach

DOI: 10.4324/9781003149828-5

and the flow approach. They measured insurance output regarding the present value of real losses incurred and average real invested assets (for the value-added approach) and rate of return on investments, amount of liquid asset and solvency score (for the flow approach). They find that "firms identified as highly efficient by the value-added approach are less likely to fail, while firms with high flow efficiency are more likely to fail" (p. 1552). The second work is by Lee (2013), who studies the interrelationship between the insurance market's development and the real aggregate output while controlling banking activities. The author uses alternative measures of real insurance premiums as proxies of insurance activity measured by life, nonlife and total insurance premiums. The author finds that insurance output as measured by life and nonlife outputs separately provides better results than combining them.

4.3. Approaches to output specification in the insurance literature

The qualifications and concerns raised in section 3.3 are as valid here as they are in the case of bank output measurement. The approaches examined below have been summarised based on the selected literature on insurance output measurement, as represented in Table 2.2.

Production approach

As discussed in section 3.3, the production approach theorises a firm as a transformer of primary inputs of labour, capital and funds into outputs. This approach specifies inputs like labour, physical capital and possibly equity in insurance literature.[3] In contrast, outputs are specified in value-form in terms of premiums received and claims or benefits paid. The discussions about the fundamental properties of the production approach in section 3.3 are equally applicable here. The inputs are generally defined in terms of labour, physical capital and financial capital.[4] The outputs for life insurers are mostly defined as the amount of premium and benefit paid. Those for nonlife insurers are defined as the amount of premium and loss/claim. Insurers are seen purely in their risk transfer and risk coverage functions. There is no recognition of the financial and risk intermediations undertaken by the insurance industry under this approach. Under the production approach, the service vector of insurers is sufficiently captured by Carrington et al. (2011). They highlight risk pooling and bearing, direct financial services and indirect financial services as the primary functions of insurers. Literature suggests that such a conceptualisation of insurance production function is ideally suitable for branch-level analysis rather than industry-level analysis. "The production approach is preferable for evaluating the efficiency of single branches, while the intermediation approach may be more appropriate for evaluating entire financial institutions" (Fiordelisi & Ricci, 2012, p. 184). Even though the authors suggested this about the banking industry, these words seem equally representative of the consensus in insurance literature. This approach to insurance output specification looks at insurers as typical production units whose primary function is to transform resources into consumption while producing directly visible and measurable output. Insurers are not seen as intermediaries of any sort under this framework. A large portion of the sample studies has employed this approach (84 out of 190), though the most popular approach is an extension of this approach called the value-added framework. It is discussed later in this chapter.

Intermediation approach

The single-most raised criticism against the production approach in insurance output specification has been its utter lack of recognition of the intermediation functions[5] performed by insurers. On the one hand, insurers collect premiums and under risk pooling to generate and fulfil claim liabilities. On the other hand, insurers use premiums to pool the funds and generate wealth and capital appreciation for policyholders and shareholders. These functions are essentially intermediation functions (Cummins et al., 2009). The former may be called the risk intermediation function, wherein insurers transform funds (premiums) into payment for liabilities (claims/losses). The latter may be called 'financial intermediation'[6] wherein insurers utilise the premiums to generate a surplus, which is then invested into various assets to maximise shareholders' wealth and improve the investment returns for policyholders in the case of life insurance. These essential functions of insurers are ignored in the production approach. However, the intermediation approach allows the recognition of this fact and thus specifies outputs and inputs in a suitable manner. As noted by Eling and Luhnen (2010b, p. 229): "intermediation approach views the insurance company as a financial intermediary that manages a reservoir of assets, borrowing funds from policyholders, investing them on capital markets, and paying out claims, taxes, and costs". Thus, the main difference between the production and intermediation approaches in insurance literature emanates from the difference in the treatment of premiums as an input rather than an output (Barros et al., 2005). Criticisms of premiums as output have been widely recognised in the literature.[7] The intermediation approach poses amount of premium as an input while treating claims as output for capturing risk intermediation and financial assets as output for capturing financial intermediation. Some studies have also recognised equity capital as an essential input for undertaking risk intermediation. This is done mainly by recognising the fact that equity capital[8] supplements premiums as a source for meeting future claim liabilities. In summary, the intermediation approach in insurance output specification recognises the amount of claim and financial assets as the correct output measures.[9]

Value-added approach

One of the dissatisfactions with the production approach was its ad hoc specification of output measures. This was addressed via the so-called value-added approach in insurance as laid down by Cummins and Weiss (2000).[10] In basic terms, "the value-added approach is derived from the micro-economic theory of the firm and is based on the theoretical premise that firms maximise profits by jointly minimising costs and maximising revenues" (Leverty & Grace, 2010). As explained in the case of bank output specification in section 3.3 earlier, the value-added approach considers all those items as output that produce revenues for the firm.[11] Literature has argued that financial intermediation is a tiny proportion of the total services provided by insurers. Thus the production/value-added approach is the correct representation of the theoretical production function of the insurance firms (Cummins & Weiss, 2000; Leverty & Grace, 2010; Carrington et al., 2011, among others).[12] In the value-added approach,[13] insurers' activities are recognised as value-producing for the final consumers, i.e. the policyholders: Risk-pooling and risk-bearing,[14] real financial services relating to insured losses and financial intermediation[15] (Mahlberg & Url, 2010; Cummins & Xie, 2008). Hence, the value-added approach treats the amount of losses/claims, assets and premiums as the correct output measures and is an extension of the traditional production approach.

National income approach

The SNA manual provides the extant wisdom on measuring life and nonlife insurance outputs under the national income accounting framework. Unlike its banking counterpart, insurance output measurement at the aggregate level is not complicated by the FISIM method. Most of the services of insurers are generally reflected in their balance sheets mainly because of the nature of pricing in insurance. Insurers, unlike bankers, do not need to charge implicitly and instead charge for all their services in the premium amount itself. This allows macro accountants to capture the majority of insurance services from the balance sheet and income statements of insurers which is not feasible in the case of banking firms. The output measures under this approach are examined later in this chapter.

4.4. Output measurement in the insurance literature

Life versus nonlife insurance output

At the outset, it is necessary to recognise that insurance output measurement is inherently different for the life and the nonlife segments. Both these segments have a very different set of services for their consumers. Both the segments are also governed by different laws and are affected by factors that may be mutually exclusive. The nature of risks covered in these segments is different, and thus their outputs must be analysed separately. However, these segments have been combined to measure total insurance output in the literature, though such studies are relatively lesser. The differences are not very large either. Some measures are used differently for these segments, mainly due to different accounting conventions and balance sheet forms across both these segments. The discussions below examine the output measures and approach considering both the segments separately but do not necessarily specify it explicitly. It is assumed that the readers will interpret the different sections while considering this.

Premium output

Premiums represent the most critical source of funds for insurers. By pooling premiums, insurers can promise claims and fulfil their liabilities. As suggested in the literature, the amount of premium collected by insurance companies can possibly represent their technical activity. The ability of insurers to fulfil their liabilities is directly conditional upon the amount of premium that they collect. Premiums have been theorised as a proxy for risk transfer and management services rendered by insurers to their consumers. It is used as a measure for output because it is assumed to be strongly and positively correlated with most services provided by insurers. This is a natural result that premiums signify the chief source of funds out of which insurers can undertake all their economic activities.

In the literature, premiums have been used in three different forms as measures of insurance output: first in the form of the amount of premium, second as a ratio measure and third in other forms, as explained in Figure 4.1. Use of premiums in the form of the amount in the literature has been either in an aggregate form for a firm or the entire industry or in disaggregated form across product groups, coverage groups or segments. The primary debate in premium output measurement has been the treatment of reinsurance claims received by the insurance firms. The gross measure of premium amount includes reinsurance benefits received by the insurance firm and removing its impact from the gross premium amount yields net premiums. Netting has also been done using other methods such as subtracting the amount of claims paid from the premiums received (life insurance) and subtracting losses incurred from premiums received (nonlife insurance), and adding financial returns to premiums to measure the total available funds with the insurers. Premiums in themselves have been defined differently in the literature. Studies have conceptualised the amount of premiums as earned premiums (Weiss, 1991; Brockett et al., 2005; Rao, 2016, among others), unearned premiums (Fenn et al., 2008; Leverty & Grace, 2010; Chen et al., 2011; Zhong & Sun, 2011; Leverty & Grace, 2012); returned premiums (Mahlberg & Url, 2003), lapsed premiums[16] and retained premiums (Ai et al., 2015). Literature has also used the premium and the amount of investments as a single output measure. This has generally been practiced to capture the total funds available with insurers to undertake intermediation activities. Some researchers have recommended adding equity capital to this measure output, but it has probably not been practised.

Another line of approach to premium output measurement is ratio measures. Two measures have been used popularly in the extant literature: the first is the ratio of gross or net premiums to losses or claims (such as in Trufin

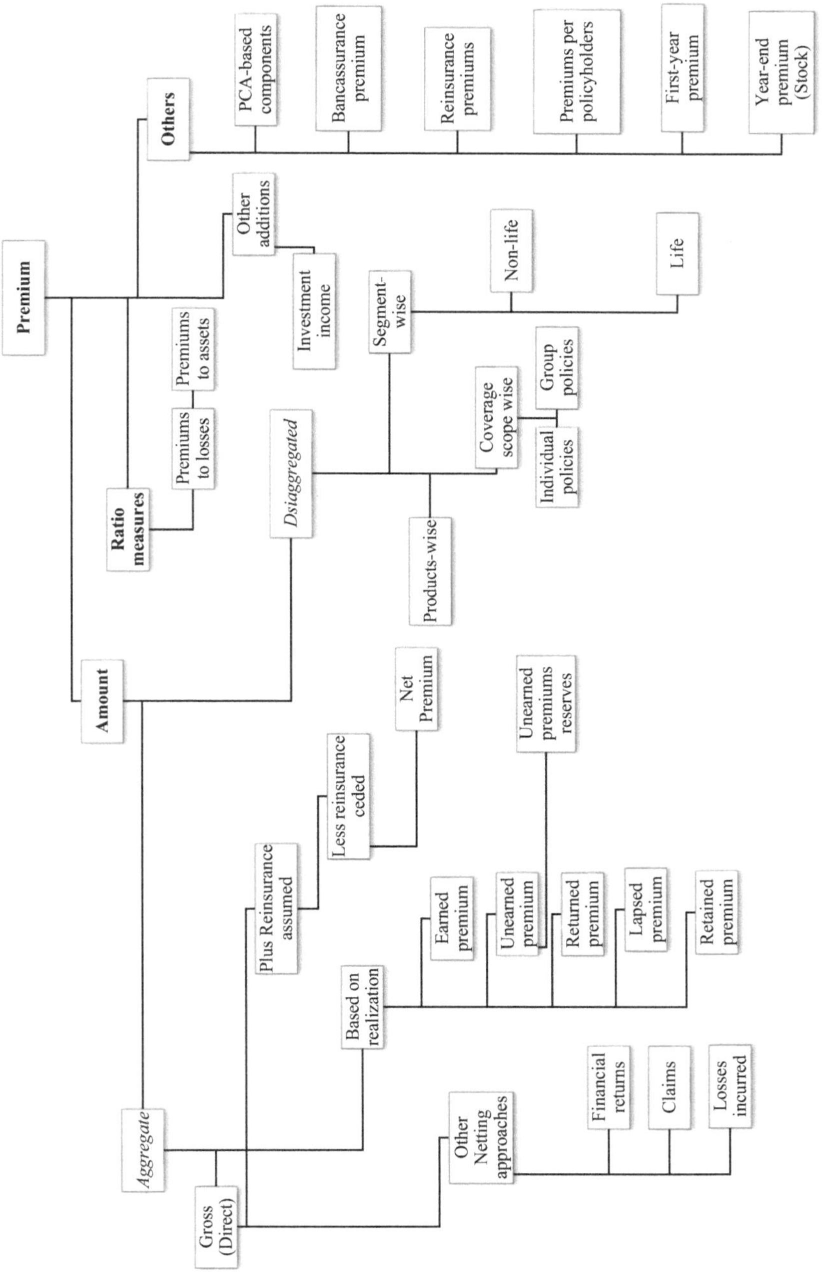

Figure 4.1 Premium output measures in insurance literature

Source: Author's analysis based on the literature survey.

et al., 2009), and the second is the ratio of premiums to total assets or only the financial assets. These two measures of insurance output have been used mainly in analysing underwriting cycles in insurance or for financial and operational performance analyses. Lastly, some novel approaches are categorized as 'others' in Figure 4.1. Among these, the Principal Components Analysis (PCA)–based measures of premium amount have been employed by Jeng et al. (2007). Some researchers have focused on the reinsurers rather than direct insurers as well on the reinsurance activities of nonlife insurers (such as Kao & Hwang, 2008; Wu & Zeng, 2011; Anandarao et al., 2018; Almulhim, 2019). Some other measures too have been used and the same may be located in the appendix to this chapter.

Claims and loss output

Conceptually, claims are the losses that insurance firms have to bear due to the liabilities arising out of insurance contracts.[17] Literature has used different concepts in its place, such as 'losses' and 'benefits paid' (in life insurance). There is a belief in the literature that there is a strong positive correlation between claims paid and insurers' losses (Wise, 2018). The frequency and severity of losses differ between life and nonlife segments and among different lines of products within the segments. This results in differences in the amount of claims or the number of claims paid by insurance firms. The term 'claim' has been used in a general sense in the literature.[18] It can be defined as claims incurred (Fenn et al., 2008) and claims paid. Incurred claims are composed of the claims paid and the additions to technical reserves.[19] Both represent claim liabilities of an insurer but in different ways. The former signifies the amount of claims due for payment by the firms (including its expectations during the current year), while the latter shows the amount paid during settlement in a given year. Similar to the premiums measure, there is a gross form and net form of the amount of claims. The gross form is unadjusted for the reinsurance[20] claims received by the firms. The net for then is the adjusted measure. There are other adjustment approaches in the literature also, as explained in Figure 4.2. These include the changes in loss reserves, loss adjustment expenses and bonuses and rebates paid by the firms.

The difference between claims and losses arises when one approaches insurers' liabilities in an ex-ante framework. Insurers expect some amount of losses to occur, whether they are life or nonlife claims inevitably. Literature has termed it expected loss (Weiss, 1990; Cummins & Xie, 2008). Studies have used two measures of expected losses[21]: first is the implicit measure which is estimated as the product of the amount of gross or net premiums and the average loss ratio (such as in Leverty & Grace, 2010); second is the present value of losses (Cummins & Nini, 2002; Choi & Weiss, 2005 across a given period. Another concept used has been 'technical losses' (Ferro & León, 2017). These concepts are different ways of approaching the financial liabilities of insurers. The choice on this account largely depends on the segment of focus and the data availability.

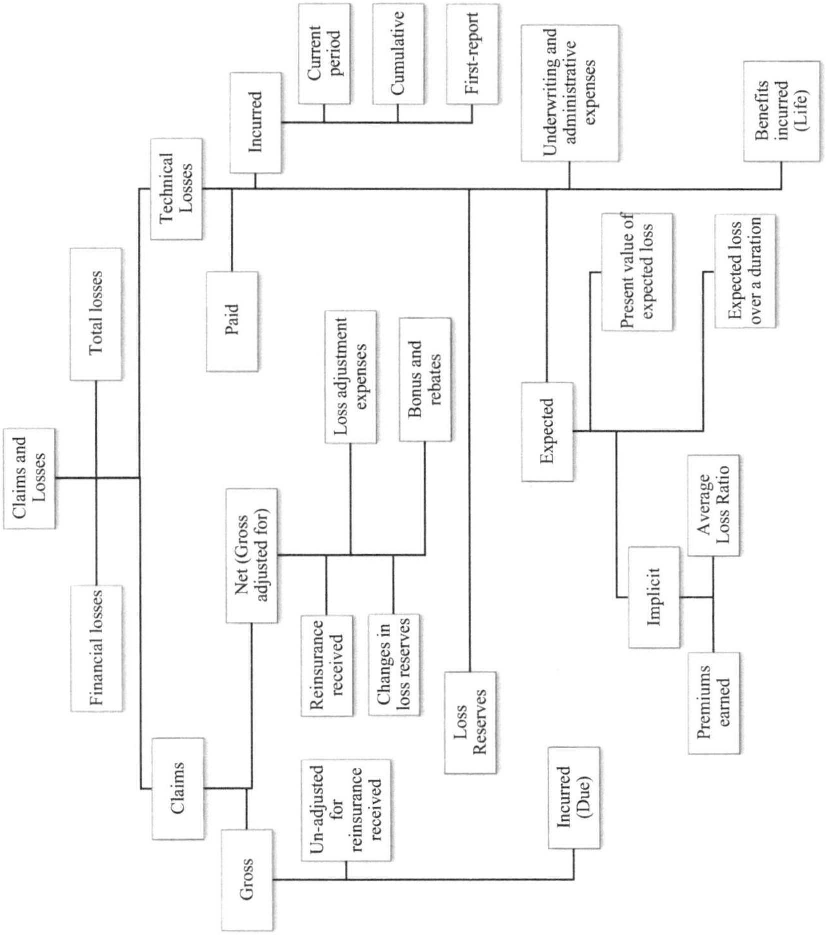

Figure 4.2 Claims and losses as insurance output in the literature

Source: Author's analysis based on the review of the literature.

In terms of popularity, the so-called real present value of losses incurred[22] and paid is the most preferred choice for capturing the financial liabilities of insurers and measuring their output. As noted by (Cummins et al., 2010, p. 1529): "Proxying output by losses incurred is appropriate because the objective of risk-pooling is to collect funds from all policyholders and redistribute them to those who incur losses". This measure is used as it is or discounted to reflect its present value. This may be necessary because one of the components of expected losses is the estimated value of liabilities for the future. This future value component requires discounting to represent its current value correctly. The choice of the discount rate and method can change the quantum of output and thus change performance estimates. Discounting is necessary[23] "for the revenue and output elements of the insurance price measure to consistently reflect present value concepts" (Cummins & Xie, 2008, p. 15). Losses have been criticised as measures of insurance output on various grounds (Cummins & Weiss, 2000; Carrington et al., 2011). The first criticism is that, like claims, this represents a bad output rather than a good output. The second issue is that it is a random variable and may have statistical noise[24] (Cummins & Weiss, 2000). The third problem with this output measure is that it can be induced by internal inefficiencies rather than external problems. As noted by (Carrington et al., 2011, p. 127): Variations in incurred losses can also be due to "lax company risk mitigation procedures or enforcement of policy conditions or both could contribute to incurred losses". The fourth criticism is that losses represent past obligations rather than current output (Carrington et al., 2011). Finally, literature has argued that losses ignore the quality of loss control and risk management. Yaisawarng et al. (2012) noted that "an insurer with excellent loss-prevention practices would have a lower amount of losses incurred and therefore produce lower output" while, in fact, it has improved.

Lastly, a scarcely used measure of loss output in the literature is the inverse loss ratio.

> The inverse loss ratio (premiums divided by losses) shows the price that an insurance firm gets for each unit of losses paid and is taken as an approximation of the unit price. It gives an indication of what customers get back from insurers for the premiums they have paid and may be regarded as a proxy for the output of the insurance industry.
>
> Trufin et al., 2009, p. 387

Shifting from value to volume measures, they include the number of claims received (e.g. Segovia-Gonzalez et al., 2009) and the number of claims paid/settled (e.g. Manikowski & Weiss, 2013). These have been utilised sparsely in the literature, though. The use of claims as an insurance output measure is generally justified because it reflects the risk pooling services undertaken by insurers. Both premiums and claims are used as proxies for measuring the output of this service in the literature. This measure of insurance output is not without its own set of criticisms. The first criticism is that claims cannot be treated as goods but must be treated as 'bads'. This is because, in terms of economic theory, an output variable must be subject to maximisation, and maximising claims seems irrational from a rational firm's perspective. Thus, this output measure does not satisfy the critical characteristic of an ideal output measure as identified in the literature, i.e. more output must be preferred over less (Gaganis et al., 2013). The second criticism has been that "claims do not represent current expenses; they measure past activity" (Wise, 2018, p. 13). The author also states that "as claims represent the end of the policy, the outcome is a loss of future profits and probably negative profits now" (p. 13). However, as stated earlier, the belief in a strong positive association between claims and losses seems to be the chief motivation for using this output measure in the literature.

The amount of losses as a measure of insurance output has a long history in the insurance literature. Notable works in this regard include Weiss (1991), Cummins and Weiss (2000), Cummins et al. (2004), Cummins and Xie (2008, 2013), Yaisawarng et al. (2012), Schlesinger (2000), Carrington et al. (2011), and Wise (2017, 2018). Three measures of prevalent in the literature. Actual losses are the losses paid by the insurers in a given period; incurred losses, broadly defined as the losses paid plus changes in technical reserves and expected losses, generally defined as the amount of liabilities to be paid ex-ante using statistical forecasting models. A few studies have also used loss adjustment expenses to measure insurance output. Pal et al. (2017) is an illustration of the same. Another novel measure in the literature is the amount of incurred losses – either on a first-reported or developed basis.[25] A vital feature of loss measures of insurance output is that these are generally flow measures.

Investment and financial assets output

The intermediation and value-added approach have popularly utilised the amount of financial assets to measure insurance output. The essence of this measure is that it proxies the wealth maximisation efforts undertaken by insurers for its owners and policyholders and represents the additional funds available with the insurers (in terms of returns generated) to handle future liabilities.[26] It is a balance sheet item and thus is a stock measure of insurance output. Studies have used flow and stock measures together in many cases. A debate in the literature has been whether to proxy the intermediation services of insurers by the amount of financial assets or to use returns on investments. The extent of financial intermediation services provided by insurers must account for the value of financial investments and the amount of funds used by the insurers to generate these investments. In that light, return on investments seems to be a relatively superior measure. Assets under management/Invested assets/Financial assets are the different terms this output measure is characterised in the literature. The essence of this output variable is that the surplus from the policyholder's money is invested in financial markets to earn a return on the idle money until claims are paid. These returns are then passed on to the owners and policyholders – whether in life or nonlife segments.[27] Figure 4.3

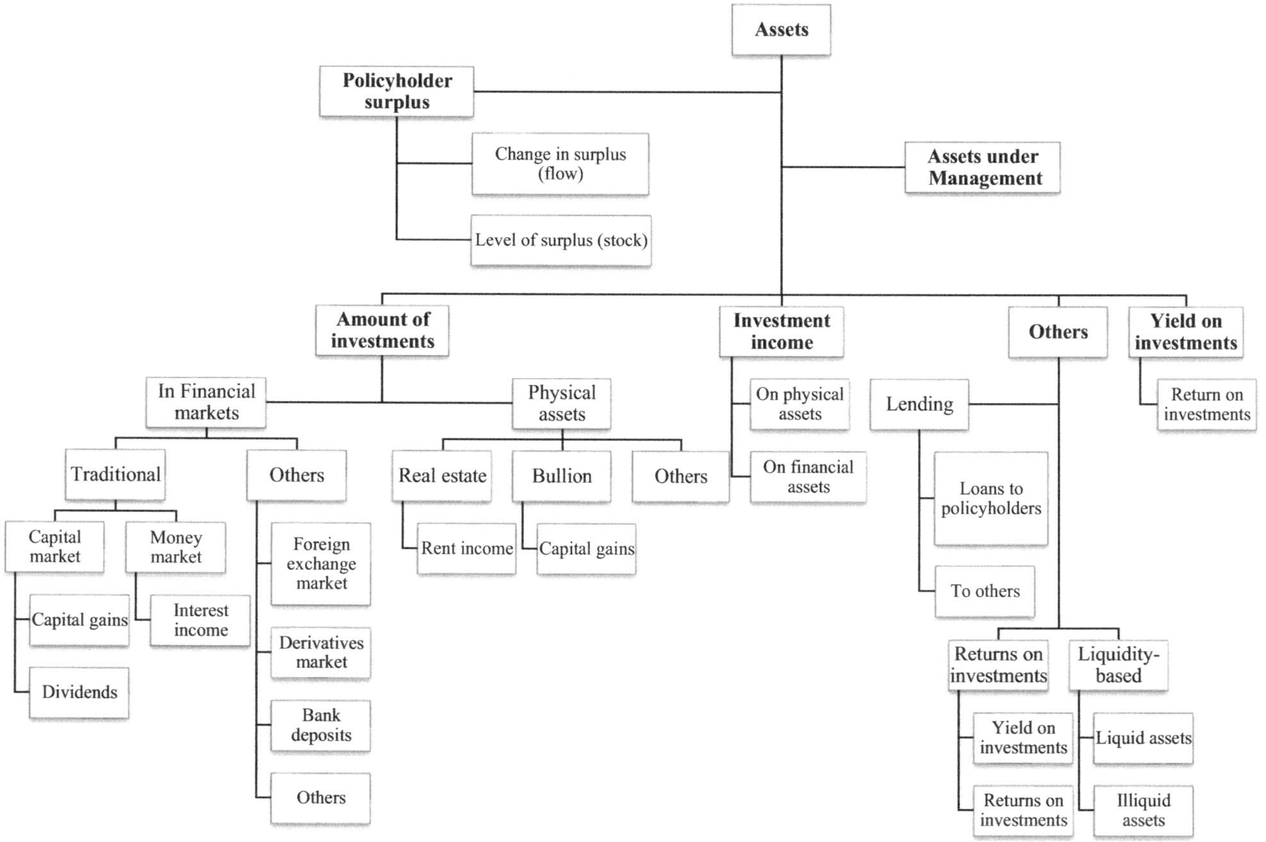

Figure 4.3 Investments and assets as insurance output in the literature

Source: Author's analysis based on the review of the literature.

summarises the primary ways in which literature has employed this variable to measure insurance output.

Reserves as output

The consensus in the literature on the use of reserves as an insurance output is presented in Figure 4.4. Another prevalent input-output dilemma in the literature has been whether to treat technical reserves as an input or an output. Essentially, the consensus has been to treat it as an input into the insurance production function. Some studies have, however, used it as an output. Notable works include Mahlberg and Url (2003) and Gaganis et al. (2013). Some notable recent studies treating it as input include Parida and Acharya (2017); Ksenija (2017); Alshammari et al. (2019); Krupa et al. (2019); Yakob et al. (2014); and Sun (2020), among many others before them. The amount of reserves is a stock variable. This is one way in which the literature has employed it. Another way literature has used this concept is through 'additions to reserves', a flow variable. The term 'reserve' can include concepts other than technical reserves, such as Incurred But Not Reported (IBNR) reserves, reinsurance reserves and reserves for primary insurance contracts. Chiefly, however, this term is used for representing technical reserves.

Technical reserves are generally statutory (and may also include voluntary) provisions made by insurers to ensure that future expected losses are fulfilled. This measure has been conceptualised as representing the risk coverage services produced by insurers. The level and movements of this measure are assumed to be strongly correlated with the amount of risk coverage that the insurance firm can provide. It may be considered a measure of insurers' productive capacity to fulfil their future liabilities. Its use as a measure of input, particularly debt capital, has been the most prevalent practice. This is because it is criticised as a measure of output on several pressing grounds. The first has been that its estimation may differ across insurers, and thus use of the same in performance analysis can generate biased and unreliable results. Another criticism has been that this variable may change due to exogenous shocks even when the amount of premiums and the number of policies issued have not changed. This can happen due to changes in risk assessment by the underwriters and risk managers in the firm. Studies have also avoided using technical reserves as an output measure due to high cross-sectional heterogeneity and differences in regulatory norms across regions.[28] Lastly, analysts have argued that technical reserves represent the future, and thus its use as a measure of current output is inconsistent with its fundamental nature (Wise, 2018).

Income output

Income output is conceptualised as operating income in the insurance literature. It has two major components: premium income (as discussed earlier) and investment income. Investment income is the flow of returns generated by the

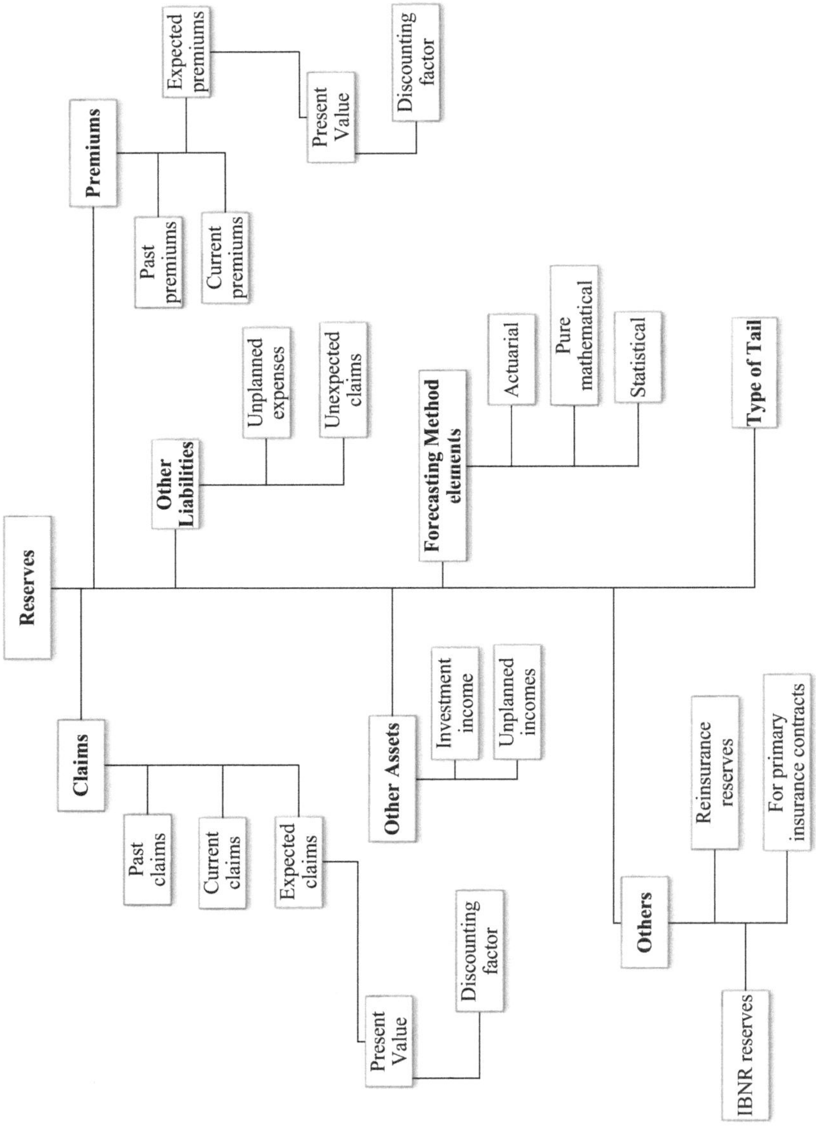

Figure 4.4 Reserves as a measure of insurance output

Source: Author's analysis based on the extant literature.

financial investments undertaken by insurers. Given that surplus will generally be available, it is invested in various financial instruments subject to the risk-preference of insurers constrained under extant regulatory norms. Investments made in financial assets will generate a flow of earnings, broadly called investment income. Given its flow nature, its use is preferable against stock variables. Investment income is generated in interest income and volatile speculative returns. Insurers tend to invest in risky (e.g. equity) and interest-bearing (debentures, bonds, etc.) assets. The different ways in which these investments can be classified are explained in Figure 4.5.

Literature has recognised the role of investment income in substituting premium income. With larger investment incomes, insurers can suppress premium rates below the competitive levels to achieve higher market share (Mahlberg & Url, 2010), mainly if the price elasticity of insurance demand is high. The portfolio of invested assets and their composition also plays a vital role in determining whether this measure can be used empirically for output analysis of insurance. There can be excessive volatility and instability if an insurer's exposure to equity and other risky assets is high. Exogenous factors might induce changes in this measure, producing biased estimates of performance parameters such as efficiency, productivity and profitability. Literature has also recognised the income from physical assets, but this dimension has not been employed frequently. Data availability and problems in computing the price and returns on physical capital might be the main reasons.

National income output of insurance

The SNA manual provides helpful notes on how national income accountants approach the issue of insurance output measurement. The broad framework is presented in Figure 4.6.

In national income accounting, the insurance sector is looked at from at least four perspectives: direct insurance, reinsurance, retrocession (insurance assumed by reinsurers) and social insurance. The largest share is occupied by direct insurers and reinsurers in the sector output of the insurance industry in any economy. The output estimation procedures for reinsurers are precisely the same for direct nonlife insurers irrespective of "whether it is life or nonlife policies that are being reinsured" (SNA, 2008, p. 119). SNA (2008) defines the output of direct insurers for the life segment as Premiums earned + premium supplements − benefits due − increases (+ decreases) in life insurance technical reserves.

Four components are there in this measurement for the life insurance industry. First is the amount of premiums earned. Second is the total premium supplement, which is additional income earned by life insurers in returns on investments, fees and other sources. The third component is the benefits (life insurance claims) due in a given year. This consists of both the death and maturity claims. Finally, the last component is the change in technical reserves. Data on all these components are estimated using accounting data reported by insurers to their regulators. The final result is a flow measure of insurance output.

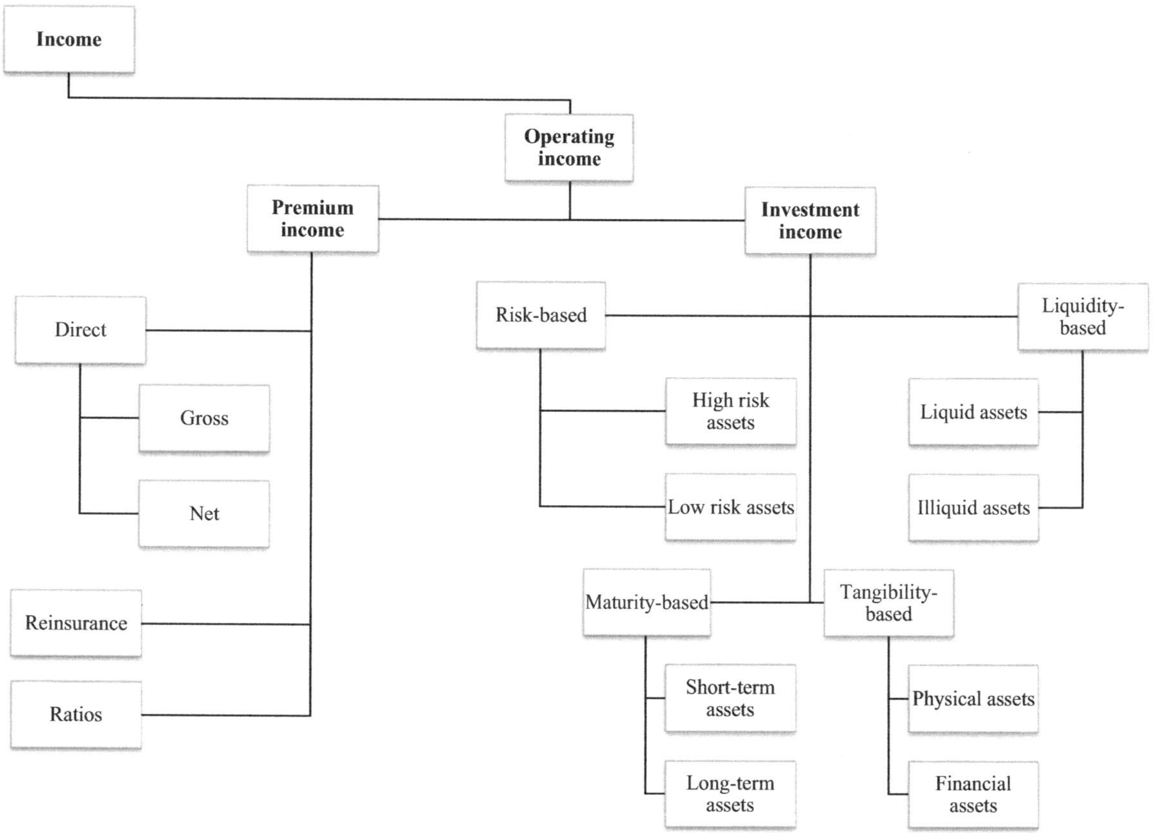

Figure 4.5 Conceptualising income output in the insurance literature

Source: Author's analysis based on the extant literature.

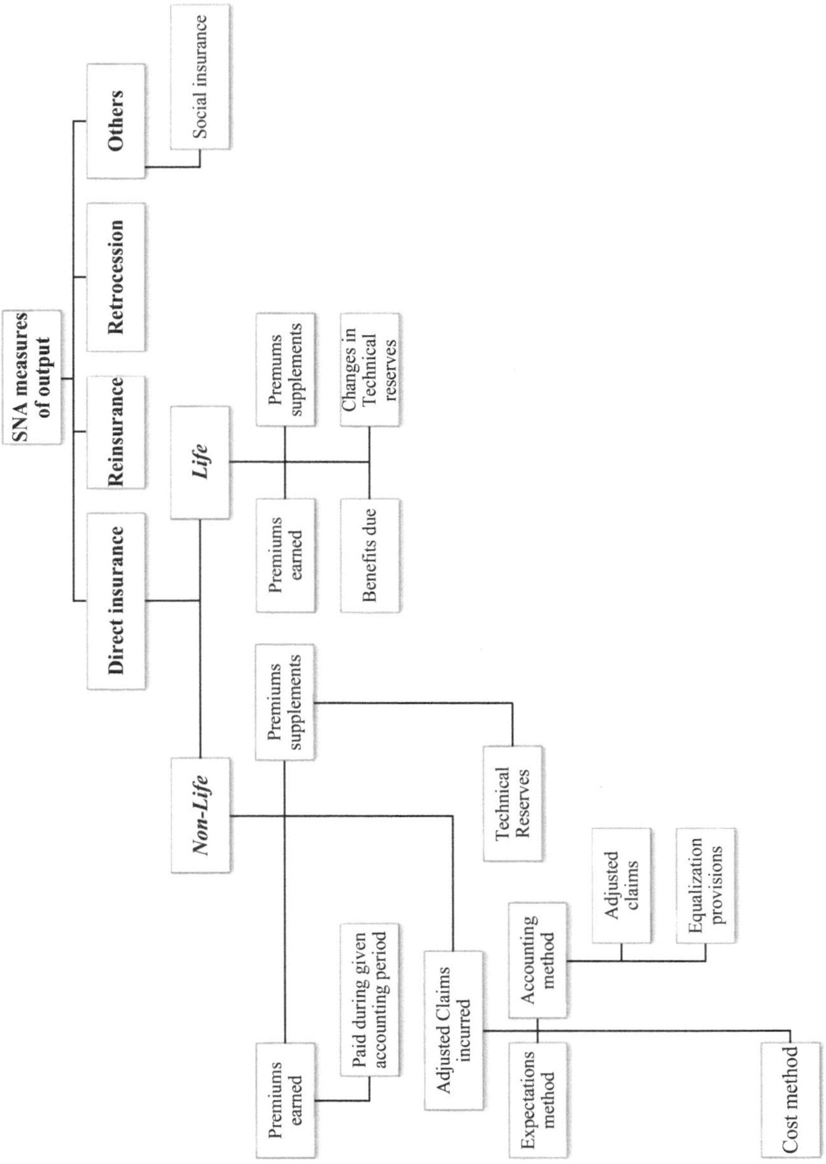

Figure 4.6 Conceptualising insurance output within the SNA framework

Source: Author's analysis based on the SNA, 2008 Manual.

As one may ascertain, the SNA uses a net premium measure of insurance output wherein gross premiums are netted out for claims and reserves. This measure is used for sectoral analysis and provides the recommended method for national economies. The same subtleties of using this measurement will differ depending on the economy. Advanced economies such as the US have very well-developed granular data on the financial service industry.[29]

Similarly, SNA recommends output measurement for the nonlife insurance industry as Total premiums earned + premium supplements – less adjusted claims incurred. This measure is also based on the framework of the net premium, where the gross premium amount is adjusted for supplementary income and incurred claims. It may also be noted that the SNA recommends using incurred claims for the nonlife segment instead of only the claims paid. As Figure 4.6 shows, the incurred claims may be estimated using the expectations method, accounting method or the cost method. The debate has been ongoing on the correct method for estimating incurred claims. Incurred claims consist of paid plus changes in reserves. The reserve component requires forecasting, and thus the methods mentioned earlier are needed. Advanced economies can utilise the accounting method relatively efficiently due to well-established data collection conventions. Emerging economies generally have to choose between the cost and expectations methods. The latter is an ad hoc method that extrapolates past patterns into the future. Given the advances in forecasting models, the expectations method might provide valuable estimates of the reserves and expected claims.

4.5. Thematic issues in insurance output measurement

Given the literature review as elaborated above, some important theoretical and empirical themes arise that may be presented as follows.

Market structure, organisational structure and performance estimation

It is well-recognised in neoclassical production theory that the market structure in which output is traded has direct implications for the quantity of that output and the method to measure it. Each insurance industry has a broadly specific market structure and showcases different degrees of integration of the firms and different intensities of competition among the firms. The way the industrial and firm-level production functions are conceptualised depends fundamentally on the industry's market structure. Aspects of a firm-level production function include substitutability among the inputs, price elasticity of demand for output, marginal rates of transformation and substitutions, exogenous factors that may affect the production function and others profoundly shaped by the market structure industry. This aspect has received limited empirical attention in the insurance literature. Firm- and industry-level production functions are generally estimated by assuming a specific market structure *a priori*. While this may provide empirical ease, it may be costing theoretical inconsistencies. The assumption of price-taking behaviour in inputs and even outputs markets, for example, has been common in insurance performance studies using trans-log cost and revenue functions.[30] Such an assumption is generally imposed on the context via stylised facts about the industry or the analyst's subjective understanding. It may so occur that if such assumptions were to be relaxed, the estimates could improve. This is an empirical question and requires more effort in the coming periods. Recognising market structure implies taking cognisance of the industry's structure and allowing that structure to shape the measure of output used in the analysis.

The implications of competition for output measurement have received some attention in the vast literature. Insurers have been found engaging in both price and non-price competition. Price competition will imply that output measures with high price elasticity of demand should be used after controlling price movements. Otherwise, excessive variability might enter into the data that could wrongly be associated with non-price factors, and the estimates of performance indicators too might be biased. As an illustration, under a continuous increase in insurance premium (the price of insurance products), the amount of total premium collected by insurers might show a large fall. Suppose these price movements were not accounted for in the production function. In that case, underestimating productivity is dangerous because the output variable (amount of total premium) is not adjusted for price movements. In case the price elasticity of demand for the chosen output variable is low, i.e., it is highly inelastic, then one would be in a better position to analyse such output variables within a production function approach, as price considerations will not be a constraint. However, demand's degree of price elasticity is an empirical question and requires estimation rather than any *a priori* assumptions. Such evidence is limited in the context of both advanced and emerging economies.

Regulators are keenly observing the market behaviour of insurers to prevent collusive behaviour. However, when collusive behaviour does occur, output determination has to account for it. The output measurement in insurance is undertaken mainly by defining each firm (in the firm- and industry-level studies) as independent output producers. Independence is conceptualised as a lack of strong interdependency between the firms' production functions. Hence, all the firms are assumed to be functioning under uncertain environments, and all the firms are assumed to be behaving as per the conditions prevailing in the market. However, at times, this may not be true. An example of this is Turkey, "where in 2000 the Antitrust Authority imposed a conspicuous fine on 39 companies for their anti-competitive behaviour deriving from ad-hoc information exchange from 1994 onwards" (Coccorese, 2010, p. 55). Kühn and Vives (1995) argue that "it is hard to find plausible business reasons, other than collusion, that might justify the exchange of individual price and output data" (p. 115). The theorisation of production functions of these colluding firms as independent would have yielded incorrect results due to simultaneity bias in determining their performance with separate and independent production functions. Under such situations, the output of the independent-appearing firms is actually collusive, and conceptual problems would arise, as examined by Coccorese (2010). First, at the industry level, the behaviour of colluding firms will not be independent of each other and will have a high degree of correlation. Comparisons among these firms might produce estimates with solid relationships, distorting the findings on competition and efficiency and productivity comparisons. Second, at the aggregate level, aggregation of the firm-level outputs into a single measure of industry-level output requires a well-defined aggregation function with theoretically correct aggregation weights. In literature, these weights are generally the price of each output. Given that price decisions might be collusive, they are expected to be highly correlated. Under such a scenario, these observed market prices or revenue shares will not provide much meaningful information on the unique weight that should be assigned to each output in the aggregate output variable. Using such weighting factors that are highly correlated and not independently determined will produce biased results. The aggregation will become all the more challenging in this case. Third, when collusion exists, price signals become inefficient and may not reflect the actual market conditions, at least for the agents other than the colluding firms. Their use as aggregation factors would probably be rendered meaningless. The fourth and last issue is that aggregation weights such as revenue shares might also reflect cost shares due to interdependent production across the colluding firms when collusion occurs. While revenue shares are suitable for output aggregation, cost shares are used for inputs aggregation. If both were highly correlated (positively or negatively), the aggregated outputs and inputs would not represent any unique information. The estimated total input and total output variables shall reflect similar kinds of information rather than information specific to the product and factor markets. An advantage of this is that either could be used for both outputs and inputs aggregation. However, such an approach in all likelihoods, will be deemed theoretically incorrect.

Another dimension in this context is the role of organisational structure in insurance performance analysis. One school of thought disregards the importance of organisational structure in determining the performance of insurers. The best consensus of this school of thought may be located in the so-called 'Demsetz and Lehn hypothesis', which "states that organisational form is not important for determination of technical efficiency, in view of the fact that regulators act as monitors" (Fukuyama, 1997, p. 490). Evidence does not show consensus on this, and this seems to hold in some advanced economies, but the findings for EMEs are weak on this account. This may become an agenda for future research. Cummins et al. (2004) have elaborated on four different hypotheses on the importance of organisational structure for the performance of insurance firms. These are the efficient structure hypothesis, expense preference hypothesis, managerial discretion hypothesis and the maturity hypothesis. Each of them is empirically tested by them in their 2004 study.

Output mix and output measures

Firm size can be a factor that affects the output mix and thus can affect the choice of output in insurance. Smaller firms might be more prone to entering into more contracts and undertaking a relatively larger amount of reinsurance to manage risks. In this case, measures such as the number of policies (life or nonlife or combined) may be useful proxies for output that can help capture the extent to which the small insurance firms can manage and allocate risks efficiently (via diversification and reinsurance). However, the same may not be accurate for larger firms, and thus the output mix can be very different in their case. For example, larger insurance firms may achieve a lower price elasticity of demand and thus may be able to charge higher prices than the smaller firms. In this case, dependency on diversification of contracts and reinsurance might not be the sole ways to manage risks efficiently. In such a case, one would find value measures of insurance output as better than volume measures. Moreover, a common criticism of volume measures in insurance is that "the number of policies does not capture meaningful differences in insurers' services" (Weiss, 1990, p. 24). However, this is true at the level of firms and groups of firms. At an industrial level (aggregate), such differences can be suppressed and averaged out to obtain a larger macroeconomic perspective.

Regulation and output measurement

Does regulation affect insurance output? Are there any implications of regulatory norms and interventions for measuring insurance output? Such concerns have been raised in the literature. An early attempt in this line of thought was in terms of the so-called 'Averch-Johnson hypothesis'. The "Averch-Johnson hypothesis" suggests links between the degree of regulation of firms and their economic behaviour. It was initially propounded by Averch and Johnson (1962) to analyse the inefficient capital accumulation behaviour of electricity utility firms due to the regulated rate of return (as against market-oriented rate of return on invested capital), which the Government guarantees. However, this hypothesis assumes single output firms and thus cannot be directly applied to banking and insurance firms which are inherently multi-output. Multi-output firms may face regulations on some outputs or different regulations on different outputs. This can make it difficult to disentangle the distortions created by such differential regulations and hence makes it difficult to estimate a pure market-oriented output measure.

Furthermore, "regulation can affect firms' incentives and costs and thereby influence productivity growth" (Weiss, 1990, p. 15). Similarly, it is possible that the regulated rate of return (e.g. premium rate charged by insurers as regulated by the regulator) may not be greater than the price of capital invested in the business. The Averch-Johnson effect may be in the form of under accumulation/utilisation of resources. Many insurance regulatory bodies stress the "fair" rate of premium, which might result in equalisation of the rate of return on capital and the cost of capital.

The nature of regulation and its underlying motivation can affect the output of banking and insurance firms and hence can make it difficult to estimate the market-oriented output. If public interests drive the regulations, the market orientation of the output variables will be weak and exogenous (not caused by market forces). However, if private interests dominate, then the market orientation of the output measures is higher even when the interests of the industry giants drive regulations. One can then use various models of market structures such as oligopoly and monopoly to measure and analyse the output behaviour of such firms. As an illustration, consider the standard solvency regulations: capital adequacy for banks and reserve determination norms for insurers. Both are generally assumed to be motivated by public interests in the EMEs. However, the efficacy of this belief is questionable and hardly any empirical pieces of evidence exist that can corroborate such an *a priori* assumption.

Insurance output measurement in advanced versus emerging economies

Compared to the emerging economies, advanced economies have several data related advantages. One of them is the availability of detailed disaggregated accounting data at the firm level for the insurance industry. As Cummins and Xie (2009, p. 135) note: "Having detailed operating data enables us to provide more accurate estimates of inputs and outputs and to account more fully for heterogeneity among the firms in the industry". This is a significant constraint for analysts focusing on emerging economies. Another advantage in analysing advanced economies is the availability of price indexes for the insurance industry and different lines of insurance. This, too, is missing in the case of EMEs.

Deflation of nominal output in insurance

The most frequently used price indexes for deflation of insurance firms and industry nominal output are CPI, WPI, insurance-specific price indexes (such as in Carrington et al., 2011) and the GDP deflator. Deflation is a necessary procedure for lending data comparable across time. This is necessary as far as time series and panel data are concerned. For cross-section data, one may use nominal variables. As expected, aggregate price indexes have been employed due to a lack of reliable and rigorous insurance-specific price indexes. To this extent, CPI has been the most frequent choice in insurance literature, followed by the GDP deflator. However, such aggregate deflation methods are not justifiable if one is interested in deriving the quantity changes of the concerned variable. They might help establish the comparability of data from different regions or countries. The use of such measures implicitly assumes a strong correlation between the aggregate price level and the price levels in the insurance industry. This generally does not hold true. Deflation of input data is at times done using input-specific price indexes. These are mainly seen in the case of the US, where firm-level disaggregated data are reliably available. In their study, Xie et al. (2011) apply such an approach to the deflation of inputs. A similar approach is also possible in the case of outputs, but hardly any study has adopted this framework. Either the CPI or the aggregate GDP deflator has been used.

Taxation and insurance output measurement

Most countries levy taxes on premium amounts. These should ideally be accounted for in the measurement of output for the industry as a whole and individual firms. Taxes are levied in indirect taxes as a proportion of the underwriting premium amount quoted by the insurer. Suppose financial statement data are used to determine the total premium amount. In that case, the value of the tax amount could be calculated, and the same be adjusted for (removed from) the observed data if already included. This is because the amount of tax on the premium is not an insurer's income, nor does it represent any value-addition by the insurer.

The following section presents the appendix on the evolution of output measurement in insurance literature from 1980 to 2022.

Appendix

Evolution of insurance output measurement in the extant wisdom from 1980 to 2022

No.	*Citation*	*Issue*	*Output Specification*	*Flow or Stock*	*Nominal or Real*	*Underlying Approach*
1	Daly and Rao (1985)	Total Factor Productivity, Economies of Scale and Technical Progress	Amount of Premium	Flow, Stock	Real	Production approach
2	Weiss (1990)	Total Factor Productivity Growth	Real expected losses proxied by relevant expenses	Flow	Real (Constant Price)	Intermediation approach
3	Diacon (1990)	Insurance Output Measurement	Ideal output measure is number of policies sold or a similar volume measure	Flow	Real (Volume)	Production
4	Hornstein and Prescott (1991)	Insurance Output Measurement	Traditional measure: Net premiums (Gross premiums net of claims paid); Suggestion: product of price and quantity of insurance contracts using hedonic pricing model	Flow	Real (Constant Price)	National income
5	Weiss (1991)	Output, Input and TFP estimation	Incurred losses and loss reserves	Flow	Real	Intermediation approach
6	Wolff (1991)	Labour Productivity growth and TFP growth	Gross National Product of insurance industry	Flow	Real	Production approach
7	Cummins and VanDerhei (1992)	Cost Efficiency	Direct Premiums; Net Premiums; Losses incurred	Flow	Nominal	Production
8	Fecher et al. (1993)	Technical efficiency for life and nonlife insurance industries	Gross Premium; Financial Returns	Stock	Nominal	Production approach

9	Kumbhakar and Hjalmarsson (1995)	Labour-use efficiency (Labour Productivity or Technical Efficiency in use of labour input) of Swedish local social insurance offices	Individual group of services provided by social insurance offices	Flow	Real (Volume)	Production approach
10	Fukuyama (1997)	Productive Effiiency and TFP growth	Reserves; Loans	Stock	Nominal	Intermediation approach
11	Toivanen (1997)	Cost Efficiency	Working time; Number of accident; Premium	Flow	Real (Volume); Real (Constant Price)	Production approach
12	Oulton (1998)	Labour productivity of aggregate economy and individual industries including insurance industry	Aggregate Value-added	Flow	Nominal	Production approach
13	Vuorinen et al. (1998)	Partial and Total Factor Productivity	Number of Applications; Turnaround time	Flow	Real (Volume)	Production Approach
14	Cummins and Zi (1998)	Technical Efficiency	Incurred Benefits; Additions to Reserves	Flow	Real (Constant Price)	Production
15	Sherwood (1999)	Insurance output measurement	Difference between amount of premiums (adjusted for rate of return on investments) and total claims paid	Flow	Nominal, Real (Constant Price)	National income
16	Acemoglu and Shimer (2000)	Effects of change in Unemployment Insurance level on aggregate output level	Amount of claims paid	Flow	Nominal	Insurance as welfare enhancing service
17	Fukuyama and Weber (2001)	Technical efficiency of nonlife insurance industries with different efficiency measures	Reserves; Loans; Investments	Flow, Stock	Real (Constant Price)	Production Approach

(*Continued*)

(Continued)

No.	*Citation*	*Issue*	*Output Specification*	*Flow or Stock*	*Nominal or Real*	*Underlying Approach*
18	Cummins and Nini (2002)	Capital Utilisation in property liability insurance	Present value of losses incurred; Amount of invested assets	Stock	Real (Constant Price)	Production approach
19	Mahlberg and Url (2003)	Technical Efficiency and Malmquist Total Factor Productivity	Sum of expenses on claims, change in reserves and returned premiums	Flow	Nominal	Production
20	Ennsfellner et al. (2004)	Technical Efficiency	Incurred benefits net of reinsurance; Changes in reserves net of reinsurance; Total invested assets; Claims incurred net of reinsurance	Both	Nominal	Intermediation
21	Cummins et al. (2004)	Technical, cost, and revenue frontiers	Assets; Premium; Income (Total, Life, Nonlife separately)	Both	Real (Constant Price)	Value Added
22	Arvanitis (2005)	Firm productivity	Amount of Sales	Flow	Nominal	Production Approach
23	Barros et al. (2005)	Technical Efficiency and Malmquist Total Factor Productivity	Claims and Profits	Stock	Real (Constant Price)	Intermediation
24	Brockett et al. (2005)	Technical Efficiency	Solvency; Liquid Assets/Liabilities; ROA	Ratio of Flow to Stock; Ratio of Stock to Stock	Nominal	Intermediation approach
25	Choi and Weiss (2005)	Cost and Revenue Efficiencies	Losses; Assets	Flow, Stock	Real (Constant Price)	Value Added
26	Jeng and Lai (2005)	Technical and Cost Efficiencies	Policies; Assets	Stock	Real (Constant Price)	Value Added
27	Tone and Sahoo (2005)	Cost Efficiency and Returns to Scale	Claims Settled, Ratio of Liquid Assets to Liabilities	Flow, Ratio of Stock to Stock	NA	NA

28	Bertschek et al. (2006)	Labour Productivity of Service industries including insurance	Sum insured	Stock	Nominal	Production approach
29	Cummins and Rubio-Misas (2006)	Cost, technical, and allocative efficiency, and Malmquist total factor productivity (TFP) change	Losses; Reserves; Assets	Flow and Stock	Real (Constant Price)	Value Added
30	Jeng et al. (2007)	Technical, Allocative and Cost Efficiencies	Benefits paid; IRIS indicators, Principal Components Analysis-based components	Flow	Real (Constant Price)	Value Added and Intermediation
31	Sinha (2007a)	Technical Efficiency	Benefits paid, Operating Income; Net Premium	Flow	NA	NA
32	Sinha (2007b)	Technical Efficiency and Malmquist Total Factor Productivity	Net Premium; Gross Income	Flow	NA	NA
33	Barros et al. (2008)	Total Factor Productivity	Profit and loss account; net premiums; settled claims; outstanding claims; investment income	Flow	Real	Production approach
34	Cummins and Xie (2008)	Total Factor Productivity, Technical Efficiency and Scale Efficiency	Expected Losses; Assets	Flow	Real (Constant Price)	Production approach
35	Maré (2008)	Labour Productivity	Value added	Flow	Nominal	Production approach
36	Chen et al. (2008)	Economies of scale and scope	Amount of Premium	Flow	Real (Constant Price)	Intermediation approach
37	ECB (2008)	Underwriting cycle in EU	Amount of Premium	Flow	NA	NA
38	Bikker and Leuvensteijn (2008)	Cost X-inefficiency and Economies of Scale	Premiums; Policies; Insured Capital; Insured Annuities	Flow, Stock	Nominal	Production
39	Fenn et al. (2008)	Cost Efficiency	Claims	Flow	Real (Constant Price)	Production

(Continued)

(*Continued*)

No.	*Citation*	*Issue*	*Output Specification*	*Flow or Stock*	*Nominal or Real*	*Underlying Approach*
40	Kao and Hwang (2008)	Technical Efficiency	Profits (Underwriting and Investment); Premiums (Direct and Reinsurance)	Flow	Nominal	Production
41	Weiss and Choi (2008)	Cost and Revenue Efficiencies	Losses; Assets	Flow, Stock	Nominal	Production
42	Cummins et al. (2009)	Cost Efficiency	Amount of assets; Amount of Asset Turnover; Return on Investment (all three for Financial Intermediation); Amount of Surplus (for Risk Management function); Amount of incurred losses (for Risk Management function)	Both	Real (Constant Price)	Both
43	Cummins and Xie (2009)	Cost and Revenue Efficiencies	Incurred Losses and Invested Assets	Stock	Real (Constant Price)	Production approach
44	Eling and Luhnen (2009)	Underwriting cycle	Amount of Premium; Amount of Losses incurred; Amount of developed incurred losses	Flow	Nominal	NA
45	Jawadi et al. (2009)	Underwriting Cycle	Direct Premiums written	Flow	Nominal	NA
46	Luhnen (2009)	Technical Efficiency and Malmquist Total Factor Productivity	Amount of Claims; Amount of Invested Assets	Flow, Stock	Real (Constant Price)	Production
47	Garg and Deepti (2009)	Total Factor Productivity	Premium; Operating income	Flow	Nominal	Production
48	Segovia-Gonzalez et al. (2009)	Efficiency	Gross and Net Premiums	Flow	Nominal	Production
49	Kasman and Turgutlu (2009b)	Total Factor Productivity	Losses paid; Benefits paid	Flow	Nominal	Production
50	Trufin et al. (2009)	Underwriting Cycle	Inverse loss ratio	NA	NA	NA

51	Cerchiara and Lamantia (2009)	NA	NA	NA	NA	NA
52	Kasman and Turgutlu (2009a)	Cost Efficiency and Economies of Scale	Losses; Benefits; Assets	Flow, Stock	Real (Constant Price)	Value Added
53	Mahlberg and Url (2010)	Technical Efficiency and Malmquist Total Factor Productivity	Amount of Claims (Losses) incurred; Amount of Technical (Actuarial) Reserves; Net Return on Financial Assets	Flow	Real (Constant Price)	Intermediation
54	Trigo-Gamarra and Growitsch (2010)	Cost and Profit Efficiencies	Incurred Benefits/Claims paid; Premiums	Flow	Real (Constant Price)	Production
55	Eling and Luhnen (2010a)	Cost and Technical Efficiency	Claims [Nonlife claims + additions to reserves]; Benefits paid [Life benefits + additions to reserves]; Investments	Flow	Real (Constant Price)	Production
56	Lin et al. (2011)	Technical Efficiency and Malmquist Total Factor Productivity	Premiums and Financial Income	Flow	Nominal	Production
57	Eslake (2010)	Labour Productivity	Gross Value Added as per SNA	Flow	Nominal	Production
58	Bates et al. (2010)	Technical Efficiency	Percentage of people reporting being healthier	Stock	Real (Volume)	NA
59	Kader et al. (2010)	Cost Efficiency	Premiums	Flow	Nominal	Production
60	Cummins et al. (2010)	Economies of scope	Incurred Benefits (claims paid); Losses; Assets	Flow, Stock	Real (Constant Price)	Production
61	Nektarios and Barros (2010)	Malmquist Total Factor Productivity	Invested assets, incurred losses, reinsurance reserves, own reserves	Flow, Stock	Real (Constant Price)	Production
62	Lei and Schmit (2010)	Financial Performance	Risk-adjusted ROA	Ratio of Flow to Stock	Nominal	NA
63	Erhemjamts and Leverty (2010)	Technical and cost efficiency	Incurred benefits	Flow	Real (Constant Price)	Value Added

(Continued)

(Continued)

No.	*Citation*	*Issue*	*Output Specification*	*Flow or Stock*	*Nominal or Real*	*Underlying Approach*
64	Leverty and Grace (2010)	Pure Technical, Allocative, Cost, Revenue and Scale Efficiencies	Value-added approach: Present Value of Real Losses Incurred; Average Real Invested Assets; Flow Approach: Rate of return on investments, Liquid assets, Solvency score	Flow, Stock and Ratio of Flow to Stock	Real (Constant Price)	Value Added and Flow
65	Xie (2010)	Technical, Allocative, Cost, Revenue and Scale Efficiencies	Losses; Assets	Flow and Stock	Real (Constant Price)	Value Added
66	Chakraborty and Sinha (2010)	Total Factor Productivity	Net Premium, Number of Products Launched	Flow	N	NA
67	Owusu-Ansah et al. (2010)	Technical	Net Premium, Claims Settled, Income on Investment	Flow	NA	NA
68	Carrington et al. (2011)	Partial and Total Factor Productivity	Amount of Premium	Flow	Real (Constant Price)	Production
69	He et al. (2011)	Cost and Revenue Efficiencies	Incurred Losses; Invested Assets	Flow, Stock	Real (Constant Price)	Production
70	Pottier (2011)	Cost, Revenue and Profit Efficiencies	Claims Incurred; Invested Assets	Flow, Stock	Nominal	Production
71	Berry-Stölzle et al. (2011)	Cost and Revenue Efficiencies	Incurred Losses; Invested Assets	Flow, Stock	Real	Production
72	Xie et al. (2011)	Cost and Technical Efficiency	Incurred Benefits; Invested Assets	Flow, Stock	Real (Constant Price)	Production
73	Eckles and Pottier (2011)	Cost Efficiency	Incurred Losses; Invested Assets	Flow, Stock	Not Clear	Production
74	Biener and Eling (2011)	Technical, Allocative and Scale Efficiencies	Incurred Benefits; Total Investments; Insured Population proportion	Flow; Stock	Real (Constant Price)	Value Added
75	Bikker and Gorter (2011)	Cost Efficiency	Incurred Losses; Premiums; Investments	Flow, Stock	Real (Constant Price)	Production

76	Chen et al. (2011)	Technical, Allocative and Cost Efficiencies	Losses; Assets; Surplus; Capitalisation; Yield; Liquid Assets	Flow, Stock and Ratio of Flow to Stock	Real (Constant Price)	Value Added; Intermediation
77	Choi and Elyasiani (2011)	Cost and Cost Scale Efficiencies	Losses; Assets	Flow, Stock	Real (Constant Price)	Value Added
78	Huang et al. (2011)	Technical and Cost Efficiencies	Losses; Assets	Flow, Stock	Real (Constant Price)	Value Added
79	Zhong and Sun (2011)	Cost Efficiency	Assets; Claims; Reserves	Flow, Stock	Real (Constant Price)	Production
80	Wu and Zeng (2011)	Technical and Scale Efficiencies	Premium; Profits; Reserves; Investment Income	Flow	Nominal	Value Added
81	Bawa and Ruchita (2011)	Technical and Scale Efficiencies	Net Premiums	Flow	Nominal	Production
82	Saad and Idris (2011)	Malmquist Total Factor Productivity	Net Premium, Net Income on Investment	Flow	Nominal	Production
83	Singh and Rajpal (2011)	Technical Efficiency	Net Premium, Income on Investment, Claims	Flow	Nominal	Production
84	Yaisawarng et al. (2012)	Technical Efficiency, Economies of Scale and Total Factor Productivity	Number of policies issued; Total invested assets	Flow, Stock	Real (Constant Price)	Hybrid of Production and Intermediary approaches
85	Chakraborty and Sengupta (2016)	Malmquist Total Factor Productivty	Premium; Number of Products	Flow	Real (Constant Price)	Production
86	Jackson (2012)	Malmquist Total Factor Productivty	Claims Incurred; Invested Assets	Flow, Stock	Real (Constant Price)	Value Added
87	Leverty and Grace (2012)	Cost, revenue, scale, technical, and allocative efficiencies	Losses; Assets	Flow, Stock	Real (Constant Price)	Value Added

(Continued)

(Continued)

No.	*Citation*	*Issue*	*Output Specification*	*Flow or Stock*	*Nominal or Real*	*Underlying Approach*
88	Al-Amri et al. (2012)	Technical Efficiency and Malmquist Total Factor Productivity	Premiums; Investment Income	Flow	Nominal	Value Added
89	Chaiyawat (2014)	Technical Efficiency	Losses; Assets	Flow, Stock	Nominal	Value Added
90	Cummins and Xie (2013)	Technical Efficiency, Economies of Scale and Total Factor Productivity	Present value of losses incurred; Amount of invested assets	Stock	Real (Constant Price)	Production approach
91	Chakraborty et al. (2013)	Technical Efficiency and Malmquist Total Factor Productivity	Benefits paid; Income from Investment	Flow	Real (Constant Price)	Value Added
92	Sinha and Khan (2013)	Malmquist Total Factor Productivty	Gross Investment income and Net Premium	Flow	Nominal	Production
93	Sinha (2013)	Cost Efficiency	Sum Assured; Incremental Assets Under Management	Flow	Nominal	Production
94	Gaganis et al. (2013)	Cost and Profit Efficiencies	Premiums; Invested Assets	Flow, Stock	Nominal	Production
95	Cummins and Weiss (2013)	Review of Evidences	Life insurance: premiums; sum of incurred benefits and additions to reserves; average invested assets; Nonlife: present value of real losses incurred;	NA	NA	NA
96	Oulton and Sebastiá-Barriel (2013)	Labour Productivity	Gross Domestic Product for financial services	Flow	Not Clear	Macro
97	Sauian et al. (2013)	Labour Productivity	Gross Domestic Product for financial services	Flow	Not Clear	Macro
98	Akotey et al. (2013)	Profitability	Investment income; underwriting profit	Flow	Nominal	NA

99	Olaosebikan (2013)	Profitability	Net Profit	Flow	Nominal	NA
100	Vencappa et al. (2013)	Total Factor Productivity Growth	Premiums; Claims	Flow	Real (Constant Price)	Production
101	Manikowski and Weiss (2013)	Underwriting Cycle	Claims, Premiums, Loss Ratios, Rates-on-Line, Capacity	Flow	Nominal	NA
102	Lee (2013)	Insurance Market Development	Premiums	NA	NA	NA
103	Dutta (2013)	Technical Efficiency	Premiums Earned; Income from Investments	Flow	NA	Reverse Intermediation
104	Bawa and Chattha (2013)	Profitability	Return on Assets	Ratio of Flow to Stock	Nominal	NA
105	Chen and McNamara (2014)	Technical and Cost Efficiencies	Benefits paid; Invested Assets	Flow, Stock	Real (Constant Price)	Value Added
106	Rahmani et al. (2014)	Financial Performance (Efficiency)	Earnings per share; Current ratio; Total income; Operating income	Flow, and Ratio of Stock to Stock	Nominal	Production
107	Porrini (2014)	Development of Insurance Market	Premiums, Claims	Flow	Nominal	NA
108	Jarraya and Bouri (2014)	Profit Efficiency	Claims; Investments	Flow	Nominal	Value Added
109	Lorson and Wagner (2014)	Sales Success	Premiums	Flow	Nominal	NA
110	Grmanová (2014)	Technical Efficiency	Premiums	Flow	Nominal	NA
111	Ma et al. (2014)	Cost, Revenue and Malmquist Total Factor Productivity	Losses; Assets	Flow, Stock	Unclear as not mentioned clearly	Value added
112	Kulvinskienė and Apčelauskaitė (2014)	Labour Productivity	Number of meetings, Number of concluded contracts	Flow	Real (Volume)	Production

(Continued)

(Continued)

No.	*Citation*	*Issue*	*Output Specification*	*Flow or Stock*	*Nominal or Real*	*Underlying Approach*
113	Javaheri (2014)	Malmquist Total Factor Productivity	Profits; Claims	Flow	Nominal	Production
114	Mandal and Dastidar (2014)	Technical Efficiency	Net Premium, Claims Processed	Flow	NA	NA
115	Nandi (2014)	NA	Net Premium, Net Benefits paid	Flow	NA	NA
116	Grmanová (2014)	Technical Efficiency	Premiums	Flow	Nominal	Production
117	Rao and Venkateswarlu (2015)	Technical Efficiency and Malmquist Total Factor Productivity	Net premium; Investment income	Flow	Real (Constant Price)	Production
118	Ai et al. (2015)	Technical Efficiency	Premiums; Policies	Flow	Real (Constant Rate based)	Production
119	Wasseja and Mwenda (2015)	Technical Efficiency and Malmquist Total Factor Productivity	Incurred benefits; Assets	Flow, Stock	Nominal	Value Added
120	Biener et al. (2015)	Cost, Technical, Allocative, Scale, Revenue and Malmquist Total Factor Productivity	Losses; Benefits; Assets	Flow, Stock	Real (Constant Price)	Value Added
121	Alhassan and Biekpe (2015)	Technical Efficiency and Malmquist Total Factor Productivity	Premiums; Claims; Investment income	Flow	Real (Constant Price)	Value Added
122	Grmanová (2015)	Technical Efficiency	Premiums; Investment Income	Flow	Nominal	Intermediation
123	Cole et al. (2015)	Profitability	Premiums; Losses incurred	Flow	Nominal	NA
124	Bruneau and Sghaier (2015)	Underwriting Cycle	Premiums written; Losses incurred	Flow	Nominal	NA
125	Bawa and Bhagat (2015)	Technical Efficiency	Net Premiums, Number of Policies Sold	Flow	Nominal	Production
126	Janjua and Akmal (2015)	Technical Efficiency and Profitability	Net Premium, Investment Income, Net Claims	Flow	Nominal	Production

127	Sinha (2015)	Technical Efficiency	Premiums Collected, Sum Assured	Flow	NA	NA
128	Noreen and Ahmad (2016)	Technical, Allocative, Cost Efficiency, and Malmquist Total Factor Productivity	Net premium; Invested Assets	Flow, Stock	Nominal	Production
129	Fier and Pooser (2016)	Advertising Efficiency	Premiums	Flow	Nominal	NA
130	Viverita et al. (2016)	Cost Efficiency and Malmquist Total Factor Productivity	Claims; Investments	Flow, Stock	Real (Constant Price)	Value Added
131	Grmanová and Hošták (2016)	Technical Efficiency	Premiums; Investment Income	Flow	Nominal	Production
132	Grmanová (2016)	Technical Efficiency	Premiums; Investment Income	Flow	Nominal	Production
133	Suárez-Álvarez et al. (2016)	Technical Efficiency	Premiums; Reserves; Assets	Flow, Stock	Nominal	Value Added
134	Chakraborty (2016a)	Technical and Scale Efficiencies and Malmquist Total Factor Productivity	Net Premiums; Investment Income	Flow	Real (Constant Price)	Production
135	Cummins and Xie (2016)	Technical, Scale, Cost, Revenue and Profit efficiencies; and Malmquist Total Factor Productivity	Losses; Invested Assets	Flow. Stock	Real (Constant Price)	Value Added
136	Chakraborty (2016b)	Financial Performance	Financial Soundness Indicators	Ratio of Flow to Stock, Stock to Stock	Nominal	NA
137	Sinha (2016a)	Technical Efficiency	Benefits paid; Asset Under Management	Flow, Stock (AUM)	Real (Constant Price)	Value Added

(Continued)

(Continued)

No.	*Citation*	*Issue*	*Output Specification*	*Flow or Stock*	*Nominal or Real*	*Underlying Approach*
138	Fernandes (2016)	Technical and Scale Efficiencies	Premiums; Benefits paid	Flow	Nominal	Value Added
139	Rao (2016)	Financial Performance	Gross Premium; Earned Premium; Profit	Flow	Nominal	NA
140	Zhang (2016)	Technical Efficiency	Net benefits plus additions to reserves; average invested assets	Flow, Stock	Real (Constant Price)	Value Added
141	Sinha (2016b)	Malmquist Total Factor Productivity	NA	NA	NA	NA
142	Parida and Acharya (2017)	Technical Efficiency and Malmquist Total Factor Productivity	Benefits; Liquidity ratio	Flow, Ratio of Stock to Stock	Real (Constant Price)	Value Added
143	Ferro and León (2017)	Technical Efficiency	Losses	Flow	Real (Constant currency)	Production
144	Nourani et al. (2018)	Technical Efficiency	Premiums; Claims; Investment income; Net profit	Flow	Nominal	Intermediation approach
145	Ksenija (2017)	Financial Performance	Equity and reserves; Business assets; Provision and liabilities; Financial incomes; Cost of insurance	Flow	Nominal	NA
146	Sinha (2017)	Technical Efficiency	Operating income; Investments, Benefits paid	Flow, Stock	Nominal	Production
147	Grmanová and Strunz (2017)	Technical Efficiency and Profitability	Premiums earned; Investment income	Flow	Nominal	Production
148	Pal et al. (2017)	Underwriting Cycle	Losses paid; Loss Adjustment expenses; Premium income	Flow	Nominal	NA
149	Chakraborty and Harper (2017)	Malmquist Total Factor Productivity	Net premium written; Income from investment	Flow	Nominal	Production
150	Wise (2017)	Technical Efficiency	Technical reserves and claims; Premiums and investment income	Flow	NA	Production, Value Added

151	Muthulakshmi (2018)	Financial Performance	Claims; Investment income; Net Premiums; Invested Assets	Ratio of flow to flow, stock to stock and flow to stock	Nominal	NA
152	Uddin et al. (2018)	Degree of Competition	Gross premium; total assets; gross claims	Flow, Stock	Nominal	NA
153	Chakraborty (2018)	Technical and Scale Efficiency, and Malmquist Total Factor Productivity	Net Premiums Earned; Income from Investments	Flow	Real (Constant Price)	Production
154	Reyna and Fuentes (2018)	Cost Efficiency	Number of Policies; Number of Claims	Flow	Real (Volume)	Production
155	Grmanová and Pukała (2018)	Technical Efficiency	Premiums earned; income from financial investments	Flow	Nominal	Production
156	Anandarao et al. (2018)	Technical Efficiency	Total Profits (excluding investment profits); Investment Profits	Flow	Nominal	Intermediation
157	Wise (2018)	Technical Efficiency	Reserves; Claims; Premiums; Investment Income; Premiums are the best measure of insurance output as per the authors	Flow	NA	NA
158	Adachi (2018a)	Cost Efficiency	Policyholders	Flow, Stock	Real (Volume)	Production
159	Adachi (2018b)	Economies of Scale	Number of Primary insured persons	Flow, Stock	Real (Volume)	Production
160	Pawirosumarto and Iriani (2018)	Labour Productivity	NA	NA	Real (Volume)	Production
161	Born and Sirmans (2018)	Underwriting performance	Premiums; Claims	Flow	Nominal	Production

(*Continued*)

(Continued)

No.	*Citation*	*Issue*	*Output Specification*	*Flow or Stock*	*Nominal or Real*	*Underlying Approach*
162	Alshammari et al. (2019)	Cost Efficiency	Claims; Assets	Flow, Stock	Nominal	Production
163	Taib et al. (2018)	Technical Efficiency and Malmquist Total Factor Productivity	Amount of premium income; net investment income	Flow	Nominal	Production
164	Krupa et al. (2019)	Investment Management Efficiency	Return on investments	Ratio of Flow to Stock	Nominal	Intermediation
165	Yakob et al. (2014)	Risk Management and Investment Management Efficiencies	Benefits paid; Investment Returns	Flow, Ratio of Flow to Stock	Nominal	Intermediation
166	Zhu (2019)	Technical Efficiency	Premiums	Flow	Nominal	Production
167	Yang and Li (2019)	Technical Efficiency and Malmquist Total Factor Productivity	Profitability; Operating Ability; Innovation Ability; ROE	Flow, Ratio of Flow to Stock	Nominal	Production
168	Oke and Abere (2019)	Operational Efficiency	Operating efficiency	Flow	Nominal	Production
169	Kozak (2019)	Cost Efficiency	Premiums; Assets	Flow, Stock	Nominal	Production
170	Sinha (2019a)	Technical Efficiency, Malmquist Total Factor Productivity and Returns to Scale	Benefits paid; Asset Under Management	Flow, Stock	Nominal	Flow and value added
171	Ilyas and Rajasekaran (2019a)	Technical Efficiency, Malmquist Total Factor Productivity and Returns to Scale	Net Claims; Invested Assets	Flow, Stock	Real (Constant Price)	Value Added

172	Ilyas and Rajasekaran (2019b)	Total Factor Productivity	Net Claims; Invested Assets	Flow, Stock	Real (Constant Price)	Value Added
173	Hasan et al. (2019)	Financial Performance	Return on Asset (ROA); Return on Equity (ROE)	Ratio of Flow to Stock	Nominal	NA
174	Lei (2019)	Financial Performance	Return on Equity	Ratio of Flow to Stock	Nominal	NA
175	Sinha (2019b)	Malmquist Total Factor Productivity	Benefits paid; Asset under management	Flow, Stock	Real (Constant Price)	Intermediation
176	Almulhim (2019)	Technical Efficiency	Premiums earned; investment and management fee income	Flow	Nominal	Production and Intermediation
177	Masud et al. (2019)	Malmquist Total Factor Productivity	Premium; Investment Income	Flow	Nominal	Production
178	Fusco and Porrini (2020)	Performance	Premiums	Flow	Nominal	NA
179	Marjanovic and Popovic (2020)	Profitability	Return on Asset	Ratio of Flow to Stock	Nominal	NA
180	Naushad et al. (2020)	Technical Efficiency	Premium; Investment income	Flow	Nominal	Production
181	Zhengyin et al. (2020)	Malmquist Total Factor Productivity	Premium income; compensation expenses; return on investment	Flow, Ratio of Flow to Stock	Nominal	Production
182	Lei and Zhanxin (2020)	Technical Efficiency and Malmquist Total Factor Productivity	Premium income; investment income	Flow	Nominal	Production
183	Sun (2020)	Malmquist Total Factor Productivity	Investment income	Flow	Nominal	Production

(*Continued*)

(Continued)

No.	*Citation*	*Issue*	*Output Specification*	*Flow or Stock*	*Nominal or Real*	*Underlying Approach*
184	Eling et al. (2020)	Malmquist Total Factor Productivity	Losses; Invested Assets	Flow, Stock	Real (Constant Price)	Value Added
185	Majid et al. (2017)	Malmquist Total Factor Productivity	Premium; Net investment income	Flow	Nominal	Production
186	Klumpes (2022)	Technical Efficiency	Losses; Claims; Assets	Flow (Losses and Claims and Stock	Real (Constant Price)	Production

Note**:** Detailed review sheet with various dimensions of output and inputs measurement used in the literature above can be availed from the author on request.

Source*:* Author's analysis of the literature.

Notes

1 Outreville (1998) elaborates on the history of the economic theory of insurance output.
2 Perhaps, the current work is the first of its kind to survey, summarize and organize a large volume of literature on this issue into a single work and similar analysis of bank output measurement.
3 As suggested by the traditional neoclassical production theory, only the essential labour and physical capital inputs are included in the performance analysis that employs the production approach (Berger & Humphrey, 1997). However, several papers have expanded the traditional input set in banking and insurance literature to include measures of financial capital like debt and equity (Carrington et al., 2011).
4 The financial capital of insurers consists of two components – equity capital and debt capital. Most of the studies either focus on equity capital per se or combine them into single financial capital input (Yaisawarng et al., 2012). Combining them implies aggregation, and the usual aggregation problems emerge.
5 "Insurers are financial intermediaries who borrow money from their policyholders in premium payments and invest the funds raised in financial assets" (Cummins et al., 2009, p. 145).
6 "The period between the date of the claim occurrence and the date of the claim payment depends on the type of insurance policy. Financial intermediation activities invest the amount of premiums received until the claim payment date" (Cummins et al., 2009, p. 149).
7 The same is discussed in the next section.
8 Equity capital is a crucial variable in the production process of insurance firms. It reflects the insolvency risk of the insurance firm and thus its ability to meet its 'promises'. Maintaining an optimal amount of equity capital has both benefits and problems. See Cummins and Nini (2002) for more details. The authors suggest that insurers tend to hold a safe or adequate amount of equity rather than an economically optimal level due to the costs of holding equity capital. This can be a source of economic shocks if claims are substantially higher than the expected level.
9 See Brockett et al. (2005) for a detailed analysis of issues involved in output choice under the financial intermediation approach and also how that approach is superior to the traditional production approach.
10 Also, see Cummins and Weiss (2013) for a review of the developments in inputs and outputs specifications under the value-added school.
11 Ideally, this should be examined empirically before permitting any item into the output vector of the insurance firm. However, many studies have used the value-added without any solid empirical justification.
12 "However, proponents of the intermediary approach . . . suggest that the objective of profit maximization associated with the value-added approach is inadequate" (Carrington et al., 2011).
13 See Cummins and Xie (2008, 2009, 2013, 2016) for empirical applications of the value-added approach and various theoretical issues in insurance output measurement under this framework.
14 For example: "Life insurers collect premiums and annuity considerations from customers and redistribute most of the funds to those policyholders who sustain losses (the risk bearing/risk pooling service)" (Cummins & Zi, 1998, p. 135).
15 For example: "Funds are collected in advance of paying benefits and invested in assets until claims are paid" (Cummins & Zi, 1998, p. 135).
16 Any of the studies have not directly used the concept of lapsed premium, but it has been proposed here as one possible measure of a 'bad output'. Policies that lapse generally result in the insurance firms' loss of future earnings. Hence, minimizing it may be a rational objective of an insurer, particularly in the case of life insurance.
17 Claims or losses have generally been treated as an output in insurance literature. But there have been arguments on treating them as an input. One of the earliest attempts in

this regard was by Müller (1981). Since then, several studies have theorised claims as an input, though the literature has primarily treated it as an output.

18 "[O]ut of the 80 studies that use the value-added approach, 46 specify output as claims (property liabilities)/benefits (life), whereas another 32 specify output as premiums/sums insured; however, there is no clear trend over time as to whether either of the two main proxies is preferred in the literature" (Gaganis et al., 2013, p. 431).

19 "The inclusion of the net change in reserves guarantees that the expected future loss from underwriting risk is appropriately accounted for as output" (Mahlberg & Url, 2003, p. 824).

20 Value measures can be adjusted for reinsurance claims received by the insurance companies to reflect the actual amount of direct losses borne by the insurers. However, the ideal adjustment should be: [Claims received by the insurer + Reinsurance premiums paid by the insurer – Reinsurance claims]. This is because if the reinsurance claims are removed from the claims received, then the reinsurance premium paid by the insurer must also be included so that the "net reinsurance gains" are accounted for. No studies surveyed have done this kind of adjustment to the claims variable.

21 Measurement of Expected losses requires knowledge about the risk preferences of the insured, while actual losses can be known directly from the financial statements. This is one reason why the actual loss measure has been more frequently used than its expected counterpart.

22 Losses incurred as a measure of output reflect "the total amount of losses expected to be distributed by an insurer as a result of their providing insurance coverage for a given year" (Cummins & Xie, 2008, p. 14).

23 "Discounting incurred losses allows for a more meaningful measure of profitability than reported (undiscounted) losses incurred since premiums reflect the expected present value of losses" (Choi & Weiss, 2005, p. 644).

24 Output smoothing procedures can be used to handle this problem. See Cummins and Xie (2008) for its empirical application. Studies that do so have generally found that smoothing of output variable (when measured by losses) does not change the final results on efficiency, productivity etc. much.

25 Developed incurred losses are defined as "losses incurred for a given year as reported several years after the close of the calendar year" (Cummins & Xie, 2009, p. 141). First incurred losses are defined as the amount of losses as reported on the first day of the year immediately succeeding the year under consideration. Differences in both these incurred loss measures represent errors in estimation of technical errors by the underwriters of the company as explained in Cummins and Xie (2009).

26 Total invested (financial) assets of insurance firms are used to measure their financial intermediation function. See Yaisawarng (2012) and Cummins and Xie (2013) for an extended perspective on this matter.

27 One aspect of this variable is that the composition of this variable can be different for life insurers and nonlife insurers. In advanced economies like the USA, nonlife insurers are more bent toward riskier instruments like stocks. In contrast, life insurers tend to invest more in relatively less risky instruments like bonds. This may or may not be accurate for emerging economies and can differ from economy to economy, region to region within a country and firm to firm. It is an empirical question and requires empirical assessment.

28 "Using reserves as an output proxy additionally leads to the significant difficulty that valuation assumptions and methods vary greatly between insurers" (Wise, 2018, p. 12).

29 Please refer to the expert contribution by Prof. Frauke Kreuter in Chapter 7 for further elaboration on this and its related matters.

30 The assumption of profit maximization has mainly been adopted without actually justifying its validity except for a cursory defence. Estimation of profit, cost and revenue efficiencies in insurance literature are among such areas. While it is necessary to assume profit maximization to make meaningful use of techniques such as DEA in emerging economies, the welfare-maximization objective may overshadow the profit maximization objective due to active regulatory control of the rate-making process. In that case,

alternative constraints on the objective function may be required to account for non-profit objectives.

References

Acemoglu, D., & Shimer, R. (2000). Productivity gains from unemployment insurance. *European Economic Review, 44*, 1195–1224.

Adachi, Y. (2018a). Expanding the scope and improving the efficiency of long-term care insurance operations. In *The economics of tax and social security in Japan* (pp. 219–237). Springer Nature Singapore Pvt. Ltd. https://doi.org/10.1007/978-981-10-7176-8

Adachi, Y. (2018b). Expanding the scope and improving the efficiency of national health insurance administrative work. In *The economics of tax and social security in Japan* (pp. 205–217). Springer Nature Singapore Pvt. Ltd. https://doi.org/10.1007/978-981-10-7176-8

Ai, J., Brockett, P. L., Golden, L. L., & Pitaktong, U. (2015). How to set rates if you must: An efficiency-based methodology for setting promulgated insurance rates with an application to title insurance. *Journal of Insurance Regulation, 34*(7), 1–39.

Akotey, J. O., Sackey, F. G., Amoah, L., & Manso, R. F. (2013). The financial performance of life insurance companies in Ghana. *The Journal of Risk Finance, 14*(03), 286–302. http://dx.doi.org/10.1108/JRF-11-2012-0081

Al-Amri, K., Gattoufi, S., & Al-Muharrami, S. (2012). Analyzing the technical efficiency of insurance companies in GCC. *The Journal of Risk Finance, 13*(4), 362–380. https://doi.org/10.1108/15265941211254471

Alhassan, A. L., & Biekpe, N. (2015). Efficiency, productivity and returns to scale economies in the non-life insurance market in South Africa. *The Geneva Papers on Risk and Insurance-Issues and Practice, 40*(3), 493–515. https://doi.org/10. 1057/gpp.2014.37

Almulhim, T. (2019). Analysis of takaful vs. Conventional insurance firms' efficiency: Two-stage DEA of Saudi Arabia's insurance market. *Cogent Business & Management, 6*(1), 1–18. https://doi.org/10.1080/23311975.2019.1633807

Alshammari, A. A., Syed Jaafar Alhabshi, S. M. bin, & Saiti, B. (2019). The impact of competition on cost efficiency of insurance and takaful sectors: Evidence from GCC markets based on the Stochastic Frontier Analysis. *Research in International Business and Finance, 47*, 410–427. https://doi.org/10.1016/j.ribaf.2018.09.003

Anandarao, S., Durai, S. R. S., & Goyari, P. (2018). Efficiency decomposition in two-stage data envelopment analysis: An application to life insurance companies in India. *Journal of Quantitative Economics*. https://doi.org/10.1007/s40953-018-0148-1

Arvanitis, S. (2005). Computerization, workplace organization, skilled labour and firm productivity: Evidence for the Swiss business sector. *Economics of Innovation and New Technology, 14*(4), 225–249. https://doi.org/10.1080/1043859042000226257

Averch, H., & Johnson, L. L. (1962). Behavior of the firm under regulatory constraint. *The American Economic Review, 52*(5), 1052–1069.

Barros, C. P., Barroso, N., & Borges, M. R. (2005). Evaluating the efficiency and productivity of insurance companies with a Malmquist index: A case study for Portugal. *The Geneva Papers on Risk and Insurance – Issues and Practice, 30*, 244–267. https://doi.org/10.1057/palgrave.gpp.2510029

Barros, C. P., Ibiwoye, A., & Managi, S. (2008). Productivity change of Nigerian insurance companies: 1994–2005. *African Development Review, 20*(3), 505–528.

Bates, L. J., Mukherjee, K., & Santerre, R. E. (2010). Medical insurance coverage and health production efficiency. *The Journal of Risk and Insurance*, 77(1), 211–229. https://doi.org/10.1111/j.1539-6975.2009.01336.x

Bawa, S. K., & Bhagat, N. (2015). Efficiency of life insurance companies operating in Punjab. *Pacific Business Review International*, 7(9), 76–85. www.pbr.co.in/2015/2015_month/March/10.pdf

Bawa, S. K., & Chattha, S. (2013). Financial performance of life insurers in Indian insurance industry. *Pacific Business Review International*, *6*(5), 44–52.

Bawa, S. K., & Ruchita. (2011). Efficiencies of health insurance business in India: An application of DEA. *American Journal of Social and Management Sciences*, *2*(2), 237–247.

Berger, A. N., & Humphrey, D. B. (1997). Efficiency of financial institutions: International survey and directions for future research. *European Journal of Operational Research*, *98*(2), 175–212.

Berry-Stölzle, T. R., Weiss, M. A., & Wende, S. (2011). *Market structure, efficiency, and performance in the European property-liability insurance industry* (Working Paper).

Bertschek, I., Fryges, H., & Kaiser, U. (2006). B2B or not to be: Does B2B E-commerce increase labour productivity? *International Journal of the Economics of Business*, *13*(3), 387–405. https://doi.org/10.1080/13571510600961395

Biener, C., & Eling, M. (2011). The performance of microinsurance programs: A data envelopment analysis. *The Journal of Risk and Insurance*, *78*(1), 83–115. https://doi.org/10.1111/j.1539-6975.2010.01404.x

Biener, C., Eling, M., & Wirfs, J. H. (2015). The determinants of efficiency and productivity in the Swiss insurance industry. In *Working Papers on Finance* (Working Paper No. 1502; Working Papers on Finance). University of St. Gallen, School of Finance. https://ideas.repec.org/p/usg/sfwpfi/201502.html

Bikker, J. A., & Gorter, J. (2011). Restructuring of the Dutch nonlife insurance industry: Consolidation, organizational form, and focus. *The Journal of Risk and Insurance*, *78*(1), 163–184. https://doi.org/10.1111/j.1539-6975.2010.01369.x

Bikker, J. A., & Leuvensteijn, M. V. (2008). Competition and efficiency in the Dutch life insurance industry. *Applied Economics*, *40*, 2063–2084. https://doi.org/10.1080/00036840600949298

Born, P. H., & Sirmans, E. T. (2018). Individual market underwriting profitability in health insurance. *Journal of Insurance Regulation*, *37*(7), 1–13.

Brockett, P. L., Cooper, W. W., Golden, L. L., Rousseau, J. J., & Wang, Y. (2005). Financial intermediary versus production approach to efficiency of marketing distribution systems and organizational structure of insurance companies. *The Journal of Risk and Insurance*, *72*(3), 393–412. https://doi.org/10.1111/j.1539-6975.2005.00130.x

Bruneau, C., & Sghaier, N. (2015). Cyclicity in the French property – liability insurance industry: New findings over the recent period. *The Journal of Risk and Insurance*, *82*(2), 433–462. https://doi.org/10.1111/j,1539–6975.2013.12027.x

Carrington, R., Coelli, T., & Rao, D. S. P. (2011). Australian private health insurance productivity growth: Is there scope to limit premium increases? *The Economic Record*, *87*(276), 125–139. https://doi.org/10.1111/j.1475-4932.2010.00684.x

Cerchiara, R. R., & Lamantia, F. (2009). *A dynamic analysis of the underwriting cycle in non-life insurance*. The Actuarial Society of Finland, Helsinki, Finland (Colloquium).

Chaiyawat, T. (2014). Corporate governance, efficiency, and firm performance in Thai property-casualty insurers. *The Journal of Risk Management and Insurance*, *18*(1), 70–85.

Chakraborty, J. (2016a). Efficiency and productivity analyses of public sector general insurance firms in India. *The IUP Journal of Applied Economics*, *15*(4), 74–92.

Chakraborty, J. (2016b). Financial efficiency of the public sector general insurance firms in India. *Pacific Business Review International*, *1*(1), 177–188.

Chakraborty, J. (2018). Efficiency and productivity analyses of general insurance firms in India: A Malmquist approach. *The IUP Journal of Applied Finance*, *24*(2), 45–56.

Chakraborty, J., & Sengupta, Dr., P. P. (2016). Measuring performance and efficiency growth of the selected Indian life insurance companies: A total factor productivity approach. *Arth Prabandh: A Journal of Economics and Management, 1*(6), 1–20.

Chakraborty, J., & Sinha, R. P. (2010). Measuring productivity and efficiency of the Indian life insurance industry: A total factor productivity approach. *SURVEY (A Quarterly Management Research Journal), 50*(3–4), 67–76.

Chakraborty, K., Dutta, A., & Sengupta, P. P. (2013). Efficiency and productivity of Indian life insurance industry. *Asia-Pacific Journal of Risk and Insurance*, 7(1), 1–26. https://doi.org/10.1515/2153-3792.1164

Chakraborty, K., & Harper, R. K. (2017). Dynamic productivity analysis of insurance firms – the effect of firm-specific and macroeconomic characteristics. *International Journal of Applied Economics, 14*(2), 37–55.

Chen, L.-R., Lai, G. C., & Wang, J. L. (2011). Conversion and efficiency performance changes: Evidence from the U.S. Property-liability insurance industry. *The Geneva Risk and Insurance Review, 36*, 1–35. https://doi.org/10.1057/grir.2010.3

Chen, L. R., & McNamara, M. J. (2014). An examination of the relative efficiency of fraternal insurers. *Journal of Insurance Issues, 37*(1), 1–31.

Chen, L. R., Peng, J. L., & Wang, J. L. (2008). Financial integration and economies of scope: A cross-industry analysis of bancassurance in Taiwan. *Journal of Insurance Issues, 31*(2), 120–151.

Choi, B. P., & Elyasiani, E. (2011). Foreign-owned insurer performance in the US property-liability markets. *Applied Economics, 43*, 291–306. https://doi.org/10.1080/00036840802552353

Choi, B. P., & Weiss, M. A. (2005). An empirical investigation of market structure, efficiency, and performance in property-liability insurance. *The Journal of Risk and Insurance, 72*(4), 635–673. https://doi.org/10.1111/j.1539-6975.2005.00142.x

Coccorese, P. (2010). Information exchange as a means of collusion: The case of the Italian car insurance market. *Journal of Industry, Trade and Competition. Springer, 10*, 55–70. https://doi.org/10.1007/s10842-008-0047-9

Cole, C. R., He, E., & Karl, J. B. (2015). Market structure and the profitability of the U.S. Health insurance marketplace: A state-level analysis. *Journal of Insurance Regulation, 34*(4), 1–30.

Cummins, J. D., Dionne, G., Gagne, R., & Nouira, A. H. (2009). Efficiency of insurance firms with endogenous risk management and financial intermediation activities. *Journal of Productivity Analysis, 32*, 145–159. https://doi.org/10.1007/s11123-009-0131-0

Cummins, J. D., Misas, M.-R., & Zi, H. (2004). The effect of organizational structure on efficiency: Evidence from the Spanish industry. *Journal of Banking and Finance, 28*(12), 3113–3150.

Cummins, J. D., & Nini, G. P. (2002). Optimal capital utilization by financial firms: Evidence from property-liability insurance industry. *Journal of Financial Services Research, 21*, 15–53. https://doi.org/10.1023/A:1014369617192

Cummins, J. D., & Rubio-Misas, M. (2006). Deregulation, consolidation, and efficiency: Evidence from the Spanish insurance industry. *Journal of Money, Credit and Banking, 38*(2), 323–355. https://doi.org/10.1353/mcb.2006.0029

Cummins, J. D., & VanDerhei, J. (1992). A note on the relative efficiency of property-liability insurance distribution systems. In *Foundations of Insurance Economics: Readings in Economics and Finance* (Soft Copy of 1st ed., pp. 1–724). Springer Science+Business Media, LLC.

Cummins, J., & Weiss, M. (2013). Analyzing firm performance in the insurance industry using frontier efficiency and productivity methods. In G. Dionne (Ed.), *Handbook of insurance* (2nd ed., pp. 795–861). Springer. https://doi.org/10.1007/978-1-4614-0155-1_28

Cummins, J. D., & Weiss, M. A. (2000). Analyzing firm performance in the insurance industry using frontier efficiency and productivity methods. In G. Dionne (Ed.), *Handbook of insurance* (pp. 767–829). Springer. https://doi.org/10.1007/978-94-010-0642-2_24

Cummins, J. D., Weiss, M. A., Xie, X., & Zi, H. (2010). Economies of scope in financial services: A DEA efficiency analysis of the US insurance industry. *Journal of Banking and Finance*, *34*(7), 1525–1539. https://doi.org/10.1016/j.jbankfin.2010.02.025

Cummins, J. D., & Xie, X. (2008). Mergers and acquisitions in the US property-liability insurance industry: Productivity and efficiency effects. *Journal of Banking & Finance*, *32*(1), 30–55. https://doi.org/10.1016/j.jbankfin.2007.09.003

Cummins, J. D., & Xie, X. (2009). Market values and efficiency in US insurer acquisitions and divestitures. *Managerial Finance, Emerald Group Publishing Limited*, *35*(2), 128–155. https://doi.org/10.1108/03074350910923482

Cummins, J. D., & Xie, X. (2013). Efficiency, productivity, and scale economies in the U.S. Property-liability insurance industry. *Journal of Productivity Analysis*, *39*(2), 141–164. https://doi.org/10.1007/s11123-012-0302-2

Cummins, J. D., & Xie, X. (2016). Efficiency and productivity in the US property-liability insurance industry: Ownership structure, product and distribution strategies. In J. Zhu (Ed.), *Data envelopment analysis: A handbook of empirical studies and applications* (Vol. 238). Springer International Publishing AG.

Cummins, J. D., & Zi, H. (1998). Comparison of frontier efficiency methods: An application to the U.S. Life insurance industry. *Journal of Productivity Analysis*, *10*, 131–152.

Daly, M. J., & Rao, P. S. (1985). Productivity, scale economies and technical progress in the Canadian life insurance industry. *International Journal of Industrial Organization*, *3*, 345–361.

Diacon, S. (1990). Insurance company output and costs. In S. Diacon (Ed.), *A guide to insurance management* (pp. 158–173). London: Palgrave Macmillan. https://doi.org/10.1007/978-1-349-07495-2_10

Dutta, A. (2013). *Efficiency and productivity analysis of Indian insurers in post reform era* [Ph.D Thesis]. National Institute of Technology.

ECB. (2008). The Euro area financial system. *Financial Stability Review*, 113–115.

Eckles, D. L., & Pottier, S. W. (2011). Is efficiency an important determinant of A.M. Best property-liability insurer financial strength ratings? *Journal of Insurance Issues*, *34*(1), 18–33.

Eling, M., Hoyt, R. E., & Schaper, P. (2020). The impact of capacity on price and productivity change in insurance markets: New firm-level evidence. *Journal of Insurance Issues*, *43*(1), 22–58.

Eling, M., & Luhnen, M. (2009). *Underwriting cycles in German property-liability insurance*. UNIVERSITAT ULM.

Eling, M., & Luhnen, M. (2010a). Efficiency in the international insurance industry: A cross-country comparison. *Journal of Banking and Finance*, *34*(7), 1497–1509.

Eling, M., & Luhnen, M. (2010b). Frontier efficiency methodologies to measure performance in the insurance industry: Overview, systematization, and recent developments. *The Geneva Papers on Risk and Insurance – Issues and Practice*, *35*(2), 217–265. https://doi.org/10.1057/gpp.2010.1

Ennsfellner, K. C., Lewis, D., & Anderson, R. I. (2004). Production efficiency in Austrian insurance industry: A Bayesian examination. *The Journal of Risk and Insurance*, *71*(1), 135–159. https://doi.org/10.1111/j.0022-4367.2004.00082.x

Erhemjamts, O., & Leverty, J. T. (2010). The demise of the mutual organizational form: An investigation of the life insurance industry. *Journal of Money, Credit and Banking*, *42*(6), 1011–1036. https://doi.org/10.2139/ssrn.1558536

Eslake, S. (2010). *An analysis of Victoria's labour productivity performance*. Presentation to a forum hosted by Victorian Department of Innovation, Industry and Regional Development.

Fecher, F., Kessler, D., Perlman, S., & Pestieau, P. (1993). Productive performance of the French insurance indus. *The Journal of Productivity Analysis*, *4*, 77–93.

Fenn, P., Vencappa, D., Diacon, S., & Klumpes, P. J. M. (2008). Market structure and the efficiency of European insurance companies: A stochastic frontier analysis. *Journal of Banking & Finance*, *32*, 86–100. https://doi.org/10.1016/j.jbankfin.2007.09.005

Fernandes, P. R. (2016). *A comparative study of performance evaluation of selected private life insurance companies and their role in economic development of India (2001–10)* [Ph.D. Thesis]. Savitribai Phule Pune University.

Ferro, G., & León, S. (2017). A stochastic frontier analysis of efficiency in Argentina's non-life insurance market. *The Geneva Papers on Risk and Insurance – Issues and Practice*, *43*, 158–174. https://doi.org/10.1057/s41288-017-0058-z

Fier, S. G., & Pooser, D. M. (2016). Advertising effectiveness for financial services firms: Evidence from the life insurance industry. *Journal of Insurance Issues*, *39*(2), 137–168.

Fiordelisi, F., & Ricci, O. (2012). *Bancassurance in Europe: Past, present and future*. Palgrave Macmillan.

Fukuyama, H. (1997). Investigating productive efficiency and productivity changes of Japanese life insurance companies. *Pacific-Basin Finance Journal*, *5*, 481–509.

Fukuyama, H., & Weber, W. L. (2001). Efficiency and productivity change of non-life insurance companies in Japan. *Pacific Economic Review*, *6*(1), 129–146.

Fusco, G., & Porrini, D. (2020). Less discrimination, more gender inequality: The case of the italian motor-vehicle insurance. *The Journal of Risk Management and Insurance*, *24*(1), 1–11.

Gaganis, C., Hasan, I., & Pasiouras, F. (2013). Efficiency and stock returns: Evidence from the insurance industry. *Journal of Productivity Analysis*, *40*(3), 429–442. https://doi.org/10.1007/s11123-013-0347-x

Garg, M. C., & Deepti, G. (2009). Malmquist indices of productivity change in Indian general insurance sector. *The IUP Journal of Management Research*, *8*(3), 21–36.

Grmanová, E. (2014). Efficiency of insurance lines in the Slovak Republic. In V. Kajurová, O. Deev, & J. Krajíček (Eds.), *European financial systems* (pp. 208–214). Masarykova univerzita. www.ceeol.com/search/chapter-detail?id=842987

Grmanová, E. (2015). Efficiency of national life insurance markets in Europe. In *European financial systems 2015: Proceedings of the 12th international scientific conference* (pp. 151–157). Masarykova univerzita. www.ceeol.com/search/chapter-detail?id=840261

Grmanová, E. (2016). Influence of selected factors on the efficiency of insurance companies. *VADYBA – Journal of Management*, *29*(2), 71–76.

Grmanová, E., & Hošták, P. (2016). Influence of selected environmental factors on the efficiency of commercial insurers. In *European financial systems 2016: Proceedings of the 13th international scientific conference* (pp. 199–206). Masarykova univerzita. www.ceeol.com/search/chapter-detail?id=839625

Grmanová, E., & Pukała, R. (2018). Efficiency of insurance companies in the Czech Republic and Poland. *Oeconomia Copernicana*, *9*(1), 71–85. https://doi.org/10.24136/oc.2018.004

Grmanová, E., & Strunz, H. (2017). Efficiency of insurance companies: Application of DEA and Tobit analyses. *Journal of International Studies*, *10*(3), 250–263. https://doi.org/10.14254/2071–8330.2017/10–3/18

Hasan, M. B., Islam, S. M. N., & Wahid, A. N. M. (2019). The effect of macroeconomic variables on the performance of non-life insurance companies in Bangladesh. *Indian Economic Review*. https://doi.org/10.1007/s41775-019-00037-6

He, E., Sommer, D. W., & Xie, X. (2011). The impact of CEO turnover on property – liability insurer performance. *The Journal of Risk and Insurance*, *78*(3), 583–608. https://doi.org/10.1111/1539-6975.2011.01411.x

Hornstein, A., & Prescott, E. C. (1991). Measures of the insurance sector output. *The Geneva Papers on Risk and Insurance. Issues and Practice, 16*(59), 191–206.

Huang, L.-Y., Lai, G. C., McNamara, M., & Wang, J. (2011). Corporate governance and efficiency: Evidence from U.S. Property – liability insurance industry. *The Journal of Risk and Insurance, 78*(3), 519–550. https://doi.org/10.1111/j.1539-6975.2011.01410.x

Ilyas, A. M., & Rajasekaran, S. (2019a). An empirical investigation of efficiency and productivity in the Indian non-life insurance market. *Benchmarking: An International Journal, 26*(7), 2343–2371. https://doi.org/10.1108/BIJ-01-2019-0039

Ilyas, A. M., & Rajasekaran, S. (2019b). Productivity of the Indian non-life insurance sector: New evidence employing Färe – Primont index approach. *International Journal of Productivity and Performance Management, 69*(4), 633–650. https://doi.org/10.1108/IJPPM-04-2019-0147

Jackson, M. I. (2012). *Total factor productivity change in the non-life insurance sector, Kenya: 2005–2009* (A Post-Graduation Research Project). Kenyatta University.

Janjua, P. Z., & Akmal, M. (2015). A comparative analysis of economic efficiency of conventional and Islamic insurance industry in Pakistan. *Pakistan Business Review*, 21–44.

Jarraya, B., & Bouri, A. (2014). Optimal production plan and profit efficiency in European non-life insurance companies. *Procedia Economics and Finance, 13*, 69–81. https://doi.org/10.1016/S2212-5671(14)00431-6

Javaheri, A. S. (2014). Productivity evaluation of Iranian insurance industry: A nonparametric Malmquist approach. *Iranian Journal of Economic Research, 18*(57), 85–95.

Jawadi, F., Bruneau, C., & Sghaier, N. (2009). Nonlinear cointegration relationships between non-life insurance premiums and financial markets. *The Journal of Risk and Insurance, 76*(3), 753–783.

Jeng, V., & Lai, G. C. (2005). Ownership structure, agency costs, specialization and efficiency: Analysis of keiretsu and independent insurers in the Japanese non-life insurance industry. *Journal of Risk and Insurance, 72*(1), 105–158. https://doi.org/10.1111/j.0022-4367.2005.00118.x

Jeng, V., Lai, G. C., & McNamara, M. J. (2007). Efficiency and demutualization: Evidence from the U.S. Life insurance industry in the 1980s and 1990s. *The Journal of Risk and Insurance, 74*(3), 683–711. https://doi.org/10.1111/j.1539-6975.2007.00230.x

Kader, H. A., Adams, M., & Hardwick, P. (2010). The cost efficiency of takaful insurance companies. *The Geneva Papers, 35*, 161–181. https://doi.org/10.1057/gpp.2009.33

Kao, C., & Hwang, S. N. (2008). Efficiency decomposition in two-stage data envelopment analysis: An application to non-life insurance companies in Taiwan. *European Journal of Operational Research, 185*(1), 418–429. https://doi.org/10.1016/j.ejor.2006.11.041

Kasman, A., & Turgutlu, E. (2009a). Cost efficiency and scale economies in the Turkish insurance industry. *Applied Economics, 41*(24), 3151–3159. http://dx.doi.org/10.1080/00036840701367663

Kasman, A., & Turgutlu, E. (2009b). Total factor productivity in the Turkish insurance industry. *International Journal of the Economics of Business, 16*(2), 239–247. http://dx.doi.org/10.1080/13571510902917558

Klumpes, P. J. M. (2022). *Consolidation and efficiency in the major European insurance markets*. Aalborg University.

Kozak, S. (2019). Efficiency of non-life insurance companies and its determinants. *Acta Scientiarum Polonorum. Oeconomia, 17*(4), 87–95.

Krupa, T., Farbarzevics, K., & Salame, B. (2019). Efficiency of German life insurance companies: Application of a two-stage SBM approach. *Współczesna Gospodarka-Contemporary Economy Review, 10*(1), 79–91. https://doi.org/10.26881/wg.2019.1.08

Ksenija, M., Boris, D., Snežana, K., & Sladjana, B. (2017). Analysis of the efficiency of insurance companies in Serbia using the fuzzy AHP and TOPSIS methods. *Economic Research-Ekonomska Istraživanja, 30*(1). http://dx.doi.org/10.1080/1331677X.2017.1305786

Kühn, K.-U., & Vives, X. (1995). *Information exchanges among firms and their impact on competition—Publications Office of the EU*. European Commission. https://op.europa.eu/en/publication-detail/-/publication/90fa6d91-de13-4c87-be75-ccb175427a61/language-en

Kulvinskienė, V. R., & Apčelauskaitė, G. (2014). Insurance intermediaries' work-related stress: Connections with labour productivity. *Ekonomika, 93*(1), 146–159.

Kumbhakar, S. C., & Hjalmarsson, L. (1995). Labour-use efficiency in Swedish social insurance offices. *Journal of Applied Econometrics, 10*, 33–47.

Lee, C.-C. (2013). Insurance and real output: The key role of banking activities. *Macroeconomic Dynamics, 17*, 235–260. https://doi.org/10.1017/S1365100511000101

Lei, Y. (2019). Reinsurance and insurers' risk-return profile. *Journal of Insurance Issues, 42*(1), 37–65. www.jstor.org/stable/10.2307/26608367

Lei, Y., & Schmit, J. T. (2010). Influences of organizational structure and diversification on medical malpractice insurer performance. *Journal of Insurance Issues, 33*(2), 152–177.

Lei, Z., & Zhanxin, M. A. (2020). Analysis on the total factor productivity of Chinese life insurance enterprises and its influence factors: Based on DEA-malmquist index and its decomposition. *SCIREA Journal of Management, 4*(2), 16–27.

Leverty, J. T., & Grace, M. F. (2010). The robustness of output measures in property-liability insurance efficiency studies. *Journal of Banking and Finance, 34*(7), 1510–1524. https://doi.org/10.1016/j.jbankfin.2009.08.015

Leverty, J. T., & Grace, M. F. (2012). Dupes or incompetents? An examination of management's impact on firm distress. *The Journal of Risk and Insurance, 79*(3), 751–783. https://doi.org/10.1111/j.1539-6975.2011.01443.x

Lin, H. D., Lee, Y., & Shih, M. L. (2011). A study on technical efficiency and productivity changes of Taiwan's life insurance industry. *Journal of Global Business Management*, 7(2), 1–8.

Lorson, J., & Wagner, J. (2014). Sales efficiency in life insurance: The drivers for growth in the German market. *The Geneva Papers, 39*, 493–524. https://doi.org/10.1057/gpp.2013.35

Luhnen, M. (2009). Determinants of efficiency and productivity in German property-liability insurance: Evidence for 1995–2006. *The Geneva Papers on Risk and Insurance – Issues and Practice, 34*, 483–505. https://doi.org/10.1057/gpp.2009.10

Ma, Y. L., Pope, N., & Xie, X. (2014). Insurer performance and intermediary remuneration: The impact of abandonment of contingent commissions. *The Geneva Papers on Risk and Insurance – Issues and Practice, 39*(2), 373–388. https://doi.org/10.1057/gpp.2013.12

Mahlberg, B., & Url, T. (2003). Effects of the single market on the Austrian insurance industry. *Empirical Economics, 28*, 813–838. https://doi.org/10.1007/s00181-003-0164-6

Mahlberg, B., & Url, T. (2010). Single market effects on productivity in the German insurance industry. *Journal of Banking & Finance, 34*, 1540–1548. https://doi.org/10.1016/j.jbankfin.2009.09.005

Majid, A. M. S., Hamid, A., & Faradilla. (2017). Assessing the productivity of insurance companies in Indonesia: A non-parametric approach. *Journal of Applied Economic Sciences, 12*(6), 1593–1605.

Mandal, S., & Dastidar, S. G. (2014). A DEA-investigation of efficiency of the Indian general insurance during recession. *Journal of Advances in Management Research, 11*(1), 115–136. https://doi.org/10.1108/JAMR-07-2012-0030

Manikowski, P., & Weiss, M. A. (2013). The satellite insurance market and underwriting cycles. *The Geneva Risk and Insurance Review, 38*(2), 148–182. https://doi.org/10.1057/grir.2013.2

Maré, D. C. (2008). Labour productivity in Auckland firms. *Motu Economic and Public Policy Research*, 1–55.

Marjanovic, I., & Popovic, Z. (2020). Profitability determinants of insurance companies in the republic of Serbia. In *Economic and financial challenges for Balkan and Eastern European countries* (pp. 133–158). Springer. https://link.springer.com/book/10.1007/978-3-030-39927-6

Masud, M. M., Rana, M. S., Mia, M. A., & Saifullah, M. K. (2019). How productive are life insurance institutions in Malaysia? A Malmquist approach. *Journal of Asian Finance, Economics and Business*, *6*, 241–248. https://doi.org/10.13106/jafeb.2019.vol6.no1.241

Müller, W. (1981). Theoretical concepts of insurance production. *The Geneva Papers on Risk and Insurance*, *6*(21), 63–83.

Muthulakshmi, P. (2018). Are general insurance companies efficient in their performance? – A comparison. *Ushus-Journal of Business Management*, *17*(2), 1–7. https://doi.org/10.12725/ujbm.44.1

Nandi, J. K. (2014). Relative efficiency analysis of selected life insurers in India using data envelopment analysis. *Pacific Business Review International*, *6*(8), 69–76.

Naushad, M., Faridi, M. R., & Faisal, S. (2020). Measuring the managerial efficiency of insurance companies in Saudi Arabia: A data envelopment analysis approach. *The Journal of Asian Finance, Economics and Business*, 7(6), 297–304. https://doi.org/10.13106/jafeb.2020.vol7.no6.297

Nektarios, M., & Barros, C. P. (2010). A Malmquist index for the Greek insurance industry. *The Geneva Papers on Risk and Insurance. Issues and Practice*, *35*(2), 309–324. https://doi.org/10.1057/gpp.2010.2

Noreen, U., & Ahmad, S. (2016). Cost efficiency and total factor productivity: An empirical analysis of Pakistan's insurance sector. *The Lahore Journal of Economics*, *21*(1), 123–150.

Nourani, M., Devadason, E. S., & Chandran, V. (2018). Measuring technical efficiency of insurance companies using dynamic network DEA: An intermediation approach. *Technological and Economic Development of Economy*, *24*(5), 1909–1904. https://doi.org/Technological and Economic Development of Economy

Oke, M. O., & Abere, M. (2019). Does consolidation have any effecton the operational efficiency in Nigerian insurance firms? *Acta Universitatis Danubius. Economica*, *15*(5), 54–72. www.ceeol.com/search/article-detail?id=855779

Olaosebikan, O. (2013). The determinants of the profitability of micro-life insurers in Nigeria. *The Geneva Papers on Risk and Insurance – Issues and Practice*, *38*(1), 140–159. https://doi.org/10.1057/gpp.2012.18

Oulton, N. (1998). *Labour productivity and foreign ownership in the UK*. NIESR (Discussion Paper No. 143, 1–22). https://citeseerx.ist.psu.edu/viewdoc/download?doi=10.1.1.156.7349&rep=rep1&type=pdf

Oulton, N., & Sebastiá-Barriel, M. (2013). *Long and short-term effects of the financial crisis on labour productivity, capital and output*. Bank of England.

Outreville, J. F. (1998). *Theory and practice of insurance*. Springer. https://doi.org/10.1007/978-1-4615-6187-3

Owusu-Ansah, E., Dontwi, I., Seidu, B., Abudulai, G., & Sebil, C. (2010). Technical efficiencies of Ghanaian general insurers. *American Journal of Social and Management Sciences*, *1*(1), 75–87. https://doi.org/10.5251/ajsms.2010.1.1.75.87

Pal, S., Bhattacharjee, K., & Pal, S. (2017). Forecasting performance of Indian non-life insurance industry – an analysis of underwriting experience of public and private insurance companies. *Asian Journal of Empirical Research*, 7(1), 10–18. https://doi.org/10.18488/journal.1007/2017.7.1/1007.1.10.18

Parida, T. K., & Acharya, D. (2017). Analysing the technical efficiency and productivity change of life insurance companies in India. In *The life insurance industry in India: Current state and efficiency* (pp. 33–72). Palgrave Macmillan imprint published by Springer Nature. https://doi.org/10.1007/978-981-10-2233-3_2

Pawirosumarto, S., & Iriani, D. (2018). The influence of work stress, working cost, compensation and work discipline on employee' productivity. *International Journal of Economics and Business Administration*, *6*(4), 62–75.

Porrini, D. (2014). The Italian motor insurance market: Will the recent interventions solve the old efficiency problems? *The Geneva Papers*, *39*, 545–568. https://doi.org/10.1057/gpp.2014.15

Pottier. (2011). Life insurer efficiency and state regulation: Evidence of optimal firm behavior. *Journal of Regulatory Economics*, *39*, 169–193. https://doi.org/10.1007/s11149-010-9139-7

Rahmani, I., Barati, B., Dalfard, V. M., & Hatami-Shirkouhi, L. (2014). Nonparametric frontier analysis models for efficiency evaluation in insurance industry: A case study of Iranian insurance market. *Neural Computing and Applications*, *24*, 1153–1161. https://doi.org/English

Rao, G. S. S. B., & Venkateswarlu, R. (2015). A study on efficiency and productivity of Indian non-life insurers using data envelopment analysis. *International Journal of Applied Operational Research*, *5*(3), 1–15.

Rao, P. H. (2016). Performance analysis of public sector general insurance companies Operating in India. *Pacific Business Review International*, *9*(5), 73–82.

Reyna, A. M., & Fuentes, H. J. (2018). A cost efficiency analysis of the insurance industry in Mexico. *Journal of Productivity Analysis*, *49*, 49–64. https://doi.org/10.1007/s11123-017-0521-7

Saad, N. M., & Idris, N. E. H. (2011). Efficiency of life insurance companies in Malaysia and Brunei: A comparative analysis. *International Journal of Humanities and Social Science*, *1*(3). 111–122.

Sauian, M. S., Kamarudin, N., & Rani, R. M. (2013). Labor productivity of services sector in Malaysia: Analysis using input-output approach. *Procedia Economics and Finance*, *7*, 35–41. https://doi.org/10.1016/S2212-5671(13)00215-3

Schlesinger, H. (2000). The theory of insurance demand. *Handbook of Insurance*, *22*, 131–151. https://doi.org/10.1007/978-94-010-0642-2_5

Segovia-Gonzalez, M. M., Contreras, I., & Mar-Molinero, C. (2009). A DEA analysis of risk, cost, and revenues in insurance. *Journal of the Operational Research Society*, *60*(11), 1483–1494.

Sherwood, M. K. (1999). Output of the property and casualty insurance industry. *The Canadian Journal of Economics/Revue Canadienne d'Economique*, *32*(2), 518–546. https://doi.org/10.2307/136434

Singh, M., & Rajpal, R. K. (2011). Efficiency analysis of the public sector general insurance companies: A comparative study of pre- and post-reform period. *The IUP Journal of Risk & Insurance*, *8*(4), 28–46.

Sinha, A. (2016b). Productivity growth assessment of public and private sector general insurance companies in India: A Malmquist index approach. *International Journal of Applied Management Sciences and Engineering*, *3*(2), 50–61. https://doi.org/10.4018/IJAMSE.2016070103

Sinha, A., & Khan, T. L. (2013). The roadmap of productivity and productivity changes of Indian non-life insurance companies: A study using bootstrapped malmquist model. *Prestige International Journal of Management & IT – Sanchayan*, *3*(2), 28–41.

Sinha, R. P. (2007a). Operating efficiency of life insurance companies: An assurance region model. *Artha Vijana*, *XLIX*(3–4), 305–320.

Sinha, R. P. (2007b). Premium income of Indian life insurance industry: A total factor productivity approach. *The IUP Journal of Financial Economics*, *V*(1), 61–69.

Sinha, R. P. (2013). Are Indian life insurance companies cost efficient? Some recent empirical evidence. *Prajnan*, *41*(3), 181–201.

Sinha, R. P. (2015). A dynamic DEA model for Indian life insurance companies. *Global Business Review*, *16*(2), 258–269. https://doi.org/10.1177/0972150914564418

Sinha, R. P. (2016a). Dynamic performance benchmarking of Indian general insurers. *Journal of Quantitative Economics, Springer, 15*(3), 543–564. https://doi.org/10.1007/s40953-016-0061-4

Sinha, R. P. (2017). Efficiency-solvency linkage of Indian general insurance companies: A robust non-parametric approach. *Eurasian Economic Review*, 7, 353–370. https://doi.org/10.1007/s40822-017-0080-2

Sinha, R. P. (2019a). Efficiency, productivity and returns to scale of Indian general insurance industry: Evidence based on panel data. *The Journal of Institute of Public Enterprise, 42*(2), 1–25.

Sinha, R. P. (2019b). Total factor productivity growth of Indian general insurance companies in the recent period: A bootstrapped approach. *Journal of Infrastructure Development, 11*(1–2), 59–80. https://doi.org/10.1177/0974930619872103

SNA. (2008). *System of national accounts*. https://unstats.un.org/unsd/nationalaccount/docs/sna2008.pdf

Spence, M., & Zeckhauser, R. (1971). Insurance, information, and individual action. *The American Economic Review, 61*(2), 380–387. www.jstor.org/stable/1817017

Suárez-Álvarez, E., Quiroga-García, R., Manzano-Pérez, I., & López-Mielgo, N. (2016). Efficiency and financial health in the European insurance market. *Journal of International Business and Economics, 4*(2), 29–40. https://doi.org/10.15640/jibe.v4n2a4

Sun, Z. (2020). Research on the factors affecting the total factor productivity of Chinese life insurance companies. *Archives of Business Research, 8*(1), 38–50. https://doi.org/10.14738/abr.81.7426

Taib, C. A., Ashraf, M. S., & Razimi, M. S. (2018). Productivity change in the efficiency of the insurance and takaful industry of Pakistan. *Academy of Accounting and Financial Studies Journal, 22*(Special Issue).

Toivanen, O. (1997). Economies of scale and scope in the Finnish non-life insurance industry. *Journal of Banking and Finance, 21*, 759–799.

Tone, K., & Sahoo, B. K. (2005). Evaluating cost efficiency and returns to scale in the Life Insurance Corporation of India using data envelopment analysis. *Socio-Economic Planning Sciences, 39*(4), 261–285. https://doi.org/10.1016/j.seps.2004.06.001

Trigo-Gamarra, L., & Growitsch, C. (2010). Comparing single- and multichannel distribution strategies in the German life insurance market: An analysis of cost and profit efficiency. *Schmalenbach Business Review, 62*, 401–417. https://doi.org/10.1007/BF03396813

Trufin, J., Albrecher, H., & Denuit, M. (2009). Impact of underwriting cycles on the solvency of an insurance company. *North American Actuarial Journal, 13*(3), 385–403. https://doi.org/10.1080/10920277.2009.10597564

Uddin, G. E., Oserei, K. M., Oladipo, O. E., & Ajayi, D. (2018). Industry competitiveness using firm-level data: A case study of the Nigerian insurance sector. In *Advances in Panel Data Analysis in Applied Economic Research* (pp. 473–492). Springer. https://doi.org/10.1007/978-3-319-70055-7_37

Vencappa, D., Fenn, P., & Diacon, S. (2013). Productivity growth in the European insurance industry: Evidence from life and non-life companies. *International Journal of the Economics of Business, 20*(2), 281–305. http://dx.doi.org/10.1080/13571516.2013.782979

Viverita, W. S., & Cabanda, E. (2016). Determinants of cost efficiency and productivity growth of the Indonesian insurance industry. *International Journal of Knowledge-Based Organizations, 6*(2), 70–82. https://doi.org/10.4018/IJKBO.2016040105

Vuorinen, I., Järvinen, R., & Lehtinen, U. (1998). Content and measurement of productivity in the service sector: A conceptual analysis with an illustrative case from the insurance business. *International Journal of Service Industry Management, 9*(4), 377–396. http://dx.doi.org/10.1108/09564239810228876

Wasseja, M. M., & Mwenda, S. N. (2015). Analysis of the efficiency of life assurance companies in Kenya using the DEA-model. *American Journal of Mathematics and Statistics*, *5*(2), 60–71. https://doi.org/10.5923/j.ajms.20150502.03

Weiss, M. A. (1990). Productivity growth and regulation of P/L insurance: 1980–1984. *The Journal of Productivity Analysis*, *2*, 15–38.

Weiss, M. A. (1991). International P/L insurance output, input, and productivity comparisons. *The Geneva Papers on Risk and Insurance Theory*, *16*(2), 179–200.

Weiss, M. A., & Choi, B. P. (2008). State regulation and the structure, conduct, efficiency and performance of US auto insurers. *Journal of Banking & Finance*, *32*(1), 134–156. https://doi.org/10.1016/j.jbankfin.2007.09.010

Wise, W. A. (2017). A survey of life insurance efficiency papers: Methods, pros & cons, trends. *Accounting*, *3*, 137–170. https://doi.org/10.5267/j.ac.2016.11.002

Wise, W. A. (2018). Life insurance company efficiency: Best method and proxies. *Insurance Markets and Companies*, *9*(1), 6–19. http://dx.doi.org/10.21511/ins.09(1).2018.02

Wolff, E. N. (1991). Productivity growth, capital intensity, and skill levels, in the U. S. Insurance industry, 1948–86. *The Geneva Papers on Risk and Insurance Theory*, *16*(59), 173–190.

Wu, H., & Zeng, X. (2011). Application of computer technology in efficiency analysis of China life insurance company. *Journal of Computers*, *6*(9), 1832–1841. https://doi.org/10.4304/jcp.6.9.1832-1841

Xie, X. (2010). Are publicly held firms less efficient? Evidence from the property liability insurance industry. *Journal of Banking and Finance*, *34*, 1549–1563. https://doi.org/10.1016/j.jbankfin.2010.01.007

Xie, X., Lu, W., Reising, J., & Stohs, M. H. (2011). Demutualisation, control and efficiency in the U.S. Life insurance industry. *The Geneva Papers*, *36*, 197–225. https://doi.org/10.1057/gpp.2011.6

Yaisawarng, S., Asavadachanukorn, P., & Yaisawarng, S. (2012). Efficiency and productivity in the Thai non-life insurance industry. *Journal of Productivity Analysis*, *41*(2), 291–306. https://doi.org/10.1007/s11123-012-0317-8

Yakob, R., Yusop, Z., Radam, A., & Ismail, N. (2014). Two-stage DEA method in identifying the Exogenous factors of insurers' risk and investment management efficiency. *Sains Malaysiana*, *43*(9), 1439–1450.

Yang, X., & Li, X. (2019). Evaluation research on optimization efficiency of human resource allocation in Marine insurance industry based on Malmquist index model. *Journal of Coastal Research, Special Issue, Selected Topics in Coastal Research: Engineering, Industry, Economy, and Sustainable Development (SUMMER 2019),94*(Special Issue), 677–681.

Zhang, Y. (2016). *Reinsurance counterparty analysis in life insurance industry: The impact on firm performance/mergers and acquisitions in global insurance industry* [Ph.D. Thesis]. The Temple University Graduate Board.

Zhengyin, W., Yan, W., & Yuna, M. (2020). Research on total factor productivity of Chinese and foreign life insurance industry analysis based on DEA and Malmquist model. *IETI Transactions on Social Sciences and Humanities*, *8*, 19–23. https://doi.org/10.6896/IETITSSH.202006_8.0003

Zhong, C., & Sun, W. J. (2011). Insurance intermediary and cost X-efficiency of China's insurance firms. *International Conference on Management and Service Science*, 1–4. https://doi.org/10.1109/ICMSS.2011.5998449

Zhu, J. (2019). *China's insurance companies' efficiency: An empirical study* [Ph.D. Thesis]. ISCTE University Institute of Lisbon.

5 Extended notes on the banking and insurance output measurement problem

5.1. Summarising the literature survey

The previous chapters have presented the key output specification approaches and output measures that have been employed in the banking and insurance literature. The fundamental aim of those chapters was to summarise and condense the voluminous works in a compact form and allow the readers access to major issues, strategies and challenges faced by output analysts in the present context. The literature survey method adopted in this work broadly corresponds to a systematic review. As highlighted in the literature, the postulates of an ideal output were presented in section 1.6 earlier. While the theory demands such rigorousness from the chosen output measures, data and empirical considerations result in divergence from such requirements. Literature on both banking and insurance has given rise to a rich set of measurements that reflect the innovation and labour work put in by analysts in bridging the gap between the theory of output measurement and its practice. The diversity of opinions and issues as presented earlier reflect the depth and breadth of the efforts made by economists and national income accountants in capturing the true economic contributions of the banking and insurance industries. Some key aspects require further commentary to summarise the seemingly most essential debates in output measurement literature on banking and insurance. The same are presented below.

5.2. Extended notes

Synthesising the concept and measure of outputs

The theory of output measurement[1] postulates certain prerequisites, as highlighted in section 1.6. However, the data availability and practical considerations result in modifications to the concept of output as postulated by the underlying theory. Yet the concept of output is critical and requires clarification before any empirical measurement is undertaken. Indeed "without a conceptual measure it is not clear what data should be collected and how they should be used to compute an output measure" (Hornstein & Prescott, 1991, p. 197). Despite

DOI: 10.4324/9781003149828-6

there being clear trends in the choice of output variables, one must be careful not to confuse popularity with validity (Eling & Luhnen, 2010). The concerns of Clark (1984, p. 54) that "no general consensus seems to have arisen regarding the appropriate definition" seems as accurate today as it was then. At the same time, one must not fall prey to the error of believing that the existence of a diversity of opinions is a reflection of a lack of agreement. A fine balance between these extreme views is necessary to make sense of the patterns and trends in the literature. Given the complexity of banking and insurance services, it is unrealistic to demand a single ideal concept and thus a single ideal measure of their outputs. Context, beliefs and data are required to choose the practically most feasible output measure in any performance analysis of the banking and insurance industries. Measurement is challenging in banking and insurance, particularly because observational data are used whose information content has to be extracted using theory rather than experimentation. There is no *a priori* control of the analyst on the behaviour of firms or industries under scrutiny. Quantitative movements in a potential output measure may emanate from multiple sources. Thus, deciding the efficacy of a particular measure for a given context has to be determined using the knowledge about the industry and the ability to make sense of the available data. These demands widen as the analysis becomes more aggregative.

Stock versus flow outputs

As examined earlier and corroborated by Tables 2.1 and 2.2, banking literature seems to have preferred the stock measures much more than the flow and ratio measures. In contrast, insurance literature has generally preferred the flow measures of output. The stock-flow dichotomy is a common theme in the banking and insurance literature. As discussed earlier, proponents of both the approaches exist, and the choice on this matter is primarily governed by the output specification approach chosen and the data availability. Another debate has been about using value or volume measures within the stock measures. Furthermore, within the value framework, there is a debate on whether to use constant or current price measures. Reconciliation of these debates suggests that, ideally, the literature would prefer flow measures for both banking and insurance analysis. Still, difficulties in locating optimal flow measures and the need to derive them from their stock counterparts have motivated the frequent use of stock measures.

Nominal versus real outputs

Do banks and insurers produce in real terms or nominal terms? This question has not been resolved yet. Factoring in that both nominal and real (volume and constant price) output measures have been frequently used, there seems to be no clear consensus on this. Some of the experts surveyed as a part of Chapter 7 held a strong view that deflation of banking and insurance output is against the nature of production in these industries. They argued that banks and insurers do not produce in real but nominal terms, and nominal considerations drive their decisions. Moreover, they argued that if deflation is undertaken for other empirical reasons, industry-specific deflators or output-specific price indexes should be employed.

Given that these are missing in the literature, they argue that leaving the data in nominal terms is the most plausible strategy.[2] Those in favour of deflation have argued that a generalised deflator is better than no deflation at all. They believe that economic theory demands the output be measured in real terms (ideally in volume terms). As quantity measures are not readily available in banking and insurance analysis, deflation with the most relevant price index is the best strategy. Among these proponents, a large majority argue for single deflation, while some have argued for double deflation. The trend in the literature surveyed in this work is evident. Single deflation is preferred over double deflation, though few studies have adopted the latter approach. Data availability in terms of the lack of industry-specific price indexes seems to be the primary determinant of the choices by analysts on this matter.

Single versus multiple outputs

As argued several times earlier in this study, banks and insurers are inherently multi-output firms. Literature has duly recognised this fact and has employed multiple measures in performance analysis – whether non-parametric (e.g. DEA-based production functions) or parametric (e.g. Stochastic Cost Frontiers). Using multiple outputs is the best strategy when analysing performance parameters such as efficiencies, productivity and others for banking and insurance firms. Modern statistical and econometric methods allow multiple outputs and inputs in production analysis. A sparsely used approach has been the index numbers measure of outputs. This may be understood in the context of the complexities involved in building output indexes for banking and insurance outputs and the data availability.

National income versus economic approaches

Economic and national income approaches to output measurement in banking and insurance have always been at odds in terms of their conceptual framework, methodology, data requirements and applicability in empirical analysis. Given that the national income approach is meant for systematising the aggregate picture of banking and insurance industries, there is considerable rigidity in this measurement approach. This is required to establish international comparability. Economic approaches, on the other hand, have been diverse and innovative. As comparability is not a concern, the economic approach to output specification has accommodated an extensive menu of choices. These alternatives have been developed to tackle different contexts and different performance issues. However, this diversity itself has led to a lack of any clear consensus and thus, synthesising the findings remains a difficult challenge. The present work has attempted to push forward the progress on this account by a small step.

Dual nature of output specification problem

An exciting aspect of the output specification problem and consequently the output measurement problem is that inputs and outputs must be defined interdependently. Banking and insurance outputs may be conceptualised as independent of inputs in purely theoretical terms. But their practical use requires establishing congruence between the chosen outputs and inputs. The output specification approaches discussed in Chapters 3 and 4 make this point abundantly clear. Literature has used these output specification approaches to choose the relevant output and related input measures. This also implies that the measurement of inputs needs to be theoretically consistent with the chosen specification approach. Otherwise, the estimating production, cost, revenue, profit or other functions will produce spurious and unreliable estimates. Input measurement issues are briefly highlighted in Chapter 10.

5.3. Background for further chapters

Given the narrative so far, it is now time to expand the scope of this work by providing opinions of selected experts on the central theme of this work. While a literature survey is necessary to summarise the extant wisdom, it is not a sufficient condition. Traditional literature reviews restrict themselves to analysing what has been done in the sample studies. Unlike the traditional approach, this work goes one step further to allow the readers to gain insights from the practitioner's point of view. Expert opinions can supplement and improve upon the issues analysed through the literature survey. It is instrumental in highlighting the debates and discussions at the frontier of a theme. With this motivation, the next part presents the contributions from carefully selected experts who were first interviewed through a semi-structured interview and were then requested to contribute their insights on the theme.

Notes

1 The theory of output measurement in economics is subsumed under the ambit of metrology, i.e. the science of measurement. See Link (2021) for a synthesis of metrology and economic measurement theory.

2 Prof. K. V. Bhanumurthy in particular held a strong view on similar lines. His contribution can be obtained from the author on request or may be included in the online resources.

References

Clark, J. A. (1984). Estimation of economies of scale in banking using a generalized functional form. *Journal of Money, Credit and Banking*, *16*(1), 53–68. https://doi.org/10.2307/1992648

Eling, M., & Luhnen, M. (2010). Efficiency in the international insurance industry: A cross-country comparison. *Journal of Banking & Finance, 34*, 1497–1509. https://doi.org/10.1016/j.jbankfin.2009.08.026

Hornstein, A., & Prescott, E. C. (1991). Measures of the insurance sector output. *The Geneva Papers on Risk and Insurance, 16*(59). www.jstor.com/stable/41952063

Link, A. N. (2021). *The economics and science of measurement: A study of metrology* (1st ed.). Routledge. https://doi.org/10.4324/9781003186953

Part II

Expert opinions and contributions

Emerging markets perspective

6 Method and rationale

6.1. Motivation and rationale

The fundamental objective of Chapters 6 and 7 is to supplement and elaborate on the issue of output measurement in banking and insurance from the practitioner's perspective. The valuable contributions made by the experts located and specifically interviewed for this study are contained in the next chapter. Instead of directly asking for contributions, as would be the case in a typical edited volume, the selected experts were first interviewed through a semi-structured questionnaire. The interviews were recorded, and the experts were then requested to submit their responses to the questionnaire. After that, each expert was requested to contribute a write-up on their insights and opinions on the theme under consideration. This draft contribution was then edited using the pre-recorded interview and response sheet. The final draft was then sent to the respective experts for their approval. The contributions received from the experts after their final approval have been presented below.[1] The chief motivation to undertake this exercise is to move beyond a review of historical evidence and present the state-of-the-art ideas and analysis directly from those engaged in these issues at both policy and academic levels.

6.2. Sampling strategy

The review of evidence undertaken in the previous chapters provided a set of analysts whose works have been regularly cited. It also allowed the author of this study to locate researchers who have been regularly contributing scholarly works on output measurement in banking and insurance performance analysis. While this method allowed locating possible contributors from academics, the policy angle also needed to be accounted for. Accordingly, using judgemental sampling, the author prepared a list of possible experts involved with banking and insurance-related regulators. This included professionals working in national income accounting, central banks across major countries, and other institutions. Both the advanced and emerging economies were targeted. The final set of potential contributors was then prepared, and each of them was contacted for this exercise. The response rate was not very high but, at the

DOI: 10.4324/9781003149828-8

same time, allowed bringing experts from diverse backgrounds on board. Once they agreed, semi-structured interviews were conducted online or offline, and the same was recorded. In the second stage, the same experts were requested to provide their responses to a detailed questionnaire which covered critical dimensions and issues on bank and insurance output measurement.[2] In the third stage, the experts were requested to contribute a draft write-up on the theme, and then edited using the pre-recorded interview and response sheet. The experts were requested to provide final comments and approval on the edited contributions in the last stage. While several potential experts were approached, the response rate was limited to around 50%.[3]

6.3. Notes for the next chapter

The next chapter presents the contributions made by each of the experts in the final sample. Each contribution is unique and covers different dimensions of the theme under consideration. There are insights on some frontier issues that can have important implications for the output measurement problem in banking and insurance literature. The narratives provided in the next chapter are a set of rich analyses by those in academics and policymaking. Each of these results from the selected expert's vast experience, subjective beliefs and wisdom. Each contribution is original and has not been published elsewhere in any form.[4]

Notes

1 It may again kindly be noted that the views expressed here are strictly personal and belong only to the expert under consideration. They are not representative of their professional opinion or the stance/opinion/beliefs of their current or any of the past institutions or employers. There is no conflict of interest of any manner.
2 The detailed methodological notes including the questionnaire used for this chapter may be made available in the online resources or can happily be availed directly from the author.
3 This was understandable given the nature of this exercise. The list of potential experts who were approached by the author and their response may be availed directly from the author on request.
4 The contact details of the experts have not been provided here. The same may be availed from the author of this book directly.

7 Expert perspectives on output measurement in banking and insurance

Barendra Kumar Bhoi

Brief Profile: Dr Barendra Kumar Bhoi is a career central banker and an economist. He served the Reserve Bank of India for more than three decades since 1984 and held several responsible positions, including Principal Adviser and Head of the Monetary Policy Department at RBI from 2014 to 2016. He also served as Visiting Fellow at IGIDR (2018–2020), Chief General Manager/ Head of the Research Department at SEBI (2005–2007) and an Economic Policy Expert at the Central Bank of Oman (2009–2012). Currently, he holds the position of RBI Chair Professor at Utkal University, Bhubaneswar, India.

Issues specific to the measurement of financial services in the system of national accounts 2008 in emerging economies

The SNA, 2008 is a foundational document for laying down the data compilation and aggregation procedures for macroeconomic accounts, and these are expected to be followed by the member countries of the United Nations (UN). This vital document recommends the principles that need to be followed for achieving a high degree of comparability of national income accounts data. Official national income accounts provide the most important estimates of the level and growth of economic activities and are critical for international macroeconomic policies and coordination. While the member countries of the UN put in a lot of effort to harmonize their statistical systems to suit the recommendations of the SNA, there is substantial inequality in the quality of data collection systems between the emerging and the developed economies. The reasons for this are well-debated in the literature. However, an essential dimension in this regard is the localized nature of data compilation by various countries. While advanced economies are in a position to implement the SNA procedures efficiently, the local differences across EMEs are far more expansive and quite heterogeneous. With tight fiscal space and relatively higher priority for welfare programmes, the financial resources for statistical system improvements take a secondary role in emerging economies. However, this also results in divergences in the institutional arrangements adopted by various EMEs for

DOI: 10.4324/9781003149828-9

data collection systems depending on their domestic budgets. Institutional arrangements for official statistical systems also differ due to considerable differences in the structures of these economies. This is all the more true for the financial services industry across the EMEs as the nature of financial intermediation[1] differs widely across these countries, unlike the advanced economies, which have experienced a more sizeable extent of financial globalization and harmonization of their data collection practices. Despite these facts, the SNA does allow for at least partial comparability for macroeconomic accounts of the EMEs. However, this is achieved only partially, and the above-raised factors remain areas requiring further improvements.

Difficulties in generating current price and constant price estimates of services output through the value-added method, including the issue of double deflation

It is well-recognized that there are three major methods for estimating GDP. They are the income method, the expenditure method and the value-added method. Theoretically sound estimates of industry-level output require reliance on the value-added method, which demands suitable data collection systems. Financial markets are more complicated than the real sector due to the intangibility of what they produce and the existence of indirect intermediation services. These services are not directly observable and are implicit in the activities undertaken by financial intermediaries, particularly in the case of banks and insurance firms. While the banking intermediation services are broadly proxied by the FISIM methodology, other intermediaries such as insurance firms remain only partially measured. Along with indirect services implicit in their operations, such services are non-marketable and require non-traditional pricing procedures. Traditionally, the observed market prices are the preferred measures for estimating current price values of output, aggregation across product segments within an industry and deflating the current price values. However, generally, banking and insurance prices cannot be ascertained simply from their observed prices in the financial markets. This is because observed prices represent the directly observable services provided by the intermediaries, while implicit services are also not accounted for by these observed prices. The FISIM approach is the best procedure that we have today, and yet it too fulfils its aims only in a limited case of the EMEs Brazil, India, Russia, Saudi Arabia, Turkey, Argentina, etc. These economies do not possess the depth and maturity of financial markets observed in advanced economies.

Consequently, deriving the implicit prices through explicitly observed data becomes a challenge for policymakers. FISIM also relies heavily on the quality of financial markets data, and that also remains a grey area for the largest of the emerging economies, particularly for the so-called BRIICS countries. Thus, the sum of value-added across all banking and insurance industries does not represent its total output under the value-added approach, as the indirect component of their total output remains unaccounted for.

Along with these issues, another critical dimension is deriving constant price estimates of banking and insurance outputs in emerging countries. Advanced economies utilize double deflators, while the developing economies still rely on single deflators. Microeconomic theory suggests that the demand and supply functions of the factor markets and product markets emerge in different ways, and hence the price behaviour of these two markets is subject to different factors. This is particularly important in the case of the determinants of inflation in factor markets versus the same in the product markets. Prices of one sector are not representative of another sector in this case due to different economic structures of both markets, different levels of development of these markets and differences in the institutional arrangements that govern the behaviour of these two markets, among others. Moreover, developing economies rely considerably on filling the gaps and insufficiencies in their official administrative data through surveys. This approach is only helpful if the surveys are undertaken in a statistically ideal sense, which is difficult to follow practically on the ground when data collectors interact with the sample respondents. Surveys are only a way of making up for the insufficiency of administrative data. They cannot substitute a matured administrative data collection system.

With a lack of sufficient statistical infrastructure to take care of the data needs for adopting the double deflation method of financial services inputs and outputs data, which is what is recommended by the SNA, 2008, emerging economies rely on the single deflation method and employ similar price indexes for both inputs and outputs data. This distorts the representativeness of the prices for estimating current price data and makes the constant price outputs and inputs data of financial services challenging to interpret meaningfully. Both the current price and constant price data are affected by using a single deflation method. This is because the countries that do not have mutually independent price indexes for inputs and outputs generally rely on the single deflation procedure. Consequently, both the current price and constant price data depend on market price indexes, which are the same for inputs and outputs for economies that rely on single deflation procedures. Estimates of financial services data, such as the amount of bank credit disbursed by the banking system, amount of premium underwritten by insurers, the value of assets owned by the banking and insurance firms and others, are critical in the estimation of the performance of the financial services. These data require deflation to be economically meaningful. The direction and quantitative extent of deflation effects will linearly affect both inputs and outputs with a single deflation approach. In reality, however, this effect should be different for inputs and outputs of the financial services industry. This is problematic because the changes in constant price estimates will be distorted across time and space to the extent that the inflation rates of inputs and outputs of financial services differ. Over time, this will particularly get blown up, resulting in incorrect policy inferences from performance indicators of financial services that use both input and output variables.

Theory and measurement of financial services output versus other services

Financial services, particularly the banking and insurance industries, present problems of output measurement that are unique to them compared to other services. There are both advantages and limitations in the output measurement of these industries. Due to their complexity on account of direct and indirect intermediation services, considerable methodological developments have occurred on their measurement issues. A well-defined FISIM approach exists for estimating the intermediation component of banking services. A similar procedure does not quite exist for other financial services, including insurance. In the case of non-banking financial services, imputations are used where needed in order to capture their non-marketable output, which is not as rigorous as that of the FISIM approach. The SNA, 2008 recognizes the indirect component of banking services and recommends the FISIM approach. However, sample estimates are blown up for other financial services to account for their non-marketable outputs. This approach is the only route for emerging countries that do not have a mature enough statistical system to handle the financial system's data complexities. For other countries such as China and Saudi Arabia, where the Government has a tight hold on the official statistics, undertaking a census may be feasible, but their data collection practices are generally not transparent to the international community.

Banks produce both marketable and non-marketable outputs. The marketable portion of their total output is well-captured by their accounting data and observed prices, such as their fees for various services and interest rates on loans and advances. However, the non-marketable portion of the output cannot be ascertained from their accounting data and thus requires external sources of information for computation through indirect methods. FISIM remains the gold standard for the measurement of this indirect component. In reality, though, the countries differ vastly in their abilities to execute the official data collection principles required for FISIM estimation. This results in a large degree of divergence in the underlying methods and data used to estimate the FISIM components across various emerging economies, making sound international comparisons difficult. Even if an international comparison is overlooked, the inability of a country to capture the true output of its banking sector can distort its understanding of the finance-growth nexus and can probably result in incorrect policy inferences so far as the growth-improving capacity of the banking sector is concerned. Despite these aspects, banks' accounting and financial data to their respective regulators in emerging nations is much more reliable than the data reported by other entities. This is mainly because of strict regulation of the banking sector in these economies. Almost every country in the category of EMEs has a central bank, and collecting and reporting data from the banking system is an essential function. The real issue arises when the estimation of the indirect services of banks is concerned, and it is here that the depth and maturity of the official statistical systems play a determining role. National income accountants handle such indirect estimations and thus largely fall outside the purview of the central banks. This may explain emerging economies having a mature central banking system but a less developed national income accounting system.

Insurance output measurement also poses unique problems for national income accountants in emerging nations. An essential element of insurance is the spreading of risk through the pooling of the same. Life insurance firms also provide investment management services, which are well-recognized by the SNA, 2008. However, countries collect data based on their local realities and practical problems, which often do not quite correspond to the actual requirements of the SNA manual. One of these aspects is the issue of treating returns versus claims as to the actual output of the insurance industry. While the SNA manual recommends measuring output through data on premiums collocated by insurance firms while adjusting the same for their technical reserves and investment services, an alternative approach can be treating the claims settled by the insurers as their true output. Both the premiums collected and the claims settled may also be employed as measures of output, but such approaches require additional official data, and this can be a problem area for emerging countries with constrained fiscal space. Compared to banking, insurers do not undertake any indirect intermediation service per se. However, they are intermediate as risk aggregators and thus help achieve a better distribution of risk that otherwise would not have been possible if these entities were absent in the economy. Such aspects are well-recognized by the SNA manual, but again, the maturity of a nation's official statistical system is the determining factor.

An essential feature of the insurance markets in emerging economies is their low penetration and density relative to banking services. This gap in the spread of insurance and banking services is a constraint on achieving the aim of financial inclusion, which is a prerequisite to ending the problem of poverty in emerging and developing nations. Both banking and insurance interact with each other and across other financial services to create an economic environment conducive to eliminating poverty, which is the very first Sustainable Development Goal (SDG) among the seventeen goals currently laid down by the United Nations. Inclusive growth is the need of the hour for many emerging economies marred by the severe rural-urban divide. Moreover, emerging markets display downwards rigidity of insurance premiums, which explains the observed low levels of its penetration. Nonlife insurance is particularly at a disadvantage because there is no investment component in these insurance products. The price elasticity of demand is exceptionally high for nonlife insurance products due to the lack of an investment component over and above risk coverage offered by most life insurance products.

The great financial recession and key performance issues of the banking sector of the emerging economies

The financial recession of 2007–08 disrupted advanced economies so that its aftereffects continue to ripple even today. The emerging economies displayed considerable immunity to the same, though they had faced a series of recessions and recessionary tendencies due to their business cycles and the world economic slowdown that began much before the COVID-19 pandemic emerged. The financial recession increased risk-aversion among banks across major developed and emerging economies. The regulatory requirements of capital adequacy, liquidity, and others have become tighter in China, India, Russia, and Brazil. Banks in the EMEs are further burdened with large NPAs that drain the productive financial resources of these firms, thereby constraining their growth and, via the finance-growth nexus, also slowing down the aggregate economic growth rate and coupled with the world economy and trade slowdown, the banking industry in the economies mentioned earlier. Hence, three chief sources of weakening performance of the banking sector may be pointed out: first, the regulatory stringency post-crisis on banking entities across their assets and liabilities management; second, the slowdown in the world economy roughly occurring in the mid-2010s; and third, the increasing burden of NPAs on their balance sheets. These issues are all the more worrying when one observes the Non-Performing Loans Ratio (NPLR) of some major emerging economies such as Russia and India. Furthermore, having a lower NPLR does not in itself imply that the banking sector is safe and healthy. Large write-offs by the banks through restructuring by the Governments are also a matter of concern in countries like China and India, which are heavily dependent on the public sector banks.

Structural changes in the composition of banking business from intermediation services to fund-based services and their implications for the importance of the FISIM approach

Traditionally, banking has been associated with financial intermediation. The FISIM approach attempts to translate the intermediation services within the national income accounting framework. However, modern banking is increasingly shifting its income base from indirect to fee-based services. Many of these services are explicitly charged by banks. Such a trend may result from the net interest margin (NIM) tendency to be on the lower end for many banks in EMEs. Low NIM is a significant constraint for any bank as it squeezes its willingness to transform deposits into credit and may result in lower profitability and possibly even weaker monitoring and selection norms for loan applications. Such factors are generally the ones that sow the seeds of the financial crisis. Banks' services across both emerging and advanced economies have diversified considerably in the last decade. Financial innovations have been a vital source of this development. The diversity of fee-based services has expanded enormously, and so has its volume in the past decade. This begs the question of whether there has been a change in the composition of the output of commercial banks in terms of the shares of fee-based and intermediation services. General macroeconomic observations do suggest that this has been the case. Fund-based services have seen a large increase with the increasing spread of universal banking in emerging economies that are generally more dependent on bank-based financial system designs than capital market-dependent designs. With such developments, output measurement that emerges from fee-based services also needs an overhaul to account for the larger share of these services in the income sources of banks. Traditional intermediation services continue to be the most crucial output generated by the banking system, but the existing national income accounting conventions in emerging nations need to adopt methodological changes to suit the proper measurement of fee-based services. A lower real rate of NIM could be considered a factor that may explain the shift in the financial dependency of banks from intermediation to fee-based services. Stringency in the regulation of the credit creation process is also a possible factor in this regard. Further research is required to understand how the banking systems in emerging economies adopt such changes and their implications for the conventional SNA, 2008-based recommendations.

Further measurement issues in the output of the banking sector

The capital formation process in emerging economies is primarily driven by the funds supplied by the banking system. Capital markets are not matured or deep enough to meet the financial needs of the entire economic system. Bank-based financial systems are thus much more sensitive to the problems of output measurement. One can theorize three different kinds of outputs as shown in Figure 7.1.

While the above discussion points out a few aspects of the measurement of non-fee and fee-based output of banks, the non-fee and non-intermediary services also need to be accounted for in the macroeconomic estimates of banking output. Consider, for example, the yield curve produced or discovered by the banking system. It plays a pivotal role in monetary policy formulation and efficiently enables capital markets to allocate financial resources. Such services are like positive externalities and thus result in underestimation of the true output produced by the banking system. While well-developed pricing procedures impute such output for public goods, even banking services need to

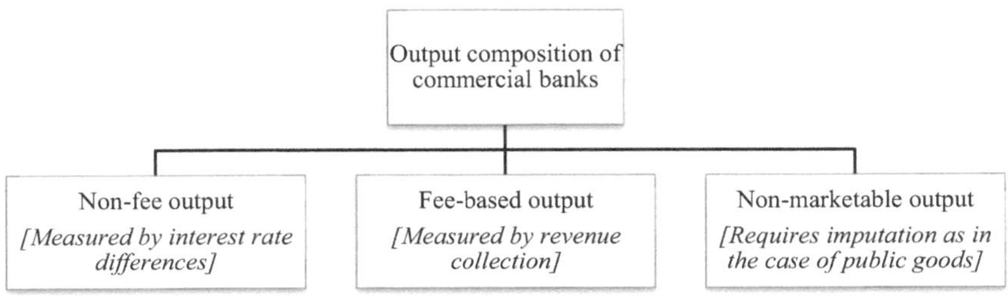

Figure 7.1 Composition of commercial bank output

Source: Analysis of the contributing expert.

be recognized as suppliers of positive externalities. Such inclusions will most probably increase the value of nominal output produced by the banks.

Similarly, the non-marketable output contributed by the central banks in terms of the regulatory and supervisory services rendered for the financial system needs more rigorous accounting procedures. While the central banks are treated separately from commercial banks, the overall output of the banking sector must include that of the central bank, as it is a critical component of the banking industry. To undertake this inclusion, possibly the user-cost approach is the best. However, emerging and developing nations are marred by constraints on the statistical system. Such computation methods demand highly disaggregated data that is observed rather than imputed. Financial sector data in developing nations, even in large and fast-growing countries such as China, India, Brazil, etc., are not collected at the degree and depth of disaggregation required for such computations. Very rigorous input-output tables at very high degrees of industrial disaggregation are required to ascertain various externalities associated with the banking sector. Input-output tables are generally more biased towards industries producing tangible outputs, especially in developing economies. Such issues need to be addressed by the policymakers on a war footing.

Some issues in the input-output debate in banking output measurement

The physical distinction between inputs and outputs is critical for empirical work on production analysis, including estimating total factor productivity. Unless this is undertaken, empirically estimating a production function for any economic output will be difficult.

In banking services, this distinction is largely blurred due to multi-stage production undertaken by banks wherein deposits, for example, maybe considered as output in one case and inputs in another. Because banks rely on financial inputs much more than physical inputs, it is tricky to measure inputs. The lack of optimal banking price indices further accentuates the problem of input measurement, as deflation of financial inputs is necessary before estimating the

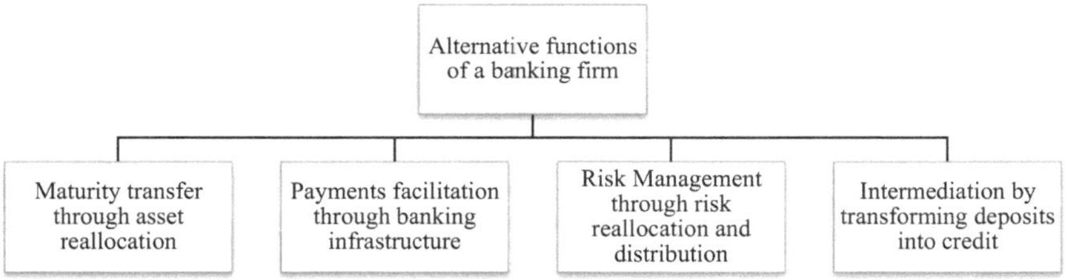

Figure 7.2 Key functions of commercial banking firms

Source: Analysis of the contributing expert.

production functions of banking output. However, this problem is dodged by the developing economies through the use of proxies, which are generally inefficient in representing the actual inflation rate of banking services. Most of such proxy deflators are price indices for other service industries or general wholesale or consumer price indices. The construction of an optimal and efficient banking price index is a critical challenge for emerging economies, and the performance of even the larger ones among them has been unsatisfactory. Even an aggregate financial services deflator could do more justice than proxy measures from non-financial services if not a banking price index.

Despite such issues, Total Factor Productivity (TFP) is estimated for the banking industries of emerging economies. Such studies generally define inputs from the deposit side and output from the credit side. However, it is only an operational approach, and like any other empirical adjustment, it is highly imperfect. One reason that may be immediately cited for this is that input requirements in a physical sense are always lesser for financial services due to their higher dependency on financial inputs in digitalization. Banking firms can serve a larger market with lower fixed costs than manufacturing and agricultural firms. This implies that traditional neoclassical production functions with labour and capital as inputs might overestimate the TFP. Hence, deflation of nominal financial inputs before their use in a production function of banking output is critical. If this deflation procedure is incorrect, one can end up with biased estimates of TFP even after accounting for financial inputs because the deflator is not optimal. This same dimension of optimal deflation is equally applicable to the measurement of the real output of the banking industry.

Debashis Acharya

Brief Profile: Debashis Acharya is currently a Professor in the School of Economics, University of Hyderabad, India. Prior to joining UoH, he taught at IIT Madras, IIT Hyderabad, mentored by IIT Madras and Panjab University, Chandigarh. He was also a UGC Visiting fellow at the Gokhale Institute of Politics and economics. His research interests are macro-monetary economics, financial economics, and inclusive finance. Some of his recent publications include Financial inclusion across major Indian states with spatial panel econometric evidence, the role of inflation targeting in the context of monetary policy and financial stability, the credibility of inflation targeting in Asian countries, near-stock properties of Bitcoin, and the future of crypto in *India in International Journal of Social Economics, Australian Economic Review, Economic Change and Restructuring, International Journal of Managerial Finance* and *EMERiCs, KIEP*. He has published about 50 papers in refereed national and international journals, including *European Journal of Operational Research, Journal of Economic Studies, Economic Change and Restructuring, Journal of Financial Economic and Policy, Indian Economic Journal, Economic and Political Weekly, Journal of Quantitative Economics* to name a few. Debashis has completed the macro research award project on financial inclusion funded by the Indian Institute of Banking and Finance. A few other sponsored research projects completed by Debashis are funded by ICSSR, UGC, DFID, UK, SICI, Calgary, and IMTFI, University of California, Irvine.

Output measurement in banking services

Banks produce a complex bundle of services that cannot be neatly divided into inputs and outputs. Depending on the perspective from which one approaches a particular service, one may consider it an input or an output. An input-output distinction is dynamic in banking, and this is both a strength and a challenge for analysts interested in measuring the output of banking services. Distinguishing inputs from outputs is necessary to establish the theoretical foundations for production analysis. Given that neoclassical theorizing essentially informs production analysis in current literature, the production frontier approach plays a dominant role in the performance[2] analysis of the banking industry. Studies focusing on technical efficiency, TFP, and other aspects of banking performance require theoretically sound measures of inputs and outputs. Irrespective of whether the theorized production frontier is parametric or non-parametric, separating observed banking services into inputs and outputs is necessary. Neoclassical production theory seems to display a broad consensus on the inputs that must be included in the production analysis. Labour and Capital are the two significant inputs on this account. As far as banking firms and industry are concerned, this should generally not be a problem for a researcher.

However, the major challenge is identifying the correct measure of output, and the mainstream pure theory of production does not directly indicate the banking firms specifically. Experience, literature, wisdom, and theoretical debates need to be carefully synthesized to identify an observed variable as an output in the case of banking services. While the pro-intermediation analysts suggest that deposits must be considered an input and credit as an output, the production approach analysts would prefer to identify both deposits and credit as outputs at different stages in the banking supply chain. Performance estimates can differ radically when output is measured from these alternative angles. Establishing the robustness of performance estimates to alternative output measures is necessary to obtain economically valid inferences about how the banks and insurance firms have performed and what policy interventions might be necessary to improve the same.

A concept that plays a fundamental role in macroeconomic research on banking and insurance performance analysis is that of value-added. This measure is derived from firm-level data and the various estimates arrived at by the official data generating agencies in a country. Generally, value-added is used for industry- and aggregate-level analysis rather than firm-level analysis. Locating the value-added for manufacturing and even agriculture is a well-researched issue, and there are many schools of thought and perspectives on this account. However, value-added accounting is quite challenging for the financial service industry, particularly for banking. The foremost reason might be that the supply chain in banking is interlaced across different verticals and horizontals and thus does not allow a clean division of the production process into various stages. This also implies that the separability conditions required for justifying aggregate output measures in an inherently multi-output industry are difficult to establish in the case of banking services.[3] Locating value-added and thus measuring output at the industry level is an identification problem. This problem has been there since a long time, and disagreement remains even to date on the optimal method to undertake it with regards to the financial intermediation services, such as banking and insurance.

The EMEs under consideration in this book have all had a broadly similar evolutionary path as far as their banking and insurance industries are concerned. These economies have been transforming from a predominantly public sector-dominated industries to increasingly market-oriented private entities-driven industries. This may be considered a rough stylized fact about these economies. To this day, the public sector dominates the scene; the determination of output is straightforward and could be explained by government policies and the behaviour of the central banks. From a structural perspective, the parameters required to estimate an output function could broadly be specified by studying the policy movements. As these economies began shifting to market-oriented competition and private ownership of banking and insurance firms, the number of parameters required to estimate the output of these industries has increased sizeably. One can no more regard the output of banks and insurers as majorly driven by the government and Central Bank's will. An extensive set of factors affect the demand and supply sides of the industrial output function, and accounting for them has become a serious challenge more than any time in the past. The output level and volatility of banking and insurance industries have increased due to the move toward privatization and market competition. The number of parameters required to specify a realistic output determination function is more prominent than ever before due to multiple determinants of both the level and volatility of the outputs in these industries.

Lastly, one must bear in cognizance that at higher levels of aggregation, the choices available for measuring outputs in the banking and insurance industries reduce to a manageable level. However, many candidates at the microeconomic level are considered outputs and even inputs. This is due to the sheer complexity and richness of activities performed by banks and insurers. For example, each fee-based service offered by a bank may be analysed as an output that the bank produces using a set of inputs. In this manner, one may locate many output variables. However, their relative importance in the aggregate production function reduces. One is left with some special measures such as the amount of deposits, amount of loans and advances and the total net worth of the firms. These observations can be corroborated by the diversity of output and even input variables employed for firm-level studies as against for industry-level studies in the present context. Corresponding to these issues is the construction of an optimal price deflator for banking and insurance outputs. Deflation continues to be a serious limitation of both disaggregate and particularly aggregate level studies. One may refer to Barman and Samanta (2004) for a brief crux of this matter in the banking context.

Some issues with aggregation and aggregation functions in the current context

Aggregating individual quantities, amounts, and entities is necessary for microeconomic and macroeconomic analyses. In the study by Acharya and Kamaiah (2001), I reflect on this point in detail. From the standpoint of microeconomic theory, demand functions faced by individual banks may need aggregation to derive a market demand function. From the macroeconomic point of view, the amount of loans disbursed across all the commercial banking firms may be aggregated to study the impact of monetary policy rates on credit flow. In either case, aggregation across individual units is required, and hence the nature of the aggregation function employed for this task must be clearly specified. Another critical dimension is the so-called hermeneutic aggregation problem (Schlicht, 1985).

Simply put, an output variable that, for example, represents the total amount of deposits across all the banking firms in the entire economy must necessarily have a microeconomic foundation. Such a variable must have been derived from the underlying deposit-collecting behaviour of individual banks. If that is not the case, then possibly such macroeconomic measures might be mere figments of our imagination rather than sound economic measurements (Menger, 1985).

Three issues deserve special attention in the current narrative. First, economic aggregation theory has to be utilized to decide the correct method for aggregation, i.e., the correct form of the aggregation function. Aggregation functions in output measurement for banking and insurance firms inevitably take the form of multiple functions that need to be themselves simultaneously aggregated.[4] Second, the method of estimating the chosen aggregation function must be carefully decided. There are generally two methods used in the literature on the present theme – parametric and non-parametric. Parametric methods require pre-defined aggregation factors to undertake aggregation across the inputs and outputs. An advantage of this method is its ability to measure aggregate input and output for performance analysis, such as required in residual Total Factor Productivity analysis. Non-parametric methods (such as Data Envelopment Analysis) can handle multiple inputs and outputs to estimate performance measures (such as technical efficiency) but cannot yield a direct measure of aggregate input and aggregate output, as is the case in the parametric case. However, one can derive non-parametric aggregation factors by using additional information related to the inputs and outputs of banks and insurance firms. For example, the ratio of individual input cost to total cost may be used to aggregate the individual inputs into aggregate input. The aggregation factor, in this case, is the ratio of the cost of individual input to the total cost and fulfils Menger's qualification above. Third, there will always be multiple choices in choosing the optimal aggregation factor – i.e., the weightage factor shall allow summation or multiplication of the individual outputs into a single output. There is no consensus on how to decide the optimal factor for aggregation in the case of output measurement in the banking and insurance industries. Using different methodologies, one may use non-parametric measures or derive many parametric aggregation factors. Output elasticities of inputs are one possible alternative in this regard, and they can be arrived at using deterministic or stochastic frontier techniques. However, in the case of parametric methods, the analyst has some amount of control over the aggregation factors. This may be considered an advantage or a possible source of bias, depending on one's perspective.

Some frontier issues in output measurement theory and practice

Here I would like to put forward some aspects pertaining to the debate at the frontier of output measurement theory and practice in a general context, rather than focusing specifically on the EMEs.

Imputed quantities and amounts are necessary for making the macroeconomic accounting measures of output theoretically consistent. Sectoral estimates of Gross Value Added (GVA) and Gross Domestic Product (GDP) for the financial services industry are frequently used by macro analysts interested in performance analysis at the industry or sectoral levels. Regarding the banking industry, there are services whose value cannot be explicitly determined by the financial statement data of banks. The intermediation services[5] that the banking system undertakes occupy a sizeable portion of the value added by the banks. However, this is not an explicit output within the production function of a typical bank and instead emerges from the inter-linkages and cross-interactions among all the banks. It is inherently an aggregate measure and thus cannot be explicitly explained via microeconomic production functions and frontiers. This issue is handled with the help of the so-called FISIM approach (Financial Intermediation Services Indirectly Measured), whose derivation is well-narrated in the literature. The basic idea underlying FISIM is that when the behaviour of individual banking firms is aggregated, their interrelationships produce additional value-added, which cannot be ascertained simply through an aggregation of their financial statements data. As noted above, the intermediation[6] between lenders and savers through mutually beneficial contracts is facilitated by the banking[7] firms. This requires measurement at the industry level by accounting for the interactions among the banks and looking at the banks as a system of firms working in cooperation to channelize scarce loanable funds rather than looking at them as individual profit-maximizing agents. Debates have primarily been undertaken on the choice of the reference rate in the estimation of the FISIM. Traditionally, a pure interest rate serves as the reference rate on this account. Locating such an interest rate is a challenge, and the most frequently employed measure is a typical risk-free interest rate such as the yield on Government bonds. However an alternative is to utilize the user cost approach, but the data requirements are even stricter in this case. Given these aspects, the user-cost approach[8] seems unsuitable for the EMEs, and the FISIM method, no matter its limitations, seems to be the best available bet in capturing the intermediation services of banks.

The emergence of Big Data is a well-known phenomenon, and the same is being slowly utilized for performance analysis in banks at the firm level. Large multi-national corporate banks are the ones who have initiated the inclusion of Big Data analytics in business decision making.[9] Another kind of data analytics that is emerging is that of thick data, "where the emphasis is not in the quantity of information but on depth and richness of insights" (Strömmer, 2019). Such emerging technologies that can be utilized for consumer behaviour analysis are banking and insurance. Notably, estimating demand functions for different outputs might become a little easier with more extensive (Big Data) and deeper (thick data) information on people's banking behaviour. Whether big or thick data, these are information in the end, and economic theory will be required to make sense of them. However, the existing data environment has considerable scope to improve and include information from such emerging technologies.[10] This might help further bridge the gap between what information the theory of output measurement demands and the knowledge that the existing data ecosystem can provide.

Edoardo Pizzoli

Brief Profile: Dr Edoardo Pizzoli is a research fellow at the University of Luxembourg, Germany, and is also working as a professional statistician at the Italian National Institute of Statistics, Italy. He has a long hands-on experience with the national income accounting process, particularly with structural statistics and has been dealing with disaggregated data across different industries in Italy.

This work on output measurement of banking and insurance activities is a welcome contribution to the existing discourse. I appreciate this opportunity to provide some notes on this theme. The discussion below is based on my experience as both a professional statistician dealing with national income accounts in Italy and my academic exposure to the University of Luxembourg and other institutions that I had the opportunity to work with. The views expressed are strictly mine and are based on my interview and discussions conducted by the author. This contribution has no association with the views of any of my past or current institutions and is purely personal.

Satellite accounts, financial services and the use of SNA in emerging economies

In terms of the National Income and Product Accounts (NIPA), emerging economies are converging to the standards of data assimilation as laid down by the SNA, 2008. Ample scope for improvement exists, but the upgrades required differ across different industries. Specific sectors such as the manufacturing sector are reasonably well-approximated by the existing data collection systems in nations such as Russia, Brazil, and others. However, significant problems arise in front of the service industry, specifically financial intermediation services. Unlike traditional services, intermediation services are not only intangible but are also difficult to track across space and time. This is mainly due to the indirect services rendered by these firms, especially the banking firms. Such services require imputation, which is one of the challenges for emerging economies. Imputation occurs primarily through existing data sources. Available information is used to produce estimates of what cannot be clearly tracked and directly observed in the economy. However, the SNA is too aggregated. While they account for the indirect intermediation services through the FISIM approach, additional data sets can help produce more disaggregated measures of the indirect intermediation services of the banking industry. Satellite accounts are a valuable means to overcome some of the constraints indicated above.[11] Achieving a healthy amount of disaggregation in banking and insurance industries will probably allow researchers to interpolate sub-industry and even firm-level FISIM estimates. While the FISIM determination is essentially an aggregate procedure, its disaggregated measures can add more dimensions to the micro-level economic analysis of banking output measurement.

Output of banks and some comments on its economic aspects

Financial services are functional to the very process of production in capitalistic organizations, i.e., organizations that work under decentralized private ownership of resources. Compared to the service industries such as education or tourism, financial services produce direct observable gains for services and non-service industries. In terms of economic theory, one may always argue that all economic activities produce externalities in some way or another; here, the direct observable effects are being focused upon. Banking services, for example, are part and parcel of all the industries that require funds. Thus, the value-addition[12] of the banking industry is not limited to itself or some pre-selected set of industries. Typical input-output analysis is also not helpful mainly because such disaggregated input-output tables are not available[13] as the value addition of banks may be inherent to the output of other industries and thus may not be directly observable. The FISIM approach roughly captures such an unobservable portion of their value-addition. However, measuring the directly observable value-addition by the banking and insurance firms is also a challenge due to the immense diversity in the use of these services. Banking, in particular, presents a stricter challenge due to the higher penetration of banking services in the EMEs than insurance penetration. This implies higher interconnections of the banking industry with other industries and thus a more complex web of value-chains that need to be delineated for estimating the final value-added by the banking industry. The use of financial statements of the banking firms is the most frequently used approach in determining their output. However, as suggested above, there are many intricate interconnections of banking activities with other industries, making it challenging to trace all the value-additions produced for different sectors. The output of non-banking industries might be overstated due to the value-added by the banking services in those industries. Such measurement issues require imputation, and even the FISIM estimation will be insufficient as it focuses only on the indirect intermediation services rather than the direct services embodied in the outputs of other industries that directly utilize banking services.

Keeping aside the empirical issues in measuring banking output, it is necessary to conceptualize what banks supply in a typical emerging economy. Smooth circulation of value[14] is a prerequisite for a healthy real sector of an economy. The networks of banks, their technological sophistication, the spread of core banking services, the depth of the financial markets and many such dimensions will determine how well the goods and services that represent the value produced in the economy circulate throughout the economy. Banks play a pivotal role in enabling this value circulation and thus allow the real sector can establish fast, efficient and stable interconnections that otherwise would be difficult to achieve. Similarly, banks play a critical role in physical and financial capital accumulation. Emerging economies generally display a higher debt-to-equity ratio, particularly for the firms in the unorganized sector of the economy. With more extensive dependence on banks for funds rather than on capital markets, the nature of the credit distribution by banks across the different industries will have a long-term impact on the structure of the economy and its growth path. Banks allow funds-scare firms to borrow money and enable them to expand their current output and invest in improving physical capital to increase future production. On similar lines, banks also provide investment opportunities to savers, thus enabling them to shift their future consumption to higher levels through financial accumulation.[15] The banking industry is an essential element in the growth story of the emerging economies that are slowly catching up with the advanced economies. They are also a solid policy tool to improve the growth process in these economies.

Notes on some allied issues

I would now like to point out some caveats and concerns for output measurement analysts and the larger audience. These are based on my experience as a professional statistician working on national income accounting as well as an academic.

One aspect that must be appreciated is that the banking industry is undergoing a tremendous transformation in terms of technological sophistication. It may not be incorrect to suggest that the banking industry will be primarily digitalised in the next decade, with physical infrastructure playing only a secondary role. In the economic sense, Output must somehow capture the value generated by the production process for its consumers. While consumer valuation is subjective, as established by the marginalist school in economics, performance analysts and national income accountants cannot fulfil their work under such a belief. An estimate of what has been produced is needed to inform the policy interventions designed to promote growth and development in fast-growing economies such as the EMEs. This task will become more complicated as the value chain shifts towards digital channels. Digitalization is not a problem for output measurement analysts at the firm and industry levels. The changes that this process brings in the value production by banks require more research and much more debate in the academic literature. Will it be feasible to specify the production function of the banking industry with physical capital as a determinant at all? What kind of technology will represent this sector's residual total factor productivity in the coming decade? Will labour, as traditionally defined, play a sizeable role as an input in the production process of this industry? How will the output be defined if banks enter an era of super-specialization due to ever-expanding market segmentation? Several such questions arise, and the output analyst will need to embrace these dimensions of banking output while expanding the scope of what is considered inputs and outputs in the banking industry of the next decade.

Frauke Kreuter

Brief Profile: Professor Frauke Kreuter is Co-director of the Social Data Science Center (SoDa) and faculty member in the Joint Program in Survey Methodology (JPSM) at the University of Maryland, USA; Professor of Statistics and Data Science at the Ludwig-Maximilians-University of Munich, Germany, and head of the statistical methods group at the Institute for Employment Research (IAB) in Nuremberg, Germany. She is an elected fellow of the American Statistical Association and the 2020 recipient of the Warren Mitofsky Innovators Award of the American Association for Public Opinion Research. In addition to her academic work, Dr Kreuter is the Founder of the International Program for Survey and Data Science, developed in response to the increasing demand from researchers and practitioners for the appropriate methods and right tools to face a changing data environment; Co-Founder of the Coleridge Initiative, whose goal is to accelerate data-driven research and policy around human beings and their interactions for program management, policy development, and scholarly purposes by enabling efficient, effective, and secure access to sensitive data about society and the economy; and Co-Founder of the German language podcast Dig Deep.

Traditional data collection systems and their emerging alternatives in the construction of macroeconomic statistics

Timely and error-free macroeconomic data are the most critical needs for macroeconomic policy formulation in both advanced and emerging economies. In reality, however, the data collected by official agencies are subject to errors – both sampling and non-sampling, as well as being constrained by a plethora of issues such as the state of the data collection infrastructure, the political will to invest in improving the same, the degree of granularity that the agencies can achieve in collecting data, among others. Despite such constraints, official macroeconomic data are the best available sources for researchers, policymakers, and other economic agents. Traditionally, physical survey-based data have been used by data collection agencies in both developed and emerging nations. Though practical considerations have made sample-based surveys the preferred approach, such data can be collected through census or sample surveys. Sample surveys are utilised from data on key aggregate economic indicators such as Gross Domestic Product (GDP), employment and unemployment, and inflation to specialized data sets on district-level development indicators. These surveys typically consist of pre-defined questionnaires through which a randomly selected[16] sample is approached physically. Their responses are collected, recorded and appropriately organised for further aggregations. In the case of industries such as banking and insurance, a census might be a feasible option as these industries are typically well-regulated and are required to report their economic activities to the designated official authorities regularly.[17] However, a large portion of economic information is obtained from survey data. Even in cases where access to population data is possible, the entire population might be too heterogeneous to be covered in a single census. Survey-based information thus remains necessary, though not a sufficient, source of information for policymaking.

While sample-based information shall continue to be the chief source of knowledge about the economic issues for macroeconomic policy, alternative sources of data are emerging in developed economies, which may help either substitute or complement the survey-based data sources. The traditional data and the data collection methodologies are now being fundamentally transformed due to the emergence of various innovative economic and financial information sources. These sources range from satellite imagery to cell phone data and have a high degree of granularity. The volume and frequency of such data are substantial compared to the traditional survey-based data. Such data are generally observational, as against experimental,[18] and require different statistical philosophies for optimal decision-making. A notable feature of these data sets is that while many statistically significant correlations are observable, causality is much more challenging to locate due to the highly complex nature of these data and the underlying data generating processes (Shriffin, 2016). A few years ago, this was true even for traditional survey data. The nature of problems associated with survey data took several decades to be understood. While some grey areas still need further research, there is also a sizeable consensus on what such data are, how their underlying data generating process is to be modelled and what various sampling and non-sampling errors may be encountered while dealing with them in official macroeconomic statistics. Today, we are facing the same situation with reference to the emerging data types and sources as highlighted above.

Merging multiple data types and data sources into macroeconomic policymaking requires an overhaul of the data collection systems and the data collection agencies that have been traditionally employed in official information assimilation, especially across emerging economies due to various well-known limitations in their information technology (IT) infrastructure and data processing capabilities.[19] It will not be a hyperbole to assert that the future of informed policymaking in various areas of macroeconomic issues shall be driven by the use of multiple data sources rather than relying primarily on survey data. Such a development has already been initiated in several corners of the world, particularly in the advanced economies. In the U.S., for example, I was a part of the US National Academy of Sciences Panel on "Improving Federal Statistics for Policy and Social Science Research Using Multiple Data Sources and State-of-the-Art Estimation Methods", out of which two reports emerged – namely Groves and Harris-Kojetin (2017a, 2017b). These two reports provide a valuable introduction to the issues that official agencies need to be prepared to handle if they wish to diversify the portfolio of information used for decision-making. One may also extrapolate these reports' ideas to the financial services industries, where observational data are the most practical way to assess economic activities. Increasingly, financial markets are moving toward digital platforms, even in EMEs. With increasing financial integration and the ongoing shift to digital delivery platforms, financial services can now be observed through multiple angles, rather than only relying upon survey methods. Data obtained through digital recording of banking services through various platforms such as mobile banking, internet banking and others are valuable information for monetary and financial authorities. Deeper patterns can be unearthed using data sources that would never be feasible in survey-based approaches. Achieving a high degree of granularity is only possible when highly disaggregated data can be reliably recorded, which is possible only through the various alternative sources as touched upon here. Survey data shall be highly costly if one attempts to achieve a high level of disaggregation. Another issue with survey data is the secular decline in the response rates (Groves & Harris-Kojetin, 2017b). The reliability of survey-based information where response rates are gradually but consistently falling is open to heavy criticism. Hence, combining alternative data sources to analyse the same economic issue is urgently needed, particularly for emerging economies with enormous scope for further economic growth and development.

The challenge of using multiple data sources is further intensified by the complexities involved in combining such sources into a single analytical framework. For illustration, consider the issue of monetary policy formulation. The central bank will typically use a macroeconomic model with well-defined structural parameters. These parameters are generally estimated using data collected using survey methods by the concerned agencies. Using multiple data sources will pose a challenge because the specified theoretical model assumes comparable and consistent data. Standardizing the same shall be needed with different data sources, which requires innovative statistical approaches beyond the traditional standardization procedures employed in official discourses on this matter.[20] Such issues present fascinating scope for further research. The US National Academy of Sciences has been working on these matters through various colloquiums, panel reports and other means. Many such organizations and agencies are working on such issues with particular reference to official macroeconomic accounts of countries.

Adoption of emerging alternative data sources in advanced economies and the emerging market economies

Another project that I have been working on is the BERD@NFID platform – namely the Business, Economic and Related Data project at the National Research Data Infrastructure, Germany. Large unstructured data sets from varied businesses and industries are becoming common today. It would be unrealistic for national income accountants, industrial economists and financial services professionals not to utilize the same. Consumer behaviour data from digital marketplaces to social media analytics – such data are not necessarily numerical. Such data break the traditional belief that a datum is a numerical piece of information. However, that is not the case anymore. Videos, images, clicks by people on online platforms, likes and dislikes on social media platforms, biometric information collected by official agencies and a host of such inherently non-numerical data sources have emerged. The BERD@NIFD platform is an ambitious attempt to systematize such information into easily usable data sets for businesses, governments and others.

Let us contextualize these ideas regarding industrial output estimation at the macroeconomic level. Theoretically, the measurement of production in any industry requires the knowledge of the cost, revenue, demand and supply functions. Without the information on these, empirical estimation of output, productivity, efficiency and other parameters is not feasible. This problem is exemplified in the case of financial services, where physically tracing these functions is not possible. The value-addition process in industries such as banking and insurance is interspersed across the supply chain. Hence, delineating the inputs and outputs at various stages of production is difficult. However, such constraints may be partially overcome if survey-based official data sources and alternative data sets such as digital purchase behaviour and social media analytics are used. The data for estimating the demand function, for example, can very well be sourced from unstructured data sets that online marketplaces such as Amazon and Walmart usually collect. While the data are large, they can be structured using AI and ML algorithms. Such data can be merged with traditional data sources. This has both economic and statistical advantages.[21]

Such ideas seem fascinating, but the data infrastructure of EMEs needs an overhaul to account for such emerging information sources. With massive development agendas on hand, the governments in emerging markets such as China, Russia, Indonesia, India and others face high costs when they may divert scarce funds from politically popular developmental projects to improve the statistical infrastructure. Political will plays a crucial role here, and it will take several years more for developing and emerging countries to garner the popular support to spend financial resources on projects that do not seem critical today in the eyes of the public. Financial resources are required because the data collection agencies need to be trained to handle novel types of information. The analytical capabilities need to be improved by investing in Information Technology.[22]

Some challenges faced by the emerging economies in traditional data collection

The opportunity cost of not protecting sensitive economic and financial data increases with the increase in the volume and flow of data. Hence, when developing, nations begin merging multiple data sources to construct macroeconomic statistics, the need to protect the microdata will increase. Such disaggregated data can also include sensitive information. Thus, safeguarding them from misuse while also allowing access to researchers, policymakers and other stakeholders is a genuine concern that the advanced economies have already been dealing with and the emerging economies are expected to deal with sooner or later. In the U.S., I have been a part of the Coleridge Initiative. This project aims to bridge the gap between how and what kind of data informs public policy decisions and how much the public knows about these policy decisions. Informing the public about the data-dependency of policy decisions is vital to flourishing a truly democratic political system. Most emerging economies, except a few, practice one or the other form of democracy. Hence, public policy measures are well-informed is a matter of interest even in developing nations.

However, the dynamics of official policy formulation are very different in the developing economies compared to their developed counterparts. Transparency in policymaking and the extent to which rigorous data is utilized to make decisions are only scarcely visible in emerging nations. This issue is pronounced when bureaucracies manage official data collection systems. Political interference and even administrative interference and errors can restrict the protection of sensitive data collected through novel sources, as highlighted earlier. Such matters are real and need a debate across the board in EMEs so that the fast-emerging data sources can be smoothly merged into their traditional data systems.

Justin Paul

Brief Profile: Prof. Justin Paul currently serves as Editor-in-Chief of the International Journal of Consumer Studies (IJCS), a 46-year-old global academic journal ranked an "A" grade by the Australian Business Deans Council (ABDC). A former faculty member with the University of Washington, he is a full professor of PhD and MBA programs, at the University of Puerto Rico, USA, with a 3-Year Visiting Professor appointment at the University of Reading Henley Business school, England. He holds two honorary titles as "Distinguished Scholar/Distinguished Professor" with the Indian Institute of Management (IIM-K) and SIBM, the premier business school in South Asia.

I welcome this opportunity to examine some aspects of the theme of this book. The views expressed below are based on my experience in academics and corporate offices of the banking firms in the US, India, and other places.

Multi-output nature of banking and insurance production

Measurement of what is produced by an individual firm is an essential prerequisite for strategizing its scarce resources in a competitive environment, assessing its performance, changing the scale of operations, and many other areas of business decision-making. In a highly competitive market, the firms face continuous pressures to innovate and provide newer products and services. Banking and insurance firms are no exception on this account. Banks and insurers invest many resources in technological upgrades on retail and corporate delivery models. This is a fact that is true for both advanced and emerging economies. It is vital for the retail segments in EMEs due to their peculiar nature.

On the one hand, these economies, such as Brazil, Russia and India, are bank-dependent on the supply of funds. Capital markets are still relatively underdeveloped, and banks play the dominant role in funding new businesses and older and established businesses. On the other hand, the retail segment is considerably more prominent in these countries than its advanced counterparts because of larger populations and market sizes. The services produced by banking firms continuously undergo fundamental changes at the firm level. Market segmentation is a fact of life in the banking industries of emerging economies. These observations imply an ever-evolving nature of the output produced by banks and even insurers. Looking from the banking angle, the value propositions embedded in the services of banks are not stable anymore, and static definitions of bank output with a univariate focus are not good enough to lend justice to the production dynamics of this industry.

Let me examine these observations further. Treating the amount of loans disbursed by a bank as its output may be correct in terms of accounting and financial senses but might not be valid from economic and marketing[23] senses. First, because each banking firm is an inherently multi-output producing entity at the microeconomic level, single-output variables will produce biased[24] estimates of performance parameters. A multi-output framework is the most realistic approach to this.[25] Second, because the value generated by these output variables are interdependent and in a single-output context, the actual value provided to consumers cannot be ascertained without accounting for the interdependence with other output variables in value formation for consumers. Thus, a multi-output approach is the most reliable approach to performance analysis of banks and insurers. Accordingly, output measurement for banking and insurance industries must be concentrated on combining the information from different output candidates into a single measure, or one should explicitly use multiple outputs in the empirical exercises on performance analysis.

Banking industry in the advanced versus emerging economies

Two factors are generally believed to differentiate emerging economies' banking industries from advanced ones. One is the pace of technological sophistication and its adoption. Second is the depth and quality of the prudential norms in the banking industry. Compared to the insurance industry, the regulatory restrictions are more prominent in the banking industry in emerging economies. The depth of these regulations can be roughly understood by the extent of the banking industry they cover,[26] and the quality of these regulations can be broadly understood in terms of the outcomes they generate over time. Emerging economies are converging technologically with advanced economies. The operational technologies, which may be considered the set of technologies that help increase the productivity of back-office operations in banks, in the EMEs are rapidly catching up with the extant practices in the more matured banking industries. Regulators in countries such as Brazil, India, Russia and even China have increasingly become aggressive in promoting state-of-the-art practices for improving operational efficiencies of their banking industry. Banks, too, have become more aware of the competitive advantages of such technologies due to competitive pressures in both the national and international markets. The use of Artificial Intelligence in risk analytics by banks and insurers is one example of operational and technological advances. Similarly, the data collection practices in the EMEs, for example, are driven mainly by digitalization, though the depth and width of the firm-level data are not as considerable as in the advanced economies.

As far as the depth and quality of prudential norms are concerned, EMEs have several challenges to be resolved. One is the issue of adverse selection which seems to be stubbornly persistent even when more efficient AI and ML algorithms are used in selecting, monitoring and pricing the products for both banks and insurers. Specifically, three areas require urgent policy overhaul in emerging nations – credit norms, retail loan assessment and corporate loan screening. The corporate segment especially brings a large share of non-performing assets (NPAs) for the banks in EMEs. NPAs directly reduce the economic value generated by various outputs of banking firms for their consumers and other stakeholders. If the observed amount of loans has increased in a particular country, but the same has been accompanied by an even larger percentage increase in NPAs, then simply inferring that the output (amount of loans in this case) has increased will be misleading. The so-called economic 'bads' must also be measured and accounted for when the economic 'goods' of the banking industry are measured.

Further remarks on measuring the output of the banking industry

The correct way to theorize about bank output, in my opinion, is to consider deposits as inputs and the loans disbursed by banks as the output. The standard inputs of labour and fixed capital shall be added to the production function along with deposits, and the amount of credit disbursed should represent the output. This is the so-called intermediation approach, which seems valid from an industrial perspective. However, at the firm level, one must be wary of the intermediation approach and instead adopt a more flexible approach depending on which aspect of banking activities is being analysed. From a branch-level perspective, the output can be measured from multiple perspectives, such as the amount of loans and deposits, the number of depositors and borrowers and various other measures. From the standpoint of the shareholders, the return on equity generated by a bank would serve as the correct measure of its output because that is the variable in whose maximization the investors would be interested. Thus, at the firm level, the diversity of output variables is large, and the banks are not limited to simply intermediating but also provide value-added services that occupy a sizeable portion of their total costs.[27]

Some issues in using financial statements as the fundamental source of output data for banks

Central banks across major economies – whether emerging or advanced, assimilate data on the banking activities from the financial statements reported by the banking companies to the authorities. The firm-level data pass through a series of aggregations until they reach the public domain through the official agencies. Central banks are generally entrusted with the responsibility of putting the best possible "estimates" in the public domain. Hence, there is strict monitoring of the quality of these data by the Central banks as well as by the internal auditors of the banking firms. Thus, the incentives to manipulate or unjustifiably transform financial data are significantly less at the firm level, mainly due to strict internal and regulator monitoring.

Given that large publicly listed commercial banks characterize EMEs, public pressure also ensures that data are reliably reported due to fears of penalties, stock market crashes and other issues. In my humble opinion, it may be correct to believe that commercial banks do not manipulate data due to both strict internal and regulatory monitoring. This lends the financial statements of banks as a valuable source of information on the production dynamics in the industry. This is one reason why premium data sources provide firm-level data on the banking industry exist, for which researchers and institutions are prepared to spend a hefty fee for access. Moreover, such databases allow researchers to build their output measures depending on the scope of their cross-section samples of banks.

Lastly, it should be pointed out that once the financial data leave the corridors of banks' corporate offices, one can never be truly sure about the quality of data. Simply looking at the extent of statistical noise in data and inferring data quality based on such a criterion will be misleading. One way to avoid such a problem is to use firm-level data to estimate aggregative measures such as industry- or sub-industry-level output measures. Literature has also used national income data for industrial performance analysis of financial services. The Gross Value Added (GVA) data is the most frequently used measure of output in this context. This measure of output is highly aggregative and is generally available only for the financial services industry.[28] Instead of using such pre-aggregated data, one can focus on firm-level information, even if limited in nature and use it for building aggregative measures for themselves. However, at the banking industry level as a whole, one is then faced with the problem of estimating the indirect output produced by banks, which is generally captured by the so-called FISIM approach in the national income accounts. Firm-level FISIM estimates are not available and difficult to derive from the sectoral GVA series and its components. Firm-level data in banking will generally fail to capture this component, and it is here that probably the superiority of output data from macroeconomic accounts is undoubtedly established.

N. R. Bhanumurthy

Brief Profile: Professor N R Bhanumurthy is currently the Vice-Chancellor, Dr B. R. Ambedkar School of Economics University (BASE University), India. He is also a professor at the National Institute of Public Finance and Policy (NIPFP), India. Prior to joining NIPFP, he worked as an Assistant and Associate Professor at the Institute of Economic Growth (IEG), India. He has worked as a macroeconomist at UNESCAP, Bangkok, and the UNDP Regional Centre for the Asia-Pacific region, Colombo. He has been a Visiting Fellow at the Foundation Maison des Sciences de l'Homme, Paris, France, and the McGill University, Montreal, Canada. He has also been a consultant to the International Labour Organization, the World Bank, and the Asian Development Bank.

Notes on national income and other macroeconomic accounts

With the increasing complexity of modern economies and the increased need for welfare interventions to induce growth and development, collecting and analysing large volumes of data are critical for sound policy formulation. Among all the different types of data collected by official authorities, the national income accounts possibly play the most important role in connecting the ground-level economic reality with those at the helm of the affairs. Different countries have different data collection capabilities, so a common standard of official data collection and reporting system is required for international comparisons. Probably, such a common international standard is also needed for supplying different countries with a statistically sound set of criteria that they should aim to follow if they wish to improve their official statistical systems. These functions are fulfilled by the System of National Accounts of the UNSC.

A concern that commonly worries the macroeconomic accountants globally, particularly in developing and emerging economies, is the measurement errors that inevitably occur in such large-scale data assimilation efforts. The more advanced economies can minimize these errors, though they cannot avoid them altogether. The developing and emerging economies are instead in a transitory stage in the evolution of their official statistical systems. Measurement errors, however, remain a matter of deep policy deliberation among macro accountants to date. One of the kinds of errors generally encountered by official statistical systems is subjective errors. Errors in recording data, using data from dissimilar sources and incorrect aggregation of unit-level information are examples of objective errors that occur mainly due to factors outside the control of the data collectors. However, a considerable amount of imputation, interpolation and extrapolation is used to adjust and organize the national income accounts before they are presented. These accounts are very keenly observed both economically and politically, and hence, the possibility of subjective errors is problematic. These errors cannot be entirely eliminated in EMEs until their economic structure shifts completely towards the organized sector.[29]

Financial services versus the tangibles in the estimation of output

The identification and quantification of unit-level information, i.e. the information on the so-called elementary units, is relatively more accessible in the case of goods with well-defined value chains and reliably differentiated production stages. Due to a clearly observable production process, determining the inputs and output at different stages in the production chain is possible in the case of Goods. This is a prerequisite to deriving estimates of value-addition at elementary levels. These estimates are then further aggregated to derive larger estimates at the industry, sector and national levels. Such a possibility is constrained in the case of services because identifying the value chain in the production of services is complex and even indeterminate in some cases. The financial services industry is perhaps the best example of this aspect. Universal banking has been an essential feature of market-oriented EMEs such as Brazil, Russia, India and others since the advent of financial globalization that roughly gained momentum in the mid-2000s. Multiple services are being provided through the same banking entity, and these services also cut across many other non-banking services. This makes it challenging to locate a single output of the banking firm; rather, its output is a combination of various activities that it performs simultaneously. This lends considerable dynamism to the very concept of banking, insurance and other financial services' outputs. A static data collection methodology that stresses identifying single output rather than considering a plethora of simultaneous activities as a measure of output will be unable to derive reliable estimates as far as financial services are concerned. Financial services need to be treated with as much aggregation as plausible given the context. Deriving highly disaggregated estimates, for example, the output from the merchant banking services of banks, will not do justice to this inherent dynamism like financial services. The interlocked nature of the production of financial services in particular and the service industries in general, does not lend itself quite well to the typical neoclassical production empirics. Thus the traditional measures of the output of financial services must be looked at simultaneously as inputs and outputs depending on the context of output analysis. The fee generated by commercial banks through merchant banking services is a measure of output so far as the total services rendered by a bank are concerned. However, they might also be theorized as inputs if one is interested in looking at the total factor productivity of a particular bank's retail banking segment because banks may channel the surplus funds from their corporate segment into their retail segment to generate loans. This is probably one reason why the literature on the measurement of banking and insurance industry output has been much more diverse than the estimation of individual firm-level output.[30]

Differences in economic structures and international comparisons

Consider India and China. Historically, both these countries have had different occupational structures of their aggregate output. The Indian economy has generally seen a larger share of services in its GDP, while China has grown on a more extensive manufacturing base. Furthermore, both these economies currently have quite the opposite policy priorities. While the Indian policymakers are incentivizing an increase in the share of manufacturing to GDP, China is pushing its service sector to contribute an increasing share to the same. Since 1980, there has been a clear difference in the service sector's contribution to their respective GDPs. India has experienced a slowdown in the share of services to GDP, while China has experienced the opposite. Both economies are well-regulated, and this difference in the way their service sectors have changed since the 1980s partly reflects the differences in their development policies. Thus, are these economies comparable even after the customary adjustments in conversion to common currency and deflation? With very different structures, macroeconomic data require more adjustments for standardization. As discussed previously, the more such adjustments are made, the higher the probability of subjective errors.

This is only one example of the ample number of differences in the economic structures across emerging economies. The structural differences in the economies are more prominent in the case of emerging countries mainly due to large differences in the level of economic development and the kind of resource endowments with which these countries began their development journeys. These differences are multiplied in the case of their financial services industry, where the EMEs have huge differences in the depth, development and penetration of this industry. In contrast to this, the advanced economies present a more coherent structure with broadly similar levels of financial development, and hence their data lend themselves to more robust international comparisons. These observations also highlight another essential feature of the EMEs: their higher dependency on the services industry for propelling economic growth compared to the commodity sector.

Input-output measurement in financial services, including the FISIM methodology

Measurement of the inputs and output of any industry are necessary elements in estimating their economic performance parameters such as their productivity, efficiency, profitability and others. In the case of services, particularly in financial services, the distinction between the two is quite subtle and generally a challenge for any economic analyst. A common approach to circumvent this problem is to estimate the output produced by the financial service firms, such as banking and insurance companies, using the data on salary and wages paid to the employees of these firms as an estimate of the output or rather the value-added of the firm. This dependency on factor market data to estimate a product market variable is probably one of the most frequently employed strategies by national income accountants across the developing economies. However, a sizeable shadow financial services segment can make such an approach to output measurement pretty unreliable. However, the EMEs are experiencing a continuous increase in the share of the organized segment to their value-added, especially for financial services.[31]

Moreover, financial services, particularly banking, do not produce only one kind of output but rather produce many different services that interchange their roles as inputs and outputs depending on the value chain stage one is looking at in this industry. For the same bank, its deposits are a product it must sell and promote with various services and features to its customers. At the same time, it must also use those deposits to produce loans and advances that its customers will utilize. From a marketing perspective, deposits are as much of a product to be sold as are various credit products. Hence, it is impossible to provide an ideal definition of input and output for a banking firm. Instead, one should adopt a flexible approach and measure inputs and output depending on the value chain stage that one is analysing.

Another actively debated matter is the preference given to the FISIM methodology in imputing the intermediation component of the value-added by the banking sector. While the FISIM was prepared to be used as a last resort, the lack of theoretical clarity on the input-output distinction has somehow made FISIM the first preference among national income accountants. Given the current state of the official statistical systems of major emerging economies, it does not seem that the FISIM will lose its dominance anytime soon. Theoretical developments on the nature of production in financial services are required before traditional or innovative approaches are employed to estimate the intermediation services supplied by the banking sector.

Despite these constraints, there are some alternatives to choose from as far as the measurement of banking output is concerned. Profit is one of the variables used to measure banks' production. Again, this approach has its limitations, mainly because of the dominance of public sector banks in major EMEs. Public sector banks are inherently driven by welfare motives rather than profit maximization motives, which is the primary aim of private sector banks. In this case, the changes in profit levels will not reflect the true extent of value-addition by the banking sector because a reduction in profit of public sector banks does not imply a reduction in the value-added by them. On the contrary, in economies with a bank-driven financial system design, a decline in profits may signal these banks' developmental role at the cost of their profit. Another approach is the use of wages paid to the employees of the banks as a measure of bank output. This approach is used chiefly by economies with a large organized labour market for financial services, making it easier to observe the market wages to estimate output.

Similarly, some alternative measures of insurance output are also used actively in academic and policy analysis. Insurance payouts during claim settlement are one possible candidate in this regard. Suppose the underlying theoretical belief is that risk coverage is the main output of insurance firms. In that case, the claim settlement amounts paid by them are an appropriate measure of their output. However, there is an ex-ante and an ex-post dimension to insurance output. In an ex-post sense, claim settlement payouts are a valid measure of insurance output, but in an ex-ante sense, they are not. In this case, the underlying theory would be that what insurance firms promise to cover is the output produced by them. Then the use of the total sum insured or assured would be a more relevant candidate. Both these approaches are challenging to apply in real time. Hence, the SNA recommends the amount of premium collected as a measure of insurance output and appropriate adjustments for the other non-insurance functions performed by the insurance firms. Currently, the premium approach is recommended by the SNA, but the forthcoming revisions of the SNA might allow recommended procedures for other approaches, too, I hope.

Some frontier issues in financial services output measurement

Emerging economies are characterized by widespread public-sector involvement in the financial services industry. The private and public firms have very different economic objectives. The very nature of their production differs considerably. The output of privately owned financial services firms can be exhaustively estimated using their observed market behaviour. However, this may not be the case with the public sector firms which the government majorly owns. The output measurement strategy for both sectors should be different even when they belong to the same industry. Thus, separate output accounting procedures for public and private financial services firms are a need of the hour. Observed market data is generally not representative of the true value added by the public firms. Public sector firms also produce non-marketable output that cannot be measured by simply using the financial market data. The FISIM approach too relies on observed market data to estimate the reference rate, which is the heart and soul of this methodology. However, it does not account for the non-marketable portion of the output produced by the public sector banks, for example. Estimating output using the neoclassical production theory relies heavily on observed market data such as the reference rate in FISIM, wages paid to employees by banks and insurance firms, and the profit earned by these firms as per their financial statements, etc. The output of public sector firms can only partially be estimated using the typical neoclassical production framework. More profound deliberations on these dimensions are needed.

Pronab Sen

Brief Profile: Dr Pronab Sen is the Programme Director for the International Growth Centre's (IGC) India Central Programme. He received his PhD in Economics from Johns Hopkins University, specializing in open-economy macroeconomic systems, international economics and public finance. He has served as the first Chief Statistician of India, acting as the functional and technical Head of the national statistical system in India and Secretary, Ministry of Statistics & Programme Implementation, Government of India (2007–2010). He recently served as the Principal Adviser, Power and Energy, at the Government of India's erstwhile Planning Commission. As a representative of the Planning Commission, he was the principal author and coordinator of the Mid-term Appraisal of the Eighth Five Year Plan, the Ninth Five Year Plan, the Mid-term Appraisal of the Ninth Five Year Plan, the Tenth Five Year Plan and the Mid-term Appraisal of the Tenth Five Year Plan.

Emerging economies and the system of national accounts

The SNA is a set of accounting principles and recommendations laid down by the United Nations Statistics Division (UNSD). The divergence between the expectations of the UNSD from the official statistical systems of the member nations and the actual data assimilation systems currently in place in major EMEs is well known both in the international policy circles and in the general academic discourse. The critical issue here is that the ability of member countries to measure their national income optimally depends not on the quality of these accounting principles but the availability of unit-level economic data.[32] An essential advantage of the SNA manual is its flexibility for member countries to adopt computation methodologies suitable to their data availability. However, despite this flexibility in methodological approaches, the differences in the availability of high-quality unit-level data are vast both among developing and developed nations on the other and among the developing nations themselves. Thus, the pertinent question is not whether the SNA is sufficient to capture the intricacies of output measurement but whether emerging countries have the infrastructure to collect the required elementary data in the first place. Methodological innovations can always be undertaken if sufficient data inputs are available. EMEs currently face the challenge of generating statistically "good" unit-level data rather than their ability or inability to adopt the SNA in the whole spirit.

The advanced economies have an inherent advantage when it comes to collecting unit-level data on the economic activities of various industries, particularly in the case of financial services. The corporate sector accounts for the bulk of its economic activities. This makes their balance sheet data quite representative of the actual economic value addition at the ground level. In the case of market-oriented EMEs such as Brazil, India, Indonesia and others, the non-corporate sector plays a sizeable role. Its contribution to the aggregate value added differs across EMEs, but it dominates in several large emerging economies. This lends their corporate sector data unrepresentative of the actual value addition undertaken by the industries, including the financial services. Another issue that arises in developing economies is that of the inter-sectoral differences in data collection systems. Agriculture data in India, Brazil, and possibly China are collected considerably longer than in other industries, given the historical dominance of agriculture until structural changes took place in these economies. Hence, the quality of non-agricultural output data in economies like India is a significant constraint.[33] The UNSC can only recommend the best practices. Its execution is local and determined by domestic factors outside its control. However, it may be noted that as far as financial services are concerned, the large bulk of aggregate value-addition comes from the corporate firms and thus, the issue of accounting for non-corporate sector output is limited only in the cases where the unorganized sector has a sizeable dominance in the provision of financial service.

Under- and overestimation of financial services output under economic shocks

In regular times, the method used to generate estimates of the non-corporate or the unorganized or the informal sector of an economy work well. This is generally in the form of extrapolation of the estimates from the corporate sector to the non-corporate sector. Hence, without any external shocks, the output measurement of the unincorporated sector is broadly representative of the true picture. This representativeness breaks down when any kind of shock is propagated through the economy. An economic shock such as the COVID-19 pandemic that has adversely affected most developing economies can impact the corporate and non-corporate sectors. Both the general observations and the economics literature suggest that this is the case. In a macroeconomic model where international economic shocks propagate freely throughout the nooks and corners of the economic structure, output measurement methodologies that proxy the value addition in the non-corporate sector break down. With differential impacts of such economic shocks and the lack of precise knowledge about the essential econometric parameters of the effects of such shocks on the non-corporate sector, extrapolation and interpolation methods will fail to capture the true size and changes in the output of the non-corporate sector. One can readily apply this logic to the financial services industries also. These problems are further intensified for financial services that provide intermediation services. Here, not only the estimates of the direct services of the non-corporate sector are distorted due to shocks, but also the estimates of their indirect intermediation services as generally measured by the FISIM approach.

Such shocks result in underestimating and overestimating the output of industries that comprise a large share of the non-corporate sector. For example, in the case of the COVID-19 shock, developing countries probably overestimate the value added by financial services as the true adverse impact on the non-corporate financial services sector is largely missing from the policy arsenal. Similarly, in the case of the 2007–08 financial recession, possibly the countries were underestimating their GDP mainly because the total impact of the same on the aggregate economy was overstated by the lack of knowledge about the structural parameters of the unorganized sector.

Defining the output of services versus other industries

Output measurement in the services sector has another challenge to overcome. While the definition of a product is quite tightly defined in the case of non-services industries, that is not the case for the services sector. What do banks actually produce? Do they produce deposit accounts held by lending customers who consume the deposit account services over many years? Do banks produce loans and advances that the borrowing customers consume? Do banks produce the transformation of deposits into credit? Similarly, do insurance firms produce coverage of risk that provides possible protection to the policyholders? Do they rather produce claim settlement services when policyholders actually face a loss? Do banks and insurance firms produce risk transformation services? Or do they rather produce efficient financial asset allocation through the financial markets?

Such questions complicate the nature of the output of financial services. With a lack of clear-cut tangible definition of what they produce, researchers and analysts have a lot of freedom to tweak the specification of the production function as per their subjective understanding of what banks and insurers produce. This makes estimates of total factor productivity, efficiency, profitability and other performance parameters difficult to synthesize for informing policy formulation. The specification of the output of financial services is further complicated by the indirect intermediation services that they supply. Not only the intermediation services but many of the positive and negative externalities of their existence are generally not well-captured by both the emerging and the advanced economies alike. Such estimation requires knowledge of the parameters of a structural macroeconomic model that can accurately specify the coefficients of the relationship between the aggregate economy and the indirect, intermediary and non-marketable output of the financial services sector. Such an expectation is far from true today. Even the best macroeconometric models used today by the OECD, EU or even the US do not account for such issues. In large part, this may be because their corporate sector is the largest contributor to the aggregate output. Thus, resolving these issues is on emerging economies and their blocs such as the BRIIC, ASEAN, etc. With proper support from the UNSC, these blocs can work deeply on these matters and possibly develop more innovative methods to account for the non-corporate sector in their national income accounts.

These problems also make it challenging to generate a well-defined price index for financial services. Index measurement is undertaken to account for the movements in a variable over time. With the lack of any commonly agreeable definition of financial service output, measurement of changes in the price of such services over time will be biased and untenable from an economic point of view. Technological shocks are perhaps the strongest and quickest in the financial services industry. For example, the same service, the home loans disbursed by banks, does not remain the same over even short time intervals. In this case, essentially, a sectoral measure that can be defined so that its value accounts for such dynamic changes in the composition of the output can do justice. Problems in the price measurement of financial services are as complicated as those on the side of their output measurement.

Another dimension in this context is the implicit pricing of various non-intermediation services provided by financial service suppliers, particularly banks. Banks offer a whole set of direct and non-fee-based and non-intermediation services. Structurally, the share of such services is different for different emerging economies. However, most EMEs have a banking sector that thrives on such services due to high competition. With the exception of perhaps China, most EMEs have both public and private banking firms in continuous competition for market share. Such services are an essential tool for the marketing strategists of banks to attract and retain customers. These services are not free of charge but are rather priced implicitly. Such implicit pricing makes it very difficult to measure an optimal Fisherian[34]-style price index. In this case, with reference to output measurement, the FISIM shall account for the implicitly priced intermediation services, but it does not account for such services that are charged implicitly but are not intermediary in nature.

Dual intermediation roles of banks and the input-output debate

As noted earlier, there are many unresolved questions about what banks produce. However, it is agreed that banks are intermediaries. They transform deposits into credit. However, while doing so, they also transform risk exposures and redistribute risks much more efficiently compared to the situation that would have prevailed in their absence. Depositors are assured of a return irrespective of how their funds perform in the loans market. Indeed, this is not always the case, as continuously loss-making banks with low net interest margins can be squeezed to the extent of insolvency. However, given that most EMEs have a well-established banking sector regulator,[35] the occurrence of such an unfortunate event at a sectoral level is complicated. This dual intermediation role of banking firms, namely the intermediation as transformers of deposits into credit and transformers of individual risk exposures into more efficiently redistributed risk exposures across depositors, requires more innovative approaches than the FISIM approach as in place right now.

Yet another debate has raged on the output measurement of banking services. It is the so-called input-output dilemma in the banking output. Are deposits inputs or output? This is a particularly persistent matter of debate. This dilemma is not a dilemma at all, as the balance sheet of a bank very well reveals the truth. Deposits are liabilities, and loans and advances are assets. Banks are essentially liability-asset transformers. Their core source of income is the extent to which they can extract net interest margins while undertaking this transformation role.

Increasingly, countries are pushing forward the digitalization of their banking and insurance industries. The COVID-19 pandemic has further given an unanticipated push to this agenda. If such a trend continues, the issue of accounting for non-corporate output and the under- or overestimation of financial services output might very well be overcome to a large extent.

Finance-growth nexus in emerging economies

Does finance cause economic growth, or is it the other way round? Or is it two-way? This is a classic matter of debate in development economics. Econometric evidence points toward a two-way causal relationship. Theory suggests that finance must react to the needs of the real sector. In terms of my experience, these questions are futile. The very nature of an economy is circular. It is further complicated by highly complex webs of inter-sectoral and intra-sectoral feedback mechanisms that the economists do not fully understand yet. With growth rate maximization being imperative for policymakers in developing nations, it is clear that whichever channels can be used to increase the growth rate must be employed.

A well-developed financial system is a necessary but not sufficient condition for economic growth. A nationwide banking system, for example, can shift funds back and forth throughout the regions of the country depending on where the funds are being generated and where they are being demanded. This can lubricate the functioning of the real sector and allow increases in the levels of "real" production and productivity. However, financial efficiency in itself does not create the factors required for economic growth, which generally emerge from the supply side. While the financial system is a vital supplier of financial capital, the ultimate supplier of human and physical capital in terms of other financial resources is the real sector. With high levels and quality of human and physical capital, finance may induce growth, but without them, finance and growth may not display any meaningful causal relationship whatsoever.[36]

Some notes on insurance output measurement

Insurance firms produce risk coverage. The amount of premium underwritten by them is generally a reliable measure of the amount of risk they cover. The non-corporate sector does not play much of a role here when it comes to insurance. Historically, insurance has been supplied by the organized sector. Thus the balance sheet data of these firms is well-representative of what they produce, unlike in the case of banking. Moreover, insurance companies may also provide risk coverage to banking firms, and in a sense, insurance firms share the risks of banks. Insurance firms also perform intermediation functions by creating a pool of funds from the insured and investing it in financial markets. However, it does not call for a FISIM-style measurement problem because the SNA, 2008 already accounts for such dimensions.

Some frontiers of banking output measurement

A final issue to be highlighted is that the nature of the output of banks when they lend for working capital versus when they lend for fixed capital is very different. The underlying production functions themselves may be considered non-aggregative. Simply adding the output data from their working capital lending with long-term lending may actually be economically incorrect. Even if such is the need, appropriate aggregation factors need to be derived that can give some meaning to such an aggregation. Short-term lending by banks is less of a concern as far as their intermediation role is concerned. Banks do not generally lend short-term working capital loans to maximize their net interest margins. These are lent more so based on the direct interest they charge and the various fee-based services they lend. Such loans are not going to be a part of the long-term assets of a bank, and hence their longer horizon decisions will be more focused on the long-term loan portfolio.

Similarly, not all deposits received by banks are long-term. Current account advances and even Savings Bank and Term deposits are not guaranteed to be stable for the banks. Variations in the withdrawal-deposit behaviour of customers are inevitable with changing economic conditions. Banks thus require a reliable long-term source of funds to underwrite long-term loan contracts such as that home loans in the retail segment and possibly project financing in the corporate segment. The extent to which short-term versus long-term funds contributes to the banks' intermediation services is an important area of further research.

R. B. Barman

Brief Profile: Dr R. B. Barman, former Executive Director, Reserve Bank of India, holds a Master's degree in Statistics and a PhD in Industrial Economics. The main areas of his professional interest include Business Information Technology and Payment Systems. Dr Barman was Vice Chairman of Irving Fisher Committee on Central Bank Statistics, Bank for International Settlements (BIS) and a Member of the International Data Forum. He has also served as an Advisor to the National Payments Corporation of India, which is entrusted with the responsibility of setting up a state-of-the-art retail payment system for India. He spearheaded the Business Intelligence initiative of the Reserve Bank of India, which in 2001 was one of the earliest such initiatives. The subject orientation and the data model thereon was a novelty, which many central banks have followed thereafter. Dr Barman has contributed richly in the area of Official Statistics – particularly on price and output statistics. His contribution in this area spans several articles. Post-retirement, Dr Barman was a Visitor at Indira Gandhi Institute of Development Research and Adviser (Research), Indian Institute of Capital Market. He is also the Adjunct Faculty of the C. R. Rao Advanced Institute for Mathematics, Statistics and Computer Applications, Hyderabad. He was the former Chairman of the National Statistical Commission and former President of The Indian Econometric Society (TIES). Dr Barman received the prestigious National Award in Official Statistics – 2021, Government of India.

Theoretical and empirical issues in the system of national accounts of emerging economies

The foundation of the System of National Accounts was laid down by the 1947 Report of the sub-committee on National Income Statistics of the League of Nations Committee of Statistical Experts entitled "Measurement of National Income and the Construction of Social Accounts". Especially important were the recommendations made by Richard Stone in the memorandum to the same report. This document provided the basic building blocks for estimation of national income accounts that most the nations today are widely undertaken. A noteworthy objective of constructing these accounts was to use these data to understand the welfare implications of development policy interventions. In the post–World War II era, many nations were burdened by the aftermath of the war. Massive development works were required to re-build these countries.[37] Accordingly, relevant data were required to understand various policy interventions' expected and actual effects. The SNA provided the basis for a systematic collection and aggregation of data to obtain vital macroeconomic estimates essential for development policies and promoting a higher economic growth rate. However, despite the focus of this report on collecting information on elementary[38] data, aggregation remained the ultimate purpose of its recommendations. Aggregation at the scales at which national income accountants undertake is extensive and presupposes many assumptions, only after which the aggregates can make any economic sense. One of these assumptions is that of symmetrical economic distributions,[39] which is assumed in the aggregation procedures. For example, actual economic distributions are generally skewed, particularly in emerging and developing economies. Adjustments in the elementary data for this skewness during aggregation into higher levels of groups such as industrial-, sectoral- and national-level estimates are not undertaken in national income accounting procedures laid down by the SNA. This was a problem with the 1949 manual, which was the first one, and it continues to be a limitation of this manual to date. Aggregation without consideration of micro-level economic distributions ends up suppressing the non-normal skewness and kurtosis in the underlying economic data.

The second aspect of the SNA procedures is the economic reductionism it implies in the macro accounting identities that it pre-supposes for national income estimation. Accounting identities are meant to resolve accounting problems and enable official agencies to construct statistically coherent estimates. However, the use of these accounting identities as representations of actual economic processes distorts the true underlying structure of the economy and possibly creates policy biases that can prove to be very costly for the welfare economic terms. While national income accountants do not advocate the accounting identities as an accurate representation of the actual economic processes, the popular political and economic discourses use such accounting ideas to interpret the success or failures of economic policies.

The third crucial theoretical issue is the blow lent to macroeconomic aggregation by the celebrated Lucas Critique, as Lucas (1976) explained. Lucas notes that "the unquestioned success of the forecasters should not be construed as evidence for the soundness or reliability of the structure proposed in that theory" (p. 23). Rightly so, this criticism led to the emergence of the Dynamic Stochastic General Equilibrium (DSGE) models for macroeconomic policy formulation. Many nations are currently building large-scale macroeconomic models for their economies to undertake policy simulations and derive the possible impact of proposed interventions on the economy and its components. Fully understanding the microeconomic foundations of aggregate data employed for macro policymaking is critically needed, especially with nations pushing for higher economic growth rates. As Lucas pointed out in his seminal work, without understanding how individual economic agents interact and their implications for macro policy, a well-specified and well-estimated macroeconomic model will not possess much economic meaning whatsoever. Not only the microeconomic foundations but inherently stochastic modelling of economic processes is required for effective macroeconomic policies. The Walrasian General Equilibrium model provides a solid theoretical tool for analysing actual economic interactions. However, economic behaviour is always undertaken under conditions of uncertainty, and this requires accounting for various probabilities associated with the modelled economic behaviour. Empirical work requires such an approach because the actual economy functions on stochastic footings rather than deterministic behaviour, which may be easily forecasted using an econometric model. The fourth issue in the present context is the emergence of Big Data, Cloud Computing and Artificial Intelligence–based data collection and analysis technologies. With large-scale disaggregated and unit-level data now available in an increasing number of emerging economies, the need for cleanly defining the micro-foundations of macro models is all the more urgent. The need for a stochastic-kind of Walrasian general equilibrium models to explain macroeconomic phenomena such as capital accumulation, aggregate GDP growth, etc., is the most pressing today than any other policy challenge.

The SNA, 2008 is now under intense pressure for revision, especially after the resolutions passed in the last few years by the United Nations Statistical Council (UNSC), particularly in 2014. It is expected that the future version of the SNA shall incorporate many of these issues. In particular, for sound measurement of output and income, three issues need to be urgently addressed by the UNSC for the revised SNA: first is the issue of economic heterogeneity in various emerging economies, particularly economies that have high occupational diversity; second is that of non-linearity in economic relationships that is observed in actual data but is generally avoided in econometric modelling; and, third is the issue of path dependency which is quite well-recognized in macroeconometric modelling nowadays. These characteristics of actual economic data demand appropriate adjustments in aggregation procedures of the SNA, and hopefully, they will be fulfilled in future revisions.

Nature of financial services output

The fundamental purpose of macroeconomic accounting is the optimal valuation of economic activities undertaken by various firms, industries, sectors and the aggregate economy. The unique contribution of each economic agent and factor in the production process is the fundamental basis of macroeconomic output measurement. In these terms, the nature of output is similar for goods and non-intermediation services. Both use explicitly defined inputs to produce explicitly observable output. In the case of intermediation services such as banking and insurance, especially for banking, the output cannot be estimated simply using the observable data.

Take the FISIM approach that relies on interest rate spreads between lending and deposit rates to proxy the amount of intermediation output generated by the banking sector. First, it is a sectoral or rather an industrial-level estimate. It is tough to distribute FISIM across each constituent bank. Second, larger spreads should imply larger value-additions. Still, if that is the case, then microfinance institutions in countries such as Bangladesh, Brazil, India and others must be contributing the highest value-addition and hence should receive large budgetary allocations in development plans. However, that is not the case because the amount of this spread is low, but the financial risks and costs involved in the microfinance industry are pretty large. What this implies is that measurement of intermediation services through an interest-margin approach (which inevitably relies on a reference-rate methodology) can capture the true quantum of intermediation but only limitedly. Third, the dependency between interest rate spreads and the risk profile of assets required to achieve those spreads demands special attention in the output measurement for intermediation services rendered by banks. For example, larger spreads are achievable only when banks presume higher risks while lending loans and advances. But such an approach can boomerang the industry and perhaps the economy itself. See for illustration the sub-prime crisis that emerged from the high-risk lending by banking institutions in the US to maximize the amount of their spreads.

The short note above highlights that statistical measurement of output under the macroeconomic accounting framework does not explain by itself the extent of value added by a firm or an industry in the economy. The implications of what is produced by these entities are equally important. In the case of intermediaries like banks, this aspect is further blurred due to indirect services rendered by them requiring indirect estimation but using directly observable data. The use of observable data for an inherently implicit activity needs a more rigorous approach than the reference rate version of FISIM, which is currently used.

Lastly, a widespread debate in the discourse on banking output measurement is identifying the inputs and outputs of a banking production function. From the perspective of direct services rendered by banks, this issue does not pose much of a problem for their output measurement. The observed data on the revenue generated by the banks for these services is a reliable indicator of value-added by the bank through these direct fee-based services. However, the production function becomes quite complicated when it comes to intermediation, as the observable bank-level accounting data is insufficient to capture the full extent of the same. In this case, a reference rate-based FISIM approach is used to measure the difference in the deposit and lending rates of the banks compared to a risk-free reference rate. In this framework, deposits act as inputs and credit lent by the banks as output. But the FISIM suggests that deposits in themselves generate returns for the depositors and hence can be considered output in that sense. The distinction between input and output is more flexible in banks' intermediation services than in direct fee-based services.

Comments on the FISIM approach in measuring banking output

FISIM is a logically coherent framework. It is internally consistent also. However, as noted above, the equalization of value-addition with interest-rate spreads is not empirically sound. As a statistician working on policymaking issues for several years, I firmly believe that the current FISIM approach needs revision to better measure the intermediation services provided over and above those proxied by interest-rate differentials. One approach to account for this could be to design macroeconometric models that can analyse the impact of the movements in interest rate spreads on economic activities and thereby adjust the estimate of FISIM for such estimated parameters. In the era of Big

Data and AI-driven software capabilities, it is not unreal to expect such models to emerge in the coming years.

Possible future developments in the output measurement of financial services

Stochastic dynamic models will and must increasingly occupy the traditional national income estimation procedures. FISIM estimation should be made more rigorous by adopting DSGE models that can dynamically adjust the traditional estimates for their complex feedback effects on other sectors. Such an approach also demands rigorous input-output tables for emerging and even advanced economies that can explain the interdependencies at higher levels of disaggregation. With large-sized unit-level banking data and the emergence of Big Data analytics in banking and finance, such an expectation is not very far-fetched from reality. Small sample constraints, for example, are not much of an issue now for advanced economies due to the large volume of unit-level data being generated for the financial services and other industries of these economies. However, this is still a constraint for emerging economies, such as China, that either do not reveal unit-level data or do not collect it altogether due to weak statistical systems. The SNA, 2008 puts a lot of expectations on the official statistical systems, and this is a significant problem for developing and emerging economies where data collection methods are not refined enough to suit the needs of such improvements. Brazil, India, Russia, Indonesia, Thailand, and other top emerging economies need to drastically overhaul their data collection systems. In particular, these nations need to produce high-frequency unit-level data for all major industries if the above improvements are adopted in the coming years. Hopefully, the SNA-2025 is underway, and such issues are expected to be included in the next revision of the SNA.

Ram Pratap Sinha

Brief Profile: Dr Ram Pratap Sinha is an Associate Professor of Economics with more than 32 years of (undergraduate and post-graduate) teaching experience. He is presently posted at the Government College of Engineering and Leather Technology. He has several journal publications to his credit and has contributed to 19 edited volumes, including on various issues in the performance analysis of insurance and banking industries. Besides, he is the author of two books. He is a reviewer of many reputed international and national journals in the area of Economics and Finance. He has taught in numerous Faculty Development Programmes and workshops in Data Envelopment Analysis and Econometrics, focusing on various performance measurements of the financial services industry of major emerging economies.

Insurance production as a multi-stage activity

What do insurance firms produce? This has been a question of policy and academic debates since long. As the insurance industry made its way into the System of National Accounts (SNA) as an explicitly-recognized industry with its own unique input-output relationships, it became a well-recognized fact that the theoretical notions adopted from the neoclassical production theory needed an overhaul, and the estimation of insurance output required newer approaches. Empirically speaking, estimation of insurance production function is more popularly undertaken using single-stage models, which posit a linear one-way input-output relationship. In such empirical models, production is theorized with a clean distinction between inputs and outputs. This representation may not always be correct and can have severe consequences if the estimates of insurance performance parameters[40] are used in firm-level or macroeconomic policymaking. The theoretically more robust approach is to consider insurance as a two-stage activity in which an intermediate output divides the total production function into two stages – the first wherein inputs are used to produce an intermediate output and the second stage wherein the intermediate output is used as an input to generate the final output. In empirical terms, the first stage is where traditional labour and capital inputs are utilized to produce an intermediate output – namely, the insurance premium collected by the firm. After that, in the second stage, the insurance premium collected is utilized for risk pooling and financing claims, thereby providing risk coverage, which is the final output. As elucidated in Figure 7.3, Stage 1 is a process which can be typically accounted for using a traditional production function approach. Inputs are processed and transformed into an output, i.e. the amount of premium collected by the firm. However, in the case of the insurance firm, value generation does not cease here. In Stage 2, the firm further transforms the premium collected into the final output, which various stakeholders consume in different forms. The policyholders consume the risk coverage services provided by the firm through the pooling of risks and losses; the shareholders consume the changes in their financial wealth depending

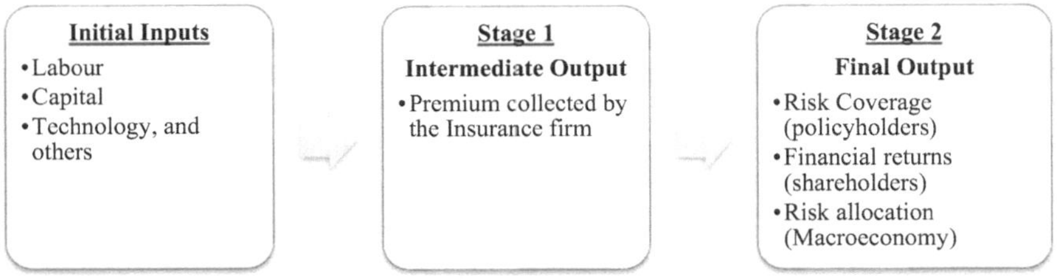

Figure 7.3 Theoretical production function of an insurance firm

Source: Analysis of the contributing expert.

on how the insurance firm is performing in and outside the stock markets and the aggregate economy obtains an efficient risk allocation.[41]

Input measurement is the first matter of concern in this context. Accounting for the inputs in official data is difficult, particularly in developing economies. The data infrastructure is often weak in their case, and the measurement practices are often inconsistent with the SNA requirements. There are many statistical practices too that render the data on inputs difficult to use for empirical studies. Furthermore, insurance is sold through many channels. Thus, many variables across each major input need to be accounted for in the production-based performance studies. Insurance branches, its employees, online platforms, third party agents and the Bancassurance model are the major channels through which insurance products are sold in most emerging economies today. Accounting for these channels in terms of official data on the financial services industry is a challenge for many countries. This is mainly due to the limited maturity of the data collection systems and a sizeable unorganized sector that cannot be easily incorporated into the official statistical design. The best approach is to use proxy measures for insurance inputs, but that may not reflect the underlying variables robustly. Capital, for illustration, can be measured as the number of branches of the insurance firm, but this does not account for other non-branch channels through which products are sold and which are essential capital inputs for the firm in providing its services.[42]

Output measurement is another and more serious challenge in the insurance industry. There are multiple perspectives through which the output of an insurance firm and the output of the entire insurance industry can be viewed. From microeconomic and macroeconomic points of view, it is possible to consider the output of insurance from the perspective of the policyholders, insurance firms, intermediate agencies and policymakers. Locating a standard measure of output that can reflect all these perspectives is difficult, primarily since insurance provides different utilities from different perspectives and measuring these using a single variable will not reflect all these different value-additions provided by insurance firms. Consider the case of insurance firm efficiency. Efficiency models can be estimated from the perspectives of different stakeholders such as the policyholders, shareholders, the employees and a host of others. The measures of inputs and outputs shall be different when looking from these different perspectives. For policymakers, efficiency measurement needs to be undertaken within a macroeconomic perspective so as to see the larger picture and the various interconnections among stakeholders. In their case, merging all these perspectives is necessary, thus demanding large-scale data with an enormous scope than the data used for microeconomic and intra-industry studies. The SNA provides one possible framework on this account. However, it relies on single variables for measuring each of the inputs and output. Such a univariate approach is computation-friendly and statistically easier to analyse but will provide a limited view of what and how insurance firms produce their outputs. It will not be incorrect to presume the existence of multiple outputs in a typical insurance firm's production function.[43]

Alternative approaches to the empirical estimation of insurance performance

Any empirical work on performance[44] measurement of a firm, industry or sector requires reliable estimates of both inputs and outputs. Models that presume single-output and single-input are generally not feasible in a multi–inputs-outputs industry such as insurance. Insurance firms can produce multiple outputs by using the same set of inputs. This complicates determining the input-output relationships while measuring insurance performance parameters. Empirical models based on data envelopment analysis (DEA), dynamic network models and two-stage econometric models infuse dynamism in the estimation process and allow modelling of multi-input–multi-output production processes to a large extent. However, the data requirements for such econometric methods are considerably strict, and EMEs, even the top-performing ones, cannot satisfactorily fulfil these requirements. A good amount of statistical adjustments to existing data are required before being used for such econometric modelling. Important information may be lost in this process. But the trade-off between information loss and the model's realism is inevitable that analysts have to face. The choice on this front largely determines the quality of the final estimates of insurance output.

Some issues in insurance input measurement

Traditionally employed measures of inputs such as labour and capital are not sufficient for accounting for the entire input vector used by insurance firms. Insurance firms transform risks of various kinds into insurable "commodities" and thus rely on various resources that might not be fully represented by the variables commonly used for insurance inputs. In EMEs such as India, Brazil and others, the net worth of an insurance firm plays a significant role as an input in the production process. The behaviour of the net worth of a firm represents the nature of Asset-Liability Management (ALM). As suggested by the Statistical Cost Accounting (SCA) model, the quality of ALM and a firm's financial performance are strongly positively correlated.[45] Another helpful variable in the context of current discussion is the total reserves of an insurance firm,[46] which can be and has been used as a proxy for debt capital by various analysts. Capital as input is embodied differently within the insurance production function, depending on whether it is debt or equity capital. Insurance firms in emerging economies rely, to a large extent, on the banking system to finance their activities. With relatively underdeveloped capital markets, banks are the chief source of finance for these firms. In such a case, the role of debt and equity capitals will differ. Both will provide funds but under different cost-benefit conditions. Aggregating both the measures into a single measure of "capital" may not be a plausible idea in such cases.[47] Thus, accounting for them separately can help in estimating the insurance output more robustly.

Some issues in insurance output measurement

As stated earlier in the discussion, differentiating the intermediate stage and final stage outputs in an insurance firm's production process is critical to achieving a realistic empirical representation of the actual reality. A two-stage model is generally the better empirical strategy in the case of insurance output measurement. One has to be clear about which stage of insurance production function they are working upon. Given that insurance firms transform risks into insurable commodities, this transformation does not occur as a one-stage event. For the studies focused on the first stage, the net premium collected by the firm is the most plausible measure. The risk pooling function of an insurance firm is undertaken, among others, using the funds collected from the policyholders. Traditional inputs of labour and capital are used to "produce" the premium income. In the second stage, the same premium income, along with other sources of funds such as debt and equity capital, and labour, are utilized to produce the final output, which is the risk coverage[48] given to the policyholder and possibly also the value generated for the shareholders,[49] to the extent of equity finance received by the firm. Insurance firms also perform the risk management function in society. This is an integral part of its total output. A helpful variable in this context is the incremental[50] Assets under management (AM) of the insurance firms. Many insurance firms in emerging and advanced economies are actively engaged in managing the funds of policyholders both directly (through investment-based life insurance policies) and indirectly (through the funds collected for general insurance policies). These firms undertake risk transformation and management functions. They pool the funds and diversify them, thereby reducing the overall variability in returns and thus the risk associated with the investment. Incremental AM is a plausible candidate in this regard, not only because it is theoretically better, but also because data are easily available in most major EMEs. AM is a critical policy lever for insurance regulators to keep an eye on the risk-taking behaviour of insurance firms. Thus data on this variable are mostly available in emerging and advanced economies.

Price measurement in insurance

Prices are critical ingredients in constructing reliable measures of the volume and value of the inputs and outputs used in the insurance industry. Deflation procedures are susceptible to the measure of price employed by the analyst. Estimates of constant-price and volume-based insurance output cannot be derived unless industry-specific standards of input and output prices exist. Across the board in EMEs, this matter is a significant constraint. Data on insurance-specific prices are generally not directly available. Analysts undertake imputations to fill this gap, but these imputed measures are largely imperfect, though they serve to some extent. For example, consider the measurement of total factor productivity in insurance. Such an exercise will require deflated measures of inputs and outputs, which in turn shall require data on input and output prices. National income data and industry-level deflators can be used for those working on sectoral data within a macroeconomic accounting framework. However, the GDP deflator is not a measure of actual observed prices but a crude aggregate proxy for a sectoral price index. Microeconomic studies require disaggregated data on prices across space and time. Such data are largely absent in the context of EMEs. This is an area that needs the urgent attention of the policymakers.[51]

Zhu Haiju

Brief Profile: Professor Zhu Haiju is currently working at the Zhejiang Gongshang University, Hangzhou, China. He specializes in monetary economics and has been working on various issues in China's financial services industry. He is also an alumnus of the Ludwig von Mises Institute, Alabama, US.

Measurement of output and its rationale

Given the initial endowments and the economic problem of scarcity, the efficiency with which a country utilizes its available resources determines its development's temporal and spatial paths. Divergence or convergence of development paths among the nations is deeply affected by the differences in the economic efficiency[52] achieved by the countries. Assessment of economic efficiency and performance is critical information for stakeholders involved in the development process. The quantities of economic outputs and the inputs are required to derive various financial performance measures. This is true in firms, industries and the aggregate economy. At the firm level, performance analysis is needed to channel the scarce resources efficiently due to competitive pressures. This is required to enable economic coordination and possibly optimal industrial policies at the industry level. At the aggregate level, performance analysis is needed to achieve the traditional macroeconomic goals of growth, low inflation and overall progress as per Keynesian policy frameworks adopted by many emerging market economies (EMEs).

Given these necessities, firms' performance analysis, industrial groupings, and aggregate economy are important considerations for any emerging economy. With the large-scale potential to increase the efficiency in resource utilization, EMEs are characterized by sub-optimal use of resources mainly due to distortions in the market process[53] created by government interventions and various internal and external shocks.[54] The effects of such interventions and shocks may have a long-lasting impact on the markets' economic coordination. These effects depend on the changes in the economic efficiency of such shocks. Studying the nature of economic efficiency is thus an inevitable necessity for any economy, particularly those on the path of economic progress but are yet to reach their potential outputs. The measurement of the output variables determines efficiency analysis in turn. At the same time, inputs measurement is also a matter of debate, the theoretical consensus in quite clear on this account. In the mainstream neoclassical models, labour and capital are considered the most fundamental inputs in any production process.[55] However, the debates on the efficiency analysis of banking and insurance industries are more tilted towards measuring outputs.

This is particularly true because the nature of the production function underlying the observed output is sensitive to the institutional arrangements under which a firm or industry functions. Wide differences on this account characterize emerging economies. While interventions in the financial services industry are shared among these economies, the degree, type and quality of policy interventions vary sizeably. The institutional environment, in terms of the participants involved, the economic freedom they enjoy in pricing their services, the degree of competition and the intensity of interventions, varies by a large margin across the EMEs. Such differences inevitably affect the quantity and composition of the output produced by the financial services industry and thus results in differences in the estimates of efficiency across these economies. Not only inter-country but the differences in the output generate even intra-industry and intra-firm differences in efficiency estimates.

Nature of output in the services industry

A common practice among mainstream economists is to treat the output of different industries in the service sector as conceptually different. This induces the need to search for the appropriate aggregation functions when analysis has to be undertaken at the industry level. While such an approach may be justified as an outcome of practical observations, the truth seems that all the outputs within the financial services industry are meant to fulfil consumer demands. Given their consumption orientation, the most practical way of aggregating them is through the weighting factors derived from the consumption side, i.e. the demand side rather than the supply side. This might better reflect the relative importance of each firm's output in the aggregate industry-level production function. However, this is easier said than done.

A reliable amount of data on various inputs and outputs is available regarding the banking and insurance industries in the significant EMEs. In China, for example, the banking and insurance industries are occupied by state-owned companies whose daily business is consolidated by the official agency – China Banking and Insurance Regulatory Commission (CBIRC). The official agency generally collects data on the assets, deposits, loans, regional distribution of the same, interest rates and other variables. Such is the case with most major EMEs such as Brazil, India and others. The issue that permeates most of these economies is that the data on possible weighting factors for aggregation are missing. On the demand side, the output price should best reflect each output's relative importance in the industry-level aggregation function. However, reliable price indices are generally missing, and the available data requires a lot of imputations to become empirically meaningful. Such concerns result in dependence on proxy measures for aggregation factors that seem to diverge from the demand-side realities rather than converging with them.

Some empirical aspects of output measurement in the EMEs

The banking industry is highly regulated. And so is the insurance industry. In China, the banking firms are essentially state-owned, and the role of the government is extremely large in channelizing the loanable funds within the economy. This is done mainly by relying on broader economic planning rather than purely through economic coordination via the market prices.[56] Price discovery is considerably distorted by state planning, though the estimates of prices for financial services can be arrived at using various proxy-pricing methods.[57]

Similarly, the insurance industry is almost monopolized by several large state-owned insurance companies, and it is difficult for private individuals to obtain licenses. This has resulted in a disproportionately higher share of public sector output in China's total financial services output. Daily banking activities such as withdrawals from private accounts are subject to strict constraints, such as limits on the amount of cash to be withdrawn per day. Such restrictions are not specific to China but are generally observed in other EMEs as well. However, the intensity of regulation differs among these economies, and this creates the need for adjustment of observed output for the impact of inflation, subsidies and other interventions. Moreover, government regulations, especially inflation and policy-induced cyclical fluctuations, make it difficult to measure the true output quantum. Such adjustments are a matter of further research, particularly for deriving the estimates of public sector output in financial services. This is necessary because, ideally, the economic theory requires the purest form of economic output, undisturbed by the non-market forces. In reality, however, the observed financial statements of banks include the impact of such interventions. Thus it might not be theoretically sound to simply use the official data on assets, deposits, premiums collected, claims paid and others without proper treatment for non-market distortions. A question immediately arises: How can this be undertaken when such impacts are embodied in the observed data themselves, and the relevant adjustment factors are unavailable? This matter requires a more exhaustive analysis, and it seems that the consensus in the mainstream is still weak on this account. One point to note here is that the structure of the financial services industry matters when judging the market-representativeness of observed financial statements. Suppose the financial system is dominated by private players with relatively minimal policy restrictions. In that case, the financial accounts of the banks and insurance firms should provide a largely reliable idea about the theoretically true level of output. The observed data, in this case, shall be least distorted by policy interventions and hence should provide a fair idea of the market forces at play. Such estimates of output should also be consistent with the neoclassical production theory. India and Brazil seem closer to this stylized approximation, while China is the diametrical opposite of these economies. Estimates of financial services output by official agencies in most economies are prepared using the firm-level financial accounts. These aspects should be borne in mind while using official industry-level data.

At this juncture, one must, however, bear in cognizance the fact that even though the official data may not be completely reliable, as incentives to 'adjust' the data by government officials or executives of state-owned enterprises will always exist, on the whole they do reflect the underlying economic performance of a region or industry. The data and experience are generally consistent on this account – for example, the economy of Northeast China is relatively backward, and this is clearly reflected in the available official economic data. However, this representativeness becomes weaker as we move towards higher levels of disaggregation, particularly in the case of output measurement of financial services. This is contributed, in part, by the sheer diversity of activities that are to be accounted for when firm-level behaviour is analysed and due to a large shadow sector that is not directly captured in the financial statements reported by the banks and insurers.

Notes

1 While theoretically, financial intermediation should work exactly the same across every economy, domestic economic conditions, the degree of financial depth, the extent of financial development, and a host of related factors cause differences in how effectively and efficiently financial intermediaries function. Such differences can be wide if one compares economies with different political regimes. India, for example, has a relatively more prominent presence of private financial intermediation firms than China. While China also follows the SNA just as India does, the dominance of public intermediaries lends a very different character to the financial services industry of China. The data on the financial services industry from both these countries thus need to be further adjusted to make them comparable in an international context. Such differences make it difficult to rely on SNA procedures and principles solely. More statistical and econometric adjustments are required to make data comparable for international macroeconomic coordination.

2 In the present discussion, the term 'performance' includes a class of measures such as technical efficiency, allocative efficiency, total factor productivity and profitability.

3 Chambers and Färe (1993) state that "the existence of an aggregate output for a multi-output technology is justified by the presumption that the underlying production technology is separable in outputs". This presumption requires rigorous justification before individual outputs can be aggregated to undertake industry-level performance analysis. An alternative in this regard is non-parametric methods such as Data Envelopment Analysis, though there are problems with it too.

4 Green (2016) provides a detailed discussion on the procedures required for consistent aggregation across different outputs and inputs to derive aggregate input and output measures for production analysis.

5 Linking the borrowers and the savers under economically efficient terms of exchange is possible due to the existence of banks, particularly in EMEs whose financial system is essentially bank-dependent rather than being more tilted towards the capital markets as is the case with the advanced economies.

6 The banking industry globally seems to be shifting towards fee-based services in modern times. It is too early to suggest that non-intermediary services have overtaken the intermediation services in the business portfolio of the banks. Still, there is a trend towards 'disintermediation' in the banking industry – i.e., the increasing share of fee-based non-intermediary services in the overall business portfolio of banks.

7 Given the focus on the banking industry, the non-banking financial intermediaries are kept outside the scope of the current narration.

8 See Supaarmorakul (2008) and Schreyer and Stauffer (2002) for more details on reference rate and user cost approaches to FISIM estimation.

9 The primary channel through which Big Data is being employed in the banking industry is via the adoption of blockchain technology in providing banking services. However, there is a serious lack of discussion on the challenges and ways of overcoming them, particularly in emerging economies (Hassani et al., 2018). Also, see Srivastava and Gopalkrishnan (2018) for significant areas where banks are harnessing the power of Big Data.

10 Technology here implies either the software or the hardware side innovations. Big and thick data may roughly be treated as software-side innovations.

11 Traditionally, satellite accounts have been used for covering non-traded inputs and outputs. However, their use in emerging economies has expanded considerably due to the limitations inherent in the developing data collection systems in such economies. Essentially, satellite accounts "provide a framework for examining difficult-to-measure

activities excluded, or inadequately treated, in the NIPA" (National Research Council, 2005). Output measurement of financial services, mainly the banking industry, is one such area.

12 Output measurement can be undertaken by the income, value-added or expenditure methods. Theoretically, all these three approaches measure the same economic phenomenon – i.e. what is produced. The value-added approach is adopted for this discussion. Adopting other approaches would not change the essence of the narration.

13 Available input-output tables for major emerging economies such as India, Brazil and Russia do not provide estimates of input-output connexions at the banking industry level but offer the same for financial services as defined in the ISIC Revision 3 or 4.

14 'Value' in this context is the use-values of commodities produced by the market economy. While the measurement of value is subjective, the amount of value produced in an economy can be approximated from the perspective of the producer. The amount of output produced by an individual firm is the practical measure of its value in the present context.

15 Banks have both direct and indirect roles in financial accumulation in an economy. They provide avenues for parking the savings in interest-bearing assets such as fixed deposits and even access to financial markets through investment account services. Banks are also intermediate as crucial players in both the money and capital markets; in countries such as India and China, they largely drive the movements in these markets. This allows financial accumulation to occur through investments in financial markets, which in themselves are enabled by the banking industry to a large extent.

16 The degree of randomization achieved in practice is a matter of debate. Even when the best efforts are invested in selecting a random sample, "randomization biases" (Banerjee et al., 2017) tend to distort the population-representativeness of the sample. As discussed later, new forms of data and data collection systems might very well be able to overcome some of these limitations.

17 One must be warned that this belief is valid only for the organized financial services sector. In emerging economies such as Brazil, China, India and others, a large portion of their financial services activities emerge in the unorganized sector. If the data from the organized sector is the only available source, then such data do not reflect the underlying population, which consists of both the organized and unorganized sectors.

18 This is not a generalized statement, and even the so-called "Big Data" sets might be generated under well-controlled experiments. However, with reference to financial services, observational data are the primary source as there is limited control that monetary authority can wield over the financial services industries. There are many aspects of the behaviour of banking and insurance firms that are not directly controllable by the monetary control, even in the most advanced economies with a high degree of financial depth.

19 This does not suggest that all the Emerging Economies are subject to the same constraints in their data collection systems. EMEs are diverse, and there are a lot of intricate differences in the problems faced by official agencies in these countries. For example, while Brazil and India have relatively transparent data assimilation and reporting systems, China, on the other hand, has a high degree of government regulation on the data that is made accessible to the public. Even though such differences exist, the overall state of development of the official data assimilation systems shows a broad macro similarity in terms of their current state of evolution across the EMEs.

20 Traditional standardization procedures involve a set of statistical treatments such as interpolation, extrapolation, imputation using proxy values, scaling of data in similar units, using ratios instead of level-form data, using first differences and growth rates instead of level-form data and others. Such procedures shall be required even when alternative data sources are employed to analyse the same variable of interest. However, when data sources are highly dissimilar, such procedures are not sufficient, though they may be necessary. For example, satellite imagery data, as a source of economic production in regions of a country, cannot be merged with the existing national accounts data simply by following the procedures mentioned earlier. One has to harmonize the definitions,

measurement units, and aggregation weights and translate the novel sources of information into a single variable which can be used as part of a typical large-scale macroeconomic model.

21 Economic advantage is on account of more disaggregated data availability with an enormous scope than what the typical consumer survey data would provide. The statistical advantage is on account of the more significant degrees of freedom and the ability to utilize the asymptomatic properties of the estimators.

22 The hardware and software components of the data collection agencies in emerging countries need to be improved for handling multiple data sources. Big Data is characterized not only by its large volume but also by its rapid frequency and flow. Data storage capacity, security, recording, analysis, and other aspects require an overhaul, which has sizeable financial implications. Emerging economies need to optimize their budgetary constraints to handle these outlays and treat them as investments rather than expenses. Such efforts will not only enhance the decision-making capabilities of policymakers at all levels of the hierarchy, but it will also create human capital in the process, as many people will get trained in using such data.

23 Given my experience as a professional in the marketing functions of several corporate banks, I must invoke the marketing perspective and try to blend it with the economic viewpoint. It is hoped that such an approach is looked at from a multidisciplinary perspective.

24 Bias in this context is the inability of the observed performance as measured by single output, to represent the true performance, which should be measured in a multi-output framework.

25 This is one of the reasons why many studies use non-parametric techniques such as Data Envelopment Analysis in the performance analysis of banking firms.

26 With the large presence of unorganized and shadow banking segments, this point implies that if regulatory actions produce desirable changes in the non-organized components, too, then such regulations may be hypothesized as deep in terms of their impact on the overall banking industry.

27 One must bear in mind that the fee-based services, although explicitly charged and taxed by authorities as products of banks, are provided as simply complementary goods and are thus not suitable for treatment as final outputs in themselves.

28 The financial services industry has a far broader scope than the banking industry. It includes insurance services, non-banking financial services, and other financial services other than traditional commercial banking.

29 ILO (2018) states that more than 60% of the employed workforce in the EMEs are engaged in the informal economy. With such a significant dependency on the informal sector, the scope for imputations and other adjustment techniques is prominent in these nations.

30 Industry-level estimates for financial services output can be interpreted more robustly than the individual firm-level data because any given financial services industry is simultaneously a supplier of inputs to other financial services and a producer of output. Whether the services rendered by a single financial service firm are input or output is thus debatable. However, it is theoretically much more convenient to consider the financial services industry as a producer of output as a whole and possibly avoid the complex interdependencies of these services at the level of firms.

31 The Global Financial Development Database of the World Bank provides information on three variables of interest in this context. First, the financial system deposits as a proportion of the GDP; second, the proportion of total firms using banks to finance their long-term investments; and third, the proportion of total firms using banks to finance their working capital requirements. On all these three accounts, major EMEs such as China, Russia, Brazil, India and Indonesia have shown a gradual and consistent increase in the last decade. This may be considered a sign of the increasing space that the organized financial sector occupies in these economies as against the so-called shadow financial sector.

32 Unit-level data are the data that correspond to individual, institutional units as defined in the SNA, 2008 manual. The quality of these data is the most crucial determinant of the ability of a nation to construct high-quality national income accounts and, through

them, derive high-quality estimates of the key macroeconomic variable. The inequality among emerging and developing countries on this account is significant. This has resulted in the call for more statistical adjustments at the end of the data compilers to make them internationally comparable.

33 With the share of non-agricultural output secularly rising against the share of agriculture in aggregate GDP in most top emerging economies, this problem becomes all the more pronounced and worrisome.

34 An economically optimal price index must fulfil critical properties which were very finely laid down by Fisher (1921) and Fisher (1922).

35 This is also one of the arguments favouring more robust financial sector regulation, which is generally disliked by the pro-market economists who would like to push forward financial deregulation instead. The financial market structure in EMEs is not strong enough in the current period to allow for further deregulation. Look at the issue of non-performing assets (NPA) in Russia, India and even Brazil. If unchecked, persistence in NPAs can very well crumble the existence of large-scale public sector banks that are generally more prone to this financial challenge.

36 These observations imply that the econometric evidence on bi-causality between finance and growth and the causal role of finance on growth should be interpreted about whether these analysts adjusted their estimated coefficients for the availability and quality of human and physical capital. Perhaps removing the intermediating role of human and physical capital in the finance-growth nexus might very well result in no causal relationship between the both whatsoever.

37 The aftermath of the war was not the only factor motivating the standardization of national income accounts through the SNA. Richard Stone put it succinctly when he noted that "The problems of war finance, full employment and the marketing of the produce of all forms of economic activity . . . have come to be discussed in terms of the concepts of national income studies" (United Nations, 1947).

38 The 1947 report stressed collecting data from the so-called elementary transactions that occur between individual accounting entities and building up the national aggregate from such building blocks. The report reads, "Experience shows that these ideas can be expounded and presented more lucidly if the elementary transactions of an economic system rather than the final aggregates of transactions, such as the national income, are made the starting-point of the enquiry". Richard Stone and his team particularly stressed this approach in the memorandum submitted as a part of this report, which is still a seminal work in national income accounting practice.

39 Economic distribution here refers to economic inequality, as Sen (1973) suggested, who defines economic inequality as a set of income, expenditure, and wealth inequalities. Hence, economic distribution is much larger than that of the popularly used notion of income inequality.

40 Insurance performance consists of efficiency, profitability, productivity, economies of scale and others.

41 Risk allocation needs to be Pareto-optimal for insurance to have a rational economic justification. There can be situations wherein a non-competitive market structure might prevent the insurance firms from allocating risks efficiently. Emerging economies can be prone to this issue, mainly where government-induced monopolies exist. Many EMEs have been opening their doors to domestic and foreign private capital. However, changes in market structure take time to occur and possibly in the coming decade, the economic efficiency of the insurance industry in EMEs will improve further.

42 Capital is used in the insurance industry in terms of physical capital and as human and financial capital. Accounting for these two kinds of capital in the insurance production function is quite challenging due to stringent data requirements that the EMEs may not be able to fulfil. For illustration, thoroughly accounting for human capital in the insurance industry requires a very well-structured, organized labour market. EMEs such as

China, where most of the labour market activities are included within the domain of the official statistical system, can probably account for this variable. However, for economies such as Brazil, Russia and India, the problem of unorganized labour markets can constrain the success of this parameter. Unorganized labour market activities are not easily accountable in terms of the official data collection, and thus the agencies need to rely on imputations such as shadow pricing, which inevitably are prone to errors.

43 Output estimation becomes more challenging when looking at investment-oriented life insurance products that produce risk coverage for their policyholders and investment returns. Here, investment risks are borne by the policyholder, but the insurance firm provides a pooling of fund services that help reduce the investor's risk exposure.

44 In the present context, 'performance' includes measuring efficiency, total and partial factor productivities, and economies of scale and scope in the current context.

45 In this context, Owusu and Alhassan (2021) is an interesting application of this model in the context of the financial services industry. Even though their paper focuses on the banking sector, their broad findings and methodological approach can also be extrapolated to the insurance industry.

46 Total reserves of an insurance firm (whether life or nonlife) is generally defined as the sum of unearned premiums and outstanding claims as underwritten by the company).

47 Such a practice can cause serious specification errors and distort the empirical foundations of the work.

48 Risk coverage provided to policyholders can be measured using the company's amount of claims actually paid. Such data are generally readily available in the major emerging economies through their official agencies or the firms' financial statements.

49 One may consider using the changes in the firm's market capitalisation in the stock exchange as a possible measure of value generated for shareholders. Alternatively, dividends and capital gains can be used during a specified period (usually a year).

50 Incremental because the Asset under Management of the insurance firm is a stock variable, while its incremental value is a flow variable. Theoretically, the output is strictly a flow concept.

51 One must bear in mind that deflation is not always required. In the case of purely cross-sectional studies, one may proceed with current price data. However, for inter-temporal models, deflation is a necessity. Inter-temporal studies occupy a large part of the extant literature on insurance performance.

52 Economic efficiency refers to the sum total of technical and allocative efficiencies in the present context. See Kalirajan and Shand (1999) for a detailed discussion on the issues in efficiency measurement.

53 Policy interventions cause distortions in the form of constraining the speed with which the markets can match the buyer's and seller's decisions, thus hampering the process of "entrepreneurial discovery" (Kirzner, 1997).

54 Shocks in this context imply exogenous shocks. It is necessary to locate the exogenous shocks as "only responses to an exogenous variable can measure the effects of policy-induced changes in that variable" (Cochrane, 1994). Exogenous shocks in the present context might include unexpected technological innovations and unforeseen changes in international trade. However, as stressed in Cochrane (1994), the specification of an unexpected event as an exogenous shock depends on how much the concerned economic agent was aware of the same and had accounted for the same in their decision-making. This is challenging for any researcher, and the slightest error in specifying the exogenous shocks will dramatically change the final analysis.

55 This is not to suggest that input measurement is a trivial task. The choice of the variables to measure the inputs, their data availability and the quality of available data pose a tough challenge for analysts in obtaining theoretically consistent measures of inputs. Mainstream neoclassical theory, for example, expects volume-based metrics of labour and capital. In reality, however, the constant-price measures are employed and the very

derivation of constant-price variables is a complicated task. However, the definition of inputs and their measurement also have consensus in the empirical literature.

56 Market prices are increasingly becoming essential components in the economic planning process in China. However, there are substantial lags in obtaining the data on prices, which creates inefficiencies in economic coordination. In the financial services industry of China, the large extent of the NPA problem and the public sector bias in the allocation of loanable funds is one example among many.

57 Such methods are used at the firm level in banking services also, and their use is not limited to industry-wide analysis only. An interesting application of the same can be found in Fragnière et al. (2011).

References

Acharya, D., & Kamaiah, B. (2001). Simple sum versus Divisia monetary aggregates: An empirical evaluation. *Economic and Political Weekly, 36*(4), 317–326.

Banerjee, A., Banerji, R., Berry, J., Duflo, E., Kannan, H., Mukerji, S., Shotland, M., & Walton, M. (2017). From proof of concept to scalable policies: Challenges and solutions, with an application. *Journal of Economic Perspectives, 31*(4), 73–102.

Barman, R. B., & Samanta, G. P. (2004). Banking services price index: An exploratory analysis for India. *IFC Bulletin* (4), 110–124.

Chambers, R., & Färe, R. (1993). Input-output separability in production models and its structural consequences. *Journal of Economics, 57*(2), 197–202.

Cochrane, J. H. (1994). Shocks. *Carnegie-Rochester Conference Series on Public Policy, 41*, 295–364.

Fisher, I. (1921). The best form of index number. *Quarterly Publication of the American Statistical Association, 17*, 533–537.

Fisher, I. (1922). *The making of index numbers*. Houghton-Mifflin.

Fragnière, E., Moresino, F., & Zheng, N. (2011). Development of pricing models for intangible services based on conjoint analysis and mathematical programming: A case study about the design of credit card services in China. In *2011 annual SRII global conference*. Retrieved January 6, 2022, from https://doi.org/10.1109/srii.2011.71

Green, H. A. J. (2016). *Aggregation in economic analysis*. Princeton Legacy Library.

Groves, R. M., & Harris-Kojetin, B. A. (2017a). *Federal statistics, multiple data sources, and privacy protection: Next steps, a consensus study report of the panel on improving federal statistics for policy and social science research using multiple data sources and state-of-the-art estimation methods*. US National Academy of Sciences, National Academies Press.

Groves, R. M., & Harris-Kojetin, B. A. (2017b). *Innovations in federal statistics combining data sources while protecting privacy, report of the panel on improving federal statistics for policy and social science research using multiple data sources and state-of-the-art estimation methods*. US National Academy of Sciences, National Academies Press.

Hassani, H., Huang, X., & Silva, E. (2018). Banking with Blockchain-ed big data. *Journal of Management Analytics, 5*(4), 256–275. https://doi.org/10.1080/23270012.2018.1528900

ILO. (2018). *World employment social outlook: Trends 2018*. Report of the International Labour Organization.

Kalirajan, K. P., & Shand, R. T. (1999). Frontier production functions and technical efficiency measures. *Journal of Economic Surveys, 13*, 149–172. https://doi.org/10.1111/1467-6419.00080

Kirzner, I. M. (1997). Entrepreneurial discovery and the competitive market process: An Austrian approach. *Journal of Economic Literature, 35*(1), 60–85.

Lucas, R. E. (1976). *Econometric policy evaluation: A critique, carnegie-rochester conference series on public policy* (Vol. 1, pp. 19–46). Elsevier.

Menger, C. (1985). *Investigations into the method of the social sciences with special reference to economics*. New York University Press.

National Research Council. (2005). *Beyond the market: Designing nonmarket accounts for the United States*. The National Academies Press. https://doi.org/10.17226/11181.

Owusu, B. F., &Alhassan, A. L. (2021). Asset-liability management and bank profitability: Statistical cost accounting analysis from an emerging market. *International Journal of Finance and Economics, 26*(1), 1488–1502.

Schlicht, E. (1985). *Isolation and aggregation in economics*. Springer-Verlag.

Schreyer, P., & Stauffer, P. (2002). *Measuring the production of financial corporations*. Progress Report by the OECD Task Force on Financial Services (Banking Services) in National Accounts.

Sen, A. (1973). *On economic inequality*. Oxford University Press.

Shriffin, R. M. (2016). Drawing causal inference from big data. *Proceedings of the National Academy of Sciences of the United States of America, 113*(27), 7308–7309. www.pnas.org/cgi/doi/10.1073/pnas.1608845113

SNA. (2008). System of national accounts. *United Nations Statistics Division*.

Srivastava, U., & Gopalkrishnan, S. (2018). Impact of big data analytics on banking sector: Learning for Indian banks. *Procedia Computer Science, 50*(2015), 643–652.

Strömmer, K. (2019). *Big or thick data? Collecting data in meaningful ways*. https://wpmu.mah.se/nmict192group6/2019/10/11/big-or-thick-data-collecting-data-in-meaningful-ways/

Supaarmorakul, P. (2008). *Estimation of financial intermediation services indirectly measured (FISIM): Thailand's case*. IFC Bulletin No. 28, 83–100.

United Nations. (1947). *Measurement of national income and the construction of social accounts*. Report of the Sub-Committee on National Income Statistics of the League of Nations Committee of Statistical Experts, United Nations, Geneva.

Part III

Empirical case studies

A BRIICS perspective

8 Empirical case studies for the banking industry on implications of using alternative output definitions

8.1. Rationale, methodologies and data

Parts I and II have provided perspectives on banking and insurance output measurement from the literature survey and insights from practitioners, respectively. Part III now provides empirical exercises on the implications of alternative output measures on various performance parameters. In the present study, performance is conceptualized in terms of efficiencies, productivities and related issues whose estimates can throw some light on how well the firms or the industry utilises their resources and progresses economically. This comprehensive conceptualization of the term 'performance' suits the present context well. Literature on banking and insurance, as summarized in Tables 2.1 and 2.2, shows the wide variety of topics that have been investigated using different output measures. Covering all of them is not feasible due to the limited space and scope of this book. Thus, three matters are looked into in this part. First is the implications of alternative output measures for separately aggregate partial factor productivities of banking and insurance industries.

Furthermore, life and nonlife insurance industries are analysed separately in the next chapter. The second is a similar exercise concerning the index-based measure of aggregate total factor productivity and parametric and non-parametric measures of aggregate technical efficiency.[1] The third is an analysis of the variations, if any, that are brought about by alternative output measures in aggregate industry-level estimates of returns to scale measured via parametric production functions. These three matters are investigated separately for the aggregate banking and insurance industries. Data used are sectoral, i.e. aggregated over the entire industry rather than firm-level.[2]

The choice of the three issues is primarily motivated by their popularity in the literature. This part of the book is presented as a case study on the empirical implications of performance estimates to alternate output measures for the banking and insurance industries. As noted by Boda and Piklova (2021, p. 1554)[3]: "the effect of adopting an approach or choosing an input-output set within an approach upon efficiency scores and results has not been consistently explored". Hence, choosing the issues that have garnered sufficient research attention seemed to be a plausible approach in this regard. The other motivating factor is the availability of data.

DOI: 10.4324/9781003149828-11

More elaboration is required on the choice of focusing upon aggregate industry-level data rather than firm-level data, which has traditionally been done in the literature. Performance estimation in banking and insurance has largely been undertaken on firm-level data. This is quite understandable because assessing technical efficiency, productivity and returns to scale requires analysing how decision-making units (DMUs) act within a production function framework. Not only theory but also the empirical methods such as DEA require data which represent individual DMUs. Firms tend to be the best representatives of the DMUs. This is the most preferred approach in the literature. However, the aggregated effects of the diverse decisions by individual firms are also matters that deserve attention. Economic theory saw a lot of analytical progress when the subject incorporated pure macroeconomic theory and released itself from its dependency on pure microeconomic logic. Such a fundamental change in perspective is necessary for the evolutionary success of a discipline. As Colander (1993, p. 447) notes: "the same reality can look fundamentally different depending on one's perspective and that revolutions in a discipline occur through these changes in perspectives". The Keynesian and the New Classical revolutions are possibly the best illustrations of such a fundamental change in economics (Colander, 1993). The current consensus is that micro-foundations are a necessary condition to contextualize macroeconomic aggregates, and in the case of performance analysis of the banking and insurance industries, one can approach industry-level aggregate as emanating from individual optimization decisions. Such aggregation is also necessary when long-term economic issues need to be assessed from a policy angle.[4] In such scenarios, policymakers would be interested in firm-level heterogeneities in the performance of banks and insurers and their sectoral performance. Production behaviour of individual firms is the level at which conscious decision-making is undertaken. However, the economic environment faced by the individual banking and insurance firms is a result of their accumulated, aggregated and interdependent actions. One way to approach these actions is to utilize a general equilibrium approach using firm-level data. Such an approach requires data which are very difficult to locate in the case of the economies under consideration here (the BRIICS countries). Another approach is to analyse how the industry as a whole is behaving instead of focusing on the individual firms. The issue under consideration here is the empirical sensitivity of performance estimates to alternate output measures for the banking and insurance industries. Suppose the industry-level estimates show considerable empirical sensitivity on this account. In that case, it may serve as a plausible justification for the existence of a similar pattern at more disaggregated levels. Hence, aggregate banking and insurance industries are analysed separately in this part of the book. The industry as a whole is treated as an aggregate DMU whose behaviour is a result of the decisions taken by individual firms composing it. The aggregate industry across each year of the time series data for the period 2000 to 2021 is treated as separate DMUs. In other words, in this study, the aggregate industry-level production function is estimated rather than the industrial production function using individual firm-level data on inputs and outputs. Aggregation is undertaken over the chosen inputs and outputs variables.

The use of the aggregate production function gives rise to the so-called "aggregation problem" (Felipe & McCombie, 2005, p. 467). It refers to the problems in building an aggregate production function from individual micro-level production functions. Traditionally, this problem has been referred to in the context of economy-wide production functions that combine inputs and outputs from heterogeneous industries. However, in the present case, one may partially dodge this problem by arguing that inputs and outputs from the same industry have been aggregated. Moreover, all the data employed in Chapters 8 and 9 have been obtained from international and national official agencies and thus represent the best possible information available.[5] Furthermore, firm-level data were not available for all the economies under consideration. Finally, efficiency and productivity analysis at the industrial level is largely missing in the literature. All these factors necessitated and motivated the adoption of an aggregative approach to performance analysis using an industry-level aggregate production function.

The present and the next chapter focus on six economies: Brazil, Russia, India, Indonesia, China and Russia (BRIICS). As shown in Tables 2.1 and 2.2, the amount of evidence on emerging economies is considerably lesser than those on advanced economies. Data constraints are the fundamental reasons for this. However, data limitations should not prevent the efforts to analyse emerging economies as the selected economies occupy, among all the major EMEs, a large majority of the share in the World real GDP.[6] Furthermore, they represent a vast untapped potential market, as discussed in Chapter 1. Lastly, the evidence on performance analysis for most BRIICS countries is quite limited. Thus, there is a considerable gap in the literature that can be fulfilled by the attempt made here in Part III.

Given the primary aim of this part is to provide a set of case studies on the empirical implications of alternating output measures in the aggregate production for banking, life and nonlife insurance industries, isolating the pure effects of variations in output definitions from other possible sources is necessary. Performance estimates such as industrial technical efficiency or total factor productivity can vary due to multiple sources, as explained in Figure 8.1.

Given these possible sources that could explain the variations in performance estimates under different output specifications, controlling for as many non-output sources as possible is necessary to isolate the pure empirical effects of variations in output measures. Hence, the most basic and common input vector of labour and physical capital is used as far as possible, particularly in analysing technical efficiency and returns to scale. The theoretical approach of specifying production function is allowed to vary to find the implications of different output measures under alternative functional forms. Both the Cobb-Douglas[7] and the Trans-logarithmic[8] production functions are employed in sections 8.4 and 9.4, while only the Cobb-Douglas[9] model is used for sections 8.3 and 9.3.[10] In terms of empirical methods, a Solow-style residual total factor productivity index[11] is built in section 8.3 for the banking industry and similarly in 9.3 for life and nonlife insurance industries. DEA,[12] Ordinary Least Squares (OLS)[13] and the Stochastic Frontier Approach (SFA)[14] methods are employed in sections 8.3 and 9.3, while OLS, Ridge Regression and SFA[15] are used in sections 8.4 and 9.4 with both the Cobb-Douglas and trans-log production functions. Ridge regression is employed to deal with the well-known multicollinearity problem in estimating trans-log production functions.[16] Finally, the data sources, variables, and definitions are presented in the appendix to this chapter.

However, all the data used in this and the next chapter have been collected from various official banking and insurance regulatory bodies of the chosen economies and diverse international sources such as the IMF, World Bank, Bank for International Settlements (BIS) and the International Labour Organization. All the inputs and outputs data used in this and the next chapter are specific to the banking and insurance industries respective. They are in aggregate form across all firms in the industry. All the nominal variables are deflated using the country-specific Consumer Price Index (CPI) available from the IMF. All the monetary variables were converted into the same measurement unit in order to facilitate intra-economy comparisons of the estimates. It may also be noted that all the subsequent empirical analyses have been undertaken in a multi-input and single output framework. This has been done to assess how each of the chosen output measures induces variations in the efficiency, productivity, and scale estimates. This applies to both – Chapter 8 and Chapter 9. Given the lack of space, only the most essential methodological details have been presented here. The rest can be availed from the author upon request.[17]

Lastly, a brief note on the output variables chosen in this part of the book is called for. The following output measures have been employed in Part III of this work.[18] The first measure is deposits and is proxied by the amount of total outstanding deposits measured in 2010 prices-based local currency units. This is a stock variable. It reflects the amount of services rendered by the banking sector to its depositors. The second measure is operating income and is proxied by the amount of net operating income after extraordinary items and taxes measured in 2010 prices-based local currency units. This is a flow variable. It represents both the interest and non-interest incomes net of interest, non-interest and other expenses, including taxes. It may also be construed as a rough measure of the amount of profits earned by banks. This variable represents the flow of services generated by banks during a given year. The third measure is the amount of loans and is proxied by the amount of total outstanding loans outstanding measured in 2010 prices-based local currency units. This measure represents the quantum of services banks provide in terms of their traditional intermediation role in the economy. It is a stock variable. The fourth measure is the financial assets of banks and is proxied by the amount of total financial assets of the banking industry measured in 2010 prices-based local currency unit. It is a stock variable. It represents both the traditional and non-traditional intermediation roles of banks in the economy. It consists of both the loans and investments.[19] The fifth measure is a volume indicator of deposits and is proxied by the number

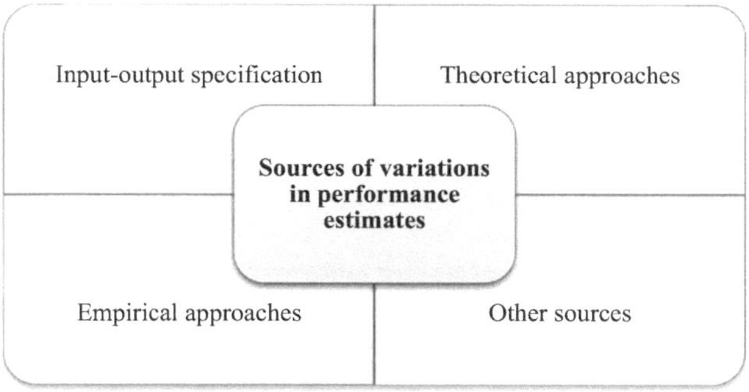

Figure 8.1 Sources of variations in performance estimates

Note: The 'other sources' represent issues such as specification errors, human error in estimation, measurement errors, etc.

Source: Author's analysis of relevant literature.

of total depositors at the end of the given year in the aggregate banking industry. This is a stock variable and is a volume measure. The sixth measure is a volume indicator of loans and is proxied by the number of borrowers.

The seventh measure is another volume indicator of deposits and is captured by the number of total deposit accounts. It is a stock variable. Finally, the last measure is another volume indicator of loans and is represented by the number of loan accounts. It is a stock variable. As one can observe, the stock variables dominate in this study and reflect the literature trend, as shown in Table 2.1. Both value and volume measures are utilized. This is an improvement over the prevalent reliance on value measures. Data on volume measures at the aggregate level are more readily available than at the firm level. These data were obtained from the databases of the World Bank, International Monetary Fund (IMF), Bank for International Settlements (BIS), and where required, from the national banking regulators of each of the chosen countries. Appropriate adjustments were made to interpolate some of the data that were found missing.[20]

8.2. Empirical sensitivity of selected partial factor productivity estimates across the banking sector of BRIICS

Partial Factor Productivities (PFPs) provide a comprehensive overview of the productivity movements in an industry. Given that these measures ascribe entire output to a single input, which violates the multi-input nature of the banking industry, their use is limited to providing preliminary findings and descriptive analysis. With the advent of multi-factor productivity measurement, the need for PFPs has reduced drastically. However, for the aggregate banking industry, labour and capital productivity can provide some evidence of the broad productivity movements in the long run. These secular movements can provide a valuable indication of the banking industry's ability to contribute to aggregate economic growth. This section thus comments on how the estimates of labour productivity (LP) and capital productivity (CP) of the aggregate banking industry vary as alternative output measures are employed within the exact definition of LP and CP. LP is defined as the ratio of the chosen output variable for the given economy to the number of employees in the banking industry for a given economy.

$$LP_{ij} = (Output_{ij}/Labour_{ij}) \quad (1)$$
$$CP_{ij} = (Output_{ij}/Physical\ Capital_{ij}) \quad (2)$$

Where i = the given country and j = chosen output measure, Labour = number of employees in the banking industry of the given economy, Capital = Number of non-branch retail agent outlets or the number of commercial bank branches or the number of ATM machines.[21]

Tables 8.1 to 8.11 in Appendix 1 provide the estimates on variations in the distribution[22] of LP and CP induced by alternative output definitions for each of the BRIICS countries. Analysis of each of the Tables 8.1 to 8.11 reveals some basic patterns. First, there are substantial differences in the mean levels of labour and capital productivities across all economies. Differences in output measures can induce large differences in the level of labour and capital productivity. Such a gap in productivity levels can cause substantial differences in how the progress of the banking industry is interpreted and the kind of policy interventions designed to improve the same. These differences can also cause wide variations in how the industry's market structure is interpreted. Low productivity levels may be interpreted as signs of a high degree of imperfections and economic barriers that could be thwarting the full realization of the industry's productive capacity. With inconsistency in productivity estimates across output measures, choosing a representative output or output vector is a critical decision in any performance analysis of the banking industry. It also does not seem that convergence could occur in these measures if sufficiently long periods were analysed. This is primarily because the trend itself is very different across these estimated series. The second key finding is that variability, as measured by the CV (coefficient of variation), in estimates of LP and CP is also disparate across the output measures but, in general, is not as heterogeneous as in the case of mean-level estimates. Third, the economic dynamics at play in productivity behaviour are different for value versus the volume output measures. Value measures show larger variability than the volume measures despite both having stock dimensions. This is particularly true when compared to their third and fourth moments of the distribution.[23]

In summary, it can be broadly concluded that differences in output measures can cause wide differences in the distribution of labour and capital productivities in the banking industry. This occurs predominantly at the first, third and fourth moments of their distribution,[24] while there is a good amount of consistency in terms of the variability measured by CV. These findings are valid across the selected emerging economies. One of the implications of these findings is that locating the critical determinants of banking productivity and inducing improvements in the same would be very difficult unless the distributional trade-offs in choosing alternative output measures are recognized.

The following section moves beyond partial productivity and incorporates total factor productivity and technical efficiency into the current narrative.

8.3. Empirical sensitivity of total factor productivity and technical efficiency estimates across the banking sector of BRIICS

Tables 8.12 to 8.28 in Appendix 2 present the estimates of the growth rate in the Solow-style residual TFP index,[25] aggregate technical efficiency scores using DEA[26] and the technical efficiency scores using a Cobb-Douglas stochastic production frontier function. Due to space constraints, only the most relevant findings and comments are mentioned here.[27]

The first issue under consideration is the growth rate in the TFP index using different output measures, as shown in Tables 8.12, 8.15, 8.18, 8.21, 8.23 and 8.26 in Appendix 2. The initial observation is that the growth rate in the TFP index shows broadly the same trend across all output measures. In very few cases, one observes a shift in the trend itself, such as in Tables 8.12 (TFPG3), 8.21 (TFPG1) and 8.26 (TFPG1). Second, financial assets, number of total deposit accounts and number of total loan accounts have caused much more variability in the distribution of estimated growth in the TFP-index compared to other output measures. Understandably, financial assets as an output variable could embody large fluctuations due to risky investments by inherently volatile banks. The finding for the number of deposit and loan accounts seems somewhat surprising. It may be on account of some structural shift in these variables. This dimension requires further research in the future. Third, the nature of skewness is very different depending on the output measure employed. Russia, for example, displays a highly skewed distribution of the growth in the TFP index across all output measures, as shown in Table 8.15. Except for it, all other banking industries show multiple types of skewness in the data ranging from highly skewed to fairly symmetrical. As shown in Table 8.12, for Brazil, the distribution of the volume measures-based growth in the TFP index is highly skewed, while the value measures-based index shows moderate to low skewness. For Russia, while all the output measures show a high degree of skewness, the volume measure shows positive while the value measures show negative skewness. In the case of India, as shown in Table 8.18, skewness is very high across most of the output measures, but it is fundamentally different for value and volume measures. As discussed earlier in the previous chapters, the value-volume difference in output measurement has many economic implications for any kind of performance analysis in banking. For China, as shown in Table 8.23, except for the financial assets output measure (TFPG3), the rest of the TFP growth estimates seem fairly symmetrical across the sample period. The nature of skewness is the opposite in the case of TFPG1 (amount of deposits) and TFPG2 (amount of loans) for South Africa, as shown in Table 8.26. Fourth, it is also necessary to verify if the information content of individual estimated TFP growth series is homogenous or unique, and one crude way of doing so is the degree of linear correlation among them. Estimates for Brazil (Table 8.12) show that the TFP growth rates under alternative output measures are not firmly correlated, and some of the series even have an almost zero correlation.

In the case of Russia (Table 8.15), however, the TFPG series with alternative output measures have very high and statistically significant correlations. The Indian banking industry (Table 8.18) also shows a similar pattern. The TFP series using the number of total loan accounts as output shows a moderately high to high correlation with all other series. For the Indonesian banking industry (Table 8.21), the number of deposit accounts and the amount of deposits based TFPG series is positively and significantly correlated. The financial assets (TFPG3) and amount of loans (TFPG2) series are also highly positively and significantly correlated. This is true across all the economies except China. It is expected because the financial assets include both loans and investments, which may be purely due to definitional similarities. In the case of China (Table 8.23), in only a few cases is, a high and significant correlation observed. Interestingly, the loan amount (TFPG2) and the number of deposit accounts (TFPG4) based series show a high and significant correlation. This has generally not been observed in other economies. Finally, in the case of South Africa (Table 8.26), all the available series show a high and significant correlation. Alternative output measures do not seem to be adding any new information to the productivity performance in this case.

The second matter estimates industry-level average technical efficiency scores across the sample period using DEA as contained in Tables 8.13, 8.16, 8.19, 8.22, 8.24 and 8.27, and with SFA as contained in Tables 8.14, 8.17, 8.20, 8.22, 8.25 and 8.28. The estimates in these tables reflect the average efficiency scores across the sample period for the aggregate banking industry. In the case of Brazil (Table 8.13), the mean level of efficiency across the sample period shows a reasonably good performance across all output measures, whether value or volume. Variability, however, is widely different. It seems that assets and the number of loan accounts-based TE scores are the most volatile (TE3 and TE5). The correlation coefficients are primarily insignificant and small. In the case of amount of deposits (TE2), efficiency scores positively correlate with volume measures-based TE scores, i.e. with TE4 and TE5.[28] Volume measures have a high and significant correlation, i.e. between TE4 and TE5 in the Brazilian banking industry. Regarding the SFA-based measures, the industry has, on average, performed well and seems to have been functioning near the average frontier. Variability is relatively low for all the reported measures. Correlation is low in all the cases, possibly implying independent information content across output measures. For the Russian banking industry,

DEA-based efficiency scores do not seem to vary much across output measures in terms of the mean levels and the variability as captured by CV. However, the correlations are negligible, even if significant, possibly indicating differences in the underlying trend in the efficiencies. Similar conclusions seem evident for SFA-based measures in Table 8.17. In the context of India, as contained in Table 8.19, performance indicators are compactly spread and do not seem to diverge much. Only a few cases show a high and significant correlation. Again, the amount of deposits is highly correlated with volume measures, and volume measures show high interrelation among themselves (TE4 and TE5). Similar results are seen for SFA-based measures, as shown in Table 8.20. Correlations are very high and significant, and it does not appear that alternating the output measures impacts the broad conclusions. Estimates for the Indonesian mainstream (excluding Islamic banking output) commercial banking sector reflect that efficiency scores using the amount of deposits and number of deposit accounts show a smaller level of TE as compared to loans and assets measures, while TE scores based on the same output measures (TE1 and TE4) show much higher variability than the loans and asset-based scores.

Similarly, in the case of China (in Tables 8.24 and 8.25), the differences in output measures do not seem to be inducing much variation in the findings. CV estimates show differences, but they are not wide enough to warrant any meaningful proof of output sensitivity. Lastly, in the South African banking industry, estimates across different output measures show quite similar behaviour, though there is some evidence of unique information contents in terms of correlations. Thus, the empirical sensitivity of efficiency estimates differs across economies but broadly suggests similarity in the final results.

8.4. Empirical sensitivity of returns to scale estimates across the banking sector of BRIICS

Industrial progress is an outcome of a large number of factors. One of them is the nature of input-output relations as summarized by Economies of Scale (EOS) for the industry as a whole. EOS can be approached from either the cost or the production function route. This is generally done under the assumption of duality. Hence, this study approaches the EOS issue via the production function route using the concept of Returns to Scale (RTS). RTS does not necessarily imply EOS. However, given the scope of this section, attention is restricted to estimating RTS instead without further linking it to EOS.

Output expansion is generally a conscious and active objective of the macroeconomic policy in emerging economies. Given the potentially large unutilized capacities across many industries, expanding inputs and improving technology is common in these economies. The banking industry also shows similar characteristics to the EMEs, and thus increasing inputs to expand output is a preferred strategy for improving the industry's performance. Moreover, given a sizeable stock of unutilized resources, understanding how the output may change due to the increase in the use of these resources is necessary for designing optimal growth and development policies. RTS provides an essential piece of information on this account. At both the microeconomic and macroeconomic levels, the nature of RTS can have profound implications for how an industry evolves and what kind of opportunities and challenges will it create for its participants. The pace of growth is also, to a large extent determined by the nature of RTS. Decreasing RTS, for example, implies that larger resource expenditures have to be incurred to achieve a given output level. This may result in a lower growth rate in output despite large resource expenditures. Achieving a particular industrial growth rate will mean expending more resources than otherwise would be necessary under constant or increasing RTS, thereby probably sacrificing efficiency. However, how RTS behaves depends largely on how the output is defined for the banking industry. Given the debates on output measurement and alternative viewpoints in the literature, this section attempts to provide a brief and elementary comment on the relation between output definition and the consequent RTS under a production function approach. RTS can be approached from two angles. First is the cost function method, wherein the total cost function would be analysed with reference to output measures to locate the nature of scale expansion. The second is through the production function, where the combined partial impacts of each input on the total output show the kind of RTS that exists. The second route has been chosen for this section. As discussed earlier and explained in the underlying estimates to the results presented here, alternative output measures have been employed. A two-inputs and one-output production function, specified in Cobb-Douglas and trans-logarithmic[29] forms, using traditional OLS, ridge regression and SFA are estimated. Appropriate methods to estimate the RTS coefficients are employed, and the results have been reported in the tables that follow. The underlying estimates are presented in Appendix 3. The inputs are restricted to labour (number of banking employees)[30] and physical capital (number of branches).[31] This has been done to present the most basic production model for this empirical case study. By keeping the framework essential in terms of variable complexity, the focus has been diverted to the issue of how different output measures cause changes in the RTS estimates if any.

The use of both Cobb-Douglas and trans-log production function specifications is in line with the literature. While the trans-log function has primarily been favoured in literature, given the aggregated nature of data, Cobb-Douglas specification seems to be a reasonably representative theorization of the underlying true production function. As is well known in the literature, the trans-log production function is characterized by very high multicollinearity. This can cause many well-recognized econometric problems in the quality of the estimated coefficients. Hence, the ridge regression method was also employed to deal with this issue. This method allows a conscious trade-off between bias and efficiency of the OLS estimators in order to reduce multicollinearity among the variables by penalizing the OLS estimators. Critiques have argued that the lasso regression is a better approach due to the non-orthogonality of the ridge estimators. However, lasso method-based estimates were also examined, and the results were broadly the same.[32] Given the reasonably simple interpretation of ridge regression estimators, the same has been used in this section and section 9.4. Time series data have been used from 2000 to 2020. Lastly, data constraints have greatly affected the choice of input and output variables.

The specifications[33] of the production functions used in this section are as below:

$$\text{In}(Y_i) = \text{In}(A) + b_1 \text{ In}(L_i) + b_2 \text{ In}(K_i) + u_i \quad (3)$$

$$\text{In}(Y_i) = b_0 + b_L \text{ In}(L) + b_K \text{ In}(K) + \frac{1}{2} b_{LL} (\text{InL})^2 + \frac{1}{2} b_{KK} (\text{InK})^2 + b_{LK} (\text{InL}) \star (\text{InK}) + u_i \quad (4)$$

Where i = the banking industry in a given year, A and b_0 are the constant parameters, u_i is the error term, L = number of employees in the aggregate banking industry, and K = number of branches in the banking industry.[34]

Brazil

Table 8.29 in Appendix 3 summarizes the findings on the variations in RTS estimates using different measures of banking industry outputs. The underlying estimations are also provided in Appendix 3 in Tables 8.35 to 8.39. The broad conclusion is that the banking industry in Brazil has recorded increasing returns to scale at the aggregate level during the sample period of 2000 to 2020. Two perspectives can be suggested here. In terms of each output variable, the RTS coefficient's robustness across different models is the robustness. In terms of each model, though, some variations in the RTS value and direction are visible. Using the financial assets, in particular, yields divergent estimates. In terms of the quantitative size of RTS, variations are clearly evident when alternative output measures are employed. The loan accounts measure is remarkably divergent from the average behaviour across other output measures.

Russia

For the Russian banking industry as a whole, Table 8.30 shows that there is no variation in the direction of RTS. Still, the quantitative size of the RTS coefficient varies considerably across models and output measures even while ignoring Model 1, which is conflated with severely high multicollinearity.[35] Intra-model variations in the value of RTS across output measures are much wider than intra-output variations across alternative models. Estimations underlying Table 8.30 are provided across Tables 8.40 to 8.43 in Appendix 3.

India

Table 8.31 presents the Indian commercial banking industry results with the related empirical estimations contained in Tables 8.44 to 8.48. Compared to

Brazil and Russia, the results here are much more similar in terms of RTS's direction and its coefficient value. Using different output measures does not seem to be causing much of a variation in RTS estimates in the case of India.

Indonesia

In the case of the aggregate Indonesian banking industry, as shown in Table 8.32 and complemented by related results in Tables 8.49 to 8.53, considerable variations in RTS estimates can be located. Whether across each model or output variable, the RTS coefficient varies in terms of the direction (increasing, decreasing or constant) and size. Compared to the economies covered previously, the Indonesian commercial banking sector shows considerable output sensitivity in estimates of RTS.

China

The Chinese commercial banking industry also shows wide variations compared to Brazil, Russia and India. Table 8.33 shows the main results, while Tables 8.54 to 8.58 provide the supplementary information. Model 1 is producing inconsistent results across all countries due to the issue of high multicollinearity. There is a good amount of variation in the RTS coefficient when the amount of deposits and loans are used versus when assets and volume measures are used.[36]

South Africa

As shown in Table 8.34, the South African banking industry does not show much variation in the RTS estimate across different models and output measures. Its supporting estimations are contained in Tables 8.59 to 8.62.

8.5. Cross-country analysis

Lastly, the six economies were utilized as a panel[37] for analysing the average growth rate of the Malmquist TFP index DEA across the sample period. The results are provided in Table 8.63 in Appendix 4. It seems that changing the output measures has a considerable effect on the nature of RTS and its size. China and India, in particular, show higher differences in RTS estimates compared to the aggregate banking industry of other economies.

The empirical case studies on the difference in performance estimates caused by alternating output measures for the aggregate banking industries across each of the BRIICS countries are thus concluded.

Appendix 1

Estimates of labour and capital (partial factor) productivities for section 8.2

Table 8.1 Estimated measures of Labour Productivity of the banking industry in Brazil during the sample period

Value Measures				
Statistic	*LP1*	*LP2*	*LP3*	*LP4*
Mean	2.87	0.43	2.44	7.29
SD	0.55	0.07	0.85	1.64
CV	19.26	16.27	34.87	22.46
Volume measures				
Statistic	*LP5*	*LP6*	*LP7*	*LP8*
Mean	161.69	297.74	96.07	487.07
SD	37.75	82.28	67.28	351.13
CV	23.35	27.63	70.03	72.09

Notes: LP1 is millions of outstanding of 2010 Brazilian reals of outstanding deposits per bank employee; LP2 is millions of 2010 Brazilian reals of net income of commercial banks per bank employee; LP3 is millions of 2010 Brazilian reals outstanding loans from commercial banks per bank employee; LP4 is millions of 2010 Brazilian reals of financial assets of commercial banks per bank employee; LP5 is Number of Depositors per Bank Employee; LP6 is Number of Deposit Accounts per Bank Employee; LP7 is Number of Borrowers from Commercial Banks per Bank Employee; LP8 is Number of Loan Accounts per Bank Employee; SD is standard deviation and CV is coefficient of variation measured in percentages.

Source: Author's estimation.

Table 8.2 Estimated measures of Physical Capital Productivity of the banking industry in Brazil during the sample period

Value Measures				
Statistic	*CPR1*	*CPR2*	*CPB1*	*CPB2*
Mean	9.76	1.56	49.49	7.49
SD	2.06	0.66	8.98	1.34
CV	21.12	42.09	18.14	17.93

(*Continued*)

Table 8.2 (Continued)

Volume Measures				
Statistic	*CPR4*	*CPR5*	*CPB4*	*CPB5*
Mean	540.12	988.23	4382.52	13246.01
SD	78.3	165.77	1575.59	6769.78
CV	14.5	16.77	35.95	51.11

Notes: CPR1 is millions of 2010 Brazilian reals of outstanding deposits of commercial banks per Retail Agent Outlet; CPR2 is millions of 2010 Brazilian reals of net income per retail agent outlet; CPR3 is millions of 2010 Brazilian reals of total assets per retail agent outlet; CPR4 is the number of depositors per retail agent outlet; CPR5 is the number of deposit accounts per retail agent outlet; CPB1 is millions of 2010 Brazilian reals of outstanding deposits per commercial bank branch; CPB2 is millions of 2010 Brazilian reals of net income per commercial bank branch; CPB3 is millions of 2010 Brazilian reals of outstanding loans per commercial bank branch; CPB4 is the number of total account holder (deposit and loans) with commercial banks per commercial bank branch; CPB5 is the number of depositors with commercial banks per commercial bank branch; SD is standard deviation, and CV is coefficient of variation which is measured in percentages.

Source: Author's estimation.

Table 8.3 Estimated measures of labour productivity of the Russian banking industry during the sample period

Statistic	*Value Measure*			*Volume Measure*
	LP1	*LP2*	*LP3*	*LP4*
Mean	35728.35	39279.85	20.67	384860.07
SD	26755.01	23528.19	13.35	63723.63
CV	74.88	59.90	64.61	16.56

Notes: LP1 is million rubles of outstanding deposits per employee in financial services; LP2 is million rubles of outstanding loans per employee in financial services; LP3 is million rubles of total bank assets per employee in financial services; LP4 is the number of bank total deposit bank accounts per employee in financial series; SD is standard deviation, and CV is coefficient of variation which is measured in percentages.

Source: Author's estimation.

Table 8.4 Estimated measures of Physical Capital Productivity of the Russian banking industry during the sample period

Measure	*Value*				
Statistic	*CPB1*	*CPB2*	*CPB3*	*CPR1*	*CPA1*
Mean	2032.26	2170.44	1.15	42607.75	523.95
SD	1891.73	1698.27	0.93	39624.09	161.12
CV	93.08	78.25	81.13	93	30.75

Measure	*Volume*		
Statistic	*CPB4*	*CPR2*	*CPA2*
Mean	19843.12	441931.72	8567.06
SD	7103.11	208026.85	4989.4
CV	35.8	47.07	58.24

Notes: CPB1 is millions of 2010 rubles of outstanding deposits per commercial bank branch; CPB2 is millions of 2010 rubles of outstanding loans per commercial bank branch; CPB3 is millions of 2010 rubles of total bank assets per commercial bank branch; CPB4 is the number of deposit bank accounts per commercial bank branch; CPR1 is millions of 2010 rubles of outstanding deposits per non-branch retail agent outlet; CPR2 is the number of deposit bank accounts per employee in financial services; CPA1 is millions of Rubles of outstanding deposits per ATM; CPA2 is the number of deposit bank accounts per ATM; SD is standard deviation, and CV is coefficient of variation which is measured in percentages.

Source: Author's estimation.

Table 8.5 Estimated measures of Labour Productivity of the Indian banking industry during the sample period

Statistic	*Value*			*Volume*		
	LP1	*LP2*	*LP3*	*LP4*	*LP5*	*LP6*
Mean	43.23	31.94	55.38	869.41	115.99	985.40
SD	6.85	6.44	8.61	334.13	25.40	355.46
CV	15.85	20.15	15.54	38.43	21.90	36.07

Notes: LP1 is millions of 2010 INR of outstanding deposits per banking employee; LP2 is millions of 2010 INR of outstanding loans per banking employee; LP3 is millions of 2010 INR of total assets per banking employee; LP4 is the number of deposit accounts per banking employee; LP5 is the number of loan accounts per banking employee; LP6 is the number of total accounts (deposit and loans) per banking employee; SD is standard deviation, and CV is coefficient of variation which is measured in percentages.

Source: Author's estimation.

Table 8.6 Estimated measures of Physical Capital Productivity of the Indian banking industry during the sample period

Statistic	*Output Perspective*				
	Value			*Volume*	
	CPB1	*CPB2*	*CPA1*	*CPB2*	*CPA2*
Mean	1659.26	1229.93	810.11	38989.5	13822.89
SD	411.25	353.41	479.79	19243.37	5776.84
CV	24.79	28.73	59.22	49.36	41.79

Notes: CPB1 is millions of 2010 INR of outstanding deposits per branch of commercial banks; CPB2 is millions of 2010 INR of outstanding loans per branch of commercial banks; CPB3 is the number of total banking accounts (deposit and loans) per branch of commercial banks; CPA1 is millions of 2010 rupees of outstanding deposits per ATM; CPA2 is the number of deposit accounts per ATM; SD is standard deviation, and CV is coefficient of variation which is measured in percentages.

Source: Author's estimation.

Table 8.7 Estimated measures of Physical Capital Productivity of the Indonesian banking industry during the sample period

Statistic	*Value*			*Volume*	
	CPR1	*CPB1*	*CPB2*	*CPR2*	*CPB3*
Mean	37251.1	167563.63	115600.37	2125.66	10576.15
SD	54468.94	85518.09	33424.15	2601.57	3725.2
CV	146.22	51.04	28.91	122.39	35.22

Notes: CPR1 is millions of 2010 rupiah of outstanding deposits per non-branch retail agent outlet; CPR2 is the number of deposit accounts per non-branch retail agent outlet; CPB1 is millions of 2010 rupiah of outstanding deposits per branch of commercial banks; CPB2 is millions of 2010 rupiah of outstanding loans per branch of commercial banks; CPB3 is the number of total accounts (deposit and loans) per branch of commercial banks; SD is standard deviation, and CV is coefficient of variation which is measured in percentages.

Source: Author's estimation.

Table 8.8 Estimated measures of Labour Productivity of the Chinese banking industry during the sample period

Statistic	*Value Measures*			*Volume Measures*		
	LP1	*LP2*	*LP3*	*LP4*	*LP5*	*LP6*
Mean	17.52	11.82	0.64	4.63	136.03	140.66
SD	6.89	5.08	0.19	2.26	35.90	34.99
CV	39.33	43.01	30.05	48.76	26.40	24.88

Notes: LP1 is millions of 2010 yuan of outstanding deposits per bank employee; LP2 is millions of 2010 yuan of outstanding loans per bank employee; LP3 is millions of 2010 yuan of total assets per bank employee; LP4 is the number of depositors per bank employee; LP5 is the number of borrowers per bank employee; LP6 is the number of customers (sum of depositors and creditors) per bank employee; SD is standard deviation, and CV is coefficient of variation which is measured in percentages.

Source: Author's estimation.

Table 8.9 Estimated measures of Physical Capital Productivity of the Chinese banking industry during the sample period

Measure	*Value*			*Volume*	
Statistic	*CPB1*	*CPB2*	*CPA1*	*CPB3*	*CPA2*
Mean	676.31	458.71	170.98	5027.67	43.48
SD	347.26	255.6	59.24	815.58	12.39
CV	51.35	55.72	34.65	16.22	28.5

Notes: CPB1 is millions of 2010 yuan of outstanding deposits per commercial bank branch; CPB2 is millions of 2010 yuan of outstanding loans per commercial bank branch; CPB3 is the number of customers per commercial bank branch; CPA1 is millions of 2010 yuan of outstanding deposits per ATM; CPA2 is the number of depositors per commercial bank branch; SD is standard deviation, and CV is coefficient of variation which is measured in percentages.

Source: Author's estimation.

Table 8.10 Estimated measures of Labour Productivity of the South African banking industry during the sample period

Measure	*Value*			*Volume*	
Statistic	*LP1*	*LP2*	*LP3*	*LP4*	*LP5*
Mean	0.71	1.09	0.01	21.47	10.67
SD	0.20	0.35	0.00	5.75	4.00
CV	28.06	32.60	31.68	26.79	37.52

Notes: LP1 is millions of 2010 rands of outstanding deposits of commercial banks per bank employee; LP2 is millions of 2010 rands of outstanding loans per bank employee; LP3 is millions of 2010 rands of total assets per bank employee; LP4 is the number of deposit accounts per bank employee; LP5 is the number of loan accounts per bank employee; SD is standard deviation, and CV is coefficient of variation which is measured in percentages.

Source: Author's estimation.

Table 8.11 Estimated measures of Physical Capital Productivity of the South African banking industry during the sample period

Measure	*Value*			*Volume*			
Statistic	*CPB1*	*CPB2*	*CPA1*	*CPB3*	*CPB4*	*CPB5*	*CPA2*
Mean	409.83	624.18	75.38	12412.65	6146.89	18559.53	2162.37
SD	97.94	177.87	27.30	3458.18	2156.70	2374.53	391.14
CV	23.90	28.50	36.22	27.86	35.09	12.79	18.09

Notes: CPB1 is millions of 2010 rands of outstanding deposits per commercial bank branch; CPB2 is millions of 2010 rands of outstanding loans per commercial bank branch; CPB3 is the number of deposit accounts per commercial bank branch; CPB4 is the number of loan accounts per commercial bank branch; CPB5 is the number of total accounts per commercial bank branch; CPA1 is millions of 2010 rands of outstanding deposits per ATM; CPA2 is the number of deposit accounts per ATM; SD is standard deviation, and CV is coefficient of variation which is measured in percentages

Source: Author's estimation.

Appendix 2

Estimates of residual total factor productivity index and technical efficiency scores for the section 8.3

Table 8.12 Residual TFP estimates under the Solow framework for the Brazilian banking industry

Descriptive Statistics					
Variable	*TFPG1*	*TFPG2*	*TFPG3*	*TFPG4*	*TFPG5*
Mean	8.72	2.79	−1.83	1.64	8.97
SD	25.49	9.94	10.20	3.35	38.63
CV	292.21	356.55	555.92	204.05	430.55
Skewness	0.86	−0.56	0.00	−1.32	1.80
Cross-Correlations					
Variable	*TFPG1*	*TFPG2*	*TFPG3*	*TFPG4*	
TFPG2	0.59***	-	-	-	
TFPG3	0.34	0.46**	-	-	
TFPG4	0.01	0.55	−0.02	-	
TFPG5	0.07	0.40*	0.29	0.14	

Notes: 1. All the variables are measured as yearly growth rates and are expressed in percentages; 2. TFPG1 is the TFP growth index with the outstanding deposits of commercial banks as an output, TFPG2 is the TFP growth index with the outstanding loans from commercial banks as an output, TFPG3 is the TFP growth index with the financial assets of commercial banks as an output, TFPG4 is the TFP growth index with the number of deposit accounts with commercial banks as an output, TFPG5 is the TFP growth index with the number of loan accounts with commercial banks as an output; 3. SD stands for standard deviation, and CV stands for coefficient of variation; 4. Wherever CV was negative, because of negative mean values, the absolute value of the same has been used; 5. *, **, and *** indicate significant at 10%, 5% and 1% levels of significance, respectively.

Source: Author's estimation.

Table 8.13 Technical efficiency estimates using multi-stage DEA for the banking industry in Brazil

Statistic	*Descriptive Statistic*				
	TE1	*TE2*	*TE3*	*TE4*	*TE5*
Mean	0.88	0.94	0.85	0.98	0.66
SD	0.10	0.06	0.14	0.03	0.33
CV	11.79	5.95	16.99	2.78	50.09
Skewness	−0.20	−1.14	−0.61	−1.58	−0.54
Variables	*Cross-correlations*				
	TE1	*TE2*	*TE3*	*TE4*	
TE2	0.07	-	-	-	
TE3	0.49*	0.08	-	-	
TE4	−0.26	0.67***	−0.25	-	
TE5	−0.12	0.71***	−0.29	0.52**	

Notes: 1. These estimates have been worked out using multi-stage output-oriented DEA under VRS assumption; 2. TE1 is TE index with outstanding deposits as an output variable, TE2 is TE index with outstanding loans as an output variable, TE3 is TE index with financial or total assets of banks, TE4 is TE index with deposit accounts with commercial banks as an output variable, TE5 is TE index with loan accounts with commercial banks as an output variable; 3. SD is standard deviation, and CV is coefficient of variation; 4. All the data are in index form, and hence unit-less, 5. *, **, and *** indicate significant at 10%, 5% and 1% levels of significance, respectively.

Source: Author's estimation.

Table 8.14 Technical efficiency estimates using the Stochastic Frontier model for the banking industry in Brazil

Statistic	*TE1*	*TE2*	*TE3*
Mean	0.96	0.95	0.89
SD	0.02	0.04	0.10
CV	2.57	4.46	10.74
Skewness	−1.05	−0.85	−1.12
Variables	*TE1, TE2*	*TE2, TE3*	*TE3, TE1*
Correlation Coefficient	0.06	−0.40*	−0.39*

Notes: 1. All the statistics are in index form and hence are unitless; 2. TE1 is TE index using SFA with deposit accounts as an output variable, TE2 is TE index using SFA with loan accounts as an output variable, TE3 is TE index using SFA with financial assets of commercial banks as an output variable wherein the amount of deposits is used as one of the input variables; 3. SD is standard deviation, and CV is coefficient of variation; 4. *, ** and *** indicate significance at 10%, 5% and 1% significance levels, respectively.

Source: Author's estimation.

Table 8.15 Residual TFP estimates under the Solow framework for the Russian banking industry

Statistic	*Descriptive Statistics*			
Mean	11.03	9.80	6.46	1.61
SD	18.63	19.72	14.35	4.79
CV	168.90	201.19	222.23	297.76
Skewness	−1.52	−1.34	−1.14	1.66
Cross-correlations				
Variable	*TFPG1*	*TFPG2*	*TFPG3*	
TFPG2	0.91***	-	-	
TFPG3	0.72***	0.81***	-	
TFPG4	0.54**	0.25	0.25	

Notes: 1. All the variables are measured as yearly growth rates and are expressed in percentages; 2. TFPG1 is the TFP growth index with the outstanding deposits of commercial banks as an output, TFPG2 is the TFP growth index with the outstanding loans from commercial banks as an output, TFPG3 is the TFP growth index with the financial assets of commercial banks as an output, TFPG4 is the TFP growth index with the number of deposit accounts with commercial banks as an output variable; 3. SD stands for standard deviation, and CV stands for coefficient of variation; 4. CV might be negative as the data are in growth-rate form; 5. *, ** and *** indicate significant at 10%, 5%, and 1% significance levels, respectively.

Source: Author's estimation.

Table 8.16 Technical efficiency estimates using DEA for the banking industry in Russia

Statistic	*Descriptive Statistics*			
	TE1	*TE2*	*TE3*	*TE4*
Mean	0.94	0.95	0.94	0.997
SD	0.10	0.04	0.05	0.01
CV	10.26	4.07	5.80	0.69
Skewness	−1.56	−0.60	−0.18	−2.36
Variable	*Cross-correlations*			
	TE1	*TE2*	*TE3*	
TE2	−0.16	-	-	
TE3	0.15	0.51**	-	
TE4	0.37*	−0.25	−0.21	

Notes: 1. These estimates have been worked out using multi-stage output-oriented DEA under VRS assumption; 2. TE1 is TE index with outstanding deposits as an output variable, TE2 is TE index with outstanding loans as an output variable, TE3 is TE index with financial or total assets of banks, TE4 is TE index with deposit accounts with commercial banks as an output variable; 3. SD is standard deviation, and CV is Coefficient of Variation; 4. All the data are in index form, and hence unit-less, 5. *, **, and *** indicate significant at 10%, 5% and 1% levels of significance, respectively.

Source: Author's estimation.

Table 8.17 Technical efficiency estimates using the stochastic Frontier model for the banking industry in Russia

Statistic	*Descriptive Statistics*			
	TE1	*TE2*	*TE3*	*TE4*
Mean	0.87	0.94	0.93	0.94
SD	0.09	0.04	0.05	0.04
CV	10.32	4.47	5.54	4.05
Skewness	−1.32	−0.81	−0.71	−1.55
Variable	*Cross-correlations*			
	TE1	*TE2*	*TE3*	
TE2	0.03	-	-	
TE3	−0.10	−0.06	-	
TE4	0.90	−0.32	0.10	

Notes: 1. All the statistics are in index form and hence are unitless; 2. TE1 is TE index using SFA with the amount of outstanding deposits as an output variable, TE2 is TE index using SFA with the amount of outstanding loans as an output variable, TE3 is TE index using SFA with financial assets of commercial banks as an output variable and TE4 is TE index using SFA with the total number of deposit accounts as an output variable; 3. SD is standard deviation, and CV is coefficient of variation; 4. *, **, and *** indicate significant at 10%, 5% and 1% levels of significance, respectively.

Source: Author's estimation.

Table 8.18 Residual TFP estimates under the Solow framework for the Indian banking industry

Statistic	*Descriptive Statistics*				
	TFPG1	*TFPG2*	*TFPG3*	*TFPG4*	*TFPG5*
Mean	1.88	1.41	0.73	5.04	1.07
SD	10.87	7.47	7.10	6.55	21.66
CV	578.75	531.64	973.43	129.93	2031.42
Skewness	−1.99	−1.58	−1.67	0.11	3.28
Variable	*Cross-correlations*				
	TFPG1	*TFPG2*	*TFPG3*	*TFPG4*	
TFPG2	0.73***	-	-	-	
TFPG3	0.33	0.59***	-	-	
TFPG4	0.60***	0.17	0.11	-	
TFPG5	−0.79***	−0.81***	−0.60***	−0.44**	

Notes: 1. All the variables are measured as yearly growth rates and are expressed in percentages; 2. TFPG1 is the TFP growth index with the outstanding deposits of commercial banks as an output, TFPG2 is the TFP growth index with the outstanding loans from commercial banks as an output, TFPG3 is the TFP growth index with the financial assets of commercial banks as an output, TFPG4 is the TFP growth index with the number of deposit accounts with commercial banks as an output variable, TFPG5 is the yearly growth rate of TFP index with the total number of loan accounts with commercial banks as an output variable; 3. SD stands for standard deviation, and CV stands for coefficient of variation; 4. CV might be negative as the data are in growth-rate form; 5. *, ** and *** indicate significant at 10%, 5%, and 1% significance levels, respectively.

Source: Author's estimation.

Table 8.19 Technical efficiency estimates using multi-stage DEA for the banking industry in India

Statistic	*Descriptive Statistics*				
	TE1	*TE2*	*TE3*	*TE4*	*TE5*
Mean	0.97	1.00	0.99	0.95	0.90
SD	0.04	0.01	0.03	0.07	0.12
CV	4.50	1.13	3.18	7.31	12.83
Skewness	−1.34	−2.91	−3.17	−1.47	−0.68
Variable	*Cross-correlations*				
	TE1	*TE2*	*TE3*	*TE4*	
TE2	0.36	-	-	-	
TE3	0.24	0.25	-	-	
TE4	0.55	−0.01	−0.09	-	
TE5	0.50	0.37	−0.08	0.78	

Notes: 1. These estimates have been worked out using multi-stage output-oriented DEA under VRS assumption; 2. TE1 is TE index with outstanding deposits as an output variable, TE2 is TE index with outstanding loans as an output variable, TE3 is TE index with financial or total assets of banks, TE4 is TE index with deposit accounts with commercial banks as an output variable, TE5 is the TE index with loan accounts with commercial banks as an output variable; 3. SD is standard deviation, and CV is coefficient of variation; 4. All the data are in index form, and hence unit-less, 5. *, **, and *** indicate significant at 10%, 5% and 1% levels of significance respectively.

Source: Author's estimation.

Table 8.20 Technical efficiency estimates using the Stochastic Frontier model for the banking industry in India

Statistic	*Descriptive Statistics*		
	TE1	*TE2*	*TE3*
Mean	0.84	0.84	0.86
SD	0.10	0.12	0.10
CV	12.23	14.25	11.94
Skewness	−0.34	−0.73	−0.48
Variable	*Cross-correlations*		
	TE1	*TE2*	
TE2	0.97***	-	
TE3	0.91***	0.90***	

Notes: 1. All the statistics are in index form and hence are unitless; 2. TE1 is TE index using SFA with the amount of outstanding deposits as an output variable, TE2 is TE index using SFA with the amount of outstanding loans as an output variable, TE3 is TE index using SFA with financial assets of commercial banks as an output variable; 3. SD is standard deviation, and CV is coefficient of variation; 4. *, ** and *** indicate significant at 10%, 5% and 1% levels of significance, respectively.

Source: Author's estimation.

Table 8.21 Residual TFP estimates under the Solow framework for the Indonesian banking industry

Statistic	*Descriptive Statistics*				
	TFPG1	*TFPG2*	*TFPG3*	*TFPG4*	*TFPG5*
Mean	−2.74	1.25	1.18	1.62	8.11
SD	13.52	10.15	15.96	18.33	87.50
CV	−493.25	814.39	1351.58	1129.54	1079.33
Skewness	−1.23	1.31	1.65	0.56	3.59
Variable	*Cross-correlations*				
	TFPG1	*TFPG2*	*TFPG3*	*TFPG4*	
TFPG2	−0.10	-	-	-	
TFPG3	−0.36	0.83***	-	-	
TFPG4	0.78***	−0.13	−0.29	-	
TFPG5	0.12	−0.21	−0.17	−0.04	

Notes: 1. All the variables are measured as yearly growth rates and are expressed in percentages; 2. TFPG1 is the TFP growth index with the outstanding deposits of commercial banks as an output, TFPG2 is the TFP growth index with the outstanding loans from commercial banks as an output, TFPG3 is the TFP growth index with the financial assets of commercial banks as an output, TFPG4 is the TFP growth index with the number of deposit accounts with commercial banks as an output variable, TFPG5 is the yearly growth rate of TFP index with the total number of loan accounts with commercial banks as an output variable; 3. SD stands for standard deviation, and CV stands for coefficient of variation; 4. CV might be negative as the data are in growth-rate form; 5. *, ** and *** indicate significant at 10%, 5%, and 1% levels, respectively.

Source: Author's estimation.

Table 8.22 Technical efficiency estimates using multi-stage DEA and SFA for the banking industry in Indonesia

Statistic	*Descriptive Statistics*					*TE using SFA*#
	TE1	*TE2*	*TE3*	*TE4*	*TE5*	*TE2*
Mean	0.74	0.98	0.97	0.70	0.97	0.97
SD	0.19	0.03	0.05	0.23	0.04	0.02
CV	26.26	2.87	4.76	32.72	3.93	1.95
Skewness	−0.29	−1.79	−2.70	0.12	−1.66	−1.03
Variable	*Cross-correlations*					
	TE1	*TE2*	*TE3*	*TE4*		
TE2	0.40***	-	-	-		
TE3	0.19	0.82***	-	-		
TE4	0.87***	0.21	0.03	-		
TE5	0.07	0.52**	0.71***	−0.04		

Notes: 1. These estimates have been worked out using multi-stage output-oriented DEA under VRS assumption; 2. TE1 is TE index with outstanding deposits as an output variable, TE2 is TE index with outstanding loans as an output variable, TE3 is TE index with financial or total assets of banks, TE4 is TE index with deposit accounts with commercial banks as an output variable, TE5 is the TE index with loan accounts with commercial banks as an output variable; 3. SD is standard deviation, and CV is coefficient of variation; 4. All the data are in index form, and hence unitless, 5. *, **, and *** indicate significant at 10%, 5% and 1% levels of significance, respectively; 6. # – SFA estimates were found statistically permissible only for the loan amount variable. The gamma statistic of the rest of the estimated frontier equations was very small and statistically highly insignificant.

Source: Author's estimation.

Table 8.23 Residual TFP estimates under the Solow framework for the banking industry of China

Statistic	*Descriptive Statistics*				
	TFPG1	*TFPG2*	*TFPG3*	*TFPG4*	*TFPG5*
Mean	11.74	16.80	4.66	13.14	1.24
SD	19.55	25.83	16.72	28.70	6.57
CV	166.54	153.76	358.77	218.51	529.25
Skewness	−0.49	−0.41	−2.41	−0.38	−0.18
Variable	*Cross-correlations*				
	TFPG1	*TFPG2*	*TFPG3*	*TFPG4*	
TFPG2	0.93***	-	-	-	
TFPG3	−0.32	−0.28	-	-	
TFPG4	0.76***	0.87***	−0.31	-	
TFPG5	−0.39*	−0.18	−0.01	−0.29	

Notes: 1. All the variables are measured as yearly growth rates and are expressed in percentages; 2. TFPG1 is the TFP growth index with the outstanding deposits of commercial banks as an output, TFPG2 is the TFP growth index with the outstanding loans from commercial banks as an output, TFPG3 is the TFP growth index with the financial assets of commercial banks as an output, TFPG4 is the TFP growth index with the number of deposit accounts with commercial banks as an output variable, TFPG5 is the yearly growth rate of TFP index with the total number of borrowers from commercial banks as an output variable; 3. SD stands for standard deviation, and CV stands for coefficient of variation; 4. CV might be negative as the data are in growth-rate form; 5. *, ** and *** indicate significant at 10%, 5%, and 1% significance levels, respectively.

Source: Author's estimation.

Table 8.24 Technical efficiency estimates using multi-stage DEA banking industry in China

Statistic	*Descriptive Statistics*				
	TE1	*TE2*	*TE3*	*TE4*	*TE5*
Mean	0.92	0.96	0.97	1.00	1.00
SD	0.12	0.05	0.06	0.00	0.00
CV	12.97	4.86	6.55	0.12	0.10
Skewness	−1.76	−1.11	−1.79	−1.20	−1.46
Variable	*Cross-correlations*				
	TE1	*TE2*	*TE3*	*TE4*	
TE2	−0.01	-	-	-	
TE3	0.28	0.38*	-	-	
TE4	0.74***	0.32	0.71***	-	
TE5	0.34	0.49**	0.82***	0.86***	

Notes: 1. These estimates have been worked out using multi-stage output-oriented DEA under VRS assumption; 2. TE1 is TE index with outstanding deposits as an output variable, TE2 is TE index with outstanding loans as an output variable, TE3 is TE index with financial or total assets of banks, TE4 is TE index with deposit accounts with commercial banks as an output variable, TE5 is the TE index with the total number of borrowers with commercial banks as an output variable; 3. SD is standard deviation, and CV is coefficient of variation; 4. All the data are in index form, and hence unit-less, 5. *, **, and *** indicate significant at 10%, 5% and 1% levels of significance, respectively.

Source: Author's estimation.

Table 8.25 Technical efficiency estimates using the Stochastic Frontier model for the banking industry in China

Statistic	*Descriptive Statistics*		
	TE1	*TE2*	*TE3*
Mean	0.73	0.74	0.82
SD	0.19	0.19	0.12
CV	25.64	25.95	14.40
Skewness	−0.47	−0.63	−1.42
Variable	*Cross-correlations*		
	TE1	*TE2*	
TE2	0.98	-	
TE3	0.48	0.47	

Notes: 1. All the statistics are in index form and hence are unitless; 2. TE1 is TE index using SFA with the amount of outstanding deposits as an output variable, TE2 is TE index using SFA with the amount of outstanding loans as an output variable, TE3 is TE index using SFA with financial assets of commercial banks as an output variable; 3. SD is standard deviation, and CV is coefficient of variation; 4. *, ** and *** indicate significant at 10%, 5% and 1% levels of significance, respectively.

Source: Author's estimation.

Table 8.26 Residual TFP estimates under the Solow framework for the banking industry of South Africa

Statistic	*Descriptive Statistics*		
	TFPG1	*TFPG2*	*TFPG3*
Mean	−1.03	0.79	5.43
SD	10.36	17.00	15.58
CV	−1008.50	2154.75	287.00
Skewness	−1.24	2.42	−0.50
Variable	*Cross-correlations*		
	TFPG1	*TFPG2*	
TFPG2	−0.83***	-	
TFPG3	0.68***	−0.66***	

Notes: 1. All the variables are measured as yearly growth rates and are expressed in percentages; 2. TFPG1 is the TFP growth index with the outstanding deposits of commercial banks as an output, TFPG2 is the TFP growth index with the outstanding loans from commercial banks as an output, TFPG3 is the TFP growth index with the number of deposit accounts with commercial banks as an output variable; 3. SD stands for standard deviation, and CV stands for coefficient of variation; 4. CV might be negative as the data are in growth-rate form; 5. *, ** and *** indicate significant at 10%, 5% and 1% significance levels, respectively.

Source: Author's estimation.

Table 8.27 Technical efficiency estimates using multi-stage DEA for the banking industry in South Africa

Statistic	*Descriptive Statistics*				
	TE1	*TE2*	*TE3*	*TE4*	*TE5*
Mean	0.95	0.98	0.96	0.92	0.91
SD	0.05	0.03	0.04	0.12	0.08
CV	5.22	3.02	4.44	12.96	8.28
Skewness	−0.71	−2.74	−0.96	−1.38	−0.46
Variable	*Cross-correlations*				
	TE1	*TE2*	*TE3*	*TE4*	
TE2	0.39*	-	-	-	
TE3	0.16	0.82***	-	-	
TE4	0.60***	0.07	−0.07	-	
TE5	0.07	−0.14	0.01	−0.32	

Notes: 1. These estimates have been worked out using multi-stage output-oriented DEA under VRS assumption; 2. TE1 is TE index with outstanding deposits as an output variable, TE2 is TE index with outstanding loans as an output variable, TE3 is TE index with financial or total assets of banks, TE4 is TE index with deposit accounts with commercial banks as an output variable, TE5 is the TE index with the total number of loan accounts with commercial banks as an output variable; 3. SD is standard deviation, and CV is coefficient of variation; 4. All the data are in index form, and hence unit-less, 5. *, **, and *** indicate significant at 10%, 5% and 1% levels of significance, respectively.

Source: Author's estimation.

Table 8.28 Technical efficiency estimates using the Stochastic Frontier model for the banking industry in South Africa

Statistic	*Descriptive Statistics*				
	TE1	*TE2*	*TE3*	*TE4*	*TE5*
Mean	0.89	0.92	0.94	0.83	0.91
SD	0.06	0.06	0.04	0.12	0.07
CV	7.18	6.71	4.04	14.98	7.90
Skewness	−1.10	−2.18	−1.88	−0.36	−0.41
Variable	*Cross-correlations*				
	TE1	*TE2*	*TE3*	*TE4*	
TE2	0.88***	-	-	-	
TE3	0.09	0.39*	-	-	
TE4	0.66***	0.56***	−0.02	-	
TE5	0.09	0.01	−0.07	−0.21	

Notes: 1. All the statistics are in index form and hence are unitless; 2. TE1 is TE index using SFA with the amount of outstanding deposits as an output variable, TE2 is TE index using SFA with the amount of outstanding loans as an output variable, TE3 is TE index using SFA with financial assets of commercial banks as an output variable, TE4 is TE index using SFA with deposit accounts as the output variable, TE5 is the TE index using SFA with loan accounts as the output variable; 3. SD is standard deviation, and CV is coefficient of variation; 4. *, ** and *** indicate significant at 10%, 5% and 1% levels of significance, respectively.

Source: Author's estimation.

Appendix 3

Estimated models for the returns to scale coefficients in section 8.4

Table 8.29 Returns to scale for the banking industry of Brazil under alternative output measures across alternative econometric models

Output Variable	*Model 1*	*Model 2*	*Model 3*	*Model 4*
	Trans-log model under standard OLS	*Trans-log model under Ridge Regression*	*Cobb-Douglas model under standard OLS*	*Stochastic Frontier Cobb-Douglas model*
Deposits (DEP)	−0.92 Negative	2.52 Increasing	9.67 Increasing	1.45 Increasing
Loans (LOAN)	2.30 Increasing	4.37 Increasing	4.42 Increasing	4.30 Increasing
Financial Assets (ASSET)	−6.62 Negative	−2.81 Negative	0.67 Decreasing	NA
Deposit Accounts (DACT)	5.58 Increasing	5.78 Increasing	5.72 Increasing	4.42 Increasing
Loan Accounts (LACT)	6.95 Increasing	15.79 Increasing	20.14 Increasing	NA

Source: Based on the author's estimation.

Table 8.30 Returns to scale for the banking industry of Russia under alternative output measures across alternative econometric models

Output Variable	*Model 1*	*Model 2*	*Model 3*	*Model 4*
Deposits	120.46 Increasing	9.40 Increasing	5.64 Increasing	5.64 Increasing
Loans	83.21 Increasing	7.86 Increasing	5.06 Increasing	5.06 Increasing
Financial Assets	122.49 Increasing	8.95 Increasing	5.34 Increasing	5.40 Increasing
Deposit Accounts	49.83 Increasing	3.20 Increasing	1.79 Increasing	1.79 Increasing

Source: Based on the author's estimation.

Table 8.31 Returns to scale for the banking industry of India under alternative output measures across alternative econometric models

Output Variable	*Model 1*	*Model 2*	*Model 3*	*Model 4*
Deposits	2.70 Increasing	2.30 Increasing	2.23 Increasing	2.30 Increasing
Loans	3.37 Increasing	2.70 Increasing	2.95 Increasing	2.96 Increasing
Financial Assets	2.88 Increasing	2.43 Increasing	2.62 Increasing	2.40 Increasing
Deposit Accounts	4.15 Increasing	3.44 Increasing	1.27 Increasing	NA
Loan Accounts	2.34 Increasing	1.95 Increasing	1.52 Increasing	NA

Source: Based on the author's estimation.

Table 8.32 Returns to scale for the banking industry of Indonesia under alternative output measures across alternative econometric models

Output Variable	*Model 1*	*Model 2*	*Model 3*	*Model 4*
Deposits	19.37 Increasing	1.02 Constant	0.97 Decreasing	NA
Loans	5.26 Increasing	0.29 Decreasing	1.36 Increasing	1.56 Increasing
Financial Assets	16.33 Increasing	0.39 Decreasing	0.88 Decreasing	NA
Deposit Accounts	−6.78 Negative	0.68 Decreasing	0.62 Decreasing	NA
Loan Accounts	20.07 Increasing	0.76 Decreasing	1.07 Constant	NA

Source: Based on the author's estimation.

Table 8.33 Returns to scale for the banking industry of China under alternative output measures across alternative econometric models

Output Variable	*Model 1*	*Model 2*	*Model 3*	*Model 4*
Deposits	−11.26 Negative	0.12 Decreasing	0.63 Decreasing	−0.29 Negative
Loans	−172.52 Negative	0.45 Decreasing	1.17 Increasing	0.11 Decreasing
Financial Assets	−285.65 Negative	1.32 Increasing	1.4 Increasing	1.92 Increasing
Deposit Accounts	−413.14 Negative	2.3 Increasing	4.55 Increasing	NA
Borrowers	−123.75 Negative	1.7 Increasing	3.27 Increasing	3.00 Increasing

Source: Based on the author's estimation.

Table 8.34 Returns to scale for the banking industry of South Africa under alternative output measures across alternative econometric models

Output Variable	*Model 1*	*Model 2*	*Model 3*	*Model 4*
Deposits (DEP)	0.15 Decreasing	0.52 Decreasing	0.76 Decreasing	NA
Loans (LOAN)	0.73 Decreasing	0.84 Decreasing	0.8 Decreasing	0.68 Decreasing
Financial Assets (ASSET)	0.56 Decreasing	0.58 Decreasing	0.67 Decreasing	0.25 Decreasing
Deposit Accounts (DACT)	1.52 Increasing	0.94 Decreasing	1.87 Increasing	1.66 Increasing

Source: Based on the author's estimation.

Table 8.35 Returns to scale with the amount of outstanding deposits as the output variable for the Brazilian banking industry

Output Variable = In(DEP)					
Input Variable	*Model 1*	*Model 2*	*Model 3*	*Model 4*	
In(LAB)	−3029.97***	0.85*	7.92***	0.26	
In(CAP)	1985.97***	3.49***	1.75**	1.19	
In(LAB)²	176.96***	0.02			
In(CAP)²	3.75	−0.16**			
In(LAB)*In(CAP)	−157.192***	0.04		**Statistic**	
RTS	**−0.92**	**2.52**	**9.67**		**1.45**
R-squared	0.95	0.55	0.60	Gamma	0.66
F-statistic	58.46***	4.01*	12.85***	Log-likelihood ratio	11.77

Notes: 1. Model 1 is the Trans-log production function using standard OLS, Model 2 is the Trans-log Production Function by Ridge Regression, Model 3 is the Cobb-Douglas production function with standard OLS, Model 4 is the MLE estimator of the Cobb-Douglas Stochastic Frontier Model; 2. The Cobb-Douglas functions include the first lag of labour variable and the second lag of the capital variable; 3. For Model 2, the final chosen k-value is 0.0005; 4. Trans-log returns to scale coefficient is estimated at mean levels of inputs; 5. Values in the bracket are standard errors; 6. *, ** and *** indicate significant at 10%, 5%, and 1% significance levels, respectively

Source: Author's estimation.

Table 8.36 Returns to scale with the amount of outstanding loans as the output variable for the Brazilian banking industry

Output Variable = In(LOAN)				
Input Variable	*Model 1*	*Model 2*	*Model 3*	*Model 4*
In(LAB)	−2919.76***	−1.02	1.01	0.79
In(CAP)	1590.76***	3.33***	3.41***	3.51***
In(LAB)²	162.74***	0.04		
In(CAP)²	6.69	-0.06		

(*Continued*)

Table 8.36 (Continued)

Output Variable = In(LOAN)					
Input Variable	*Model 1*	*Model 2*	*Model 3*	*Model 4*	
In(LAB)*In(CAP)	−131.48***	0.10***		Statistic	-
RTS	**2.30**	**4.37**	**4.42**		**4.3**
R-squared	0.98	0.90	0.90	Gamma	0.51
F-statistic	187.06***	27.32***	81.27***	Log-likelihood ratio	13.04

Notes: 1. Model 1 is the Trans-log production function with standard OLS, Model 2 is the Trans-log production function with ridge regression, Model 3 is the Cobb-Douglas production function with standard OLS, Model 4 is the MLE estimator of the Cobb-Douglas Stochastic Frontier Model; 2. When the Model 3 is estimated under the intermediation approach by including the amount of outstanding deposits as a regressor, the R^2 turns out to be 0.99. The coefficient of amount of deposits is worked out to be 0.75 and is found to be significant at 1% level. The F-statistic is 589.60 and is also significant at 1% level. The size of the labour coefficient is -0.39 which is insignificant even at 10% level. The estimated coefficient of capital is 2.89 which is significant at 1% level. However, this specification has been excluded throughout the book to maintain consistent presentation; 3. Similarly, Model 4 was re-estimated under the intermediation approach, and the MLE coefficient of deposit variables was found to be 0.82 and is significant at 1% level. Labour coefficient is worked out to be -0.42, and that of Capital is 2.81, and both are significant at 1 % level. The log-likelihood ratio is 40.16 while the LR test statistic is 3.47, which is significant at 5% significance level as per critical values given in Kodde and Palm (1986); 4. For Model 2, the final chosen k-value is 0.0005; 5. Trans-log returns to scale coefficient is estimated at mean levels of inputs; 6. *, ** and *** indicate significant at 10%, 5% and 1% levels of significance, respectively

Source: Author's estimation.

Table 8.37 Returns to scale with the amount of financial assets of banks as the output variable for Brazilian banking industry

Output Variable = In(ASSET)			
Input Variable	*Model 1*	*Model 2*	*Model 3*
In(LAB)	−1384.10*	−0.11	−2.08***
In(CAP)	1585.13***	4.72***	2.75***
In(LAB)²	99.68**	−0.21***	
In(CAP)²	0.20	−0.09#	
In(LAB)*In(CAP)	−120.91**	−0.003	
Estimated Returns to Scale	**−6.62**	**−2.81**	**0.67**
R-squared	0.88	0.34	0.48
F-statistic	22.95***	1.68	8.89***

Notes: 1. Model 1 is the Trans-log production function with standard OLS, Model 2 is the Trans-log production function with ridge regression, Model 3 is the Cobb-Douglas production function with standard OLS; 2. When the Model 3 is estimated under the intermediation approach by including the Amount of outstanding deposits as a regressor, the R^2 turns out to be 0.77. The coefficient of Amount of Deposits is worked out to be 0.83 and is found to be significant at 1% level. The F-statistic is 20.201 and is also significant at 1% level. The sign of the other coefficients remains the same though. The size of the labour coefficient is -7.14 and that of capital is 2.17. Both are significant at 1% level. However, this specification has been excluded throughout the book so as to maintain consistence of presentation; 3. Model 4 produced a very low and an insignificant gamma statistic, and hence have been excluded. It was estimated also re-estimated under the intermediation approach and the MLE coefficient of deposit variables was found to be 0.93 and is significant at 1% level. Labour coefficient is worked out to be -6.69 and that of Capital is 1.52 and both are significant at 1 % level. The log-likelihood ratio is 23.93 while the LR test statistic is 11.32 which is significant at 1% level of significance as per critical values given in Kodde and Palm (1986). Thus RTS worked out to be -4.24, thus implying DRS; 4. For Model 2, the final chosen k-value is 0.0005; 5. Trans-log returns to scale coefficient is estimated at mean levels of inputs; 6. *, ** and *** indicate significant at 10%, 5% and 1% levels of significance respectively, and # indicates significant at 15% level.

Source: Author's estimation.

Table 8.38 Returns to scale with the number of deposit accounts as the output variable for Brazilian banking industry

Output Variable = In(DACT)					
Input Variable	*Model 1*	*Model 2*	*Model 3*	*Model 4*	
In(LAB)	−807.46***	0.44	4.67***	2.70***	
In(CAP)	174.40*	0.59	1.05***	1.72***	
In(LAB)^2	30.81**	0.15***			
In(CAP)^2	−8.69***	−0.04*			
In(LAB)*In(CAP)	0.40	0.07***		**Statistic**	-
RTS	**5.58**	**5.78**	**5.72**		**4.42**
R-squared	0.99	0.95	0.96	Gamma	0.99***
F-statistic	1039.16***	64.20***	213.55***	Log-likelihood ratio	37.87

Notes: 1. Model 1 is the Trans-log production function with standard OLS, Model 2 is the Trans-log production function with ridge regression, Model 3 is the Cobb-Douglas production function with standard OLS, Model 4 is the stochastic frontier Cobb-Douglas model. 2. Trans-log returns to scale coefficient is estimated at mean levels of inputs. 3. In Model 2, the k-value is 0.0005; 4. *, ** and *** indicate significant at 10%, 5% and 1% levels of significance respectively

Source: Author's estimation.

Table 8.39 Returns to scale with the number of loan accounts as the output variable for Brazilian banking industry

Output Variable = In(LACT)			
Input Variable	*Model 1*	*Model 2*	*Model 3*
In(LAB)	−6141.69***	−11.85***	14.79**
In(CAP)	−85.89	1.30*	5.35**
In(LAB)^2	207.08*	0.46**	
In(CAP)^2	−39.52$^{\#\#\#}$	0.07	
In(LAB)*In(CAP)	69.25	0.55***	
Estimated Returns to Scale	**6.95**	**15.79**	**20.14**
R-squared	0.97	0.66	0.74
F-statistic	92.32***	6.27***	25.18***

Notes: 1. Model 1 is the Trans-log production function with standard OLS, Model 2 is the Trans-log production function with ridge regression, Model 3 is the Cobb-Douglas production function with standard OLS; 2. Model 3 has been estimated with Cochrane-Orcutt adjustment for serial correlation. When estimated under the intermediation approach by including the Amount of outstanding deposits as a regressor, the R^2 turns out to be 0.67. The coefficient of Amount of Deposits is worked out to be 0.56 and is found to be not significant even at 10% level. The F-statistic is 12.22 and is also significant at 1% level. The labour coefficient is -6.92 and that of capital is 9.57. Only the capital coefficient is significant at 1% level. Other two coefficients are insignificant event at 10% level. However, this specification has been excluded throughout the book so as to maintain consistence of presentation. 3. Model 4, under the production approach produces a very low and highly insignificant gamma statistic. However, when it is re-estimated using amount of outstanding deposits as an input variable, its MLE coefficient is worked out to be 0.47 which is not significant even at 10% level. Labour coefficient is found to be -6.56 and that of Capital is 9.41, and both are significant at 1% level. The log-likelihood ratio is 18.41. This implies RTS of 3.32 which signifies IRS; 4. Trans-log returns to scale coefficient is estimated at mean levels of inputs; 5. *, ** and *** indicate significant at 10%, 5% and 1% levels of significance respectively. 6. For Model 2, the chosen k-value is 0.0005.

Source: Author's estimation.

Table 8.40 Returns to scale with amount of outstanding deposits as the output variable for the Russian banking industry

Output Variable = In(DEP)					
Input Variable	*Model 1*	*Model 2*	*Model 3*	*Model 4*	
In(LAB)	−78.33	2.81***	7.15***	6.99***	
In(CAP)	97.11	−1.19***	−1.51***	−1.35***	
In(LAB)^2	14.38	0.21***			
In(CAP)^2	−0.19	−0.06***			
In(LAB)*In(CAP)	−12.39	0.12***		**Statistic**	-
RTS	**120.46**	**9.40**	**5.64**		**5.64**
R-squared	0.99	0.98	0.98	Gamma	0.93***
F-statistic	243.64***	204.86***	642.27***	Log-likelihood	15.73

Notes: 1. Model 1 is the Trans-log production function with standard OLS, Model 2 is the Trans-log production function with ridge regression, Model 3 is the Cobb-Douglas production function with standard OLS, Model 4 is the stochastic frontier Cobb-Douglas model; 2. Trans-log returns to scale coefficient is estimated at mean levels of inputs; 3. All the coefficients were found to be statistically insignificant in Model (1) after which It was re-estimated using only the interaction term and excluding the polynomial terms. Another variant of the same model with cubic terms was tested for. Still, the results did not improve. Hence, it was excluded; 4. For Model 2, the k-value is 0.002; 5. *, ** and *** indicate significant at 10%, 5% and 1% levels of significance respectively.

Source: Author's estimation.

Table 8.41 Returns to scale with amount of outstanding loans as the output variable for the Russian banking industry

Output Variable = In(LOAN)					
Input Variable	*Model 1*	*Model 2*	*Model 3*	*Model 4*	
In(LAB)	−39.16	2.66***	5.92***	5.89***	
In(CAP)	82.99$^{\#\#\#}$	−0.77***	−0.86***	−0.83***	
In(LAB)^2	11.98*	0.16***			-
In(CAP)^2	0.67	−0.03***			
In(LAB)*In(CAP)	−12.84**	0.08***		**Statistic**	
RTS	**83.21**	**7.86**	**5.06**		**5.06**
R-squared	0.99	0.99	0.99	Gamma statistic	0.94***
F-statistic	488.61***	328.41***	1089.53***	Log-likelihood ratio	24.19

Notes: 1. Model 1 is the Trans-log production function with standard OLS, Model 2 is the Trans-log production function with ridge regression, Model 3 is the Cobb-Douglas production function with standard OLS, Model 4 is the stochastic frontier Cobb-Douglas model; 2. When the Model 3 is estimated under the intermediation approach by including the Amount of outstanding deposits as a regressor, the R^2 turns out to be 0.99. The coefficient of Amount of Deposits is worked out to be 0.48 and is found to be significant at 1% level. The F-statistic is 1633.95 and is also significant at 1% level. The size of the labour coefficient is 2.47 which is significant at 1% level. The estimated coefficient of capital is -0.13 which is insignificant even at 10% level. This model suffers from a high degree of multicollinearity as indicated by the Variance Inflation Factors. Furthermore, the same model is estimated using Ridge Regression with the k-value of 0.02. The R^2 is 0.98 and the sign of the coefficients remains the same. The size of the coefficient is reduced sizeably, however. These specifications have been excluded here so as to maintain consistency of presentation; 3. Similarly, Model 4 was re-estimated under the intermediation approach and the MLE coefficient of deposit variables was found to be 0.50 and is significant at 1% level. Labour coefficient is worked out to be 2.34 which is significant at 1% level while that of Capital is -0.15 which is highly insignificant. The log-likelihood ratio is 35.84 while the LR test statistic is 2.52 which is significant at 10% level of significance as per critical values given in Kodde and Palm (1986); 4. For Model 2, the final chosen k-value is 0.002; 5. Trans-log returns to scale coefficient is estimated at mean levels of inputs; 6. *, ** and *** indicate significant at 10%, 5% and 1% levels of significance respectively.

Source: Author's estimation.

Table 8.42 Returns to scale with amount of financial assets of banks as the output variable for the Russian banking industry

Output Variable = In(ASSET)					
Input Variable	*Model 1*	*Model 2*	*Model 3*	*Model 4*	
In(LAB)	−91.74*	2.23***	6.35***	6.34***	
In(CAP)	117.07*	−0.73**	−1.01***	−0.94***	
In(LAB)^2	12.84###	0.19***			
In(CAP)^2	−2.36###	−0.06***			
In(LAB)*In(CAP)	−8.96	0.13***		**Statistic**	-
RTS	**122.49**	**8.95**	**5.34**		**5.40**
R-squared	0.99	0.99	0.99	Gamma	0.83***
F-statistic	383.64***	247.80***	771.34***	Log-likelihood	19.41

Notes: 1. Model 1 is the Trans-log production function with standard OLS, Model 2 is the Trans-log production function with ridge regression, Model 3 is the Cobb-Douglas production function with standard OLS, Model 4 is the stochastic frontier Cobb-Douglas model; 2. When the Model 3 is estimated under the intermediation approach by including the Amount of outstanding deposits as an input variable, the R^2 turns out to be 0.99. The coefficient of Amount of Deposits is worked out to be 0.68 and is found to be significant at 1% level. The F-statistic is 1619.48 and is also significant at 1% level. Labour coefficient is 1.52 and that of capital is 0.009. Only the coefficient of Labour is significant at 1% level in this case. The coefficient of Capital is highly insignificant. However, this specification has been excluded so as to maintain consistency of presentation; 3. Similarly, Model 4 was re-estimated under the intermediation approach and the MLE coefficient of deposit variables was found to be 0.70 and is significant at 1% level. Labour coefficient is worked out to be 1.41 which is significant at 5% level while that of Capital is 0.04 which is insignificant. The log-likelihood ratio is 36.38 while the LR test statistic is 6.65 which is significant at 1% level of significance as per critical values given in Kodde and Palm (1986); 4. For Model 2, the final chosen k-value is 0.002; 5. Trans-log returns to scale coefficient is estimated at mean levels of inputs. 6. *, ** and *** indicate significant at 10%, 5% and 1% levels of significance respectively.

Source: Author's estimation.

Table 8.43 Returns to scale with the number of deposit accounts as the output variable for the Russian banking industry

Output Variable = In(DACT)					
Input Variable	*Model 1*	*Model 2*	*Model 3*	*Model 4*	
In(LAB)	−39.60#	0.66***	2.13***	2.08***	
In(CAP)	36.74	−0.30**	−0.34***	−0.29***	
In(LAB)^2	5.07	0.07***	-	-	-
In(CAP)^2	−0.58	−0.02***			
In(LAB)*In(CAP)	−3.26	0.05***		**Statistic**	
RTS	**49.83**	**3.20**	**1.79**		**1.79**
R-squared	0.98	0.97	0.97	Gamma	0.89***
F-statistic	132.12***	105.60***	318.16***	Log-likelihood	34.65

Notes: 1. Model 1 is the Trans-log production function with standard OLS, Model 2 is the Trans-log production function with ridge regression, Model 3 is the Cobb-Douglas production function with standard OLS, Model 4 is the stochastic frontier Cobb-Douglas model; 2. Trans-log returns to scale coefficient is estimated at mean levels of inputs; 3. In Model 2, the k-value is 0.002; 4. ** and *** indicate significant at 10%, 5% and 1% levels of significance respectively.

Source: Author's estimation.

Table 8.44 Returns to scale with amount of outstanding deposits as the output variable for the banking industry of India

Output Variable = In(DEP)					
Input Variable	*Model 1*	*Model 2*	*Model 3*	*Model 4*	
In(LAB)	−95.64$^{\#}$	0.30**	0.80**	0.81***	
In(CAP)	320.98***	0.62**	1.43*	1.49***	
In(LAB)^2	0.87	0.01**	-		
In(CAP)^2	−20.27**	0.03			
In(LAB)*In(CAP)	7.00	0.02***		**Statistic**	-
RTS	**2.70**	**2.30**	**2.23**		**2.30**
R-squared	0.95	0.84	0.63	Gamma	0.99**
F-statistic	59.41***	17.04***	15.43***	Log-likelihood	17.58

Notes: 1. Model 1 is the Trans-log production function with standard OLS, Model 2 is the Trans-log production function with ridge regression, Model 3 is the Cobb-Douglas production function with standard OLS, Model 4 is the stochastic frontier Cobb-Douglas model; 2. Trans-log returns to scale coefficient is estimated at mean levels of inputs; 3. The trans-log function was re-estimated using only the interaction term and excluding the polynomial terms. Another variant of the trans-log function with cubic terms was tested for. Still, the results did not improve. 4. For Model 2, the k-value is k = 0.095818.5. Model 3 has been estimated with Cochrane – Orcutt adjustment for auto correlation; 6. *, ** and *** indicate significant at 10%, 5% and 1% levels of significance respectively, and # indicates significant at 15% level.

Source: Author's estimation.

Table 8.45 Returns to scale with amount of outstanding loans as the output variable for the banking industry of India

Output Variable = In(LOAN)					
Input Variable	*Model 1*	*Model 2*	*Model 3*	*Model 4*	
In(LAB)	−87.88	0.28**	0.69*	0.66	
In(CAP)	398.77***	0.84***	2.26***	2.30**	
In(LAB)^2	0.58	0.01**			
In(CAP)^2	−24.05*	0.04***			
In(LAB)*In(CAP)	7.03	0.02***		**Statistic**	-
RTS	**3.37**	**2.70**	**2.95**		**2.96**
R-squared	0.94	0.85	0.85	Gamma	0.99***
F-statistic	53.06***	18.29***	54.17***	Log-likelihood	15.41

Notes: 1. Model 1 is the Trans-log production function with standard OLS, Model 2 is the Trans-log production function with ridge regression, Model 3 is the Cobb-Douglas production function with standard OLS, Model 4 is the stochastic frontier Cobb-Douglas model; 2. When the Model 3 is estimated under the intermediation approach by including the Amount of outstanding deposits as a regressor, the R^2 turns out to be 0.99. The coefficient of Amount of Deposits is worked out to be 1.18 and is found to be significant at 1% level. The F-statistic is 684.10 and is also significant at 1% level. The size of the labour coefficient is -0.26 which is significant at 5% level. The estimated coefficient of capital is 0.51 which is significant at 5% level. It been excluded here so as to maintain consistency of presentation; 3. Similarly, Model 4 was re-estimated under the intermediation approach and the MLE coefficient of deposit variables was found to be 1.14 and is significant at 1% level. Labour coefficient is worked out to be -0.23 which is significant at 5% level while that of Capital is 0.51 which is significant at 1% level. The log-likelihood ratio is 41.83 while the LR test statistic is 0.18 which is insignificant as per critical values given in Kodde and Palm (1986); 4. For Model 2, the chosen k-value is 0.195328; 5. Trans-log returns to scale coefficient is estimated at mean levels of inputs; 6. *, ** and *** indicate significant at 10%, 5% and 1% levels of significance respectively, and # indicates significant at 15% level.

Source: Author's estimation.

Table 8.46 Returns to scale with financial assets of commercial banks as the output variable for the banking industry of India

Output Variable = In(ASSET)					
Input Variable	*Model 1*	*Model 2*	*Model 3*	*Model 4*	
In(LAB)	−148.34**	0.15	0.19	0.53***	
In(CAP)	400.58***	0.81***	2.43***	1.87***	
In(LAB)²	−2.04	0.006#		-	
In(CAP)²	−32.91***	0.04***			
In(LAB)*In(CAP)	19.98**	0.02***			
RTS	**2.88**	**2.43**	**2.62**	**Statistic**	**2.40**
R-squared	0.93	0.81	0.64	Gamma	0.99***
F-statistic	44.78***	14.09***	16.23***	Log-likelihood	19.35

Notes: 1. Model 1 is the Trans-log production function with standard OLS, Model 2 is the Trans-log production function with ridge regression, Model 3 is the Cobb-Douglas production function with standard OLS, Model 4 is the stochastic frontier Cobb-Douglas model; 2. When the Model 3 is estimated under the intermediation approach by including the Amount of outstanding deposits as an input variable, the R^2 turns out to be 0.98. The coefficient of Amount of Deposits is worked out to be 0.91 and is found to be significant at 1% level. The F-statistic is 306.45 and is also significant at 1% level. Labour coefficient is -0.39 and that of capital is 0.78. Both are significant at 1% level. This specification has been excluded so as to maintain consistency of presentation. Researchers can access the actual data from the accompanied e-resources and estimate further extensions and variations of the empirical case studies presented herein; 3. Similarly, Model 4 was re-estimated under the intermediation approach and the MLE coefficient of deposit variables was found to be 0.90 and is significant at 1% level. Labour coefficient is worked out to be -0.11 which is insignificant. Output elasticity coefficient of Capital is 0.42 which is significant at 5% level. The log-likelihood ratio is 42.24 while the LR test statistic is 9.54, which is significant at 1% level of significance as per critical values given in Kodde and Palm (1986); 4. For Model 2, the final chosen k-value is 0.131441; 5. Trans-log returns to scale coefficient is estimated at mean levels of inputs; 6. Model 3 has been estimated with Cochrane – Orcutt adjustment for auto correlation; 7. *, ** and *** indicate significant at 10%, 5% and 1% levels of significance respectively, and # indicates significant at 15% level.

Source: Author's estimation.

Table 8.47 Returns to scale with total loan accounts with commercial banks as the output variable for the banking industry of India

Output Variable = In(LACT)			
Input Variable	*Model 1*	*Model 2*	*Model 3*
In(LAB)	-134.04***	0.36***	1.38***
In(CAP)	364.31***	0.42**	0.14
In(LAB)²	2.94**	0.01***	
In(CAP)²	-21.20***	0.02***	
In(LAB)*In(CAP)	5.19	0.02***	
RTS	**2.34**	**1.95**	**1.52**

(Continued)

Table 8.47 (Continued)

Output Variable = In(LACT)			
Input Variable	*Model 1*	*Model 2*	*Model 3*
R-squared	0.98	0.69	0.48
F-statistic	177.50***	7.15**	8.36***

Notes: 1. Model 1 is the Trans-log production function with standard OLS, Model 2 is the Trans-log production function with ridge regression, Model 3 is the Cobb-Douglas production function with standard OLS, Model 4 is the stochastic frontier Cobb-Douglas model; 2. When the Model 3 is estimated under the intermediation approach by including the Amount of outstanding deposits as an input variable, the R^2 turns out to be 0.83. The coefficient of Amount of Deposits is worked out to be 0.81 and is found to be significant at 1% level. The F-statistic is 27.66 and is also significant at 1% level. Labour coefficient is 0.50 and that of capital is -1.07. Both are significant at 5% level. This implies RTS of 0.25, i.e. DRS. This specification has been excluded so as to maintain consistency of presentation; 3. Model 4 produced very poor results and the stochastic frontier model did not seem to be suitable. It was also re-estimated under the intermediation approach and the MLE coefficient of deposit variables was found to be 0.98 which is insignificant even at 10% level. Labour coefficient is worked out to be 0.85 while that of Capital is -1.27, both of which are insignificant at 10% level. The log-likelihood ratio was found to be 23.45; 4. For Model 2, the final chosen k-value is 0.916500; 5. Trans-log returns to scale coefficient is estimated at mean levels of inputs; 6. *, ** and *** indicate significant at 10%, 5% and 1% levels of significance respectively, and # indicates significant at 15% level.

Source: Author's estimation.

Table 8.48 Returns to scale with total deposit accounts with commercial banks as the output variable for the banking industry of India

Output Variable = In(DACT)			
Input Variable	*Model 1*	*Model 2*	*Model 3*
In(LAB)	-245.16***	0.58***	0.70**
In(CAP)	316.77***	0.76***	0.57
In(LAB)²	0.33	0.02***	
In(CAP)²	-30.96***	0.04***	
In(LAB)*In(CAP)	23.13***	0.03***	
RTS	**4.15**	**3.44**	**1.27**
R-squared	0.98	0.83	0.27
F-statistic	213.48***	16.16***	3.38*

Notes: 1. Model 1 is the Trans-log production function with standard OLS, Model 2 is the Trans-log production function with ridge regression, Model 3 is the Cobb-Douglas production function with standard OLS, Model 4 is the stochastic frontier Cobb-Douglas model; 2. Trans-log returns to scale coefficient is estimated at mean levels of inputs; 3. In Model 2, the k-value is 0.606159; 4. Model 3 has been estimated using Cochrane-Orcutt adjustments for autocorrelation. An ARMA (1, 1) model was also estimated for the same model and in both the cases, the results do not improve; 5. Model 4 yielded did not produce good results. The gamma statistic was very low and insignificant and the resultant MLE coefficients were very small and insignificant even at 10% level. Hence, it has not been presented; 6. *, ** and *** indicate significant at 10%, 5% and 1% levels of significance respectively.

Source: Author's estimation.

Table 8.49 Returns to scale with amount of outstanding deposits commercial banks as the output variable for the banking industry of Indonesia

Output Variable = In(DEP)			
Input Variable	*Model 1*	*Model 2*	*Model 3*
In(WAGE)	-206.46***	-0.25##	0.67***
In(CAP)	67.90**	0.22***	0.30***
In(WAGE)²	9.17***	-0.007	
In(CAP)²	1.21*	0.11**	
In(WAGE)*In(CAP)	-6.25**	0.008***	
RTS	**19.37**	**1.02**	**0.97**
R-squared	0.93	0.57	0.97
F-statistic	44.02***	4.21**	232.88***

Notes: 1. Model 1 is the Trans-log production function with standard OLS, Model 2 is the Trans-log production function with ridge regression, Model 3 is the Cobb-Douglas production function with standard OLS, Model 4 is the stochastic frontier Cobb-Douglas model; 2. Trans-log returns to scale coefficient is estimated at mean levels of inputs; 3. For Model 2, the k-value is 0.118012; 4. In Model 3, the labour variable has been taken at its second lag; 5. *, ** and *** indicate significant at 10%, 5% and 1% levels of significance, respectively, and ## implies significant at 13% level; 6. Values in the bracket are standard errors. 7. Model 4 produced poor estimates. The gamma statistic was very small and highly insignificant, while the coefficients were statistically insignificant even at the 10% level.

Source: Author's estimation.

Table 8.50 Returns to scale with the amount of outstanding loans from commercial banks as the output variable for the banking industry of Indonesia

Output Variable = In(LOAN)					
Input Variable	*Model 1*	*Model 2*	*Model 3*	*Model 4*	
In(WAGE)	7.78**	-1.16**	0.86***	0.49***	
In(CAP)	0.24*	0.17	0.50***	0.15***	
In(WAGE)²	-0.69***	0.02*		†0.92***	
In(CAP)²	-1.26***	0.01		-	
In(WAGE)*In(CAP)	1.53***	0.03***		Statistic	-
RTS	**5.26**	**0.29**	**1.36**		**1.56**
R-squared	0.99	0.85	0.98	Gamma	0.91***
F-statistic	250.89***	17.71***	333.51***	Log-likelihood	51.69

Notes: 1. Model 1 is the Trans-log production function with standard OLS, Model 2 is the Trans-log production function with ridge regression, Model 3 is the Cobb-Douglas production function with standard OLS, Model 4 is the stochastic frontier Cobb-Douglas model; 2. Trans-log returns to scale coefficient is estimated at mean levels of inputs; 2. In(LAB) is with second lag in Model 3. When the same model is estimated under the intermediation approach by including the Amount of outstanding deposits as a regressor, autocorrelation appears to be a serious problem. Accordingly, the Cochrane-Orcutt Serial Correlation adjustment procedure is used to tackle this problem. The resulting model provides an R^2 of 0.98. The coefficient of Amount of Deposits is worked out to be 0.80 and is found to be significant at 1% level. The F-statistic is 235.51 and is also significant at 1% level. The size of the labour coefficient is 0.73, which is significant at 1% level. The estimated coefficient of capital is 0.14 which is significant at 15% level. It been excluded here to maintain consistency of presentation. Researchers can access the data from the accompanied e-resources and estimate more extensions and variations of the empirical case studies presented herein; 3. Model 1 has been estimated with Cochrane-Orcutt adjustment for autocorrelation, and In(CAP) is with first lag; 4. For Model 2, the final chosen k-value is 0.002; 5. † – Model 4 is reported with intermediation approach results, and the third variable is In(DEP); 6. Trans-log returns to scale coefficient is estimated at mean levels of inputs; 7. *, ** and *** indicate significant at 10%, 5% and 1% levels of significance, respectively.

Source: Author's estimation.

Table 8.51 Returns to scale with amount of financial assets of commercial banks as the output variable for the banking industry of Indonesia

Output Variable = ln(ASSET)			
Input Variable	*Model 1*	*Model 2*	*Model 3*
ln(WAGE)	-167.06***	-0.15	0.46**
ln(CAP)	58.47**	0.18**	0.42***
ln(WAGE)²	7.72**	0.002**	
ln(CAP)²	1.43*	0.01	
ln(WAGE)*ln(CAP)	-5.88**	0.01***	
RTS	**16.33**	**0.39**	**0.88**
R-squared	0.93	0.83	0.93
F-statistic	45.10***	15.52***	46.98***

Notes: 1. Model 1 is the Trans-log production function with standard OLS, Model 2 is the Trans-log production function with ridge regression, Model 3 is the Cobb-Douglas production function with standard OLS, Model 4 is the stochastic frontier Cobb-Douglas model; 2. Trans-log returns to scale coefficient is estimated at mean levels of inputs; 2. When the Model 3 is estimated under the intermediation approach by including the Amount of outstanding deposits as an input variable, the R^2 turns out to be 0.98. The coefficient of the amount of deposits is worked out to be 0.70 and is found to be significant at 1% level. The F-statistic is 245.71 and is also significant at 1% level. Labour coefficient is 0.53 and that of capital is 0.05. Labour coefficient is significant at 1% level. However, the output elasticity coefficient of capital is highly insignificant. However, when the first lag of the capital variable is used, its coefficient turns out to be 0.13 and becomes significant at 5% level. The signs of other two coefficients do not change. This specification has been excluded to maintain consistency of presentation; 3. For Model 2, the final chosen k-value is 0.013861; 4. Trans-log returns to scale coefficient is estimated at mean levels of inputs; 5. *, ** and *** indicate significant at 10%, 5% and 1% levels of significance, respectively; 6. ln(WAGE) in Model 3 is in first lag.

Source: Author's estimation.

Table 8.52 Returns to scale with the total number of loan accounts with commercial banks as the output variable for the banking industry of Indonesia

Output Variable = ln(LACT)			
Input Variable	*Model 1*	*Model 2*	*Model 3*
ln(WAGE)	-99.01***	0.27***	0.90***
ln(CAP)	55.20***	0.09***	0.17**
ln(WAGE)²	5.09***	0.009***	-
ln(CAP)²	0.89**	0.004***	-
ln(WAGE)*ln(CAP)	-4.79***	0.005***	-
RTS	**20.07**	**0.76**	**1.07**
R-squared	0.98	0.83	0.95
F-statistic	202.62***	15.46***	197.41***

Notes: 1. Model 1 is the Trans-log production function with standard OLS, Model 2 is the Trans-log production function with ridge regression, Model 3 is the Cobb-Douglas production function with standard OLS, Model 4 is the stochastic frontier Cobb-Douglas model; 2. Trans-log returns to scale coefficient is estimated at mean levels of inputs; 2. When the Model 3 is estimated under the intermediation approach by including the Amount of outstanding deposits as an input variable, the coefficient of Amount of Deposits is worked out to be 0.11 and is found to be insignificant even at 10% level. The labour coefficient is 1.02 in this case and is significant at 1% level. However, this model suffers from autocorrelation problem and even after undertaking the Cochrane-Orcutt adjustments, the coefficients behaved similarly. 2. For Model 2, the final chosen k-value is 0.651838; 3. Trans-log returns to scale coefficient is estimated at mean levels of inputs; 4. *, ** and *** indicate significant at 10%, 5% and 1% levels of significance, respectively.

Source: Author's estimation.

Table 8.53 Returns to scale with the total number of deposit accounts with commercial banks as the output variable for the banking industry of Indonesia

Output Variable = In(DACT)			
Input Variable	*Model 1*	*Model 2*	*Model 3*
In(WAGE)	-71.59	0.12	-0.12
In(CAP)	-34.16	0.17***	0.74**
In(WAGE)^2	1.29	0.005	
In(CAP)^2	-0.90	0.009***	
In(WAGE)*In(CAP)	3.57	0.008***	
RTS	**-6.78**	**0.68**	**0.62**
R-squared	0.97	0.51	0.58
F-statistic	93.64***	3.37**	12.91***

Notes: 1. Model 1 is the Trans-log production function with standard OLS, Model 2 is the Trans-log production function with ridge regression, Model 3 is the Cobb-Douglas production function with standard OLS, Model 4 is the stochastic frontier Cobb-Douglas model; 2. Trans-log returns to scale coefficient is estimated at mean levels of inputs; 3. In Model 2, the k-value is 0.423110; 4. Model 1 has also been estimated without the intercept term. With the intercept term, all the coefficients are statistically insignificant as shown in the table at even 10% level. By excluding the constant term, the coefficients become significant, but the signs of these coefficients change. Hence, it was thus decided to exclude that specification, because it deviates the sign and even the size of the coefficients considerably; 5. *, ** and *** indicate significant at 10%, 5% and 1% levels of significance, respectively.

Source: Author's estimation.

Table 8.54 Returns to scale with the amount of outstanding deposits with commercial banks as the output variable for the banking industry of China

Output Variable = In(DEP)					
Input Variable	*Model 1*	*Model 2*	*Model 3*	*Model 4*	
In(LAB)	-119.62**	1.17***	2.78***	2.97***	
In(CAP)	-129.22	-1.98***	-2.15**	-3.26***	
In^2(LAB)	7.66**	0.04***			
In^2 (CAP)	7.03	-0.09***			
In(LAB)*In(CAP)	-2.40	0.04***	-	**Statistic**	-
RTS	**-11.26**	**0.12**	**0.63**		**-0.29**
R-squared	0.87	0.75	0.82	Gamma	0.99***
F-statistic	20.99***	9.72***	41.42***	Log-likelihood	1.33

Notes: 1. Model 1 is the Trans-log production function with standard OLS, Model 2 is the Trans-log production function with ridge regression, Model 3 is the Cobb-Douglas production function with standard OLS, Model 4 is the stochastic frontier Cobb-Douglas model; 2. Trans-log returns to scale coefficient is estimated at mean levels of inputs; 3. For Model 2, the k-value is 0.049336; 4. Models 1 and 3 have been estimated with Cochrane-Orcutt adjustments for autocorrelation problem. The unadjusted standard OLS model showed strong evidence of autocorrelation, and hence the same was appropriately treated for. The signs of the coefficients are the same in both the cases for both models. Hence the Model 2 has also been estimated; 5. *, ** and *** indicate significant at 10%, 5% and 1% levels of significance, respectively.

Source: Author's estimation.

Table 8.55 Returns to scale with the amount of outstanding loans with commercial banks as the output variable for the banking industry of China

Output Variable = In(LOAN)					
Input Variable	*Model 1*	*Model 2*	*Model 3*	*Model 4*	
In(LAB)	-223.23***	0.99***	2.90***	3.04***	
In(CAP)	-266.85	-1.93***	-1.73**	-2.93***	
In(LAB)^2	9.12***	0.05***			
In(CAP)^2	14.23	-0.09***			
In(LAB)*In(CAP)	-4.21	0.05***	-	Statistic	-
RTS	**-172.52**	**0.45**	**1.17**		**0.11**
R-squared	0.89	0.78	0.86	Gamma	0.99***
F-statistic	26.79***	11.43***	55.42***	Log-likelihood	1.85

Notes: 1. Model 1 is the Trans-log production function with standard OLS, Model 2 is the Trans-log production function with ridge regression, Model 3 is the Cobb-Douglas production function with standard OLS, Model 4 is the stochastic frontier Cobb-Douglas model; 2. Trans-log returns to scale coefficient is estimated at mean levels of inputs; 2. When the Model 3 is estimated under the intermediation approach by including the Amount of outstanding deposits as a regressor, the resulting model provides an R^2 of 0.99. The coefficient of Amount of Deposits is worked out to be 1.02 and is found to be significant at 1% level. The F-statistic is 1500.36 and is also significant at 1% level. The size of the labour coefficient is 0.12 which is insignificant even at 10% level. The estimated coefficient of capital is 0.33 which is significant at 10% level. It been excluded here to maintain consistency of presentation. Researchers can access the actual data from the accompanied e-resources and estimate more extensions and variations of the empirical case studies presented herein. However, when the fourth model is estimated in the same context, the results are not good and the gamma statistic is highly insignificant along with insignificant coefficients; 3. For Model (2), the final chosen k-value is 0.007755; 4. Trans-log returns to scale coefficient is estimated at mean levels of inputs; 5. Model 3 has been estimated with Cochrane-Orcutt adjustments for serial correlation. In either case, the signs of the coefficients do not change and sizes are roughly similar; 6. *, ** and *** indicate significant at 10%, 5% and 1% levels of significance, respectively.

Source: Author's estimation.

Table 8.56 Returns to scale with the amount of financial assets with commercial banks as the output variable for the banking industry of China

Output Variable = In(ASSET)					
Input Variable	*Model 1*	*Model 2*	*Model 3*	*Model 4*	
In(LAB)	-17.42	1.07***	2.65***	2.46***	
In(CAP)	-523.99	-1.11**	-1.25*	-0.54	
In(LAB)^2	0.03	0.03***			
In(CAP)^2	21.73	-0.04**			
In(LAB)*In(CAP)	1.67	0.05***	-	**Statistic**	-
RTS	**-285.65**	**1.32**	**1.4**		**1.92**

Output Variable = In(ASSET)					
Input Variable	*Model 1*	*Model 2*	*Model 3*	*Model 4*	
R-squared	0.86	0.84	0.84	Gamma	0.90***
F-statistic	19.33	16.63***	50.32***	Log-likelihood	5.95

Notes: 1. Model 1 is the Trans-log production function with standard OLS, Model 2 is the Trans-log production function with ridge regression, Model 3 is the Cobb-Douglas production function with standard OLS, Model 4 is the stochastic frontier Cobb-Douglas model; 2. Trans-log returns to scale coefficient is estimated at mean levels of inputs; 3. When the Model 3 is estimated under the intermediation approach by including the Amount of outstanding deposits as an input variable, the R^2 turns out to be 0.87. The coefficient of the amount of deposits is worked out to be 0.33 and is found to be significant at 5% level. The F-statistic is 42.28 and is significant at 1% level. Labour coefficient is 1.63 and that of capital is -0.09. Labour coefficient is significant at 1% level while the coefficient of capital is highly insignificant. If the first lag of the capital variable is used, the results deteriorate considerably. This specification has been excluded to maintain the consistency of the presentation. Similar exercise for Model 4 results into poor estimates. The gamma statistic is very small and highly insignificant. Labour and Deposit coefficients are found to be positive and significant while capital coefficient is negative and insignificant; 4. For Model 2, the final chosen k-value is 0.006076; 5. The significance level of LR-test statistic has been undertaken using mixed-chi square distribution values given in Kodde and Palm (1986); 6. Trans-log returns to scale coefficient is estimated at mean levels of inputs; 7. Models 1 and 2 have been estimated with the first lag of the labour variable; 8. *, ** and *** indicate significant at 10%, 5% and 1% levels of significance, respectively, and ## indicates significant at 12% level.

Source: Author's estimation.

Table 8.57 Returns to scale with the total number of deposit accounts with commercial banks as the output variable for the banking industry in China

Output Variable = In(DACT)			
Input Variable	*Model 1*	*Model 2*	*Model 3*
In(LAB)	-287.31***	1.19***	3.28***
In(CAP)	-672.62*	-0.82	1.27*
In(LAB)^2	14.05***	0.04***	
In(CAP)^2	36.81**	-0.03	
In(LAB)*In(CAP)	-11.54#	0.06***	-
RTS	**-413.14**	**2.30**	**4.55**
R-squared	0.94	0.69	0.91
F-statistic	55.62***	7.16***	78.99***

Notes: 1. Model 1 is the Trans-log production function with standard OLS, Model 2 is the Trans-log production function with ridge regression, Model 3 is the Cobb-Douglas production function with standard OLS, Model 4 is the stochastic frontier Cobb-Douglas model; 2. When the Model 3 is estimated under the intermediation approach by including the Amount of outstanding deposits as an input variable, the coefficient of the amount of deposits is worked out to be 0.11 and is found to be insignificant even at 10% level. The labour coefficient is 1.02 in this case and is significant at 1% level. However, this model suffers from the autocorrelation problem, and even after undertaking the Cochrane-Orcutt adjustments, the coefficients behaved similarly; 3. For Model 2, the final chosen k-value is 0.249917; 4. Trans-log returns to scale coefficient is estimated at mean levels of inputs; 5. Model 3 has been estimated using the Cochrane-Orcutt adjustments for dealing with the problem of autocorrelation in the non-adjusted model. The capital variable is in its second lag; 6. *, ** and *** indicate significant at 10%, 5% and 1% levels of significance, respectively, and # indicates significant at 15% level.

Source: Author's estimation.

Table 8.58 Returns to scale with the total number of borrowers from commercial banks as the output variable for the banking industry in China

Output Variable = In(BOR)					
Input Variable	*Model 1*	*Model 2*	*Model 3*	*Model 4*	
In(LAB)	-85.25***	-0.07	0.40**	0.002	
In(CAP)	-210.29**	1.16***	2.87***	2.99***	
In(LAB)^2	3.21***	-0.002			
In(CAP)^2	9.98***	0.05***			
In(LAB)*In(CAP)	-1.01	0.008**	-	**Statistic**	-
RTS	**-123.75**	**1.70**	**3.27**		**3.00**
R-squared	0.98	0.67	0.84	Gamma	0.99***
F-statistic	133.32***	6.41***	42.36***	Log-likelihood	19.11

Notes: 1. Model 1 is the Trans-log production function with standard OLS, Model 2 is the Trans-log production function with ridge regression, Model 3 is the Cobb-Douglas production function with standard OLS, Model 4 is the stochastic frontier Cobb-Douglas model; 2. Trans-log returns to scale coefficient is estimated at mean levels of inputs; 3. In Model 2, the k-value is 0.603455; 4. Model 1 has also been estimated without the intercept term. With the intercept term, all the coefficients are statistically insignificant, as shown in the table at even 10% level. By excluding the constant term, the coefficients become significant, but the signs of these coefficients change. Hence, it was decided to exclude the specification because it deviated from the theoretical expectations on the expected sign and the size. Similarly, when the model fourth is estimated, the results are insignificant from an economic point of view, though the gamma statistic is high and significant; 5. Model 3 has been estimated with the second lag of capital variable. The model has been estimated with Cochrane-Orcutt serial correlation adjustment; 6. *, ** and *** indicate significant at 10%, 5% and 1% levels of significance, respectively.

Source: Author's estimation.

Table 8.59 Returns to scale with the amount of outstanding deposits of commercial banks as the output variable for the banking industry of South Africa

Output Variable = In(DEP)			
Input Variable	*Model 1*	*Model 2*	*Model 3*
In(WAGE)	13.61	-0.04	0.43***
In(CAP)	12.98*	0.13***	0.33**
In(WAGE)^2	-0.24	-0.002	
In(CAP)^2	-0.13	0.008***	
In(WAGE)*In(CAP)	-1.17**	0.02**	-
RTS	**0.15**	**0.52**	**0.76**
R-squared	0.83	0.60	0.85
F-statistic	15.50***	4.80***	45.53***

Notes: 1. Model 1 is the Trans-log production function with standard OLS, Model 2 is the Trans-log production function with ridge regression, Model 3 is the Cobb-Douglas production function with standard OLS, Model 4 is the stochastic frontier Cobb-Douglas model; 2. Trans-log returns to scale coefficient is estimated at mean levels of inputs; 3. For Model 2, the k-value is 0.233219; 4. Models 3 has been estimated with Cochrane-Orcutt adjustments for the autocorrelation problem. The unadjusted standard OLS model showed strong evidence of autocorrelation, and hence the same was appropriately treated for. The sign of the coefficients is the same in both the cases; 5. For model 3rd, the labour variable has been specified at its 3rd lag. Even with its current value and for lags up to 3rd, the sign remains the same. The size of the labour coefficient increases slightly, at the cost of the size of the capital coefficient; 6. *, ** and *** indicate significant at 10%, 5% and 1% levels of significance, respectively, and # indicates significant at 15% level.

Source: Author's estimation.

Table 8.60 Returns to scale with the amount of outstanding loans from commercial banks as the output variable for the banking industry of South Africa

Output Variable = In(LOAN)					
Input Variable	*Model 1*	*Model 2*	*Model 3*	*Model 4*	
In(WAGE)	21.25*	0.04†	0.31***	0.29*	
In(CAP)	9.99$^{\#\#}$	0.12***	0.49***	0.39***	
In(WAGE)^2	-0.67$^{\#\#}$	0.003†			
In(CAP)^2	0.03	0.007***			
In(WAGE)*In(CAP)	-1.10**	0.03***	-	Statistic	-
RTS	**0.73**	**0.84**	**0.80**		**0.68**
R-squared	0.77	0.66	0.69	Gamma	0.86***
F-statistic	10.52***	6.26***	21.03***	Log-likelihood	22.40

Notes: 1. Model 1 is the Trans-log production function with standard OLS, Model 2 is the Trans-log production function with ridge regression, Model 3 is the Cobb-Douglas production function with standard OLS, Model 4 is the stochastic frontier Cobb-Douglas model; 2. When the Model 3 is estimated under the intermediation approach by including the amount of outstanding deposits as a regressor, its coefficient is worked out to be 0.62 and is found to be significant at 1% level. The rest of the estimated coefficients are positive and highly significant. Similarly, when Model 4 is estimated similarly, the coefficients are insignificant, and the overall model seems poor due to a very low and insignificant gamma statistic. The individual coefficients are, however significant at 1% level; 3. For Model 2, the final chosen k-value is 0.059198; 4. Trans-log returns to scale coefficient is estimated at mean levels of input; 5. Model 3 has been estimated with Cochrane-Orcutt adjustments for serial correlation. In either case, the signs of the coefficients do not change, and sizes are roughly similar; 6. Models 1 and 2 have been estimated with the first lag of the labour variable. In the case of Model 1, this allowed the suppression of the degree of multicollinearity to a great extent, though it remained high; 7. *, **, and *** indicate significant at 10%, 5% and 1% levels of significance, respectively, and †indicates significant at 16% level.

Source: Author's estimation.

Table 8.61 Returns to scale with the amount of financial assets of commercial banks as the output variable for the banking industry of South Africa

Output Variable = In(ASSET)					
Input Variable	*Model 1*	*Model 2*	*Model 3*	*Model 4*	
In(WAGE)	21.36††	0.03	0.22**	0.02	
In(CAP)	7.20	0.15***	0.45***	0.23*	
In(WAGE)^2	-0.66	0.004			
In(CAP)^2	0.24	0.01***			
In(WAGE)*In(CAP)	-1.16*	0.01	-	**Statistic**	-
RTS	**0.56**	**0.58**	**0.67**		**0.25**
R-squared	0.72	0.61	0.62	Gamma	0.99***
F-statistic	8.23***	4.93***	15.37***	Log-likelihood	22.72

Notes: 1. Model 1 is the Trans-log production function with standard OLS, Model 2 is the Trans-log production function with ridge regression, Model 3 is the Cobb-Douglas production function with standard OLS, Model 4 is the stochastic frontier Cobb-Douglas model; 2. When the Model 3 is estimated under the intermediation approach by including the Amount of outstanding deposits as an input variable, the R^2 turns out to be 0.86. The coefficient of Amount of Deposits is worked out to be 0.69 and is found to be significant at 1% level. The F-statistic is 38.57 and is significant at 1% level. Labour coefficient is 0.16, and that of capital is 0.12. Labour coefficient is significant at 5% level while the coefficient of capital is significant at 15% level. Similarly, the fourth model is also estimated in the same context, and the model seems to be alright. The gamma statistic turns out to be 0.83 and is significant at 1% level. For Model 2, the final chosen k-value is 0.025251; 3. Trans-log returns to scale coefficient is estimated at mean levels of inputs; 4. *, ** and *** indicate significant at 10%, 5% and 1% levels of significance, respectively, and †† indicates significant at 13% level.

Source: Author's estimation.

Table 8.62 Returns to scale with the number of deposit accounts of commercial banks as the output variable for the banking industry of South Africa

Output Variable = In(DACT)					
Model 3	*Model 1*	*Model 2*	*Model 3*	*Model 4*	
In(WAGE)	13.05	-0.30***	0.39	0.71***	
In(CAP)	1.28	0.44***	1.48***	0.95***	
In(WAGE)^2	-0.16	-0.02***			
In(CAP)^2	0.76	0.03***			
In(WAGE)*In(CAP)	-1.29	0.04**	-	Statistic	-
RTS	**1.52**	**0.94**	**1.87**		**1.66**
R-squared	0.95	0.82	0.91	Gamma	0.99***
F-statistic	59.33	14.20***	98.25***	Log-likelihood	14.27

Notes: 1. Model 1 is the Trans-log production function with standard OLS, Model 2 is the Trans-log production function with ridge regression, Model 3 is the Cobb-Douglas production function with standard OLS, Model 4 is the stochastic frontier Cobb-Douglas model; 2. When the Model 3 is estimated under the intermediation approach by including the Amount of outstanding deposits as an input variable, the coefficient of amount of deposits is worked out to be 0.11 and is found to be insignificant even at 10% level. The labour coefficient is 1.02 in this case and is significant at 1% level. However, this model suffers from the autocorrelation problem, and even after undertaking the Cochrane-Orcutt adjustments, the coefficients behaved similarly; 3. For Model 2, the final chosen k-value is 0.387843; 4. Trans-log returns to scale coefficient is estimated at mean levels of inputs; 5. Model 3 has been estimated using the Cochrane-Orcutt adjustments for dealing with the problem of autocorrelation in the estimated residuals of the base model. The capital variable is in its second lag; 6. *, ** and *** indicate significant at 10%, 5% and 1% levels of significance, respectively.

Source: Author's estimation.

Appendix 4

Estimates for section 8.5

Table 8.63 Average change in the Malmquist Index of total factor productivity for the panel of selected economies across the sample period

Country	*DMTFP*	*LMTFP*	*DAMTFP*	*LAMTFP*	*AMTFP*
Brazil	0.3	2.4	2.6	3	2.6
Russia	12.3	9.4	3.7	NA	4.9
India	0.6	1.0	5.1	2.8	3.0
Indonesia	-6.7	-4.8	-3.1	-1.8	-2.5
China	6.0	6.6	-0.2	-0.2	6.1
South Africa	-3.1	-3.8	3	-3.3	-1.5

Notes: 1. All the variables represent the Malmquist Total Factor Productivity Index as estimated using the DEA approach; 2. In terms of the underlying output variables, DMTFP represents the amount of outstanding deposits with the commercial banks, LMTFP represents the amount of outstanding loans with the commercial banks, DAMTFP represents the number of total deposit accounts with the commercial banks, LAMTFP represents the number of total loan accounts with the commercial banks and AMTFP represents the amount of financial assets owned by the commercial banks.

Source: Author's estimation.

Appendix 5[38]

Input variables and estimates of output elasticities of inputs used in the construction of the total output index for section 8.3

Table 8.64 Cobb-Douglas production function estimates used in the estimation of weights for total inputs index for residual TFP index for Brazil and Russia

Brazil		*Russia*	
Output Elasticities for Inputs Aggregation		*Output Elasticities for Inputs Aggregation*	
All variables are in millions of their respective Units		*All variables are in millions of their respective Units*	
Inputs	**Output 1: Log of outstanding deposits**	***Inputs***	**Output 1: Log of outstanding deposits**
Real Mean Wage Rate	0.22	Bank employees	6.21
Bank Branches in Millions	-1.53	Commercial Bank Branches	-0.97
Total Equity in Millions	0.81	Number of total electronic terminals (self-service, POS, etc.)	0.15
Inputs	**Output 2: Log of Deposit Accounts with Commercial Banks**	***Inputs***	**Output 2: Log of Outstanding Loans (in millions)**
Real Mean Wage Rate	0.08	Bank employees	6.02
Bank Branches in Millions	1.20	Commercial Bank Branches	-0.80
Total Equity in Millions	0.43	***Inputs***	**Output 3: Total Bank Assets**
Inputs	**Output 3: Log of Outstanding loans with Commercial Banks**	Bank employees	0.97
Real Mean Wage Rate	0.16	Commercial Bank Branches	0.20
Bank Branches in Millions	2.67	Outstanding Deposits	0.75

Brazil		*Russia*	
Outstanding deposits	0.73	***Inputs***	**Output 4: Total Bank Accounts**
Inputs	**Output 4: Log of Loan Accounts (in millions)**	Bank employees	2.13
Real Mean Wage Rate	2.45	Commercial Bank Branches	-0.34
Bank Branches in Millions	3.69		
Number of depositors	0.99		
Inputs	**Output 5: Log of Total Assets (in millions of LCU)**		
Real Mean Wage Rate	-0.33		
Bank Branches in Millions	4.36		
Total Equity in Millions	-0.58		
Amount of Deposits per deposit account	1.30		

Table 8.65 Cobb-Douglas production function estimates used in the estimation of weights for total inputs index for residual TFP index for India and Indonesia

India		*Indonesia*	
Output Elasticities for Inputs Aggregation		*Output Elasticities for Inputs Aggregation*	
All variables are in millions of their respective Units		*All variables are in millions of their respective Units*	
Inputs	**Output 1: Log of outstanding deposits**	***Inputs***	**Output 1: Log of outstanding deposits**
Bank employees	0.80	Mean Real Wages	0.59
Commercial Bank Branches	1.49	Branches of commercial banks	0.51
Inputs	**Output 2: Log of Outstanding Loans**	***Inputs***	**Output 2: Log of Outstanding Loans**
Bank employees	-0.26	Mean Real Wages	-0.31
Commercial Bank Branches	0.51	Branches of commercial banks	0.38

(*Continued*)

Table 8.65 (Continued)

India		*Indonesia*	
Amount of outstanding deposits	1.18	Amount of outstanding deposits	0.84
Inputs	**Output 3: Log of Total Bank Assets**	***Inputs***	**Output 3: Total Bank assets**
Bank employees	-0.39	Mean Real Wages	-0.28
Commercial Bank Branches	0.78	Branches of commercial banks	0.27
Amount of outstanding deposits	0.91	Amount of outstanding deposits	0.61
Inputs	**Output 4: Log of Deposit Accounts**	***Inputs***	**Output 4: Log of Deposit accounts**
Bank employees	2.15	Mean Real Wages	1.16
Commercial Bank Branches	1.19	Branches of commercial banks	0.85
		Inputs	**Output 5: Log of Loan accounts**
		Mean Real Wages	-0.43
		Branches of commercial banks	0.44
		Deposits per borrower	0.18

Table 8.66 Cobb-Douglas production function estimates used in estimation of weights for total inputs index for residual TFP index for China and South Africa

China		*South Africa*	
Output Elasticities for Inputs Aggregation		**Output Elasticities for Inputs Aggregation**	
All variables are in millions of their respective Units		***All variables are in millions of their respective Units***	
Inputs	**Output 1: Log of outstanding deposits**	***Inputs***	**Output 1: Log of outstanding deposits**
Bank employees	3.55	Employees in Finance and Insurance	0.55
Commercial Bank Branches	-5.30	Branches of Commercial Banks (2nd lag)	0.33
Inputs	**Output 2: Log of Outstanding Loans**	***Inputs***	**Output 2: Log of Outstanding Loans**
Bank employees	3.77	Employees in Finance and Insurance	-0.37

China		*South Africa*	
Commercial Bank Branches	-5.16	Branches of Commercial Banks	0.07
Inputs	**Output 3: Log of Bank Assets**	Amount of deposits	0.73
Bank employees	2.65	***Inputs***	**Output 3: Log of Deposit accounts**
Commercial Bank Branches	-1.26	Employees in Finance and Insurance	1.37
Inputs	**Output 4: Log of Deposit Accounts**	Branches of Commercial Banks	0.90
Bank employees	2.66		
Commercial Bank Branches (2nd lag)	-3.53		
Inputs	**Output 5: Log of Borrowers from commercial banks**		
Bank employees	0.94		
Commercial Bank Branches (2nd lag)	2.80		
Amount of deposits	-0.21		
Inputs	**Output 6: Log of Depositors with banks**		
Bank employees	3.29		
Commercial Bank Branches	-1.78		

Notes

1 For an overview and application of the aggregate industry-wide approach to technical efficiency adopted here, please see Méon and Weill (2010).

2 It is duly recognized at this stage that aggregation generates some insurmountable problems. First, it gives rise to the aggregation problem as initiated by the Cambridge Capital controversy. Second, there are very strict conditions to be fulfilled to prove that the estimated coefficients represent technological relationships rather than mere accounting identities. Both these matters are examined in detail in Felipe and McCombie (2014). However, these criticisms are generally levied against the use of aggregate production functions for deriving microeconomic inferences. No such attempt is made in the Part III of this study. First, data constraints have forced the use of this approach. The ideal approach is always to prefer firm-level information rather than industry-level data. If high-quality, consistent and reliable firm-level data are unavailable, one then needs to adopt a more accommodative approach. Second, the primary aim of Part III is to show how empirical estimates of performance parameters change when alternative output

measures are used. Suppose the evidence on aggregated data shows meaningful impact of changing output measures on selected parameters. In that case, it does provide a preliminary case for such an impact at a more disaggregated level of data. Macroeconomic literature has evolved considerably since the early critiques on aggregation. If aggregation were an economically non-useful approach, then macroeconomic theory's entire edifice, including national income accounting, could crumble down. As argued in Colander (1993), economists have been equally vociferous on the existence of a separate and independent macroeconomic reality, which is an outcome of interactions among individual actions but may evolve independently of those individual actors. The present work has adopted this rather optimistic view toward aggregation. Due to data constraints and providing a fresher perspective, the study has adopted the use of aggregate industry-level data. A final reason for this choice was that the author wanted to use data from the same source as far as possible so that comparability of results across economies could be maintained. Thus, given the above qualifications, the analysis in Chapters 8 and 9 must be interpreted as brief case studies rather than rigorous economic analysis of the chosen performance issues, which is far beyond the scope of this work.

3 Boda and Piklova (2021) find higher variability in efficiency scores based on the production approach mainly caused when the number of labourer variables is used along with the total asset variable. In the present study, similar findings are obtained concerning the variation in output measures only rather than both outputs and inputs. This has been done by keeping the input vector constant across all specifications.

4 Lawrence Klein's works are generally referred as the seminal works on this issue in applied macroeconometrics. Since being in the Cowles commission, he aimed to link the macroeconomic issues with the microeconomic, optimizing logic of economic agents into "properly measured" macro aggregates (Visco, 2014). To date, the debate on this issue has continued. One school of thought asserts that macro aggregates are meaningless without microeconomic foundations. The other states that macroeconomic reality can be theorized independently of pure microeconomic behaviour within minimalistic micro-foundations. "The new macro perspective allowed one to talk about interrelationships among aggregates without specifying the underlying individual choice theoretic framework" (Colander, 1993, p. 447). See the author's work for more detail on these two schools of thought in macroeconomic theorizing.

5 A frequently used data source in the literature is BankFocus (earlier BankScope) by Moody's Analytics. While this is a useful source for firm-level information in banking and insurance, criticisms have been levied on its unqualified use. The same has been highlighted earlier in Chapter 2. Furthermore, the author could not fully access the source to verify the complete availability of firm-level data and its quality. Hence, it seemed best to use data from national and international official agencies.

6 There are multiple definitions of EMEs in the literature. The exact definition used here is based on the multi-dimensional procedure and accounts for both the economic and financial characteristics of the economies. The online resources may provide the details on the procedure used to define and then select the emerging economies. The same can also be obtained from the author upon request.

7 The Cobb-Douglas functional form possesses several strengths. The "Cobb-Douglas production function is robust to duality" (Kouki et al., 2014, p. 357). Furthermore, it has been suggested in works on macroeconometrics by Klein and others that Cobb-Douglas is ideal for aggregate economic analysis.

8 This functional form is theorized as a second-order Taylor series approximation to an unknown underlying true production function. For more details on its properties and issues in constructing and using it in production analysis, see Boisvert (1982).

9 The Cobb-Douglas production function has a rich history. It has transcended many barriers and has passed through many stages of conceptual metamorphosis. The evolution of this function can be located in Felipe and McCombie (2014) and, more recently, in Biddle (2021).

10 Cobb-Douglas production function was the primary choice. The trans-log function was adopted to provide additional insights.
11 See the seminal work of Solow (1957) for more details.
12 In sections 8.3 and 9.3, the chosen DEA model is output-oriented under Variable Returns to Scale (VRS) on the lines of Fare et al. (1994, Chapters 4 and 6). The DEAP Version 2.1 software was used.
13 All econometric estimations reported in this and the next chapter were tested for econometric diagnostics, and due care was taken to ensure that the key econometric issues of normality of estimated residuals, autocorrelation, multicollinearity and specification error tests were handled appropriately. The estimated results are robust to alternative specifications in terms of the variables. Sensitivity tests to alternative specifications were undertaken to ensure that the estimated coefficients and results are reliable on the lines suggested by Magnus and Vasnev (2015). Due to space restrictions, the same has not been reported but can be happily obtained from the author on request.
14 There are some works, such as Fecher (1993), that have used a Cobb-Douglas based SFA for estimating industry-level production functions. Similarly, Kumbhakar and Hjalmarsson (1995) use a trans-log SFA with only interactive terms.
15 There are two key choices to be made when using the SFA: first is the functional form, and the second is the distributional assumption for the inefficiency term (Eling & Luhnen, 2010). In sections 8.3, 8.4, 9.3, and 9.4, the Battese and Coelli (1992) error components model under SFA is employed using the FRONTIER 4.1 software. More details may be availed from the author on request.
16 The detailed definitions and explanations of each of the variables used, the procedures employed for dealing with missing data, the data source for each variable and other important methodological issues can be obtained from the author on request. This choice was made due to space restrictions.
17 The detailed definitions and explanations on each of the variables used, the procedures employed for dealing with missing data, data source for each variable and other important methodological issues can be obtained from the author on request. This choice was made due to space restrictions.
18 The choice of these variables is largely based on the production approach; though, in section 8.4, the intermediation approach is also tested. The production approach has been used as it lends itself to the objective of these empirical case studies. Each of the chosen output measures requires being included in the production function alternatively to study the impact that this can have on performance estimates. The production approach can allow such an exercise more conveniently than other output specification approaches. Furthermore, given that the nature of the analysis is aggregative rather than firm-level, the production approach seems to rationalize the behaviour of the aggregate banking industry quite well. Data constraints have played a pivotal role in choosing the final set of output variables in Part III.
19 The data on this variable were obtained from the Global Monitoring Report on Non-Bank Financial Intermediation dataset of the Financial Stability Board. This dataset provides rich insights into the financial structure of various intermediaries, including commercial banks.
20 Details on the variable-wise issues, adjustments and other dimensions may be available in the online resources. Alternatively, they can be obtained directly from the author upon request.
21 The exact output variable and the definition of each labour and capital productivity measure used have been clearly stated in notes to each of the supporting tables in the appendix at the end of this and the next chapter.
22 Only the first and second moments are analysed here. The primary reason for this is that the data are industry-level aggregates rather than firm-level estimates. Going beyond the second moment did not seem to make much sense as the disaggregated information is unavailable. Reading too much in too little data may not be a plausible approach, so further moments are not presented.

23 The use of traditional descriptive statistics and the associated distribution theory for social data (information derived from human behaviour) has been criticised because data in social sciences do not easily lend themselves to the statistical assumptions demanded by traditional distributions theory. Various conceptual and philosophical issues are raised when mainstream statistical theory is applied to economic and social data without recognising the pitfalls. Winkler (2009) analyses these issues in detail and provides a heterodox view on analysing social science data. The author argues for an alternative narrative in analysing economic and social data that does not demand the strict assumptions required by the traditional statistical theory for data in pure sciences.

24 Estimates of skewness and kurtosis have not been reported here but may be provided in the online resources or can directly be obtained from the author on request.

25 The residual TFP index was built as a ratio of the total output index (wherein only one output measure has been used at a time) and a total inputs index (with multiple inputs that include labour, physical capital and financial capital). The main debate is on the choice of the weights for aggregating the inputs into the index of the total input. This study uses the output elasticities of each of the chosen inputs estimated using a Cobb-Douglas production function under Ordinary Least Squares. Some mathematical and economic conditions need to be fulfilled while using this approach. The first is that the sign of the output elasticity coefficient for each chosen output should be positive. The second and weaker condition is that failing the first requirement, at least the sum of output elasticities of inputs should be positive. The second condition was consistently fulfilled across most of the cases. In cases where it couldn't be fulfilled, lags of the input variables were tried to overcome the problem. The estimated weights used for aggregating inputs into a total inputs index are presented in Appendix 5.

26 A rigorous survey of the evolution of the DEA method and its empirical applications can be found in Emrouznejad and Yang (2017).

27 Detailed analysis and extended comments may be obtained from the online resources or can be availed from the author upon request. The purpose of Chapters 8 and 9 is to indicate the broad analytical dimensions of the issue under investigation. Higher levels of disaggregated data are required to infer any further insights than presented here.

28 Such observations are purely statistical. The economic content of the same needs further investigation. As the primary aim of this part of the book is to provide case studies on the empirical implications of alternative output measures, the economic issues of such findings are much beyond the scope. Further research can address these concerns.

29 Another approach could have been to use the Fourier flexible form employed alternatively in the literature. However, "a disadvantage (of Fourier flexible form of production function) is that the number of Fourier terms can become very large, causing degrees of freedom problems. Consequently, the method cannot be used for small datasets" (Cummins & Weiss, 2013, p. 810).

30 In the case of some economies, data on the number of employees in the banking industry were not available. Only in such cases have the data on the number of employees in the financial services industry. Data on the number of branches were not available in all the cases. Due to data constraints, the number of banking institutions was used as a rough proxy for the size of physical capital employed by the banking industry.

31 Literature on banking has treated the number of branches as both input and output. Use of the same as output is defended on the grounds that the number of branches is representative of convenience (Fixler & Zieschang, 1999). However, this study uses the number of branches to measure quasi-fixed capital input, which is presumed to vary broadly (but slowly) in direct correlation to the demand for outputs (whether an asset, liability or others). Technological advances and digitalisation of banking processes might cast disagreement on such a belief. However, for the EMEs under consideration, physical infrastructure can be assumed to have a large scope for expansion due to under reach of core banking services. Thus it might not be too unrealistic to assume that branch

expansion is a key input change for inducing larger outputs of the banking industry as a whole. For a defence of this variable as an output measure, see Srivastava (1999), Kumbhakar and Sarkar (2003), and Asaftei and Kumbhakar (2008), among others. For those who favour its use as an input, see the discussion and references in Chapter 10.

32 These estimates can be obtained from the author on request.

33 Please see Barua et al. (2015) for the form of the trans-log function used here and the methodology to estimate returns to scale from the same.

34 In a few cases where consistent and continuous data on the number of branches were not available, the data on the number of banking firms were used.

35 Multicollinearity is measured in terms of the value of Variance Inflation Factors.

36 The analysis in this section and in 9.4 has been kept basic and limited to statistical notes rather than economic inferences. Such an exercise will require much more space and data, which is outside the scope of this book.

37 Building international or global production frontiers in an industry such as banking is difficult to justify theoretically. Banking activities are generally localised in terms of the policies, institutions, markets and price determination. External shocks may impact these elements, but in broad terms, the industry is specific to local conditions, and conceptualising an international or global frontier seems unreliable. "One has to account for country-specific differences in the environments in which firms operate in order to make a global frontier meaningful" (Gaganis et al., 2013, p. 430). Very few studies have adopted such an approach in the banking performance literature, maybe due to such concerns.

38 Detailed estimated models can be obtained from the author on request.

References

Asaftei, G., & Kumbhakar, S. C. (2008). Regulation and efficiency in transition: The case of Romanian banks. *Journal of Regulatory Economics*, *33*(3), 253–282. https://doi.org/10.1007/s11149-007-9041-0

Barua, A., Goldar, B., & Sharma, H. (2015). *The role of technological conditions of production in explaining India's manufacturing growth, 1998–99 to 2007–08: Some policy perspectives*. Centre for International Trade and Development (Discussion Paper No. 15–04).

Battese, G. E., & Coelli, T. J. (1992). Frontier production functions, technical efficiency and panel data: With application to paddy farmers in India. *The Journal of Productivity Analysis*, *3*, 153–169.

Biddle, J. E. (2021). *Progress through regression the life story of the empirical Cobb-Douglas production function* (1st ed.). Cambridge University Press. https://doi.org/10.1017/9781108679312

Boda, M., & Piklova, Z. (2021). Impact of an input-output specification on efficiency scores in data envelopment analysis: A banking case study. *RAIRO Operations Research*, *55*, S1551–S1583. https://doi.org/10.1051/ro/2020040

Boisvert, R. N. (1982). *The Translog production function: Its properties, its several interpretations and estimation problems*. New York State College of Agriculture and Life Sciences (Working Paper No. A.E. Res. 82–28). https://ecommons.cornell.edu/bitstream/handle/1813/65165/Cornell_Dyson_rb8228.pdf?sequence=1&isAllowed=y

Colander, D. C. (1993). The macrofoundations of micro. *Eastern Economic Journal*, *19*(4), 447–457. www.jstor.org/stable/40325524

Cummins, J. D., & Weiss, M. A. (2013). Analyzing firm performance in the insurance industry using frontier efficiency and productivity methods. In *Handbook of insurance* (2nd ed., pp. 795–858). Springer.

Eling, M., & Luhnen, M. (2010). Efficiency in the international insurance industry: A cross-country comparison. *Journal of Banking and Finance*, *34*(7), 1497–1509.

Emrouznejad, A., & Yang, G. (2017). A survey and analysis of the first 40 years of scholarly literature in DEA: 1978–2016. *Socio-Economic Planning Sciences*. https://doi.org/10.1016/j.seps.2017.01.008

Fare, R., Grosskopf, S., & Lovell, C. A. K. (1994). *Production frontiers* (1st ed.). Cambridge University Press.

Fecher, F., Kessler, D., Perlman, S., & Pestieau, P. (1993). Productive performance of the French insurance indus. *The Journal of Productivity Analysis, 4*, 77–93.

Felipe, J., & McCombie, J. S. L. (2005). How sound are the foundations of the aggregate production function? *Eastern Economic Journal, 31*(3), 467–488.

Felipe, J., & McCombie, J. S. L. (2014). The aggregate production function: 'Not even wrong'. *Review of Political Economy, 26*(1), 60–84. https://doi.org/10.1080/09538259.2013.874192

Fixler, D., & Zieschang, K. (1999). The productivity of the banking sector: Integrating financial and production approaches to measuring financial service output. *The Canadian Journal of Economics, 32*(2), 547–569.

Gaganis, C., Hasan, I., & Pasiouras, F. (2013). Efficiency and stock returns: Evidence from the insurance industry. *The Journal of Productivity Analysis, 40*, 429–442. https://doi.org/10.1007/s11123-013-0347-x

Kodde, D. A., & Palm, F. C. (1986). Wald criteria for jointly testing equality and inequality restrictions. *Econometrica, 54*(5), 1243–1248.

Kouki, M., Park, S. S., & Renault, E. (2014). Estimating scale economies in financial intermediation: A doubly indirect inference. *The Journal of Productivity Analysis, 41*, 351–365. https://doi.org/10.1007/sl 1 123-013-0345-z

Kumbhakar, S. C., & Hjalmarsson, L. (1995). Labour-use efficiency in Swedish social insurance offices. *Journal of Applied Econometrics, 10*, 33–47.

Kumbhakar, S. C., & Sarkar, S. (2003). Deregulation, ownership, and productivity growth in the banking industry: Evidence from India. *Journal of Money, Credit and Banking, 35*(3), 403–424.

Magnus, J. R., & Vasnev, A. L. (2015). Interpretation and use of sensitivity in econometrics, illustrated with forecast combinations. *International Journal of Forecasting, 31*, 769–781. http://dx.doi.org/10.1016/j.ijforecast.2013.08.001

Méon, P.-G., & Weill, L. (2010). Does financial intermediation matter for macroeconomic performance? *Economic Modelling, 27*, 296–303. https://doi.org/10.1016/j.econmod.2009.09.009

Solow, R. (1957). Technical change and the aggregate production function. *The Review of Economics and Statistics, 39*(3), 312–320.

Srivastava, P. (1999). *Size, efficiency and financial reforms in Indian banking*. Indian Council for Research on International Economic Relations (Working Paper No. 49).

Visco, I. (2014). Lawrence R. Klein: Macroeconomics, econometrics and economic policy. *Journal of Policy Modeling, 36*, 605–628. http://dx.doi.org/10.1016/j.jpolmod.2014.03.003

Winkler, O. W. (2009). *Interpreting economic and social data a foundation of descriptive statistics* (1st ed.). Springer. https://doi.org/10.1007/978-3-540-68721-4

9 Testing the empirical sensitivity of major performance indicators of the insurance industry under alternative output definitions

Selected exercises

9.1. Background

Continuing the analysis undertaken in Chapter 8, a similar framework is applied to the insurance industry in this chapter. The fundamental aims are twofold: first is to find whether performance measures such as efficiency, productivity and scale vary on account of different output measures of the aggregate insurance industry, and the second is to know the extent of such variations if any. This chapter investigates the above two objectives by adopting the similar methodological, econometric and data-oriented approach as Chapter 8. In terms of partial factor productivities, labour, physical capital, financial capital and operational productivities are defined using the ratios as shown in equations 1 and 2 in Chapter 8, but with output and inputs pertaining to the insurance industry as discussed later. TFP is defined as explained in Chapter 8. Using only the Cobb-Douglas production function, technical efficiency is measured under both the standard OLS and SFA approaches. Unlike the banking production analysis in the previous chapter, this chapter does not consider trans-logarithmic function. There are two major reasons for this: first is that the true underlying production function seemed fairly well-represented by the Cobb-Douglas specification in both economic and econometric terms; second is that the econometric results using the trans-log function yielded inconsistent and highly problematic estimates. Using the principle of Occam's razor, it was decided to adopt the Cobb-Douglas specification, given its ability to explain a large portion of the aggregate output variations in the insurance industry in the present study.[1]

Estimates in this chapter are reported separately for the total insurance industry, life insurance industry and nonlife insurance segment. The insurance output measures employed in this chapter for the total insurance industry are the amount of total gross premiums, total net premiums, total claims, total net claims (net of reinsurance received), total financial assets and the number of total policies; for the life insurance industry they are amount of premiums, net premium (net of commercial expenses), claims, financial assets/assets under management (AUM) and the number of policies underwritten; for the nonlife insurance industry they are amount of premiums, net premiums, claims, financial assets/assets under management and the number of policies underwritten.

DOI: 10.4324/9781003149828-12

The output set in this chapter largely consists of value measures. As noted in the previous chapter, all the monetary variables are deflated in 2010 prices using country-specific CPI and are expressed in local currencies. The data sources are as per the discussion in the previous chapter.

9.2. Partial factor productivity estimates for the insurance industry

Other than labour and physical capital productivities, operational productivity (using the amount of real commercial expenses as an input) and financial capital productivity (using the amount of real equity capital) is also estimated in this section as and where data were available. Labour is defined as the number of employees in the concerned insurance industry (total, life or nonlife). In cases where data were unavailable, the number of employees in the financial services sector or real wage rate of the financial services sector was employed. Physical capital is defined as the number of branches of the insurance industry or the number of total retail agent outlets or insurance corporations (where data on branches were either unavailable or not consistently available for the sample period). Tables 9.1 to 9.4 in appendix 1 present data on various partial factor productivities at the aggregate industry level for Brazil, Russia, India and China. Due to data issues for Indonesia and South Africa, their results have not been reported.

Table 9.1 (Brazil) presents the estimates of labour and operational productivities for total, life and nonlife segments separately. In terms of the mean productivity levels, estimates within each industry segment and within each productivity measure show wide differences on account of differences in output measures.[2] Financial assets have larger labour productivity than others, which probably reflects the impact that stock versus flow output measures can have on performance estimates. In terms of variability as shown by CV, except LPLC and OPNLP, all other productivity estimates show fairly similar behaviour. In the case of the Russian insurance industry, as shown in Table 9.2, when labour productivity estimates are looked at in terms of their levels, financial assets stand out (LPTFA). In terms of variability across all reported estimates, financial assets-based and total claims-based estimates show the largest CV (LPTFA and LPTC). Table 9.3 (India) shows that the financial assets-based estimate has a larger size than premiums. Using stock versus flow measures of output can make a large difference in the final results. Surprisingly, volume-based output measures generally show higher variability than the value measures. In the case of China (Table 9.4), both the mean and variability of financial assets is the highest. It seems that this output measure can induce large variations in productivity estimates if not adjusted appropriately.[3]

9.3. Total factor productivity and technical efficiency estimates for the insurance industry

Residual TFP index,[4] DEA-based technical efficiency and SFA-based efficiency results with regard to the insurance industry are presented in this section.

As explained in section 8.3 in Chapter 8, the methodological framework is extended here to the insurance industry. As clarified earlier in this chapter, only the Cobb-Douglas production specification is used mainly due to the aggregate nature of the data and lack of theoretically acceptable results in using the trans-log and even the Constant Elasticity of Substitution (CES) functions.

Table 9.5 estimates the average annual growth rate of the residual TFP index for Brazil using alternative insurance output measures. Compared to the life and nonlife segments individually, the total insurance segment shows a much larger variation in the mean growth levels of the TFP index (TFPG1, TFPG2 and TFPG3). In this case (TFPG3), financial asset shows lesser variability than premiums and claims while recording the highest average growth rate during the sample period among the three estimates. In the case of the life insurance segment, the mean growth rates are fairly similar, but in terms of variability, the net life premiums-based measure (TFPG6) displays a very high variability. Estimates for the nonlife segment (TFPG7 and TFPG8) seem fairly robust to output specifications. In terms of the skewness of the distribution of estimated TFPG series using different output measures, while all the series show moderate to high skewness, the asset output for the total insurance segment and all the estimates for the life segment show high skewness. Depending on the output measure used and the insurance segment focused upon (total, life and nonlife), skewness changes drastically from being negative to positive. One can only appreciate the policy and analytical implications of such dramatic shifts in TFP growths under different output measures.

Regarding the uniqueness of information content, as measured by the correlation coefficient, it appears, at least for within-segment estimates, that changing the output definitions adds new information due to the low and insignificant correlation coefficient. Regarding the estimates of technical efficiencies, in Table 9.6, within each segment, the first and third moments show a fair amount of similarity, though there are some differences among them. These differences may possess sizeable implications given that these data represent the entire segments in aggregated form. For the life segment, however, the third moment of the distribution of the estimated TE index shows an appreciable difference (TED3 and TED4). Using premiums versus claims can induce significant differences in how the efficiency is concentrated around its mean. The correlation coefficients are generally positive, high and significant, and thus it seems that irrespective of the chosen output measure, efficiency shall behave quite similarly.

In the case of Russia, as shown in Table 9.7, the sensitivity of mean levels of growth in the TFP index is quite high wherein, at times, the average growth is positive, and for some outputs, it is negative. This difference is sizeably wide too. The differences in variability are also quite wide when different output measures are employed. The premium output for total and nonlife segments seems to be introducing considerable change in the distribution, as shown by their positive and large skewness value. In terms of their cross-correlations, only two pairs show a high correlation, namely TFPG1 (total premium) and TFPG5 (nonlife premium), and TFPG2 (gross claims) and TFPG3 (net claims). Thus, the TFP growth has different paths on average when different output measures are employed. Concerning the efficiency estimates as shown in Table 9.8, for the total insurance segment (life plus nonlife), premiums and assets show much higher variability than claims output measures. However, claims-based efficiency shows a much higher mean level of achievement on this account. The correlations are largely low and signify substantial differences, and probably independent, in the temporal movements of aggregate technical efficiency across the same period. In the Indian insurance industry context, as contained in Table 9.9, the mean, variability and skewness in the residual TFP growth are all considerably sensitive to the choice of output measure. Correlations being quite weak, different output measures seem to be expressing different information content and thus cannot serve meaningfully as simple alternatives to each other in productivity analysis of the insurance industry. Choice of output will deeply affect the behaviour of the productivity growth. From the perspective of efficiency analysis, as shown in Table 9.10, variability is largely stable across the estimated efficiencies using different output measures except in the case of premium output measures (TED2, TED3 and TES3). Mean levels of efficiencies are largely high in all the cases. Correlations are also largely weak, though it is moderately high in some cases, such as between claims (TED4) and assets under management (TED5). Some degree of independence in the movements of these efficiencies seems evident. For the Indonesian mainstream insurance industry (excluding Takaful insurance), as shown in Table 9.11, average mean and variability are widely fluctuating across output measures, and some evidence of independence in the distribution of these estimates is visible. From the angle of efficiency estimates in Table 9.12, the nature of skewness, variations in mean levels and the variability of estimated efficiency series seem to be implying quite a similar behaviour.

In the case of China, differences in output measures seem to be inducing considerable heterogeneity in the estimated average growth in the TFP index, as shown in Table 9.13. Mean levels show diametrically opposite performance. In terms of the analysis segment, the individual segments show larger variability than when the composite of life and nonlife segments is analysed (TFPG3 and TFPG4 versus TFPG1 and TFP2). Skewness also shows some evidence of sensitivity to the choice of output measure. On the empirical sensitivity of efficiency estimates to alternative output measures as per Table 9.14, the first and second moments show some sign of sensitivity, while at the higher moments, this difference seems to vanish. This is reflected in the high and significant correlation coefficients. There does not seem to be much impact of using different output measures in this case. Evidence in Table 9.15 for the South African insurance industry shows a higher impact of changes in output definitions on mean, variability and skewness. However, efficiency estimates in Table 9.16 suggest otherwise.

9.4. Returns to scale estimates for the insurance industry of selected EMEs

Extending the discussion in section 8.4 of Chapter 8, this section presents the estimates on the returns to scale for the total insurance, life insurance and nonlife insurance industries in Table 9.17 in Appendix 3. The underlying estimations are reported in Tables 9.18 to 9.23 in appendix 3. The very nature of RTS, i.e. whether increasing, decreasing or constant, changes for Brazil's total insurance industry when one switches from premiums to claims and assets. In the case of life and nonlife segments separately, however, RTS remain increasing while the size changes considerably. Premium output appears to be inducing the largest RTS for Brazil. Except for the claims measure, all other outputs yield a decreasing RTS for Russia. Claims-based RTS has the largest size. In the case of India, RTS are negative and thus decreasing. Premiums-based estimates are such across the segments. The magnitudes of the RTS coefficients are also wide even when most of them are showing decreasing returns. Though the RTS is largely increasing, the magnitudes vary considerably in Indonesia, China and South Africa.

Appendix 1

Estimates for Section 9.2

Table 9.1 Partial factor productivity estimates for the insurance industry of Brazil

Statistic	*Aggregate insurance industry*					
	LPTP	*LPTNP*	*LPTC*	*LPTFA*		
Mean	83330.59	69209.96	31229.31	147082.85		
SD	34642.95	27028.52	15979.39	76972.73		
CV	41.57	39.05	51.17	52.33		
Statistic	*Life Insurance industry*					
	LPLP	*LPNLP*	*LPLC*	*OPLP*	*OPLC*	*OPNLP*
Mean	850.73	518.70	338.42	3.47	1.37	2.44
SD	442.80	268.30	249.54	0.81	0.49	1.86
CV	52.05	51.72	73.74	23.49	35.99	75.96
Statistic	*Nonlife industry*					
	LPNP	*LPNNP*	*LPNC*	*OPNP*	*OPNC*	*OPNNP*
Mean	82479.85	68691.26	30890.89	7.41	2.76	6.41
SD	34227.32	26783.65	15779.13	2.46	1.15	2.46
CV	41.50	38.99	51.08	33.16	41.45	38.34

Notes: 1. All the variables are measured in terms of 2010 constant Brazilian reals per unit of input, wherein LP stands for Labour Productivity, and the concerned measures are in terms of per employee in the insurance industry, while OP stands for Operational Productivity and the concerned measures are in terms of per real of commercial expenses in life and nonlife segments; 2. Each variable represents a measure of partial factor productivity with different output variables; 3. The various measures represent the following output variables: LPTP – total premium per insurance industry employee, LPTNP – total net premium per insurance industry employee, LPTC – total claims per insurance industry employee, LPTFA – total financial assets of aggregate insurance companies per insurance industry employee, LPLP – life insurance premium collected per insurance industry employee, LPNP – nonlife premium collected per insurance industry employee, LPLC – life insurance claims per insurance industry employee, LPNC – nonlife insurance claim per insurance industry employee, LPNLP – net life premium collected per insurance industry employee, LPNC – nonlife claims per insurance industry employee; 4. OPLP – life premium collected per Brazilian real of commercial expenses of life insurers, OPLC – life insurance claims per Brazilian real of commercial expenses of life insurers, OPNLP – net life premium per Brazilian real of commercial expenses of life insurers, OPNP – nonlife premium per Brazilian real of commercial expenses of life insurers, OPNC – nonlife insurance claims per Brazilian real of commercial expenses of life insurers, OPNNP – net nonlife premium per Brazilian real of commercial expenses of life insurers; 5. All the variables are measured in 2010 Brazilian reals of the concerned output variable per employee in the insurance industry, including health and reinsurance; 6. SD is standard deviation; CV is the coefficient of variation measured in percentages.

Source: Author's estimation.

Table 9.2 Partial factor productivity estimates for the insurance industry of Russia

Statistic	*LPTP*	*LPTFA*	*LPTC*	*LPPOL*	*IATP*	*IAPOL*
Mean	10.01	24.60	10.13	2137.80	3.61	697.56
SD	5.52	14.92	8.33	1251.43	1.45	164.77
CV	55.17	60.65	82.20	58.54	40.14	23.62

Notes: 1. LPTP is millions of constant 2010 Brazilian reals of total premium per employee in insurance organisations, LPTFA is millions of constant 2010 Brazilian reals of financial assets of insurance companies per employee in insurance organisations, LPTC is millions of constant 2010 Brazilian reals of total claims paid by insurers per employee in insurance organisations, LPPOL is the number of total policies per employee in insurance organisations, IATP is millions of 2010 Brazilian reals of total premium per insurance agent in the country and IAPOL is the number of total policies per insurance agent in the country. 3. SD is standard deviation; CV is the coefficient of variation measured in percentages.

Source: Author's estimation.

Table 9.3 Partial factor productivity estimates for the insurance industry in India

Statistic	*Total Insurance Labour Force*			*Life Insurance Labour Force*	
	TLP	*TLA*	*TLPO*	*LLP*	*LLPO*
Mean	8.21	67.46	2364.58	8.13	2811.89
SD	3.81	30.18	422.32	3.62	414.91
CV	46.35	44.74	17.86	44.45	14.76
Statistic	*Total Insurance Physical Capital*		*Total Insurance Financial Capital*		*Life Insurance Financial Capital*
	TBP	*TBPO*	*FEPP*	*FEPA*	*LEPP*
Mean	84.75	28050.75	7.05	59.89	6.67
SD	22.36	10284.70	1.77	18.60	2.26
CV	26.38	36.66	25.06	31.06	33.92
Statistic	*Life Insurance Physical Capital*		*Nonlife Insurance Labour Force*		
	LBLP	*LBLPO*	*LNP*	*LNPO*	*LNAUM*
Mean	116.16	56862.59	8.37	1440.86	15.83
SD	30.55	45019.13	4.80	934.84	8.87
CV	26.30	79.17	57.29	64.88	56.04
Statistic	*Nonlife Insurance Financial Capital*				
	NEP	*NEAUM*			
Mean	8.03	15.37			
SD	1.20	1.88			
CV	14.96	12.23	-		

(*Continued*)

Table 9.3 (Continued)

Statistic	*Nonlife Insurance Physical Capital*		
NBP	*NBPO*	*NBAUM*	
Mean	62.59	10542.10	118.88
SD	20.23	3819.15	35.71
CV	32.32	36.23	30.04

Notes: 1. TLP is millions of 2010 constant INR of total premium per insurance industry employee, TLA is millions of 2010 constant INR of financial assets of insurance industry per insurance industry employee, TLPO is the number of total policies per insurance industry employee, LLP is millions of 2010 constant INR of total premium per life insurance industry employee, LLPO is the number of life insurance policies per life insurance industry employee, TBP is millions of 2010 constant INR of total premium per branch in insurance industry, TBPO is the number of total policies per branch of the insurance companies, FEPP is millions of 2010 constant INR of total premium per INR of equity capital of all insurers, FEPA is millions of 2010 constant INR of financial assets per INR of equity capital of all insurers, LEPP is millions of 2010 constant INR of life insurance premium per INR of equity capital of life insurers, LBLP is millions of 2010 constant INR of life insurance premium collected per branch of life insurers, LBLPO is number of life insurance policies underwritten per branch of life insurers, LNP is millions of 2010 constant INR of nonlife insurance premium per employee in the nonlife insurance industry, LNPO is the number of nonlife policies underwritten per employee in nonlife insurance companies, LNAUM is millions of 2010 constant INR of total assets under management of nonlife insurance companies per employee in the nonlife insurance industry, NEP is millions of 2010 constant INR of nonlife premium underwritten per INR of equity capital of nonlife insurers, NEAUM is millions of 2010 constant INR of total assets under management of nonlife insurance companies per INR of equity capital of nonlife insurers, NBP is millions of 2010 constant INR of total premium per branch of nonlife insurers, NBPO is number of nonlife policies underwritten per branch of nonlife insurance companies, and NBAUM is millions of 2010 constant INR of total assets under management of nonlife insurance companies per branch of nonlife insurers; 2. All the variables are expressed in terms of the underlying output variable per unit of the concerned input variable. 3. SD is standard deviation, and CV is the coefficient of variation expressed in percentages.

Source: Author's estimation.

Table 9.4 Partial factor productivity estimates for the insurance industry of China

Statistic	*LTP*	*LLP*	*LNP*	*LTA*
Mean	2.45	1.88	1.24	7.32
SD	0.62	0.70	0.41	5.09
CV	25.18	37.06	33.45	69.55

Notes: 1. LPT is millions of 2010 constant yuans of the total premium underwritten in the insurance industry per employee in the insurance industry, LLP is millions of 2010 constant yuans of life insurance premiums underwritten per employee in the insurance industry, LNP is millions of 2010 constant yuans of nonlife insurance premiums underwritten per employee in the insurance industry, LTA is millions of 2010 constant yuans of total financial assets per employee in the insurance industry; 2. All the variables are expressed in terms of the underlying output variable per unit of the concerned input variable. 3. SD is standard deviation, and CV is the coefficient of variation expressed in percentages.

Source: Author's estimation.

Appendix 2

Estimates for section 9.3

Table 9.5 Residual TFP estimates for the insurance industry of Brazil for the sample period under alternative measures of output

Descriptive Statistics				*Cross-correlations*			
Statistic	*TFPG1*	*TFPG2*	*TFPG3*	*Variables*	*TFPIG1*	*TFPG2*	*TFPG3*
Mean	3.54	6.74	20.63	TFPG2	-0.13		
SD	14.36	21.62	59.02	TFPG3	0.05	0.01	
CV	405.99	320.94	286.11	TFPG4	0.14	-0.49**	0.19
Skewness	-0.83	0.96	1.81	TFPG5	0.16	0.29	0.19
Statistic	**TFPG4**	**TFPG5**	**TFPG6**	TFPG6	0.68***	-0.04	0.21
Mean	14.93	16.21	17.7	TFPG7	0.99***	-0.13	0.05
SD	29.25	25.89	56.38	TFPG8	0.99***	-0.16	0.04
CV	195.87	159.7	318.57	**Variables**	**TFPG4**	**TFPG5**	**TFPG6**
Skewness	1.63	1.78	1.78	TFPG5	0.25		
Statistic	**TFPG7**	**TFPG8**		TFPG6	0.39*	0.26	
Mean	3.50	3.21		TFPG7	0.13	0.15	0.68***
SD	14.40	16.30		TFPG8	0.16	0.18	0.69***
CV	412.01	508.35		**Variables**	**TFPG7**		
Skewness	-0.85	-0.82		TFPG8	0.99***		

Notes: 1. TFPG is the yearly growth rate in the Total Factor Productivity Index; 2. In terms of the underlying output variable, TFPG1 represents premium collected by life and nonlife insurers combined, TFPG2 represents claims paid by all insurers, TFPG3 represents financial assets of all insurers, TFPG4 represents premium collected by life insurers, TFPG5 represents the claims paid by life insurers, TFPG6 represents net premium collected by life insurers, TFPG7 represents premium collected by nonlife insurers, and TFPG8 represents net premium collected by nonlife insurers; 3. SD is standard deviation, and CV is the coefficient of variation expressed in percentages; 4. ***, ** and * imply significance at 1%, 5% and 10% levels, respectively; 5. All the variables are in percentage terms.

Source: Author's estimation.

Table 9.6 Technical efficiency estimates for the insurance industry of Brazil using multi-stage DEA and Cobb-Douglas SFA under alternative measures of output

Statistic	*Descriptive Statistics*							
	TED1	*TED2*	*TED3*	*TED4*	*TED5*	*TED6*	*TES1*	*TES2*
Mean	0.87	0.77	0.81	0.65	0.87	0.81	0.60	0.59
SD	0.15	0.17	0.21	0.25	0.15	0.17	0.23	0.24
CV	16.89	21.91	26	38.97	16.9	20.8	38.10	41.52
Skewness	-0.73	-0.15	-1.12	0.56	-0.73	-0.26	0.20	0.07
Variables	*Cross-correlations*							
	TED1	*TED2*	*TED3*	*TED4*	*TED5*			
TED2	0.64***							
TED3	0.84***	0.48**						
TED4	0.47*	0.75***	0.21					
TED5	0.99***	0.64***	0.84***	0.47**				
TED6	0.3	0.78***	0.19	0.71***	0.3			

Notes: 1. TED is the Technical Efficiency Index derived using the DEA framework, and TES is the Technical Efficiency Index derived using the SFA framework; 2. In terms of the underlying output variables, TED1 represents the total premium collected by all insurers, TED2 represents total claims paid by all insurers, TED3 represents the amount of premium collected by life insurers, TED4 represents the amount of claims paid by life insurers, TED5 represents the amount of premium paid by nonlife insurers, TED6 represents the amount of claims paid by nonlife insurers, TES1 represents the amount of premium paid by life insurers, and TES2 represents the amount of net premium paid by life insurers; 2. SD is standard deviation, and CV is the coefficient of variation expressed in percentages; 3. ***, ** and * imply significance at 1%, 5% and 10% levels, respectively; 4. All the variables are in percentage terms.

Source: Author's estimation.

Table 9.7 Residual TFP estimates for the insurance industry of Russia for the sample period under alternative measures of output

Statistic	*Descriptive Statistics*			*Variables*	*Cross-correlations*		
	TFPG1	*TFPG2*	*TFPG3*		*TFPG1*	*TFPG2*	*TFPG3*
Mean	16.31	-4.81	-4.70	**TFPG2**	0.59***		
SD	74.25	7.55	9.79	**TFPG3**	0.50**	0.92***	
CV	455.35	-156.91	-208.19	**TFPG4**	-0.17	0.04	0.12
Skewness	2.84	0.04	0.15	**TFPG5**	0.93***	0.43**	0.35
Statistic	**TFPG4**	**TFPG5**	**TFPG6**	**TFPG6**	-0.17	-0.07	-0.10
Mean	-1.10	71.36	-1.94	**Variables**	**TFPG4**	**TFPG5**	
SD	37.65	310.79	12.78	**TFPG5**	-0.23		
CV	-3421.58	435.55	-658.51	**TFPG6**	0.30	-0.09	
Skewness	0.09	4.20	0.72				

Notes: 1. TFPG is the yearly growth rate in the Total Factor Productivity Index; 2. In terms of the underlying output variable, TFPG1 represents the amount of premium collected by insurers, TFPG2 represents the amount of total claims paid by insurers, TFPG3 represents the amount of net claims paid by insurers, TFPG4 represents the amount of premium collected by life insurers, TFPG5 represents the amount of premium collected by nonlife insurers, and TFPG6 represents the amount of financial assets of owned by insurers; 3. SD is standard deviation, and CV is the coefficient of variation expressed in percentages; 4. ***, ** and * imply significance at 1%, 5% and 10% levels, respectively; 5. All the variables are in percentage terms.

Source: Author's estimation.

Table 9.8 Technical efficiency estimates for the insurance industry of Russia using multi-stage DEA and Cobb-Douglas production function with SFA under alternative measures of output

Statistics	*Descriptive Statistics*						
	TED1	*TED2*	*TED3*	*TED4*	*TED5*	*TES1*	*TES2*
Mean	0.81	0.98	0.98	0.72	0.6	0.86	0.85
SD	0.18	0.05	0.05	0.23	0.37	0.08	0.1
CV	22.49	4.9	4.9	32.6	62.31	9.08	12.19
Skewness	-0.12	-2.45	-2.42	0.17	-0.06	-1.07	-0.6
Variables	*Cross-correlations*						
	TED1	*TED2*	*TED3*	*TED4*			
TED2	0.28						
TED3	0.31	0.97***					
TED4	-0.44**	-0.01	-0.02				
TED5	0.22	0.34	0.35	0.24			

Notes: 1. TED is the Technical Efficiency Index estimated using DEA, while TES is the Technical Efficiency Index estimated under the SFA framework; 2. In terms of the underlying output variable, TED1 represents the amount of premiums collected by all the insurers, TED2 represents the amount of claims paid by all the insurers, TED3 represents the amount of net claims paid by all the insurers, TED4 represents the amount of financial assets owned by all the insurers, TED5 represents the amount of premium collected by life insurers, TES1 represents the amount of claims paid by all the insurers while TES2 represents the amount of net claims paid by all the insurers; 3. SD is standard deviation, and CV is the coefficient of variation expressed in percentages; 4. ***, ** and * imply significance at 1%, 5% and 10% levels respectively; 5. All the variables are in percentage terms.

Source: Author's estimation.

Table 9.9 Residual TFP estimates for the insurance industry of India for the sample period under alternative measures of output

Statistic	*Descriptive Statistics*			*Variable*	*Cross-correlations*		
	TFPG1	*TFPG2*	*TFPG3*		*TFPG1*	*TFPG2*	*TFPG3*
Mean	-0.96	14.98	7.36	TFPG2	0.52**		
SD	20.93	30.83	18.03	TFPG3	-0.35	0.05	
CV	-2176.24	205.75	245.12	TFPG4	-0.05	-0.02	0.16
Skewness	1.00	1.61	0.28	TFPG5	-0.41*	-0.30	0.28
Statistic	**TFPG4**	**TFPG5**		**Variable**	**TFPG4**		
Mean	12.08	1.02		TFPG5	-0.04		
SD	6.49	5.60					
CV	53.72	550.01					
Skewness	0.67	1.32					

Notes: 1. TFPG is the yearly growth rate in the Total Factor Productivity Index; 2. In terms of the underlying output variable, TFPG1 represents the amount of financial assets owned by all the insurers, TFPG2 represents the amount of premium collected by life insurers, TFPG3 represents the amount of claims paid by life insurers, TFPG4 represents the amount of premium collected by nonlife insurers, TFPG5 represents the assets under management of nonlife insurance companies; 3. SD is standard deviation, and CV is the coefficient of variation expressed in percentages; 4. ***, ** and * imply significance at 1%, 5% and 10% levels, respectively; 5. All the variables are in percentage terms.

Source: Author's estimation.

Table 9.10 Technical efficiency estimates using multi-stage DEA and Cobb-Douglas production function using SFA for the insurance industry of India for the sample period under alternative measures of output

Statistics	*Descriptive Statistics*			
	TED1	*TED2*	*TED3*	*TED4*
Mean	0.98	0.85	0.84	0.96
SD	0.05	0.16	0.24	0.08
CV	4.83	19.26	28.09	8.63
Skewness	-2.75	-0.63	-1.45	-3.05
Statistics	*TED5*	*TES1*	*TES2*	*TES3*
Mean	0.99	0.91	0.90	0.81
SD	0.02	0.09	0.07	0.12
CV	2.13	9.76	7.42	15.45
Skewness	-1.68	-1.06	-2.38	-0.45
Variable	*Cross-correlations*			
	TED1	*TED2*	*TED3*	*TED4*
TED2	-0.16			
TED3	-0.30	-0.46		
TED4	0.18	0.12	-0.24	
TED5	0.07	0.45	-0.36	0.66
Variable	*TES1*	*TES2*		
TES2	0.07			
TES3	-0.38	-0.24		

Notes: 1. TED is the Technical Efficiency Index estimated using DEA, while TES is the Technical Efficiency Index estimated under the SFA framework; 2. In terms of the underlying output variable, TED1 represents the amount of financial assets owned by all the insurers, TED2 represents the amount of premium collected by life insurers, TED3 represents the amount of premium collected by nonlife insurers, TED4 represents the amount of claims paid by life insurers, TED5 represents the amount of assets under management of nonlife insurance companies, TES1 represents the amount of financial assets owned by all the insurers, TES2 represents the amount of benefits paid by life insurers, and TES3 represents the amount of premium collected by nonlife insurers; 3. SD is standard deviation, and CV is the coefficient of variation expressed in percentages; 4. ***, ** and * imply significance at 1%, 5% and 10% levels, respectively; 5. All the variables are in percentage terms.

Source: Author's estimation.

Table 9.11 Residual TFP estimates for the insurance industry of Indonesia for the sample period under alternative measures of output

Statistics	*Descriptive Statistics*		
	TFPG1	*TFPG2*	*TFPG3*
Mean	0.18	4.87	0.91
SD	12.22	36.02	16.13
CV	6874.77	739.98	1781.09
Skewness	-0.57	1.81	1.03

Variable	*Cross-correlations*	
	TFPG1	*TFPG2*
TFPG2	-0.17	
TFPG3	0.14	-0.06

Notes: 1. TFPG is the yearly growth rate in the Total Factor Productivity Index; 2. In terms of the underlying output variable, TFPG1 represents the amount of premium collected by nonlife insurers, TFPG2 represents the amount of financial assets owned by all the insurers, and TFPG3 represents the total number of policyholders of all insurers; 3. SD is standard deviation, and CV is the coefficient of variation expressed in percentages; 4. ***, ** and * imply significance at 1%, 5% and 10% levels, respectively; 5. All the variables are in percentage terms.

Source: Author's estimation.

Table 9.12 Technical efficiency estimates for the insurance industry of Indonesia using multi-stage DEA and Cobb-Douglas production function based SFA for the sample period under alternative measures of output

Statistic	*Descriptive Statistics*					
	TED1	*TED2*	*TED3*	*TES1*	*TES2*	*TES3*
Mean	0.96	0.92	0.83	0.87	0.90	0.74
SD	0.10	0.09	0.19	0.10	0.07	0.19
CV	10.15	10.23	23.12	11.06	7.60	25.51
Skewness	-3.22	-0.67	-1.22	-1.60	-1.49	-0.65
Variable	*Cross-correlations*			*Variables*	*Cross-correlations*	
	TED1	*TED2*			*TES1*	*TES2*
TED2	-0.28		TES2		-0.12	
TED3	0.16	0.32	TES3		-0.02	0.30

Notes: 1. TED is the Technical Efficiency Index estimated using DEA, while TES is the Technical Efficiency Index estimated under the SFA framework; 2. In terms of the underlying output variable, TED1 represents the amount of financial assets owned by all the insurers, TED2 represents the total number of policyholders of all insurers, TED3 represents the amount of premium collected by nonlife insurers, TES1 represents the amount of financial assets owned by all the insurers, TES2 represents the total number of policyholders of all insurers, and TES3 represents the amount of premium collected by nonlife insurers; 3. SD is standard deviation, and CV is the coefficient of variation expressed in percentages; 4. ***, ** and * imply significance at 1%, 5% and 10% levels, respectively; 5. All the variables are in percentage terms.

Source: Author's estimation.

Table 9.13 Residual TFP estimates for the insurance industry of China for the sample period under alternative measures of output

Statistic	*Descriptive Statistics*			
	TFPG1	*TFPG2*	*TFPG3*	*TFPG4*
Mean	-1.29	7.67	0.42	-0.29
SD	10.70	16.68	13.43	10.99
CV	-832.38	217.43	3182.85	-3787.80
Skewness	0.47	-2.39	0.06	0.67
Variables	*Cross-correlations*			
	TFPG1	*TFPG2*	*TFPG3*	
TFPG2	0.27			
TFPG3	0.33	-0.12		
TFPG4	0.57***	-0.01	0.75***	

Notes: 1. TFPG is the yearly growth rate in the Total Factor Productivity Index; 2. In terms of the underlying output variable, TFPG1 represents the amount of premium collected by all insurers, TFPG2 represents the amount of financial assets owned by all insurers, TFPG3 represents the amount of premium collected by life insurers, and TFPG4 represents the amount of premium collected by nonlife insurers; 3. SD is standard deviation, and CV is the coefficient of variation expressed in percentages; 4. ***, ** and * imply significance at 1%, 5% and 10% levels, respectively; 5. All the variables are in percentage terms.

Source: Author's estimation.

Table 9.14 Technical efficiency estimates for the insurance industry of China using multi-stage DEA and Cobb-Douglas production function based SFA for the sample period under alternative measures of output

Statistic	*Descriptive Statistics*		
	TED1	*TED2*	*TED3*
Mean	0.86	0.76	0.73
SD	0.16	0.35	0.27
CV	19.17	45.93	36.90
Skewness	-0.50	-1.02	-0.06
Statistic	*TED4*	*TES1*	*TES2*
Mean	0.77	0.84	0.87
SD	0.23	0.09	0.10
CV	29.27	10.78	11.01
Skewness	-0.15	-1.06	-0.74
Correlation Coefficient (TES1, TES2)			-0.10
Variables	*Cross-correlations*		
	TED1	*TED2*	*TED3*
TED2	-0.56***		
TED3	0.92***	-0.70***	
TED4	0.95***	-0.67***	0.98***

Notes: 1. TED is the Technical Efficiency Index estimated using DEA, while TES is the Technical Efficiency Index estimated under the SFA framework; 2. In terms of the underlying output variable, TED1 represents the amount of premium collected by all insurers, TED2 represents the amount of financial assets owned by all insurers, TED3 represents the amount of premium collected by life insurers, and TED4 represents the amount of premium collected by nonlife insurers; 3. SD is standard deviation, and CV is the coefficient of variation expressed in percentages; 4. ***, ** and * imply significance at 1%, 5% and 10% levels, respectively; 5. All the variables are in percentage terms.

Source: Author's estimation.

Table 9.15 Residual TFP estimates for the insurance industry of South Africa for the sample period under alternative measures of output

Statistics	*Descriptive Statistics*		
	TFPG1	*TFPG2*	*TFPG3*
Mean	-4.30	1.08	-1.42
SD	11.51	12.22	11.25
CV	-267.86	1133.98	-793.31
Skewness	0.79	1.90	-2.07
Variables	*Cross-correlations*		
	TFPG1	*TFPG2*	
TFPG2	0.47*		
TFPG3	0.07	0.20	

Notes: 1. TFPG is the yearly growth rate in the Total Factor Productivity Index; 2. In terms of the underlying output variable, TFPG1 represents the amount of premium collected by life insurers, TFPG2 represents the amount of premium collected by nonlife insurers, and TFPG3 represents the amount of financial assets owned by all the insurers; 3. SD is standard deviation, and CV is the coefficient of variation expressed in percentages; 4. ***, ** and * imply significance at 1%, 5% and 10% levels, respectively; 5. All the variables are in percentage terms.

Source: Author's estimation.

Table 9.16 Technical efficiency estimates for the insurance industry of South Africa using multi-stage DEA and Cobb-Douglas production function based SFA for the sample period under alternative measures of output

Statistics	*Descriptive Statistics*				*Variables*	*Cross-correlations*	
	TED1	*TED2*	*TED3*	*TES1*		*TED1*	*TED2*
Mean	0.88	0.92	0.91	0.91	TED2	0.27	
SD	0.11	0.07	0.10	0.07	TED3	0.24	0.75***
CV	12.73	7.57	11.16	7.45			
Skewness	-0.85	-0.86	-1.00	-0.67			

Notes: 1. TED is the Technical Efficiency Index estimated using DEA, while TES is the Technical Efficiency Index estimated under the SFA framework; 2. In terms of the underlying output variable, TED1 represents the amount of financial assets owned by all the insurers, TED2 represents the amount of premium collected by life insurers, TED3 represents the amount of premium collected by nonlife insurers, TES1 represents the amount of premium collected by life insurers; 3. SD is standard deviation, and CV is the coefficient of variation expressed in percentages; 4. ***, ** and * imply significance at 1%, 5% and 10% levels, respectively; 5. All the variables are in percentage terms.

Source: Author's estimation.

Appendix 3

Estimates for section 9.4

Table 9.17 Estimated returns to scale coefficients across alternative measures of output for the insurance industry of the selected emerging economies

Perspective	*Output Variable*	*Country*					
		Brazil	*Russia*	*India*	*Indonesia*	*China*	*South Africa*
Total Insurance Industry	Premium (TPREM)	3.45	0.27	-3.39	NA	1.9	NA
	Claims (TCLAIM)	-0.63	1.94	NA			
	Net Claims (TNCLAIM)	NA	2.01	NA			
	Financial Assets (TFAST)	0.12	0.96	-0.97	1.19	3.9	1.04
Life Insurance Industry	Premium (LPREM)	3.58	-0.75	-7.49	NA	1.22	0.42
	Net Premium (LNPREM)	5.84	NA				
	Policyholders (LPOL)	NA			1.53	NA	
	Claims (LCLAIM)	2.32	NA	3.98	NA	NA	
Nonlife Insurance Industry	Premium (NPREM)	3.48	-0.56	-1.42	4.17	1.86	1.35
	Net Premium (NNPREM)	4.02	NA				
	Claims (NCLAIM)	-0.41	NA				
	Assets under management (NAUM)	NA		0.25	NA		

Table 9.18 Estimated returns to scale for the Brazilian insurance industry under alternative output measures

Input Variable	*Output Variables*					
	Total Insurance			*Life Insurance*		
	In(TPREM)	*In(TCLAIM)*	*In(TFAST)*	*In(LPREM)*	*In(NLPREM)*	*In(LCLAIM)*
In(LAB)	0.71***	-0.41***	-0.49*** 1st lag	0.52***	0.85***	1.19*** 1st lag
In(PCAP)	2.74#	-		3.06** 1st lag	4.99*** 1st lag	-
In($TRES_{total}$)	-	-0.22** (0.087)	-			
In($TRES_{life}$)	-					0.47***
In($PREM_{total}$)	-		0.61***	-		
In($PREM_{life}$)	-					0.66*** 1st lag
Estimated RTS	**3.45**	**-0.63**	**0.12**	**3.58**	**5.84**	**2.32**
F-statistic	6.38***	10.25***	33.36***	11.16***	19.60***	105.50***
R^2	0.87	0.81	0.79	0.98	0.97	0.85

Input Variable	*Output Variables*		
	Nonlife Insurance		
	In(NPREM)	*In(NNPREM)*	*In(NCLAIM)*
In(LAB)	0.71***	0.86***	-0.47***
In(PCAP)	2.77#	3.16#	-
In($TRES_{nonlife}$)			-0.13**
In($PREM_{nonlife}$)	-		0.19** 1st lag
Estimated RTS	**3.48**	**4.02**	**-0.41**
F-statistic	6.39***	7.33***	39.70***
R^2	0.87	0.84	0.92

Notes: 1. In(LAB) is the natural log of the total number of labourers in life, nonlife, health and reinsurance industries; 2. ***, ** and * imply significance at 1%, 5% and 10% levels, respectively.

Source: Author's estimation.

Table 9.19 Estimated returns to scale for the Russian insurance industry under alternative output measures

Input Variables	*Output Variable*					
	Total Insurance				*Life Insurance*	*Nonlife Insurance*
	In(TPREM)	*In(TCLAIM)*	*In(TNCLAIM)*	*In(TFAST)*	*In(LPREM)*	*In(NPREM)*
In(LAB)	0.44^{***} Real Wage	0.13^{*}	0.17^{**}	-0.99^{***} Real Wage	0.40^{*}	-0.96^{***} Real Wage
	1st lag					
In(AGENT)	0.13 2nd lag	-				
In(PCAP)	-0.30^{***}	0.88^{***}	0.89^{***}	-	-1.15^{**}	0.40^{***}
In($TRES_{total}$)		0.93^{***}	0.95^{***}	-		
In($PREM_{total}$)	-			0.58^{***}	-	
In(TPOL)	-			1.37^{***}	-	
Estimated RTS	**0.27**	**1.94**	**2.01**	**0.96**	**-0.75**	**-0.56**
F-statistic	140.01^{***}	98.99^{***}	76.23^{***}	43.64^{***}	4.04^{**}	107.10^{***}
R^2	0.96	0.94	0.93	0.88	0.90	0.92

Notes: 1. In(LAB) is the natural log of the average number of employees in insurance organisations across the country; 2. ***, ** and * imply significance at 1%, 5% and 10% levels, respectively.

Source: Author's estimation.

Table 9.20 Estimated returns to scale for the Indian insurance industry under alternative output measures

Input Variables	*Output Variable*					
	Total Insurance		*Life Insurance*		*Nonlife Insurance*	
	In(TPREM)†††	*In(TFAST)*††	*In(LPREM$_{new}$)*	*In(LBEN)*	*In(NPREM)*	*In(NAUM)*†
In(LAB$_{total}$)	-4.17***	-1.74 1st lag	-			-0.72
In(LAB$_{life}$)	-		-8.34***	2.79$^{\#\#\#}$	-	
In(LAB$_{nonlife}$)	-				-1.92*	-
In(PCAP$_{life}$)	0.55***	-	0.85***	-		
In(PCAP$_{nonlife}$)	(life + nonlife branches)	-			0.50$^{\#}$	-
In(AGENT$_{life}$)	-			0.24*	-	
In(TRES$_{total}$)	-	0.48	-			
In(TRES$_{life}$)	-			0.95***	-	
In(TRES$_{nonlife}$)						0.18
In(FCAP$_{total}$)	0.23***	0.14	-			
In(FCAP$_{nonlife}$)	-					0.30
In(PREM$_{total}$)	-	0.15 1st lag	-			
In(PREM$_{nonlife}$)	-					0.49
Estimated RTS	**-3.39**	**-0.97**	**-7.49**	**3.98**	**-1.42**	**0.25**
F-statistic	21.96***	21.85***	88.68***	194.16***	356.25***	99.94***
R^2	0.79	0.84	0.90	0.97	0.97	0.96

Notes: 1. ***, ** and * imply significance at 1%, 5% and 10% levels, respectively; 2. † – Ridge regression model due to high collinearity among regressors under the standard OLS specification and the k-value is 0.069 which was found to be the optimum value; 3. †† – Ridge regression model due to high collinearity among regressors under the standard OLS specification and the k-value is 0.272 which was found to be the optimum value; 4. ††† – Shows the estimates of the ridge regression model due to high collinearity among regressors under the standard OLS specification. Chosen k-value is 0.285, which was found to be the optimum value.

Source: Author's estimation.

Table 9.21 Estimated returns to scale for the Indonesian insurance industry under alternative output measures

Input Variable	*Output Variables*		
	Total Insurance	*Life Insurance*	*Nonlife Insurance*
	In(TFAST)	*In(LPOLH)*	*In(NPREM)*
In(LAB)	0.97^{***}	0.16^{***}	0.38^{***}
In($TRES_{nonlife}$)	-0.25^{**}	-	
In($TRES_{life}$)	0.47^{**}	-	
In($PCAP_{total}$)	-	1.37^{**}	3.79^{**}
Estimated RTS	**1.19**	**1.53**	**4.17**
F-statistic	123.76^{***}	4.98^{**}	6.26^{***}
R^2	0.95	0.34	0.40

Notes: 1. In(LAB) is the natural log of the total number of employees in the country's Financial Intermediation sector, which includes insurance, banking, and other financial services. This variable has been used as a proxy for employment in the insurance industry due to a lack of data; 2. ***, ** and * imply significance at 1%, 5% and 10% levels, respectively.

Source: Author's estimation.

Table 9.22 Estimated returns to scale for the insurance industry of China under alternative output measures

Input Variable	*Output Variable*			
	Total Insurance		*Life Insurance*	*Nonlife Insurance*
	In(TPREM)	*In(TFAST)*	*In(LPREM)*	*In(NPREM)*
In(LAB)	0.63^{*}	-0.83	2.14^{***} 2nd lag	2.33^{***} 1st lag
In($PCAP_{total}$)	1.27^{***}	6.22^{***}	-0.92^{***}	-0.47^{**}
In(TPREM)	-	-1.49^{***}	-	
Estimated RTS	**1.9**	**3.9**	**1.22**	**1.86**
F-statistic	21.25^{***}	210.02^{***}	124.70^{***}	113.78^{***}
R^2	0.97	0.97	0.94	0.93

Notes: 1. In(LAB) is the natural log of the total number of employees in insurance companies; 2. ***, ** and * imply significance at 1%, 5% and 10% levels, respectively.

Source: Author's estimation.

Table 9.23 Estimated returns to scale for the insurance industry of South Africa under alternative output measures

Input Variable	*Output Variable*		
	Total Insurance	*Life Insurance*	*Nonlife Insurance*
	In(TFAST)	*In(LPREM)*	*In(NPREM)*
In(LAB)	0.45* 2nd lag	0.86***	2.07***
In(TPREM)	0.59***	-	
In($PCAP_{total}$)	-	-0.44##	-0.72
Estimated RTS	**1.04**	**0.42**	**1.35**
F-statistic	37.92***	35.19***	15.86***
R^2	0.82	0.79	0.76

Notes: 1. In(LAB) is the natural log of the number of employees in the country's service sector is available from the International Labour Organization database; 2. ***, ** and * imply significance at 1%, 5% and 10% levels, respectively.

Source: Author's estimation.

Notes

1 The detailed empirical results on the trans-log specification can be obtained from the author on request.

2 This point is made here and in all further sections while keeping in mind that value and volume measures of output cannot be compared in terms of mean levels.

3 One of the ways to deal with this can be to index both the output and input and then calculate their ratio. In this case, one can estimate the growth in labour productivity and make these diverse output measures possibly more comparable in terms of mean levels. However, productivity per se is a level form-based economic concept, and its growth rate throws very different economic dimensions than its absolute level. Hence, absolute level-form partial factor productivity estimates are reported instead of their growth rates. The estimates of growth in these partial factor productivity indexes can be obtained from the author on request. The divergence in these estimates widens much more when estimating growth rates in productivities.

4 Due to space constraints, the estimated output elasticities of inputs used as weighting factors in constructing the total inputs index are not reported here. The same may be made available in the online resources and can happily be obtained from the author upon request.

Part IV

Extended notes and concluding remarks

10 Inputs measurement issues

10.1. Introductory note

The previous chapters have analysed the literature on output measurement in banking and insurance performance analyses. Contributions from selected experts were also presented, after which case studies were elaborated on the empirical implications of using different output measurements for performance estimation. Another closely related element in the larger debates on production analysis of banking and insurance industries is the measurement of inputs. Given that the production process cannot be conceptualised without sound measures of both outputs and inputs, it is natural for performance analysts to be concerned with both these dimensions. Contrasted with the diversity of opinions on the outputs of banks and insurers and how to measure them, there clearly appears to be a consensus on how to measure the inputs (Eling & Luhnen, 2010). This chapter briefly summarises the various dimensions of inputs measurement[1] in banking and insurance literature on performance analysis.

10.2. Inputs measurement in the banking and insurance literature

The most fundamental inputs vector consists of volume measures of labour and capital. Given the paucity of data, researchers have used value measures instead. Labour input, in volume terms, is generally conceptualised in terms of the employees' working hours. The problem with this measure, other than data availability, is that banks and insurers do not rely only on the labour of employees who work from the physical premises of the firms but also on those who are not employees but provide labour services from outside the premises. Insurance agents, brokers, banking correspondents, retail agent outlets, and various other intermediaries provide valuable labour services by dedicating their time to realising the business objectives of banking and insurance firms. Reliable measurement of the time input of such labour services is difficult. This has motivated analysts to conceptualise labour input in terms of the number of labourers. Unlike the time-based measures, the headcount measure of labourers in banks and insurance firms is relatively easier to locate. Reliable data are

DOI: 10.4324/9781003149828-14

generally available. Labourers, in this context, include not just the employees working physically on the premises of the firm but also the intermediaries, as stated above. In many countries, official agencies require banks and insurers to report such data. Thus, data constraints are somewhat lesser than the time-based labour inputs. When information on the number of labourers is also unavailable, another alternative in the literature in such cases has been the monetary value of expenditure on labour services. This measure is a value measure expressed in monetary terms rather than quantity terms. The use of this approach to measure labour input reflects the amount of funds spent by a bank or an insurance firm on compensating their employees for their time and services. Concerning the intermediary labour services, data on commissions are generally available. Thus, labour or personnel expenses have been a frequently employed labour input measure.

The problem with this approach is that it is a nominal value and requires appropriate deflation. Literature on firm-level studies has found it useful to use specific input prices to deflate expenses' nominal value. These prices are used as deflators for each specific input variable. For more aggregative studies, the traditional deflators of CPI and GDP deflator have been among the popular choices. Ideally, inputs specific deflation must be adopted, but except for a few advanced economies, hardly any economy can boast of such disaggregated input price data for banking and insurance firms. In summary, labour has been conceptualised in three major ways in the literature on banking and insurance performance analysis: first is in terms of the time spent on performing labour services; second is in terms of the number of labourers (both direct and intermediary); and, third is in the form of nominal expenses on personnel deflated by an appropriate deflator. Each has its own advantages and constraints, and the choice on this account is largely driven by data availability.

As per the extant literature, the second element in the traditional input vector of banks and insurers is a volume measure of physical capital. The existing literature has conceptualised physical capital mostly as fixed assets in this sense. Generally, the expenses on or value of these assets are used as input. However, this begs the question: what is capital for banks and insurers? It is well-recognised in the literature discussed in previous chapters that the measurement of capital input is quite complicated when it comes to banks. For example, as captured by the number of branches, its physical premise was a favoured measure when digitalisation was not a large-scale phenomenon. However, the role of information and communications technology (ICT) as a capital input is increasingly being recognised in the literature. ICT does not lend itself easily to quantification and further complicates the problems associated with the measurement of traditional capital inputs. Among these problems, the issue of incorporating quality changes in the quantity estimates is more serious for ICT, where quality improvements are frequent and rapid. To dodge these constraints, researchers have largely avoided including ICT in the banking production function and have allowed its impact on the residual technology parameter instead.

On the other hand, several studies have included the monetary value of ICT assets such as computers and various payment terminals in the fixed assets variable. The notable studies that have stressed the importance of including ICT-related measures in the capital input variable of bank production function include Brand and Duke (1982), Oral and Yolalan (1990), Anthanassopoulos (1998), Thanassoulis (1999), Athanassopoulos and Giokas (2000), Allen and Liu (2007) and Aksoy et al. (2022). In the case of insurance literature on similar lines, some notable works on this account include Arvanitis (2005), Bertschek et al. (2006) and Noreen and Ahmad (2016).[2]

The traditional input vector exhausts at this point, and new inputs have been proposed in the literature that captures the specificities of the production process in the banking and insurance industries. Capital has been expanded to include financial capital[3] also. Financial equity capital is considered an important input in modern financial theory (Hughes & Mester, 1998) and was subsequently incorporated into banking and insurance production analyses. This variable has been measured by equity capital as per the balance sheet of the individual banks and insurers.[4] This is a stock variable specified in nominal terms in most sample studies, as examined in Chapters 3 and 4. The importance of this variable in a bank's or the banking industry's production function has been well argued by Hartwick (1996). Equity capital is also hypothesised as a measure of the risk management function of banks, while it is theorised as a representation of solvency for insurers. As discussed in the previous chapters, equity capital has been accepted as a critical element of the inputs vector of banks and insurers, which cannot be ignored. It was noted in Chapters 3 and 4 that the so-called output specification approaches also define the relevant inputs. Hence, outputs and inputs are specified simultaneously. The set of inputs discussed till now is accepted universally by all the output specification approaches. This set includes labour, physical capital and equity capital. Beyond these inputs, disagreements on what inputs must be included in the production function of banks and insurers arise. The intermediation approach in banking and insurance suggests that deposits and premiums must be treated as inputs for banks and insurers. The same variables are treated as output in the production and value-added approaches in banking and insurance literature. Lastly, an input variable that has been less frequently employed in literature is the value of materials. This variable consists of intermediate goods and services used by insurers, such as lawyer fees, telephone use, stationary expenses, etc. It is frequently used in the case of studies on advanced economies. However, data on this input are not reliably available for economies like Brazil, China, Russia and other EMEs. In insurance performance studies, there is another debate on treating technical reserves as an input or an output.[5] When treated as an input, it is proxied as a measure of debt capital.

Another approach to input specification has been less frequently used explicitly in the literature. It is the so-called operating expenses approach, and it suggests that all the inputs that occupy a sizeable share in the total operating expenses of the insurance firm must be included because "It is misleading and incorrect to omit an input that accounts for a significant proportion of operating expenses" (Cummins & Weiss, 2013, p. 821). However, this is an empiricist approach and requires information on each item's total operating expense function and share. Such an approach for specifying inputs is plausible for firm-level studies but may not suit industry or sectoral studies in banking and insurance performance analysis. Finally, the national income approach has been used to specify outputs rather than outputs and inputs. No studies were found that claimed to have used the national income approach to specify inputs in their study – either at the firm level or sectoral analysis.

10.3. Concluding remarks

The scope of discussion on inputs measurement in banking and insurance literature is large. There are many theoretical and empirical challenges that researchers have to deal with when specifying the inputs to be included in the production function. Depending on the performance parameter being studied, the economy being analysed and the data availability, different permutations and combinations are possible that will lead to alternative input vectors. However, there is considerable agreement in the literature on the major inputs. This agreement has been presented in this chapter. Given the primary focus of this work on output measurement issues, the input measurement dimension has only been briefly reviewed in this chapter.

Notes

1 See Maroto-Sánchez (2011) for a discussion on various issues in inputs measurement when estimating performance of services industries in general.
2 Please refer to the appendices to Chapters 3 and 4 and the reference list given in those chapters for more details on these studies.
3 Financial capital of banks and insurers consists of two major components – equity capital and debt capital. Most of the studies either focus on equity capital per se, or combine both of them into single financial capital input. For an illustration in insurance literature, see Yaisawarng et al. (2012).
4 The use of equity capital in banking and insurance production processes as an input has been briefly discussed in Chapters 3, 4, 8 and 9, and thus has not been elaborated on here.
5 See Berry-Stölzle et al. (2011) for use of technical reserves as a measure of debt capital. See Mahlberg and Url (2003) for use of technical reserves as a measure of output. Please also see Alshammari et al. (2018).

References

Aksoy, E. E. A., Dirik, C., & Göker, I. E. K. (2022). Opening the black-box of bank efficiency in Turkey with two-stage data envelopment analysis: A study on capital adequacy ratio. *EGE Academic Review*, *22*(1), 75–91. https://doi.org/10.21121/eab.1064816

Allen, J., & Liu, Y. (2007). Efficiency and economies of scale of large Canadian banks. *The Canadian Journal of Economics*, *40*(1), 225–244.

Alshammari, A. A., bin Syed Jaafar Alhabshi, S. M., & Saiti, B. (2018). The impact of competition on cost efficiency of insurance and takaful sectors: Evidence from GCC markets based on the stochastic frontier analysis. *Research in International Business and Finance*, 1–29. https://doi.org/10.1016/j.ribaf.2018.09.003

Anthanassopoulos, A. D. (1998). Nonparametric frontier models for assessing the market and cost efficiency of LargeScale Bank branch networks. *Journal of Money, Credit and Banking*, *30*(2), 172–192.

Arvanitis, S. (2005). Computerisation, workplace organisation, skilled labour and firm productivity: Evidence for the Swiss business sector. *Economics of Innovation and New Technology*, *14*(4), 225–249. https://doi.org/10.1080/1043859042000226257

Athanassopoulos, A. D., & Giokas, D. (2000). The use of data envelopment analysis in banking institutions: Evidence from the commercial bank of Greece. *Interfaces*, *30*(2), 81–95.

Berry-Stölzle, T. R., Weiss, M. A., & Wende, S. (2011). *Market structure, efficiency, and performance in the European property-liability insurance industry* (Working Paper).

Bertschek, I., Fryges, H., & Kaiser, U. (2006). B2B or not to be: Does B2B E-commerce increase labour productivity? *International Journal of the Economics of Business*, *13*(3), 387–405. https://doi.org/10.1080/13571510600961395

Brand, H., & Duke, J. (1982). Productivity in commercial banking: Computers spur the advance. *Monthly Labor Review*, *105*(12), 19–27.

Cummins, J. D., & Weiss, M. A. (2013). Analysing firm performance in the insurance industry using frontier efficiency and productivity methods. In *Handbook of insurance* (2nd ed., pp. 795–858). Springer.

Eling, M., & Luhnen, M. (2010). Efficiency in the international insurance industry: A cross-country comparison. *Journal of Banking and Finance*, *34*(7), 1497–1509.

Hartwick, J. M. (1996). *The financial capital constraint and the valuation of commercial banking activity*. Queen's Economics Department (Working Paper No. 942).

Hughes, J. P., & Mester, L. J. (1998). Bank capitalization and cost: Evidence of scale economies in risk management and signaling. *The Review of Economics and Statistics*, *80*(2), 314–325.

Mahlberg, B., & Url, T. (2003). Effects of the single market on the Austrian insurance industry. *Empirical Economics*, *28*, 813–838. https://doi.org/10.1007/s00181-003-0164-6

Maroto-Sánchez, A. (2011). Productivity in the services sector: Conventional and current explanations. *The Service Industries Journal*, *32*(5), 719–746. https://doi.org/10.1080/02642069.2010.531266

Noreen, U., & Ahmad, S. (2016). Cost efficiency and total factor productivity: An empirical analysis of Pakistan's insurance sector. *The Lahore Journal of Economics*, *21*(1), 123–150.

Oral, M., & Yolalan, R. (1990). An empirical study on measuring operating efficiency and profitability of bank branches. *European Journal of Operational Research*, *46*, 282–294.

Thanassoulis, E. (1999). Data envelopment analysis and its use in banking. *Interfaces*, *29*(3), 1–13.

Yaisawarng, S., Asavadachanukorn, P., & Yaisawarng, S. (2012). Efficiency and productivity in the Thai non-life insurance industry. *The Journal of Productivity Analysis*, *41*(2), 291–306. https://doi.org/10.1007/s11123-012-0317-8

11 Limitations, future scope and concluding remarks

11.1. Limitations and future scope

The analysis presented in this work is subject to constraints that must be brought to the notice of the readers at this juncture. Every research attempt is subject to factors that may be out of the researcher's control or maybe controllable but still must be sacrificed due to time and space restrictions. The insights provided in this work are also subject to such constraints, and a short note on them may help clarify some of the concerns in advance. Lack of conscious recognition of limitations leads to various barriers and biases (Singh, 2015).

The first point in this regard is that this work has not attempted to build a consensus on the issue of output measurement in banking and insurance performance[1] analysis. Rather, the aim has been to summarise the ideas, debates, agreements and disagreements on the theme. While broad patterns in the literature have been highlighted and explained, locating a consensus on a topic of such rich analytical diversity will require a work of a much larger scope. The author of this work found that there did not exist any reference on output measurement issues in banking and insurance performance analysis that could be utilized not only for systematization of the thoughts on this subject but also to obtain a summary account of the voluminous literature in this area. Such concerns have motivated this work. The second point is that literature reviews are also expected to critique the extant wisdom, which is an essential step in any systematic review work (Machi & McEvoy, 2022). While providing critical comments and notes on various issues across the chapters, this work is not a formal critique of what has been done on output measurement in banking and insurance literature. A formal critique is beyond the scope of this book. Furthermore, without having a compact summary of what has been done so far, critiquing the extant literature would be unrealistic. It is hoped that this work will provide some background and foundations for more rigorous analytical attempts.

The third matter is the sample size of studies included in this book. While the author is motivated by the fact that the combined sample size (for banking and insurance literature) of approximately 500 high-quality scholarly works is possibly the first attempt of its kind, particularly when coupled with contributions from

DOI: 10.4324/9781003149828-15

practitioners and policymakers and also accompanied by empirical case studies, it is also duly recognized that a larger sample could have been analysed to incorporate more diversity in the analysis. On this account, it may kindly be pointed out again that the number of studies reviewed was 872, but they had to be downsized due to space restrictions.[2] The fourth point is that the present work does not attempt to delve into meta-analysis of the empirical evidence, which is also a possible agenda for future research. Meta-analytic reviews are extremely demanding in terms of time and prone to various errors if the samples of a large number of diverse studies are not synthesized correctly. Such an attempt would fall far outside the scope of this work, and the objectives of this study seem better suited to a systematic review rather than a meta-analytic approach.

Further research can be undertaken on quantitatively synthesizing the empirical sensitivity of various performance parameters to alternative output measures by using the empirical findings of the extant literature itself. Such research will provide fascinating insights on this subject. It may also reveal the biases that differences in output measures can bring into the estimates of performance parameters such as efficiencies, productivity, scale and scope economies, competitiveness, profitability and others. However, such a review work shall have to build a very large sample to undertake a meaningful exercise of such scale.

The fifth observation is that the Part III of this work analysed banking and insurance industries using aggregate industry-level data rather than firm-level data.[3] Generally, aggregation tends to smoothen out the heterogeneity in firm-level data. This may be an information loss.[4] Aggregated data also imply that the quantitative production relations as estimated in Part III, are average relationships and thus represent the aggregate average production function. However, it also provides a fresh vantage point to approach the banking and insurance production process. The industry level point of view has largely been ignored in the literature. While performance estimates from firm-level data are extremely valuable, the insights from an industry-level aggregate point of view are equally useful. As argued earlier in Chapter 8, industry-level performance movements can provide worthwhile information for macroeconometric works that incorporate banking and insurance industries in analysing the growth and development process of the aggregate economy. Aggregate industry-wide findings are also important for firm-level decision making as they largely shape the external environment that banking and insurance firms shall face. Hence, given the lack of attention on aggregate analysis on the subject matter in particular and its usefulness for macroeconomic analysis in general, the present study made the current choice.

Further research can investigate the empirical sensitivity of performance estimates to different output measures using a large panel of firms for various economies. Data constraints, however, shall be a major concern for such an attempt. Sixth, this study has not delved deeper into two issues close to output measurement: inputs measurement (which has been briefly reviewed in Chapter 10) and output price measurement. Further research must also study how variations in inputs and output prices affect empirical estimates of efficiencies, productivities and other performance parameters. Seventh and last is that the empirical case studies in this book are confined to a multi-input–single-output framework. Future research can also examine the issues covered in this work within a multi-input–multi-output approach.

Given these constraints and the possibilities for future efforts, the next section concludes this study with final remarks.

11.2. Final concluding remarks

The present work has provided a summarization of a voluminous literature on banking and insurance output measurement. Various approaches to the specification of output were reviewed in Part II, along with alternative output measures by invoking the practices in the extant literature. Conceptual schemas were constructed and elaborated on that capture the consensus and debates on output measurement in banking and insurance performance analysis. After that, various thematic issues were also analysed to bring attention to some of the most pressing matters. While reviews of literature generally restrict themselves to what has been presented in Part I, this book also attempted to enrich the narrative by inviting and providing contributions of various academics, policy-makers and practitioners in this area from various countries and backgrounds. Part II of this work thus enlarged the scope of review by allowing selected professionals to provide their insights, experience and wisdom on this matter. Part III supplied selected empirical case studies on how the empirical estimates of partial factor productivities, total factor productivity, technical efficiency and returns to scale may change when the underlying production function is modelled using alternative output measures and alternative empirical methods methodologies. The three parts combined summarize a substantial volume of literature by bringing together a traditional review of literature, contributions by selected professionals and empirical case studies on the BRIICS countries together into a single work.

Several tentative findings may be summarized as follows. The first is that systematic approaches largely drive the output vector for banks and insurers to output specifications rather than ad hoc choices. Second, while output specification approaches are used, their economic rationale is generally not rigorously defended in a sizeable portion of the sample studies. Third, the stock-flow dimension of output measurement requires much more attention and cannot be ignored. There are large variations in performance estimates between stock and flow measures of banking and insurance outputs. Similarly, the value-volume dimension and nominal versus real output measures are found to be inducing wide dispersion in the performance estimates. Fourth, clear patterns in output choices are evident, as highlighted in Chapters 3 and 4. In other words, output choices are not random in the literature and have meaningful patterns over space and time. Fifth, a clear consensus on this subject matter is yet to be established, but given the evolution of the practices in literature, agreements in output measurement are overcoming the disagreements, though gradually. Sixth, well-defined output measures exist in the literature, and each measure has been innovated to account for more complexities of banking and insurance production. These innovations have been summarized in various figures and narrations in Chapters 3 and 4. The seventh key finding is that on changing the output measure, the empirical estimates of performance analysis change by wide margins in the case of the BRIICS economies. Particularly, the distributional characteristics of estimated technical efficiency and productivities change noticeably when alternative output measures are employed in the underlying production function. The differences seem to be more pronounced at the first and third moments of estimated productivities and efficiency distribution. Analysis of RTS shows mixed results, and there is some degree of consistency in terms of the nature of RTS (increasing, decreasing or constant), while the size of the scale coefficient varies widely for most of the selected emerging economies.

The attempts made in this work are hoped to extend further the research on the underlying theme in newer and fascinating directions. Until now, what has been done has probably been compactly summarized in this work. What needs to be done has been suggested across this work. What will be done shall now be determined by the directions that future research assumes on this matter.

Notes

1 Again, kindly note that performance parameters have been defined in this study to include efficiencies, productivities, profitability, competitiveness, scale and scope economies, and other related matters. Thus this term is not limited to only financial performance as is common practice in the literature.
2 The author's review sheet with detailed comments on all 872 studies is available on request.
3 The rationale for adopting such an approach and its advantages and problems have been provided in Chapter 8.
4 This also raises the question of the degree of "descriptive realism" (Broer, 1987) that an aggregate empirical analysis can achieve. The answer to this question is open-ended and must be analysed by keeping the context of the empirical analysis in mind. Regarding the present study, no explicit attempt is made to achieve a high degree of realism in the economic description laid down in Part III of the book. Rather, a broad set of case studies are provided to elaborate on the issues examined in the previous sections. The issues such as efficiency, productivity and returns to scale are very complex and will require a more rigorous empirical strategy than the one adopted here if a full-fledged analysis is to be undertaken.

References

Broer, D. P. (1987). *Neoclassical theory and empirical models of aggregate firm behaviour*. Kluwer Academic Publisher. doi:10.1007/978-94-009-447-7

Machi, L. A., & McEvoy, B. T. (2022). *The literature review: Six steps to success*. SAGE.

Singh, S. (2015). Hello, limitations! The paradoxical power of limits in scientific writing. *Indian Journal of Dermatology, Venereology and Leprology*, *81*, 4–6. https://doi.org/10.4103/0378-6323.148555

Index

Note: Page numbers in *italics* indicates figures and page numbers in **bold** indicates tables on the corresponding page.